The Origins of Southern Evangelicalism

The Origins of Southern Evangelicalism

Religious Revivalism in the South Carolina Lowcountry 1670–1760

Thomas J. Little

THE UNIVERSITY OF SOUTH CAROLINA PRESS

Published by the University of South Carolina Press
Columbia, South Carolina 29208

www.sc.edu/uscpress

Manufactured in the United States of America

22 21 20 19 18 17 16 15 14 13
10 9 8 7 6 5 4 3 2 1

Library of Congress Cataloging-in-Publication Data

Little, Thomas J. (Thomas James), 1963–
The origins of southern evangelicalism : religious revivalism in the South Carolina lowcountry, 1670–1760 / Thomas J. Little.
pages cm
Includes bibliographical references and index.
ISBN 978-1-61117-274-4 (hardback) — ISBN 978-1-61117-275-1 (ebook) 1. South Carolina—Church history—17th century. 2. South Carolina—Church history—18th century. 3. Evangelicalism—Southern States—History—17th century. 4. Evangelicalism—Southern States—History—18th century. I. Title.
BR555.S6L58 2013
277.57'07—dc23

2013013550

For Sally and John

Now, I sincerely wish that things were better in this region with regard to religion than is the actual case. I would to God that there were many righteous preachers to be found here, who were really seriously concerned about the glory of God and the arch-shepherd Jesus. Then one could be hopeful that things would get better than they are now. The most distressing thing is the fact that there are preachers who do not preach and live properly in every respect; but there are also those who proclaim the word of God purely and sincerely. Among the latter one can justifiably include Mr. Whitefield, an English preacher. . . . In America, by means of the gospel, he brought about a great awakening in an area around 1,400 miles wide. And in a very few years, very many were converted to the true God.

John Tobler, "A Description of South Carolina" (1754)

Contents

Preface

Although evangelical Christianity has long been and continues to be "the predominant religious mood of the South," historians have traditionally described it as a comparatively late-flowering development in the Atlantic Protestant world.[1] Donald G. Mathews in his seminal *Religion in the Old South* (1977), for example, described prerevolutionary southern revivals as evolving only after the mid-1740s. Samuel S. Hill in his influential coda to *Religion in the Southern States: A Historical Study* (1983) stated that "if one wanted to pinpoint the salient beginning [of southern Christian evangelicalism], he would turn to the 1750s or perhaps the years just after 1800." Similarly, Christine Leigh Heyrman in her award-winning *Southern Cross: The Beginnings of the Bible Belt* (1998) writes that "evangelicalism came late to the American South, as an exotic import rather than an indigenous development."[2]

Such descriptions of evangelical ascendancy in the colonial South are demonstrably deficient. Indeed, one of principal aims of this book is to show that Protestant evangelicalism had much earlier beginnings in prerevolutionary southern society than historians have traditionally understood. At the heart of the work is a detailed examination of key efforts at religious renewal and revival in the colonial South Carolina lowcountry from roughly 1670 to 1760. Stemming from the colony's pluralistic religious heritage and all of them equally expressions of a desire for religious reform, these efforts constituted an important first step in the process by which evangelical Christianity eventually came to dominate southern religion. As we shall see, the rise of evangelical Christianity in colonial South Carolina was shepherded in by a diverse group of hitherto obscure and half-forgotten people, people who came from both the Old World and the New. It reached a climax in what Pietist leader John Tobler described for a Swiss almanac as a "great awakening."[3] And, of even greater, long-term significance, it foundationally shaped the evolution of organized Christianity in the Lower South.

This polyethnic region, comprising southern North Carolina, South Carolina, Georgia, and, after 1763, East and West Florida, was not only one of the most dynamic regions in eighteenth-century colonial British America but also an area of intense geopolitical rivalry involving England, France, Spain, and America's native population.[4] What is more, by the late colonial period the Lower South in general and South Carolina in particular were societies with tremendous wealth, an extraordinarily large African American slave population, and a strong tradition of religious revivalism and pluralistic religious expression. In his lengthy account of religion in South Carolina, the economic and cultural center of the lower southern colonies, John Tobler described a bewildering array of European religious groups including Anglicans, Baptists, Catholics, Jews, Presbyterians, and, of course, "the Pietists." Halfway through his description, as he turned his attention to the Seventh Day Baptists and the Church of the Brethren (or "Dunkards"), the New Windsor mathematician publicly wondered, "And who could enumerate all the religions?"[5]

Its dynamism, diversity, and geopolitical importance notwithstanding, the Lower South has unfortunately not received the same scholarly attention as most other areas of colonial British American settlement, particularly with regard to the study of religion. Since the 1960s there has been a fairly steady stream of scholarly articles exploring various aspects of religion in the colonial lower southern colonies, and there are insightful chapters on these colonies' prerevolutionary religious history in several important books by such scholars as Jon Butler, Thomas S. Kidd, and Sylvia R. Frey and Betty Wood.[6] Yet except for S. Charles Bolton's comprehensive *Southern Anglicanism: The Church of England in Colonial South Carolina* (1982), Daniel B. Thorpe's important study *The Moravian Community in Colonial North Carolina: Pluralism on the Southern Frontier* (1995), and, more recently, Nicholas M. Beasley's imaginative analysis of liturgical Christianity in seventeenth- and eighteenth-century Barbados, Jamaica, and South Carolina, *Christian Ritual and the Creation of British Slave Societies, 1650–1780* (2009), there has been remarkably little serious study of religion in the Lower South.[7]

By studying the origins and evolution of evangelical Christianity in colonial South Carolina this book focuses attention on a neglected aspect of the Lower South's religious history that is vitally important for achieving a fuller understanding of the region's complex religious past. In addition, it moves the religious history of the Lower South more fully into the mainstream of early American and Atlantic historiography by showing how South Carolina revivalism developed along the same lines as revivalism in the northern colonies, grew out of both local and continental forces, and was directly linked to the international history of the early modern era. These are especially important contributions because even more than the written history of religion in the Lower South region as a whole, the literature on colonial South Carolina revivalism is unusually thin and sporadic when compared to that of colonies in other regions of British America. Moreover, those works which do presently exist have unfortunately not had a significant scholarly impact. As a result historians have often simply assumed that religious revival had less effect in South Carolina than in any other mainland colony. In the main this is true of historians whose interests lay in social, political, and economic history as well as of those who have specialized in intellectual and cultural themes. Even scholars of colonial South Carolina's religious history have sometimes tended to minimize the impact of revivalism in the colony, partly because of the poverty of scholarship, partly because of a certain habituation, partly for other reasons. In stressing that "the Church of England was a major cultural force in South Carolina," for instance, S. Charles Bolton asserted that "the Great Awakening had few lasting effects in the low country," though he earlier did acknowledge that it "remained a permanent influence." In particular, Bolton observed, "the *South Carolina Gazette* continued to carry debates about Whitefield, an Anglican school for Negroes came into existence, stimulated in part by the need to compete with Whitefield's good works, and evangelical ministers began to enter the province."[8]

While readily agreeing with Bolton's main point about the cultural importance of the Anglican church in eighteenth-century South Carolina, the present book vigorously disputes his commonplace notion that the Great Awakening made little lasting impact on the colony, arguing instead that evangelical revivalism of a wide swath ended up counting for a great deal. For example, it describes the religious experiences of a substantial number of men and women from every social order who were increasingly taken with revivalistic Christianity, including such well-known social figures as Henry Laurens, who, the North Carolina Moravians declared, "had been awakened by Whit[e]field."[9] It also points out that the Great Awakening reinvigorated the colony's dissenting majority while effectively stymieing Anglican efforts to consolidate the Church of England's ecclesiastical position as eighteenth-century South Carolina's state church. Furthermore, it documents the corrosive effect that the Awakening had on the relationship between the laity and "unrighteous preachers" who trusted "more in human powers and works than they should according to scripture," a significant aspect of the revival which John Tobler and many other Atlantic migrants wrote about in offering an explanation for why "things were [not] better . . . with regard to religion"—including, as Tobler put it, "work on [converting] the black slaves."[10] This doctrinal issue became especially obvious during George Whitefield's famous preaching tour of the colony in the years 1740 and 1741, but it had "disturb'd and inflam'd several Churches" well in advance of his coming. In fact, it had divided the South Carolina Presbytery during the 1720s, appeared with the arrival of group of Appenzellers and other emigrants from eastern Switzerland in 1737, and split up South Carolina Baptists the previous year.[11]

If the poverty of scholarly literature on the rise of evangelical Christianity in colonial South Carolina has lent credence to the notion that religious revivalism had no lasting impact on the colony in the prerevolutionary era, this idea has developed in tandem with, and may also have been in part a direct consequence of, another core belief in the study of early American religious history. In the past several decades modern scholars have continued to emphasize that, in contrast to New England and the Middle Colonies, "religious awakening came later to the colonial South, starting in the mid-1740s with Presbyterian itinerants and reaching full pitch in the 1760s and 1770s with the Baptist and Methodist revivals."[12] Underpinning this continuing emphasis is a rather chauvinistic view that religious developments in the colony of Virginia—which has been the recipient of scholarship of extraordinarily high quality over the past generation and almost always figures prominently in accounts of the South's early religious experience—exemplified religious developments elsewhere in southern society.[13] Indeed it is probably no exaggeration to say that much of the scholarship on religion in the colonial South has been shaped by an assumption that Virginia was representative of the region.

This is certainly the case in the study of the origins and evolution of southern evangelicalism. At least since southern religious history was first "discovered" in the 1960s and 1970s, most writers have followed the lead of historian Wesley M. Gewehr in describing the rise of evangelical Christianity in the early South, helping to explain why they have continually emphasized the extent to which Protestant evangelicalism came late to the region. In his impressive early study of southern revivalism, *The Great Awakening in Virginia, 1740–1790* (1930), Gewehr traced evangelical ascendancy in colonial Virginia through three discrete phases of growth in the decades immediately preceding the signing of the Declaration of Independence. First there was a "militant Presbyterian" phase, which began among the people of Hanover County in eastern Virginia and was brought to maturity after 1748 by New Side minister Samuel Davies, a young evangelist from the Delaware Valley region of Pennsylvania. Second there was "an even more popular and extravagant phase," that of the Separate Baptists, a missionary group from New England who established themselves at Sandy Creek, North Carolina, in 1755 and quickly began to spread new, more powerful forms of revivalism throughout the southern backcountry. After a particularly fraught period of opposition in the Old Dominion, the Separate Baptist movement eventually took hold in the eastern and central parts of Virginia by about 1770, when the Separates counted three churches north of the James River. Finally there was "the great Methodist awakening," the last phase of the Chesapeake Bay area's prerevolutionary evangelical revivals. This final phase, commencing in the spring and summer of 1772 when Wesleyan itinerants began preaching at Norfolk, Portsmouth, and other places in tidewater Virginia, continued until the outbreak of the American Revolutionary War, as did the contentious and belated Separate Baptist phase.[14]

Recent scholarship has consistently shown that Gewehr's three-phase model of late colonial evangelical Christian development is still largely appropriate for eighteenth-century Virginia and the Chesapeake Bay region more generally.[15] In the pluralistic colonies of the Lower South, however, another, earlier pattern of revivalism and evangelicalism emerged in the prerevolutionary era, one that is significantly different from the traditional Gewehrian formulation that historians are prepared to find. The object of the present book is to highlight this earlier Lower South pattern, which has been obscured and foreshortened in the historiography of American religion by a scholarly preoccupation with the Chesapeake colony, and to look at some of evangelicalism's key originary moments in southern society. In this connection colonial South Carolina could hardly have offered a greater contrast to Virginia. Not only did South Carolina have a stronger evangelical background than Virginia, a difference derived in large measure from the character of its European population, but it also early acquired a cosmopolitan diversity that was largely missing in the Chesapeake colony. There dissenters were much less a factor in the overall process of colonial religious development, the white population was much more homogeneously Anglican until after 1750, and Christian worship was characterized by a much higher degree of ecclesiastical uniformity. Nor does it seem that the two colonies shared the same interest in religion, perhaps in part because of the number of spiritual choices available and the relative intensity of religious competition. By the middle decades of the eighteenth century South Carolina had almost twice as many churches per capita as Virginia.[16] Furthermore, the multiple attempts at religious revival during the formative period in South Carolina history bespeak a greater concern for the strength of organized Christianity. As for the Great Awakening itself, it was as much an evolution from South Carolina's background and circumstances as an exogenous development produced by religious activity outside the colony, though, as in the case of the Chesapeake revivals, the Awakening cannot properly be understood apart from the mutually constitutive forces at work throughout the prerevolutionary Atlantic world.

No less than the Great Awakening, this transatlantic frame of reference is especially important for understanding certain religious developments in the Carolina lowcountry, beginning with the founding of the colony in 1670 and the Lords Proprietors' efforts to encourage immigration and continuing with other developments, such as the legal establishment of the Church of England, all of which, taken together, vividly testify to the growing interconnections and exchanges between the Old World and the New World in the seventeenth and eighteenth centuries. Yet despite its obvious importance, relatively few studies of colonial American religion are cast in terms of an Atlantic framework, and this is especially true of the colonial South. In recent years the field of Atlantic world studies has significantly enhanced and reshaped historical understanding of the American colonies by situating their history in a transnational imperial context. Even so, the religious dimensions of early American history remain underexplored in the scholarship of this emerging field.[17]

Some recently published works have begun to correct this disciplinary imbalance. Ned Landsman's *Crossroads of Empire: The Middle Colonies in British North America* (2010) includes an important discussion of how evangelical religion and religious pluralism helped shape the complex development of colonial New York, New Jersey, and Pennsylvania as well as their place in the Atlantic world. Richard A. Bailey's *Race and Redemption in Puritan New England* (2011) contributes to the historiography by showing how religion was both the principal point of contrast and a key source of identity formation in the encounters between Europeans, Native Americans, and enslaved Africans living in colonial New England. In addition, Chris Beneke and Christopher S. Grenda's edited volume, *The First Prejudice: Religious Tolerance and Intolerance in Early America* (2011), provides significant new insights into the dynamic role of religious difference in Atlantic history, while Linda Gregerson and Susan Juster's edited collection, *Empires of God: Religious Encounters in the Early Modern Atlantic* (2011), underscores the close connections between religion and colonialism in the formative period of European conquest and colonization in the Americas. Like Gregerson and Juster's volume, Carla Gardina Pestana's insightful *Religion and the Making of the British Atlantic World* (2009) also considers religion and empire in a transatlantic imperial framework, focusing on the intricate religious consequences of early modern British expansion.[18]

Along with a few other important books such as W. R. Ward's *Protestant Evangelical Awakening* (1992) and Mark Noll's *The Rise of Evangelicalism: The Age of Edwards, Whitefield, and the Wesleys* (2003), these works have shown how an Atlantic perspective can help historians understand the transnational imperial evolution of Protestant evangelical revivalism in North America, Europe, and beyond, as well as the many effects of this momentous religious development.[19] They have also provided a solid foundation for better understanding the unique regional growth of early evangelicalism in eighteenth-century colonial British America. One of the aims of the present study is to illuminate the Atlantic contours of colonial South Carolina's religious development by focusing attention on the cosmopolitan and multicultural elements of evangelicalism's complex beginnings in the lowcountry, in addition to the transatlantic imperial dynamics that fueled prerevolutionary revivalism in the Lower South. This international approach to the colony's early religious history adds an important dimension to the book's focus on the manifold ways in which indigenous developments gave rise to evangelical Christianity in the South Carolina lowcountry.

Portions of the epilogue, as wells as parts of chapters 2, 3, and 5, are based on some of my earlier work on the religious history of the Lower South which appeared in the following publications: "'Adding to the Church Such As Shall Be Saved': The Growth in Influence of Evangelicalism in Colonial South Carolina, 1740–1775," in Jack P. Greene, Rosemary Brana-Shute, and Randy J. Sparks, eds., *Money, Trade, and Power: The Evolution of Colonial South Carolina's Plantation Economy* (Columbia: University of South Carolina Press, 2001), 362–82; and "The Origins of Southern Evangelicalism: Revivalism in the South Carolina Lowcountry, 1700–1740," *Church History* 75 (December 2006), 768–808. A Mednick Fellowship from the Virginia Foundation for Independent Colleges allowed me to pursue research and writing on the rapid spread of evangelical churches and itinerants in the Carolinas and Georgia after 1740. A James Still Fellowship at the University of Kentucky and a John B. Stephenson Fellowship from the Appalachian College Association made it possible to carry out research on early attempts at religious renewal and revival in the South Carolina lowcountry. The Historical Commission of the Southern Baptist Historical Collection in Nashville, Tennessee, also provided resources and support. I am grateful to all these institutions and to Emory & Henry College for their sponsorship and generous financial assistance.

The staffs of the Kelly Library at Emory & Henry College and the Hodges Library at the University of Tennessee were especially helpful in securing sources for the present book. Archivists and librarians at the the Fondren Library at Rice University, the Furman University Library, the Presbyterian Library and Archives at Montreat, North Carolina, the South Carolina Department of Archives and History, the South Carolina Historical Society, and the South Caroliniana Library and the Thomas Cooper Library at the University of South Carolina also rendered invaluable assistance. My time at the NEH Summer Institute for College Teachers at Haverford College, the International Seminar on the History of the Atlantic World at Harvard University, and the Jessie Ball Dupont Summer Seminar for Liberal Arts College Faculty at the National Humanities Center in Research Triangle Park, North Carolina, opened up broad new vistas and stimulated my thinking deeply and in a variety of different ways. Special thanks go to historian Jon Butler for reading an earlier version of this manuscript and offering his advice and encouragement. I am also thankful to the peer reviewers commissioned by the University of South Carolina Press for their useful suggestions, as well as to Alex Moore for his continuing support and guidance. Most of all, however, I am thankful for my family, friends, and colleagues, and for having had the opportunity to study at the University of South Carolina and at Rice—my Harvard and my Yale College.

1

Libertines, Sectaries, and Enthusiasts

The Formation of an Evangelical Tradition

The People here, generally speaking, are the Vilest race of Men upon the Earth they have neither honour, nor honesty nor Religion enough to entitle them to any tolerable Character, being a perfect Medley or Hotch potch made up of Bank[r]upts, pirates, decayed Libertines, Sectaries and Enthusiasts of all sorts who have transported themselves hither from Bermudas, Jamaica, Barbados, Montserat, Antego, Nevio, New England, Pensylvania & c; and are the most factious and Seditious people in the whole World. Many of those that pretend to be Churchmen are strangely cripled in their goings between the Church and Presbytery, and as they are of large and loose principles so they live and Act accordingly, sometimes going openly with the Dissenters . . . against the Church.

Carolina commissary Gideon Johnston to the
bishop of Sarum [Salisbury], September 20, 1708

Colonial South Carolina had a stronger evangelical background than historians have traditionally recognized. Most of the colony's early settlers were Protestant dissenters, and most South Carolina Anglicans had deep reformed convictions, being "actually Joyned and linked with the Dissenters."[1] At the turn of the eighteenth century, when the colony's European population numbered about 3,250, Presbyterians, Congregationalists, French Huguenots, Baptists, and Quakers counted more than ten times as many congregations as Anglicans.[2] At the same time South Carolina Anglicans were pressing their ministers "to baptize their Children without Godfathers and God Mothers and the Sign of the Cross," demanding that they preach and pray extemporaneously, and—worse—asking them, "What has the Bp [of] London . . . to do with us?" In fact, Commissary Gideon Johnston, the bishop of London's agent in South Carolina (1708–1716), frequently commented on the reforming temperament of his South Carolina parishioners. In his "long and Tedious Letter" of September 20, 1708, to Gilbert

Burnet, bishop of Salisbury, for instance, he spoke of the ease with which they moved from one church to another, contemning the strange cripplings "half faced Churchmen" displayed in their comings and goings "between Church and Presbytery." He also spoke about their unprecedented (mis)use of the holy sacraments and dilated at length on the "large and loose principles" informing such behavior, not to mention the "ill usage" he met with from the colonists, especially the Protestant reformers and fanatics—the "Libertines, Sectaries, and Enthusiasts of all sorts."[3]

During the seventeenth century a heterogeneous mixture of Protestant dissenters flooded into the South Carolina lowcountry, helping to give distinctive shape to a unique New World society in the Atlantic basin. Very early, the Carolina proprietors sought to recruit nonconformists to the colony by granting freedom of religion and liberty of conscience, a policy that was later codified in the Fundamental Constitutions (1669) and encouraged many pioneer settlers to immigrate. Virtually all had economic as well as religious reasons for coming, of course, and from one perspective there are certainly some grounds to suggest, as historian Peter A. Coclanis has written, "that the desire for greater economic opportunity, the quest for material gain, was to Carolina's early immigrants the most important factor by far in their decisions to settle in the colony."[4] Nevertheless it remains true that many early immigrants moved to the colony in search of religious freedom. In 1697, for example, a provincial law stated that "several of the present Inhabitants of this Country [that is, a great many] did transport themselves into this Province in hopes of enjoying the Liberty of their Consciences according to their own Persuasions, which the Royal King Charles the Second . . . was pleased to impower the Lords Proprietors of this Province to grant to the Inhabitants of this Province, for to encourage the settlement of the same."[5] Similarly, when Anglicans later sought to secure legal establishment for their church in 1704, South Carolina dissenters protested to the House of Lords on the grounds that after the restoration of Charles II "and the re-establishment of the Church of England by the Act of Uniformity, many of the subjects of this kingdom, who were so un-happy as to have some scruples about conforming to the rites of the said church, did transplant themselves and families into the . . . colony, by means whereof the greatest part of the inhabitants there were Protestant dissenters from the Church of England."[6]

Early South Carolinians were an extremely "factious and Seditious people."[7] Throughout much of the seventeenth century an Anglican faction known as the Goose Creek Men, comprising mostly immigrants from Barbados and some "high church" English Episcopalians, engaged in a tug of war for control of the colony's government with a dissenting faction, which included several dissident Anglicans who were generally sympathetic to nonconformists and who, like their dissenting allies, tended to support the proprietary regime. (For the late-seventeenth century, the term *"high church" Episcopalian* may be briefly defined as an adherent of the Church of England who advocated an episcopal form of church government and placed emphasis on complete adherence to the established church position, including the liturgy of the 1662 Prayer Book.) In 1694, after a protracted struggle that involved an open challenge to proprietary authority, a declaration of martial law, and the overthrow of a governor, James Colleton, a spirit of compromise prevailed. In the last years of the century, with dissenters securely at the helm South Carolina entered into a period of peace and prosperity.[8] The economy grew; Anglicans and dissenters cooperated to establish an Anglican ministry; and, as one Protestant dissenter put it a few years later, "all the inhabitants . . . lived in great peace."[9] Gone, at least for a moment, was the vicious factionalism that had led to the overthrow of Governor Colleton.

It was in the middle and late 1690s that substantial numbers of New England settlers began to arrive in the colony. Along with earlier emigrants from the region, including a group of Baptists from Kittery, Maine, they swelled South Carolina's non-Anglican population, probably by no fewer than five hundred people. Adding considerable strength to the colony's seventeenth-century background of religious nonconformity and sectarian dissent, these new migrations forwarded an "infant Reformation" begun in 1670, when South Carolina's earliest Protestant comers vicariously struggled to countenance "the Arke of God."[10] Perhaps most important, they gave rise to episodes of both individual and collective spiritual excitement as New England ministers embarked on an energetic program of experiential conversion work. Yet also important, they helped set the stage for the advance toward later evangelical awakenings as well as a much more forceful confrontation in the political arena over the legal establishment of the Church of England.

Hoping to establish "an ample Colony" of English subjects along the southeast coast of North America, the eight men to whom Charles II granted Carolina on March 24, 1663, professed not only material but also religious inspiration when they "humbly besought" a royal charter, the eight, in the words of the charter, "being excited with a laudable and pious zeal for the propagation of the Christian Faith and the enlargement of our Empire and Dominions . . . in the parts of AMERICA not yet cultivated or planted, and only inhabited by some barbarous People, who have no knowledge of Almighty God." All adhered firmly to the Anglican church and quite naturally believed that they might effect this "pious and noble purpose" by establishing a staple-producing agricultural colony in the New World, as all imagined that Christian missionizing—the preaching and propagation of the Christian gospel—would accompany English settlement of the region, no less than mercantile profits.[11]

To encourage such settlement while at the same time minimizing their investment in the transatlantic imperial venture, the proprietors, being enterprising Protestants, hoped to recruit seasoned English colonists who would settle at their own expense. Consequently they sought to attract colonists from New England, the Chesapeake, and the Atlantic and Caribbean islands by offering land on liberal terms, promising representative self-government, and granting liberty of conscience to all would-be adventurers, for under the charter they enjoyed broad discretionary powers concerning ecclesiastical matters—"and in as ample a manner as any Bishop of Durham . . . ever . . . enjoyed." These included the patronage and power to license the organization and building of all churches and "to cause them to be Dedicated and Consecrated according to the Ecclesiastical Laws of our Kingdom of England." They also included the power to safeguard the liberty of persons who stood outside the Restoration church, one of the chief distinguishing features of the Carolina charter. Using their influence at court, the proprietors won important concessions from Charles II in this regard, despite the fact that the crown was facing domestic pressure from the Cavalier Parliament (which was dominated by Episcopalian MPs) and the bench of bishops to curb the strength of English nonconformity. Specifically they won "full and free License, liberty, and Authority, by such legal ways and means as they shall think fit" to grant reasonable "Indulgences and Dispensations" to any "Person and Persons, inhabiting and being within the said Province . . . Who really in their Judgments, and for Conscience sake, cannot or shall not Conform . . . to the Public Exercise of Religion, according to the Liturgy, forms and Ceremonies of the Church of England, or take and subscribe the Oaths and Articles made and established in that behalf."[12]

Having secured such authority, the Lords Proprietors included an extraordinary provision in "A Declaration and Proposal to all that will Plant in Carolina," an informal plan of government that was drafted shortly after the royal charter was granted, the king sharing their "pious and good intention for the propagation of the Christian faith amongst the barbarous and ignorant Indians." Not only does it reveal one of the principal ways in which the proprietors hoped to recruit settlers to develop their colony, but it also speaks directly to their religious commitments. "We will grant, in as ample manner as the undertakers shall desire," the provision in the August 25, 1663, Declaration and Proposal states, "freedom and liberty of conscience in all religious or spiritual things, and to be kept inviolably with them, we having power in our charter so to do."[13] Whether the provision was written as a specific overture to New England Puritans (which seems likely, as a group of Massachusetts Bay colonists had already attempted to settle in Carolina) or whether it simply represents a general policy statement remains somewhat unclear.[14] But the Declaration and Proposal's religious provision proved to be precedent-setting nevertheless. Furthermore, even if the provision represents a generic policy statement, it stands in vivid contrast to the ecclesiastical spirit prevailing in England at the time. Following the restoration of Charles II, Parliament passed a series of four statutes designed to strengthen the position of the episcopal Church of England. Known collectively as the Clarendon Code, they were named after Edward Hyde, 1st Earl of Clarendon, Lord High Chancellor and one of the eight Carolina proprietors. The Corporation Act (1661) excluded nonconformists from municipal office. The Act of Uniformity (1662) provided for the issuance of a new Book of Common Prayer and required all clergy to affirm it publicly or resign. The Conventicle Act (1664) forbade dissenting religious services, while the Five Mile Act (1665) prohibited nonconforming ministers who refused to subscribe to the new prayer book from coming within five miles of a town or parish where they had held their livings. As the king's chief minister, Clarendon enforced the measures, though as the Declaration and Proposal would suggest, he was personally disposed to be tolerant and disapproved of their passage.[15]

In the face of this growing body of legislation, the Lords Proprietors reaffirmed their commitment to freedom and toleration in "The Concessions and Agreement of the Lords Proprietors," an important statement of settlement conditions issued on January 7, 1665. Significantly, the Concessions and Agreement added to the proprietors' earlier religious assurances, with the most important additions being outlined in a "General clause of Liberty of Conscience." The clause provided that no one would "be any ways molested, punished, disquieted or called in question for any differences in opinion or practice in matters of religious Concernment" and that all would "freely and fully have and enjoy his and their Judgements and Consciences in matters of religion." What is more, the proprietors vowed in a subsequent clause not to use their right of patronage and power of advowson (that is, the power of presenting a nominee to an ecclesiastical benefice) to infringe upon people's consciences and, further, granted provincial representatives the "power, by act, to constitute and appoint such and so many Ministers or Preachers as they shall think fit, and to establish their maintenance, Giving Liberty besides to any person or persons to keep and maintain what preachers or Ministers they please."[16] Here the evidence is more than suggestive: in these early years the proprietors believed that their colony would be inhabited by a substantial number of New Englanders. "We have ... indeavoured to comprehend all Interests," they wrote of the Concessions and Agreement, "especially that of New England from whence the greatest stocke of people will in probability come." There were many other potential peopling fields, of course, especially Barbados, where the sugar revolution of the 1640s had persuaded many islanders to emigrate and where interest in settling a provision-growing colony on the North American mainland was widespread. However, the proprietors seem to have focused their early recruiting efforts not on the West Indies but on New

England, supposing that relatively few people would leave the sugar islands for Carolina, "our more southerne plantations being already much drayned."[17] The second royal charter of June 30, 1665, tends to confirm that the English proprietors of Carolina hoped New England might become a major recruiting ground for the settlement of their colony in America. Whereas the first charter comprehended punishment for anyone who might "scandalize or reproach" the "Liturgy, forms, and Ceremonies" of the established church without specifying conditions of nonconformity and religious dissent, the second charter explicitly guaranteed protection for prospective settlers' different opinions concerning religious matters, English laws "to the contrary hereof, in any-wise, notwithstanding." Such specific legal protection provides further evidence that the proprietors secured additional rights for dissenting Protestants contemplating removal, particularly the New England Puritans they spoke of with regard to the Concessions and Agreement (which was undoubtedly the source of the 1665 charter language).[18] Theirs was to be a colony of wide religious tolerance, and they persuaded Charles II to concede just that, which is all the more striking given the hatred and fear of nonconformity in Restoration England. For example, a 1666 promotional tract printed in London for Robert Horne extolling the benefits of settling in Carolina cited "full and free Liberty of Conscience" as one of "the chief and Fundamental privileges" offered in the new colony, and it was listed with ordinal priority, first. "No man," Horne's *Brief Description of the Province of Carolina* states, "is to be molested or called in question for matters of Religious Concern; but every one to be obedient to the Civil Government, worshiping God after their own way."[19] Other early promotional papers describing Carolina, such as Samuel Wilson's *An Account of the Province of Carolina* (1682), continued holding up this chief privilege.

Taking into account the royal charters, the 1663 Declaration and Proposal, and the 1665 Concessions and Agreement serves to illuminate the central premise underpinning the religious provisions of the Fundamental Constitutions, a remarkable document drafted in 1669 by Anthony Ashley Cooper (afterwards 1st Earl of Shaftesbury) with the help of his personal secretary, John Locke. As the historian Charles H. Lippy has recently written, these provisions "become hallowed icons that paved the way for robust pluralism to emerge in Carolina."[20] Yet it is important to note that long before they were composed the proprietors had resolved to sanctify "freedom and liberty of conscience in all religious or spiritual things." Indeed, as early as August 1663 they had vowed "to be kept inviolably" bound to the principle of religious freedom, and when Lord Ashley drew up new settlement terms some six years later he proceeded from this basic premise. As he later explained it to South Carolina's first governor, Captain William Sayle, who had written him to enlist financial support to recruit a minister named Sampson Bond, "in answer to your Desires concerning Mr Samson Bond wee writt formerly both to him and you to let you know that if he would come to Carolina he should have 500 acres of land £40. per annum and an house but though we allow him this Salary and Alotment of land to be the Preacher among you yet wee give neither him nor you Authority to compell any one in matters of Religion having in our Fundamental Constitutions granted a freedom in that Pointe which wee resolve to keep inviolable."[21]

On the basis of this inviolable freedom, Lord Ashley drafted an elaborate set of fifteen constitutional provisions designed to safeguard the liberty of colonists who would "unavoidably be of different Opinions concerning Matters of Religion," maintain peace amid theological and ecclesiastical diversity, and, most important, provide "heathens Jews & other dissenters from the purity of Christian Religion . . . an oppertunity of acquainting themselves with the truth & reasoanbleness of its doctrines." (In the earliest version of the Fundamental Constitutions dated July 21, 1669, these fifteen provisions appear as Articles 61 to 75.)[22] To achieve these goals, the constitutions provided that any seven or more people "agreeing in any Relig [ion] shall Constitute a Church or profession." Consequently, almost all of its articles pertaining to religion deal with the terms of church membership and communion, thus establishing legal boundaries for potential congregants. At a minimum, colonists in Carolina had to "Acknowledge a god, And that God is publickely & Solemnly to be worshipped," and it was automatically assumed that all adults would belong to a church.

In addition to prohibiting unbelief and presupposing church membership, the constitutions stipulated that the terms of admittance and fellowship of each religious community must be "written in a book" and "subscribed by all members of the said Church or Profession," along with the date of each communicant's subscription. This record was to be kept by a provincial official known as a precinct register, who was also charged with maintaining a registry of all births, marriages, and deaths. In order to become a formal member of a church every person had to subscribe publicly to its terms of communion "before the precinct Register & any one Member of the sd Church." Anyone who struck out his or her name from the church book, or had his or her name struck out by a religious official, would cease to be a formal member. Such action however would result in dire consequences, because nonmembers were denied all legal rights and liberties. Article 66 states that "Noe person above Sixteen yeares of Age shall have any benefitt or Protection of the law or be capeable of any place of profitt or honnor who is not a member of some Church or Profession haveing his name recorde in some one & but one Religious record at once."

In drawing up terms of fellowship the constitutions commanded each church or profession to observe three general rules that Lord Ashley imagined would be sufficiently broad to allow virtually any like-minded group to assemble for religious worship or exercise, including Anabaptists, Quakers, and other radical groupings (all of whom could vote and hold public office, provided they met certain social and legal qualifications). Religious toleration would extend to any church or profession affirming that "there is a god," that "God is publickely to be worshipped," and that "it is lawfull & the duty of every man being thereunto called by those that Governe to beare wittnesse to truth." Although no religious group could legally assemble without setting "downe the externall way whereby they Witnesse a truth," those who refused to swear oaths would be permitted to do so in any "Sensible" manner. What is more, they would be permitted to worship freely as long as they did not "speak any thing in their Religeous Assembly Irreverently or Seditiously of the Government." Article 68 forbade colonists from disturbing or molesting "any Religeous Assembly," while Article 75 prohibited anyone from persecuting "another for his speculative opinions in Religion or his way of Worship." Dissenters would later cite Article 75 as the constitutional basis for religious freedom in Carolina.[23]

No less than in demanding religious adherence, Ashley took great care in his efforts to ensure that all colonists in Carolina would behave themselves with "peaceablenesse & inoffencivenesse," hoping to facilitate proselytizing; and in formulating the proprietors' policy of indulgences he remained deeply devoted to propagating Christianity among "the Natives of the place," heathens who, like enslaved Africans, might "by good Usage & perswasion & all those convinceing Methods of Gentlenesse & Meeknesse Suitable to the rules and designes of the gospell be wonn over to embrace & unfeignedly receive the truth." Toward this end the constitutions forbade the use of "any reproachfull reviling or Abusive language against the Religion of any church or profession that being the certaine way of disturbing the publick peace & of hindering the conversion of any to the truth by Engadgeing them in Quarrells & animositys to the hatred of the professors & that profession wch otherwise they might be brought to assent to." The constitutions further provided that it would be "lawfull for Slaves as all others to enter themselves & be of what Church any of them shall thinke best . . . but be in all other things in the same state & condition."[24] The inclusion of this provision makes it abundantly clear that Ashley was conscious of the historic role that religion played in determining social status.

Although Ashley designed the Fundamental Constitutions with the express intention of trying to persuade non-Christians to embrace the truth of the Bible, and although he believed that hindering their conversion "cannot be wthout great Offense to Almighty god," he initially made no provision for an establishment of religion, not even the limited sort outlined in the 1665 Concessions and Agreement (which contained a clause authorizing the Carolina assembly to enact legislation to pay for clerical salaries, with dissenting congregations having the right to maintain their own ministers).[25] However, in the official version of the constitutions sealed on March 1, 1670, the proprietors adopted an additional article empowering the provincial legislature "to take care for the building of churches, and the public maintenance of divines, to be employed in the exercise of religion, according to the Church of England." The article goes on to stipulate that since the Anglican church was "the only true and orthodox and the national religion of all the King's dominions, it is so also of Carolina; and, therefore, it alone shall be allowed to receive public maintenance, by grant of parliament." John Locke reportedly claimed that this clause was added "contrary to his judgment," and its insertion proved a cause of dismay to many potential settlers on both sides of the Atlantic.[26] Yet nothing in the article suggests that the proprietors suddenly began hedging on toleration. Nor is there any indication in this period that they thought of the Church of England in strictly exclusive terms, at least not in the way that the architects of the 1662 Act of Uniformity did. Though the article precluded multiple establishment, it merely suggested that state church ministers might exercise religion according to Anglican liturgical and ceremonial practice, generally undertaking to use the Book of Common Prayer. Moreover, it was framed in such a way as to allow for a comprehensive establishment in Carolina, one which might encompass a wide variety of Anglican opinion. The proprietors had in fact demonstrated a commitment to such inclusiveness in framing the Concessions and Agreement a few years earlier.

While the Fundamental Constitutions was nearing completion, the project to settle Carolina proceeded apace. Having ultimately resolved to plant a colony at their own expense, the proprietors pledged £10,400 to sponsor an expedition to Port Royal and soon began considering Ashley's new frame of government, commonly called the Grand Model.[27] In mid-August 1669 they sent out a fleet of three vessels—the *Carolina*, the *Port Royal,* and the *Albemarle*—and more than one hundred passengers and crew under the command of Captain Joseph West. A Puritan follower who conceived of the undertaking as a godly mission, West first led the fleet to Kinsale, Ireland, in hopes of recruiting indentured servants, and then to Bridgetown, Barbados. Here Captain West relinquished command of the expedition to Sir John Yeamans, a leading Barbadian planter to whom the proprietors entrusted the management of their new colony in America. Shortly thereafter, on November 2, the *Albemarle* was broken up in foul weather. Hiring another ship, the *Three Brothers*, to take its place, Yeamans set sail from Barbados about three weeks later. The fleet obtained Nevis in early December and made a brief stop at the island before proceeding to Carolina. On the way stormy seas wrecked the *Port Royal* in the Bahamas and scattered the other ships, whereupon Affra Harleston, a passenger aboard the *Carolina* cried out, "God will preserve me as he hath in many great Dangers when I saw his wonders in ye Deepe & was by him Delivered."[28]

As did many men and women at the time, Harleston boldly invoked the power of religion in seeking deliverance, showing how vital Christian referents made the Atlantic crossing, and in the wake of the storm the *Carolina* providentially arrived at Bermuda along with Yeamans and others in the ship's company in the winter of 1699–1670. Mooring in Castle Harbor, the port for the town of St. George's, Bermuda, the Carolina colonists spent several weeks on the island while preparing to sail for the southeast, during which time they repaired to a local parish church for Sabbath services and Wednesday evening lectures.[29] Here they quickly fell under the spell of the Reverend Sampson Bond, being "exceedingly affected with him and his Ministry all the tyme they were in Barmudas."[30] An Oxford man who was ordained by the bishop of Exeter in 1641, Bond had been for many years very "painefull in the worke of the Ministry." Originally sent to Bermuda in 1662 by Edward Montagu, 2nd Earl of Manchester, under a three-year commission from the Somers Islands Company, he was a charismatic Puritan preacher who excelled in art of casuistical divinity.[31] According to one Carolina colonist, "Sr. John Yeoman was soe much affected with him, that he promised . . . he would procure [him] a Comission from the King to make him our minister and to the vttmost endeauor to procure him a Coniderable Sallry for his incouragemt."[32]

Yeamans meanwhile had decided to forsake the venture and return to Barbados, naming Captain William Sayle, a prominent Bermudian, as governor. Nearly eighty years old, Sayle was a veteran of colonial government and "well Experienced in new Settlemnts."[33] He had served as councilman, sheriff, and three-time governor of Bermuda (1640–1642, 1643–1645, and 1658–1662), and in 1648 he founded the Puritan colony of Eleuthera (from *eleuthros*, Greek for "freedom") in the Bahamas, where he and other Eleutherian pioneers famously worshiped "at a cave."[34] Yet Sayle's appointment was complicated by questions about his fitness to assume the position, by jealously and intrigue, and by bitter religious differences. The difficulties began when two "troublesome spirritts," William Owen and William Scrivener, attempted to foment division by urging "the people to a Publicke difference or Suit" against Yeamans, "nott regarding the discouradgmt & ill opinion, that therevpon might arise."[35] Specifically they argued that Sayle's old age, poor health, and radical religious views disqualified him from office and that Yeamans, in naming him governor, had breached the proprietors' instructions to make "choise of a person as Governor fitt for such an Imployment." Owen denounced Sayle as an "overgrowne zealote" and asserted that his appointment would discourage settlement of the new colony because Sayle had openly "declared he had bein an independent these 24 years," a fact which Owen claimed "was verie well knowne att Ronoake and Virginia and in som other places" where the Church of England was established by law or practice.[36]

Despite their best efforts, Owen and Scrivener failed to persuade the leaders of the Port Royal expedition to bring a suit against Yeamans, "Coll Sayle being a p'son of good report." And they readily agreed to embrace the newly commissioned governor "rather then this designe should fall."[37] A seasoned politician, Sayle possessed rare qualities of leadership, and, although he was not "a man . . . of great sufficiency" like Yeamans, one of the biggest sugar planters in Barbados, he was certainly a man of high social station, managing to build up a small fortune through shipping, trade, whaling, provisioning, and tobacco cultivation.[38] Further, Sayle was particularly well positioned to take advantage of the widespread interest in the Carolina project, Owen's contentions to the contrary aside. He had powerful connections among lay and clerical leaders in New England, where a great "Concourse of people" soon began "fitting for [the] Country."[39] No less important, he stood ready to play an active role in promoting the colonizing effort in the Atlantic and Caribbean islands, enjoying any number of important contacts throughout the region.

Beyond the West Indian sugar colony of Barbados, which saw a mass exodus of perhaps ten thousand people during the middle decades of the seventeenth century, Bermuda was potentially one of the most promising recruiting grounds among the islands. With many men going down to the sea in ships and fewer and fewer opportunities for upward social mobility, it had a population numbering as high as five thousand to six thousand people, including a substantial number of African and Native American slaves.[40] In early 1669 Sampson Bond corresponded with his brother-in-law John Wolstencraft in New York and indicated that he "himselfe and some hundreds of people" were ready to quit the colony and remove to the North American mainland.[41] Eager to encourage immigration, Wolstencraft immediately brought the matter to the attention of Governor Francis Lovelace, who made it known through an intermediary, Samuel Maverick, that he would gladly allot Bond "a proportion of land (accordinge to the families [he] should bringe) on an Iland called States Iland, about 3 or 4 leagues from this cittie." Maverick, one of the first Puritan settlers in Massachusetts, was vitally concerned in the project to reduce Dutch influence in New Netherland. Asserting that the "greatest want heare is good, honest, ingenious people, and some good ministers," his letter to the prospective settlers reveals that—while they were certainly interested in economic opportunities—their principal concerns had more to do with religious matters, as they indicated that they chiefly wanted "directions from some person well accquainted in the cuntery, as to the priviledges and libertyes of the Inhabitants." "I haue beene heare from the very first settling of N: England, by the English," Maverick thus reported to Bond in May 1669, "and could giue you an account of all the privilidges injoyed and bondagess imposed in the severall Gouerments there, but . . . I shall only informe you what is allowed, and may be expected to be enjoyed by the Inhabitants, within his Royal Highnes his territories heare." Quite remarkably, Maverick's informal listing of indulgences in the colony sounds much like those formally prepared by the Carolina proprietors in the Fundamental Constitutions, reading as follows: "Ecclesiastical liberties are, 1. Liberty of conscience to all, prouided they rase not fundamentalls in religion, nor disturbe the publique peace. 2., Cerimonies may be used or omitted. 3., The Booke of Common Prayer may be made vse of or not." An old Cornwall man and a former neighbor of two families of Bonds in Saltash, England, Samuel Maverick was no Lord Ashley or John Locke. Nevertheless he clearly understood as well as they did the lure of religious toleration, one of the mainsprings in the workings of colonial British American promotion and recruitment that underscores the interconnections between religion and empire in the early modern Atlantic world. In addition Maverick understood on both an individual and collective level the popular demand for clergymen, ending his letter to Bond with the comment, "though (if you should come) you resolve not to be tyed to any people, yett many might reape benefitt by you."[42]

A prominent layman in Bond's congregation who was anxious to acquire new lands with his two sons, Nathaniel and James, William Sayle was undoubtedly among the Bermudians interested in the possibility of settling in New York—or elsewhere in the Americas. Year by year more and more colonists were leaving the island to acquire land in the Bahamas, the Leeward Islands, and Jamaica. At the same time ecclesiastical affairs in Bermuda became increasingly conflicted, with Quakers suffering active persecution and an acrimonious struggle erupting among the colony's Puritan parishioners. This controversy raised serious questions about liberty of conscience and caused many to consider emigrating to safeguard their religious future. Later, in a letter to Lord Ashley dated June 25, 1670, for example, William Sayle spoke of himself and a number of Charleston's original settlers as being sufferers under an intolerant Presbyterian majority on the island, claiming abuse by "some who are now in Authority in Barmudas." Sampson Bond similarly discovered "a great discouragement" to stay in the colony, which, as Sayle put it, was immediately "taken notice oft in other places." In the winter of 1669–1670 Bond was "inuited to Boston in New England," where he subsequently traveled to preach a trial sermon at the city's First Church. In the meantime Francis Lovelace wrote from New York "with tenders of Large incouragement," and at one point Lovelace even sent a ship to Bermuda to accommodate Bond and his family.[43] By this time, however, Bond was being "tould he must depart" by Bermuda's governor, Sir John Heydon, whereupon the strong-willed minister hotly retorted that "he would not goe," threatening Heydon and the Governor's Council by saying that "if they did send him awaie, they should pull him out of his house and carrie him, and if they did soe he was a man."[44]

The history of Sampson Bond's wrangling with these officials gives some unique insight into the nature and character of Puritan religiosity in Bermuda, an especially illustrative example because the tiny island supplied a good number of settlers to Carolina, including William Sayle and his family, who happened to be among the earliest known slave owners in Charleston.[45] Following the Restoration, an increasingly fierce, complicated debate involving Calvinist reform, Christian ritual, and African slave proselytization broke out in the colony, prompting the governor and some of the council to call for Bond's expulsion. In the spring of 1670 the Somers Islands Company received a letter from Bond's opponents to the effect that he was "endangering . . . the publick peace, And causeing the contempt of the Gospel," and on the basis of his accusers' testimony it ordered that "Mr Sampson Bond be forthwith dismissed [from] the Islands, And that . . . the Governor and Concell take care to see the same performed accordingly." According to the company's order, Bond had "shewed himself upon all occasions a person of a factious and contentious spirit fomenting divisions between Governor and Governor, people and people." Additionally, he had "made it his practise to prosecute quarrells, and to egg on the people to needless Suits of Law in the Courts of the Sommer Islands." "But principally," the 1670 order goes on to say,

> [He] hath bin an instrument to discontent all the ministers sent over thither by the Company, by distilling into the eares of the Governor and Concell such things as might tend thereunto, And hath appeared active therein, And further hath occasioned the imprisonment of one of them for the space of 8 months. And, as these were not crimes enough, he the said Sampson Bond hath bin an Instrument lately to present the Governor upon the Bench for some proclamacons made and issued out touching liberty to be granted to Negroes, embracing the Christian faith. And thereupon he the said Mr. Bond hath come into open court, and owned his contrivance of, and avowed the said Presentment. And further did alleadge that the breeding up of such children in the Christian religion makes them stubborne. The contrivance of which presentment this Court doth adjudge seditious, and the uttering of the prealleadged work impious.[46]

Governor Heydon and the council immediately acted to remove Bond for the "severall Crimes and Miscarriages Charged upon him in the said Order," issuing a warrant to the colony's sheriff "to Charge and Command him to depart these Islands forthwith."[47] These men were predominantly Presbyterians who were deeply troubled by Bond's raucous criticism of the ecclesiastical order in Bermuda. They were also put out with his not so subtle murmurings against the Reverend Samuel Smith, son of a prominent company shareholder and the leading proponent of slave Christianization in Bermuda. In petitioning the company to send another minister to replace Bond, an Independent, Governor Heydon and his supporters complained of Bond's scandalous attacks on the Book of Common Prayer as well as his willingness to "clamor against . . . Mr. Samuel Smith (for whom he hath not any loue) being a person desirous to promote the designe of Mr. Smiths enemies."[48] However, their efforts to remove the troublesome minister created a popular uproar, with several of Bond's supporters forming a mob in St. George's.

Among the mob were "some of . . . the cheefe persons that imprisoned Mr. Smith."[49] Smith, a moderate Puritan with Presbyterian or reforming Anglican leanings and pastor of St. George's church from 1663 to 1671, had stirred up a good deal of anxiety among Bermuda's English inhabitants in his effort to baptize and convert slaves. In 1668, on the pretext of defying "an order . . . for Preaching in vacant churches," Captain Samuel Whaley, Heydon's predecessor as governor, and a majority of the council voted to arrest Smith on charges of contempt. (Later, in June 1669, Smith brought actions against these men for false imprisonment.)[50] Setting forth his case in several letters to England, Smith alleged that "there was partiall dealing in itt," indicating that one reason for the proceedings against him was his failure to repudiate the Church of England as thoroughly as some of the authorities might have wished.[51] Captain Whaley and several members of the Governor's Council were ardent Puritans and Congregationalist sympathizers, and two of the councillors—former governors William Sayle and Florentius Seymour—were leading Independents. These powerful men formed the nucleus of Sampson Bond's nascent Bermuda "partie."[52]

When the Governor's Council determined to commit Smith to jail, "he sayd, (thretningly), That once within these six or seven Moneths hee should stand uppon eaven ground with the Government."[53] At the time, the Somers Islands Company was undertaking a series of reforms to assert its sovereignty, making new laws for Bermuda and appointing an all-powerful governor, Sir John Heydon, to rule the colony. After many months of delay, Heydon arrived on May 15, 1669, with instructions for Smith's "speedy enlargement," the company finding "nothing of Crime" in his actions and "leaving him to take his remedy against the p[e]rsons that caused his imprisonment," an extraordinary step without precedent in Bermuda law. The company's decision provoked anger, a lawsuit involving Whaley and eight councilmen, and many months of litigation, as Smith's cause raised the controversial issue of whether the defendants could be sued "for anything done in the execution of their Offices," particularly when acting as part of an official court of judicature.[54]

In the meantime Governor Heydon's arrival sparked rumors that "the Negroes . . . should be made free." After the new governor was installed and five new councilmen were sworn in, Heydon, having read his orders and instructions and having secured Smith's release, made his way to King's Castle to assume command of the fort from Captain Sayle, then commander-in-chief of the island's militia. Shortly thereafter, on June 9, the Governor's Council heard a complaint against a colonist named George Garrett who "about three weeks last past" had reported that Bermuda's slaves would be freed "at the next mustering, when the Governnor should cum upp." Whipped and stigmatized (the miscreant had a paper pinned on his chest), Garrett proved to be the least of council's concerns. For in the ensuing weeks Samuel Smith touched off a sustained public debate over slave baptism, one that reached a dramatic climax in the winter of 1669–1670—just as the Port Royal expedition landed on the island with planters looking to establish a new colony in Carolina.[55]

In late October, Smith sought official permission to extend his missionary work by introducing a motion before the Governor's Council asking "whether hee may proceede to the Baptizeing of Molattoes, Indians, (and more especiallie) Negroes, or not." The council acted predictably: it "unanimously determined at present, not posetively to Determine in and about the motion."[56] About the same time some slaves professing Christianity began petitioning the governor for freedom on the grounds that they had been baptized, the petitioners "alledging . . . the Gospel allowes noe bondmen."[57] Virginia Bernhard documents a few early slave baptisms in Bermuda, despite a 1647 law prohibiting the "Baptizing of Bastards or Negroes children," and there were undoubtedly some significant advances in Christianizing slaves in the mid-1660s before the authorities rudely interrupted Smith's labors. Indeed, it was probably the newer slave converts who spearheaded what Bernhard identifies as "an extraordinary bid for freedom in 1669."[58]

At any rate these two events forced Governor Heydon's hand. Thus on November 13 he issued an official proclamation regarding "all persons professing Christianity . . . in the discharge of their duties," an important document stressing Christian obligation and obedience and commanding all "Masters and Servants . . . to live in peace, mutuall love and respect to each other, Servants submitting to the condition wherein God hath placed them." Noting that he had been shown "divers petitions . . . desireing liberty and freedom," Heydon began his proclamation by defending slavery. He reminded the petitioners of slave owners' rights and the custom of New World slaveholding. He also made it clear that he was primarily addressing white individuals, not black persons. "The petitioners," he said in the preamble to the document, had not well weighed "the just Interests of their respective Owners and Masters to their persons, being purchased by them *without condition or limitation*, . . . It [slavery] being likewise soe practiced in these American Plantations, and other parts of the world." "And they nothing regarding the great benefitt they might be capable of," he continued,

> being admitted into the Christian State, and uppon demonstration of knowledge and ffaith in the holie Scriptures with life and conversation, to Baptisme, and other holie Ordinances of Christ, whereas heathenish Masters, that know not the Scriptures, would keepe them in ignorance and

> blindnes, enslaveing the soules as well as the bodies. But Christians are under Evangelicall restraints to have a respect to both. Yet some make use of this holie profession as an argument to free themselves from their severall duties . . . which is a gross mistake, and their Judgments may be rectified in rightly perusing the 6th Chap[te]r to the Ephesians.

Heydon went on to quote Paul's teaching to the early Christians of Ephesus (Ephesians 6:5–8), "Servants bee obedient unto them that are your Masters . . . knowing that whatever good thing any man doth, the same shall hee receive of the Lord, whether hee bee bond or free," and cited other biblical references (1 Corinthians 7:20–22 and 1 Peter 2:17–18) to make a point, namely that "such Negroes as formerlie, or lately have bin baptized by severall Ministers, should not thereby think themselves more free from their Masters and Owners, but rather, by the means of their Christian profession, obliged to a more strict bond of fidelity and service." "Likewise," he said, "Masters may beare a recipricall tenderness and care to their faithfull servants," because, Heydon instructed, Paul also wrote in his letter to the Ephesians, "And ye Masters doe the same [good] unto them, forbearing threatings, knowing that your Master also is in Heaven, neither is there respect of persons with him" (Ephesians 6:9).[59]

Imploring Bermudians to live in unity, loyalty, and "fear of God," Heydon sought to promote "what concerns us all, the peace, tranquilitie and welfare of these Islands," and in issuing his proclamation he stressed that if planters and slaves would fulfill their relative duties "true religion and civil conversation would be encouraged [and] the service of God would be esteemed the greatest freedome."[60] But events over the next few months soon dispelled any hope of peace and unity. As early as the mid-1660s Sampson Bond had led Bermuda planters in opposition to slave conversion. In 1670 the Somers Islands Company noted that because of his "prealleged work"—a reference to his claim that Christian instruction made slaves difficult to manage—he had "by publick Letter from this Court Anno 1666 bin admonished . . . in order to his reforming, and the leaving of such practices." Despite this transatlantic censure, however, the incorrigible minister "persisted in those former courses," maintaining that slave Christianization empowered slaves and undermined planter authority, thus endangering the social fabric.[61] After the issuance of Governor Heydon's proclamation, Bond circulated a paper entitled "A Public Grievance," which was later presented at the Court of Assizes by another colonist, John Stowe. It argued that "ye Negroes taking occasion from the Proclamation set forth by ye Governor, touching there liberty, but besides ye intent thereof, may Committ many Inslovencies againsnt there Masters and Mistresses."[62] The circular had an explosive impact, and when the governor sent it to the company so that "they might better know" the fractious minister, Heydon asked, revealingly: "If Mr. Sampson

Bond the person that said the Book of Common Prayer was a mass Boooke, or a company of packet praires made vp by the pope and the words Godfather and Godmother be blasphemy . . . [be heard] what condition shall your servants here live vnder if such practices are suffered vnder your Gouernment?"[63]

Sampson Bond gave voice to an argument that would soon become rather familiar in South Carolina, where the popular minister was encouraged to settle at "the most hearty request of ye Colony in Generall."[64] On Saturday, February 4, 1670, Governor Heydon announced that the *Carolina*, having been blown off the North American coast and presently at anchor in Castle Harbor, was preparing to set sail for Port Royal, and that since its arrival many "Servants, and others engaged in the aforesaid Honorable Expedition [had] bin dispersed abroad in these Islands, and by the Inhabitants entertained." Calling on the colonists to return to St. George's by Monday, February 14, he likewise announced that Captain Sayle was now in command of the expedition and offered free passage to any settlers resolved to join him, including any "two or ffoure capable persons [who] shall be pleased to goe . . . And take a view of the place . . . in order to the incourageing Inhabitants with us for their transplanting themselves and ffamilies according to the Report of the said two or ffour persons."[65] There was widespread interest in settling Carolina throughout Bermuda. This interest had been evident for some time. In October 1663, for example, Charles II issued a warrant to Florentius Seymour, then governor of colony, instructing that he "hinder not any free and disengaged person or persons from going out of the Island of Bermudas to Carolina." "We are informed that divers persons under your government have a desire to goe unto that place & settle their," an official wrote from Whitehall.[66]

After rounding up "all manner of persons" and enduring a two-week delay, the *Carolina* finally weighed anchor on February 26, along with a two-masted Bermuda boat purchased to replace the *Port Royal*.[67] The two vessels arrived off the southeast coast in seventeen days and made landfall at Seewee, welcomed by a group of Indians of the same name. Sailing southward to Port Royal in mid-March, the colonists discovered a place at St. Helena where "there was a mile & a half of Cleare Land fitt & ready to Plante," in addition to an abundance of timber, fruit trees, oysters, fish, and turkey. It appeared an ideal location, but the Indians they met there confirmed what the Seewee had previously reported: the site was well within the striking distance of the Westoes, "a rangeing sort of people" who had recently attacked St. Helena and were likely to strike again. "They hoped by our Arrivall to be protected from ye Westoes," Nicholas Carteret, a passenger aboard the *Carolina*, reported, "often making signes they would ingage them with their bowes & arrows, and wee should with our guns." Meanwhile the Bermuda sloop was dispatched to take a view of Kiawah, an Indian village on the west bank of a river about twenty leagues farther north, and when it brought back a favorable report a debate immediately arose over whether to quit Port Royal and begin a new settlement. Though there was considerable opposition, "the rule of ye Inconsiderate multitude cryed out for Kayawah," with Governor Sayle and majority of the settlers voting to remove northward.[68]

South Carolina's first law established the rule of religion, and no sooner had the colony been started than there was a grassroots effort to settle a minister and set up a church. Reaching Kiawah in April 1670, the early Carolina colonists chose to create their new settlement at a place they called Albemarle Point, on a low bluff several miles up the Ashley River, where they occupied a nine-acre site next to the village of the Kiawah Indians. They began building a town (which the proprietors named Charles Towne), planting provisions, and attempting to recruit more settlers from abroad. Governor Sayle immediately wrote "to the people of the Somers Islands & New England to gaine what people we may to promote the designe," and he and other leaders of the Carolina venture quickly began making plans to recruit settlers from Barbados, the Bahamas, and other English colonies in the New World.[69] "Though we are (att present) under some straight for want of provision," Sayle reported to the proprietors in late June, "yet, we doubt not (through the goodness of God) of recruits from sundry places to which we have sent."[70] Yet though the governor was optimistic about South Carolina's future prospects, the English foothold at Kiawah remained tenuous, with the population numbering no more than 140 people or so. Two days after Sayle wrote, Joseph West reported that the food supply was running precariously low; at one pint of peas per person per day, he estimated that there remained only about seven weeks of produce (about thirty barrels). With the colonists on the verge of starvation, the *Carolina* was dispatched to Nansemond, Virginia, to secure provisions and other supplies, and the *Three Brothers*, shortly after its arrival at Charleston in late May, was sent to Bermuda.[71]

At the same time South Carolina public officials sought to "propagate and cherish the service of God . . . and root out evill and wickedness," which they considered absolutely essential to the success of the undertaking.[72] On July 4, 1670, after discovering "how much the Sabboth Day was Prophanely violated, and of divers other grand abuses, practised by the people, to the greate dishounour of God Almighty," the governor and council "did make such orders . . . to suppress the same," promulgating an ordinance for strict observance of the Sabbath. The measure was read "to all the People" and published with the consent of a majority of the colony's freeholders.[73] It had an immediate impact, as it helped to facilitate what the authorities described as "an infant Reformation." Yet though the law established the rule of religion, contemporaries realized that until a maintenance was settled on an accredited minister this early religious reformation could never obtain "soe much strength as to walk alone."[74] "Pray send us a minister," surveyor general Florence O'Sullivan wrote to the proprietors. "We are in great want of an able minister," the provincial council said.[75] The substance of these and other early pleas for settling a minister varied. There were deep concerns about "stirring and awakening poore people that are dead in their trespasses and sinnes," for example, and there were many other concerns too. "The Israelites prosperity decayed when their prophets were wanting," the council proclaimed, "for where the Arke of God is, there is peace and tranquility."[76]

William Sayle and Joseph West spearheaded the effort to countenance "the Arke of God," and by "curbing the vicious" and "countenancing the vertuous" both men helped to sustain a vital religious community in South Carolina.[77] William Sayle worked tirelessly to promote Christianity, so much so that he literally "lost himself in his government."[78] And Joseph West, Sayle's handpicked successor as governor, showed himself similarly absorbed, as did many members of the council, especially including Paul Smith, a lay leader who served as the colony's unofficial chaplain and spiritual advisor. Opprobriously labeled "a knave and arrant preacher" by one of his Anglican opponents, Smith held religious views that were obviously not acceptable to everyone.[79] But his preaching helped fill the spiritual void created by the absence of an ordained minister and established a vital, empowering tradition of such popular religious action. Many early settlers like William Sayle turned to Smith to satisfy their spiritual needs, demonstrating that South Carolina was ripe for a "powerfull and soul-edefying" ministry. "There is one thing which lyes very heavy upon us," Sayle reported to Lord Ashley in the summer of 1670, "the want of a Godly and orthodox Minister which I and many others of us have ever lived under, as the greatest of our Mercyes." Hoping that the proprietor might provide financial support to settle a maintenance on Sampson Bond, Sayle wrote "in the name of all ye rest . . . most humbly to beseech your Lordship to put on bowells of great Goodness and Compassion towards your Colony here, in procuring (which your Lordship may easily and speedly doe) a Comission and Competent Sallary for him for about five or seven years (till the Lord shall enable us to mayntayne him ourselves)." "I doe most faythfully assure your Lordship," Sayle continued, "that this Mr. Bond is so well known, well reported off, and so beloved in most the Carabee Islands that were it known abroad that he were your Minister here, It is the judgment of sundry prudent persons, It would (in a little tyme) gaine many hundreds of Considerable persons to this place."[80]

In turn the council issued an even more insistent request. Ministers, the councilmen wrote in early September, were the "means corrupted youth might be vary much reclaimed." They represented empirical symbols of Christianity's presence, proclaiming its truth through catechism, instruction, and the regular performance of "the Sabbaoth and service of Almighty God."[81] Florence O'Sullivan wrote that the colony urgently needed a minister to compose quarrels, beseeching Lord Ashley to send "a minister qualified according to the Church of England and an able Counsellor to end controversies amongst us and putt us in the right way of the management of your Colony." Joseph West asked that a minister be settled to awaken sinners. Singling out William Owen for consideration, he noted that "some . . . persons being ambitious of perpetuating theire owne wicked Inclinacons spurned at all order & good Government fearing to be reduced from a sordid beastly life."[82] The surveyor John Culpepper's map of circa July or August 1671 shows that the governor and council set aside lands for public support of a minister, in addition to a four-acre lot for a church yard. Also in the winter of 1670–1671 the authorities found occasion to introduce another Sabbath law to reinforce Christian practice.[83]

In early March, after a substantial number of new immigrants landed, Governor West and the council revised and republished the 1670 orders "for ye better keeping of the Sabbath," as officials feard that the immoral, blasphemous "disorders" that had prompted the passage of the first law were "likely to bee renewed." They also worried that the newcomers might plead ignorance should proceedings be brought against them, or, worse, refuse to consent to the law. The governor's council included five elected representatives, but because the colony's population was so small there had not been a sufficient number of South Carolina freeholders to hold a parliament, raising a controversial issue concerning the legality of the 1670 ordinance. To these ends Governor West made "a Speech to the . . . people," promising to hold parliamentary elections once "opportunity did serve."[84] He also made it known "that he would afflict and inflict punishment upon them if they did sweare and profane," publishing a revised Sabbath law soon thereafter. This law included even stiffer fines for transgressors and sanctioned both whipping and gagging for nonpayment. "The freehoulders . . . were called in before the Councell Table where our Governor setting aside elocution said they had made verie good lawes for the beating doune of sinn and sweareing," one contemporary reported.[85]

Subsequent legislation from the 1680s and 1690s throws retrospective light on these early measures, for which there is no statutory evidence; and it speaks to the silent assumptions and fears that gave them added meaning, as well as the genuine spiritual aspirations of the lowcountry's first settlers.[86] These laws commanded colonial South Carolinians to "apply themselves" in worship and prayer every Sabbath, prohibiting them from working, traveling in a boat, and engaging in "vicious exercises, pastimes and meetings," such as drinking, hunting, and gaming. They forbade the selling of goods on Sunday under penalty of forfeiture and prohibited the sale of "any wine, beere, punch or other liquor whatsoever." As well, they condemned profanity and drunkenness and prescribed punishments for these and other "enormous sins."[87]

Seventeenth-century legal proscriptions served several important functions in colonial South Carolina, particularly in the early 1670s when Protestant comers attempted to secure a place for the ark of God in the new settlement at Charleston. The context of events in these years demanded practical solutions to peculiar problems created by the unsettled conditions of the colony's fledgling society, and officials sought to ensure that the laws of the civil government were set in accordance with living in a godly community. Sumptuary laws preserved "order & good Government," prevented the "destruction of good Neighbourhood," and encouraged pious practice. Their cordoning off of sacred time and prohibitions against sin supported efforts to maintain vital religious traditions in an especially uncertain environment. The "making of all such Acts," Governor West and the provincial council said, availed "the people's good." For without "some good orders" it was widely believed that the "just judgement of Almighty God may reasonably be expected to fall upon this land."[88]

However, the efforts of William Sayle and Joseph West to promote Puritan Christianity and establish a commonwealth of God met with considerable opposition, stirring conflicts that facilitated the development of rival political factions. Their leadership helped to sustain religious practice and discipline into the 1680s, when a new era of church building and ministerial activity began. Even so, there were complaints about the governors' zealousness, their reforming religious views, and their priorities—their "desires to feare God above all worldly Interest."[89] There were further complaints about the sumptuary laws. Some charged that the council did not have the authority to pass these laws without calling a parliament. Others complained about the penalties. Still others claimed that the measures were "made post factum" and saw in their passage a puritanical design to deprive freeholders of their liberties. Maurice Mathews believed that the "pecuniary fines and corporeal punishments" were intentionally "designed on freemen without their consent." William Owen charged that they "imported equall fines upon poore people here as the greatest of estates are subject to in England." Owen also maintained that English law "knew noe such thing as gagging."[90]

Owen, Mathews, and a few other leading men such as William Scrivener immediately set themselves up as a "contrary party" in a bid to seize control of local government. This group included both English and English West Indian immigrants. The latter were part of steady stream of immigration from the Caribbean Islands, especially Barbados. As M. Eugene Sirmans has observed, most opposition party activists were firmly Anglican and generally viewed both Sayle and West as religious extremists who pressed their Puritan beliefs too far.[91] Owen openly called upon the proprietors to appoint a man of "moderate zeal" as governor. He suggested that the ideal candidate would be neither "strickt episcopalle nor yet licentious nor rigid presbiterian nor yet hypocriticall" but would steer "in an even Ballance betweene all opinions . . . [while] turneing his face to the Liturgie of the Church of England."[92]

Shortly before he died on March 4, 1671, William Sayle chose Joseph West to succeed him as temporary governor, and over the following year leaders of the opposition party endeavored to turn him out of office. This effort took shape after West began "feeling authority creeping upon him" and at some length declared "that he did very suddenly intend to have a book where everyman should *subscribe religion,*" indicating that he not only intended to coerce others into leading godly lives through sumptuary legislation, but that he also intended to go much further by enforcing the religious provisions of the Fundamental Constitutions regarding mandatory church membership. The new governor, at the height of his young political career but acknowledged only by his own supporters, was determined to maintain firm control over the settlers by demanding ecclesiastical conformity. With this new apprehension appearing, his opponents quickly threw their support behind the candidacy of Sir John Yeamans, the Barbadian Anglican who most everyone believed would be commissioned again as governor upon his arrival in the colony. As the chief proprietor's deputy and the only Landgrave (or provincial noble) in Carolina, Yeamans had a legitimate claim to the governorship, because the proprietors had not yet named Sayle's permanent replacement. Yet to the dismay of Yeamans and his supporters, when Sir John asserted his right to the position in June the "people did not incline to salute him as Governor." What is more, West stubbornly refused to relinquish his office without proprietary instructions.[93] Frustrated, the Yeamans group had no choice but to continue pressing the governor to hold parliamentary elections, hoping to capture control of the legislature and challenge West in the assembly.

As pressure from the opposition mounted, as South Carolina's population continued to increase, and after months of delay, Governor West was forced to make good on his promise to call a parliament. His critics were undoubtedly correct in asserting that he had long "denyed a Parliament for feare his election or actions should be questioned," for the colony had grown significantly in the winter of 1670–1671, and no sooner had the first assembly met in early July than the representatives began debating whether West "was made Governor according to the Lords Proprietors directions."[94] It was obvious where Yeamans and his party stood, but they quickly found themselves in the minority. Thus, after failing a second time to persuade West that he should surrender his position voluntarily, the Yeamans group stormed out of the assembly in protest.

In advancing his claim Yeamans exacerbated the partisan tone of South Carolina politics and contributed to increasing sectarianism. "The people," West reported, "did all resent this distraction and began to murmur," saying that Yeamans's actions were threatening to destroy the indeterminate settlement.[95] Having predicted that his political adversary might someday be commissioned governor and pursue worldly interests with ungodly zeal, the embattled governor perceived the contest as a righteous one. If Yeamans succeeded, he suggested, "wee must not expect a blessing on our undertakings."[96]

While West's opponents undoubtedly held a different view, it is clear that Sir John did little to endear himself among provincial freeholders. Not that it mattered—Yeamans was making "a party to outrule the vote." Already benefitting from the support of William Owen, Maurice Mathews, and other Englishmen who stood "at the greatest distance from the Governor," he was aligning himself with newcomers who were arriving in the colony from Barbados. These immigrants included "many considerable men" who, like Yeamans, were members of the Caribbean island's planter class. They augmented the influence of Sir John's political faction, which West dubbed the "Barbados Party."[97] This group gained increasing strength as the number of West Indians coming into South Carolina continued to grow.

Unlike Governor West, most seventeenth-century Barbadians were committed Anglicans who professed adherence to the Church of England. By the time of the Restoration the Barbados assembly had enacted a series of laws creating a traditional parish and vestry system and had formally provided for an Anglican establishment. Early legislation commanded all residents to "give due Obedience, and conform themselves unto the Government and Discipline of the Church of England, as the same hath been established by several Acts of Parliament." Justices of the peace, ministers, and other officials were called upon to impose uniformity of practice in public worship in accordance with the Book of Common Prayer. The island assembly made church attendance compulsory, enjoined "Masters and Overseers of Families to have Prayers openly said or read every Morning and Evening with his Family, upon Penalty of Forty Pounds of Sugar," and ordered constables, churchwardens, and sidesmen to canvass the island every Sunday to search for people who were "Drinking, Searing, Gaming, or otherwise misdemeaning themselves."[98] In South Carolina, Barbadian Anglicans affirmed similar legislation but were nonetheless offended by the rigidity of Governor West's theological outlook. Scarcely had the first substantial group of Barbadian immigrants arrived when they drew together into a hard core of opposition under the leadership of Sir John Yeamans.

The Carolina proprietors disavowed Yeamans's "too forward Grasping at the Government," and they soon came to understand something of the depth and breadth of his unpopularity in the colony, but they decided to honor his legal claim to the governorship nevertheless. Unaware of proprietors' decision, Yeamans became ever more insistent and demanding, building up his so-called Barbados party, while the political faction that formed around the authority of Governor West grew in response. More than six months passed before Yeamans's commission arrived, during which time partisan jealousies mounted and confessional tensions increased. By the spring of 1672, when Sir John was finally proclaimed governor by the South Carolina council, these divisive ambiences had done much to "discompose the quiet of the settlement."[99]

Most of the blame fell on Yeamans. No sooner had they commissioned him than the proprietors were expressing misgivings about their decision to put the government under his control. It quickly became clear that his appointment was far from being "acceptable to the whole plantation." It also became clear that it would be exceedingly difficult "for Jealousy to be removed and Factions united" as long as he remained in office. Under West, government of the colony had "thriven very well." With Yeamans, "the face of things" changed. What particularly concerned the proprietors were "all the divisions" in South Carolina. Partisanship had grown immensely since Sir John began organizing his Barbados faction. To make matters worse, the proprietors were starting to realize that they had unintentionally compounded the problem. By replacing West not only had they alienated and embittered his supporters; they had removed a counterweight to one-party dominance of the provincial government. Now there was little to "balance one another's powere to prevent the ingroseing it into any one hand," which jeopardized proprietary authority.[100]

In considering solutions to the problem they were facing the proprietors seized upon the obvious: finding a new governor, someone "indifferent to the whole plantation" and not "suspected or disgusted by any of the Planters." But this involved consequences that raised other problems of equal, if not greater, difficulty. Yeamans had been heavily engaged in the Carolina venture from the beginning and had led efforts to colonize the Lower South in the 1660s, a fact to which the proprietors remained indebted. More important, the elite West Indian sugar planter was seen on both sides of the Atlantic as the "most considerable man" in South Carolina. As well, Yeamans had enlisted a substantial number of Barbadians to settle in the colony and was likely to do still more. As a result the proprietors were more than a little bit concerned about offending him. Yet even at a distance Yeamans's actions gave them "some umbrage." Colony officials were "making themselves but Cyphers" to him, and now that Yeamans had been given the upper hand he was expanding his power and dispatching his duties in ways that the proprietors had "never intended."[101]

Equally wary and circumspect, the proprietors could take heart from reports that reached them concerning their efforts to recruit settlers in New England, the Chesapeake, the Middle Colonies, and the Atlantic islands. John Dorrell and Hugh Wentworth, Puritan merchants who underwrote the peopling of the Bahamas, claimed in a letter they wrote in 1670 to Anthony Ashley Cooper that Bermuda was "yearly able to spare a Hundred inhabitants for the settlement of new Plantations." Dorrell and Wentworth noted that many colonists had previously emigrated from their home island to St. Lucia, Trinidad, Antigua, and Jamaica.

They also noted that in less than four years they had transported upwards of three hundred Bermudians to New Providence. Shortly after receiving the news, the proprietors contacted Sir John Heydon of Bermuda to enlist his support in recruiting settlers.[102] Similar, if less direct, efforts were undertaken in Virginia, New York, New Jersey, and the New England colonies, with the success of these efforts starting to show just as Governor Yeamans was attempting to consolidate his position. By January 1672 the population increased to about four hundred, and immigration from various quarters tended to check the "overruling power" of any one individual or group, impeding the ability of Sir John to control local government.[103]

These early recruiting efforts constituted the initial step in the formulation of a policy that profoundly shaped the future of South Carolina. They were anticipations of what eventuated in a full-blown campaign to enlist settlers in an effort to build up a proprietary party in the colony to offset the Barbados faction. The proprietors assured West that he and his supporters would not suffer to be "borne downe."[104] They had committed themselves to establishing a "faire and equall Government," holding out this promise to all prospective colonists, especially including Protestant dissenters. Resolving that none should be "deceived," they wrote to West: "Whatever cause there is of any jealousy we will provide the best we cann against all inconveniencys that may happen . . . and you may be sure we will maintaine and support you." To the council the proprietors promised to "countenance and assist" all those who promoted "the common good of the place" and to "study the good of those men who shall endeavour to signalize themselves that way."[105]

Although reluctant to dismiss Yeamans, the proprietors generally tried to be as good as their word. Immigration ensured the welfare of the colony and seemed likely to produce a balanced government, just the sort of solution the proprietors were looking for. Additionally, the proprietors studied the latest accounts from Carolina. Consistent with their promise, they assigned praise to provincial leaders whose efforts advanced their interests and contributed to the colony's well-being. In this way they came to identify with the strangely assorted group that coalesced around the leadership of Joseph West, whom they ultimately commissioned again as governor in 1674. Increasingly dissatisfied with Yeamans's administration of the colony and having earlier recognized West as "the person to whom we principally owe the settlement of that plantation," the proprietors felt obligated to reconsider their commitment to Yeamans and concluded that West was "the fittest man there for this trust."[106] As the leader of the political faction that opposed Yeamans's Barbados party, he was the natural and logical choice, and the proprietors had every reason to believe that his appointment would effect political change. But the council and parliament were dominated by West's political opponents, nearly all of whom were Anglicans. They vigorously pursued the profitable abuses of politics, dominating the Indian trade, ignoring proprietary instructions, and employing an unbuttoned, aggressive style of partisan politics that, together with the continuing flow of Barbadians into the colony, enabled them to retain control of local government.[107]

✢

The 1680s and 1690s saw an intensification of proprietary efforts to recruit settlers, an intensification of partisan broils, and the beginnings of sustained public worship, formalized Christian practice, and evangelization. As before, the proprietors found themselves faced at the opening of the period by the perennial problem of local government, a problem partly of their own making and one that might easily have been foreseen. In 1671 a sea captain in their employ, John Coming, had warned them of the potential danger of what was presently the source of their greatest concern. "The Barbadians," Coming reported, "do endeavour to rule all."[108] Governor West made essentially the same observation a few months earlier. Now, to an alarming extent, these Barbadians had come to dominate the political system, and they were generally held to blame for many of the colony's ills.

Even after they decided to replace Yeamans in 1674, the proprietors openly acknowledged "how industrious and usefull . . . the generallity of the people that came from Barbados have been." And in a letter they wrote to the governor and council explaining their decision to commission West they indicated, in a rather troubled and somewhat less than enthusiastic tone, that they were "still willing to encourage" others to immigrate.[109] But by 1680, after another group of islanders came to South Carolina, many of whom settled along Goose Creek and established one of the first major inland settlements, it became distressingly evident that some of their leaders had formed a powerful political cabal. While Barbadians probably accounted for less than one half of South Carolina's white population, which might have reached more than one thousand at this time, they held a solid majority in legislature, opposing Governor West and the proprietors alike.[110]

The proprietors sought to curb the growing influence of these troublesome West Indians and recover their authority to set the direction of their colony. They redoubled their efforts to recruit more inhabitants, mindful of the potential of cultivating new alliances and of the extent to which the pace of immigration had slowed. They also revised the Fundamental Constitutions, liberalizing further their plan of government and their policy of religious toleration. Finally, the proprietors initiated several political, legal, and economic reforms designed to establish a more effective system of administration and control.[111]

The proprietary recruiting drive turned up hundreds of immigrants. Most came directly from Europe, and most were Protestant dissenters. At least five hundred English Puritans arrived in the early and mid-1680s, from the gentry and lesser social classes, in addition to about 150 Scottish Covenanters. The former were largely Presbyterians and Independents, but there were substantial numbers of Baptists and other sectaries among the English immigrants as well. They were joined by a comparable number of French Huguenots who were seeking refuge from Louis XIV's violent persecution of Protestants, which culminated with the revocation of the Edict of Nantes in 1685. Settlers from some of the older colonies came too. Quakers arrived from Barbados and elsewhere, while a significant number of Baptist families removed from Kittery, Maine, after their minister, William Screven, was cited for his "offensive speeches," fined, and forbidden from keeping "any private exercise at his house or elsewhere, . . . either in Kittery, or any other place within the limits of [the] Province." Many other New Englanders followed, settling in Charleston and at Wappetaw, Cainhoy, and Dorchester. Nearly all of these were Congregationalists of firm convictions. One of the earliest substantial companies arrived in 1691 with Benjamin Pierpont, a graduate of Harvard College who had recently completed his clerical training. A native of Roxbury, Massachusetts, Pierpont assumed the pastorate of the Independent Church in Charleston, where he served until his death in 1698.[112]

Among the English Puritans who migrated to the colony in the early 1680s were prominent men of the gentry and business classes suffering disabilities and persecution under the Stuart monarchy, such as Joseph Morton and Daniel Axtell. In 1681 both men were created landgrave by the Lords Proprietors and reportedly "brought five hundred people to Carolina in a month." Morton subsequently served two terms as governor (1682–1684, 1685–1686) and, like Axtell, he appears to have shared extensive kinship and friendship connections with many of the Puritans who came. Axtell was a merchant in Stoke Newington, Middlesex, a village on the outskirts of London. He was the son of a Baptist from Hertfordshire. His father had served as an army officer at the trial of Charles I and was executed as a regicide in 1660 for his role in the death of the king. In 1678 Axtell removed from England after authorities searched his house for seditious libels. His wife, Rebecca (Blake) Axtell, was the daughter of Benjamin Blake, another prominent leader among the dissenters who migrated during these years.[113]

Blake was a captain in Oliver Cromwell's navy and the younger brother of the famous Admiral Robert Blake, a soldier in the New Model Army who took to the sea to lead the English battle fleet. He decided to emigrate from Somersetshire after Parliament failed to exclude James, the Catholic Duke of York, from the throne. In his *British Emire in America* (London, 1708), contemporary historian John Oldmixon, who was also a native of Somersetshire, recalled:

> 'Twas about this time, that the Persecution rais'd by the Popish Faction, and their Adherents, in England, against the Protestant Dissenters, was at

> the height; and no Part of this Kingdom suffer'd more by it than Somersetshire. The Author of this History liv'd at that time with Mr. Blake . . . being educated by his Son-in-law, who taught School in Bridgewater, and remembers, tho then very young, the Reasons old Mr. Blake us'd to give for leaving England: One of which was, That the Miseries they endur'd, meaning the Dissenters then, were nothing to what he foresaw would attend the Reign of a Popish Successor; wherefore he resolv'd to remove to Carolina.

Captain Blake sat on the provincial council and was appointed clerk of the Crown and Peace for South Carolina, and he was a man of considerable standing and influence—"so great an Interest among Persons of his principles," Oldmixon said, "that many honest substantial Persons engaged to go over with him." These English Old World immigrants likely included Thomas Smith, another prominent Puritan from Somersetshire. Like Blake, Smith was made landgrave by the proprietors, and, like Morton, he later served as the colony's governor (1693–1694), as did Blake's son, the second Landgrave Joseph Blake (1696–1700). A proprietary deputy, Daniel Axtell did not hold a major political office, but by all accounts he played a key role in recruiting settlers, having extensive kinship, friendship, and trading connections throughout the English Atlantic. In fact he and his wife Rebecca actively encouraged New Englanders to settle in Carolina. Thomas Smith may well have done the same. Shortly after arriving in the colony in 1684, Smith visited Boston with his wife Barbara and their two sons, Thomas and George. Here it appears that he deeded his interest in some property belonging to his grandparents to his uncle, and it is entirely possible that he promoted immigration during his visit.[114] What is certain is that Smith was a member of an elite group of nonconformists in South Carolina in the late 1600s.

Though their total numbers were comparatively more modest (perhaps about one hundred at the turn of the eighteenth century), Quakers formed a significant part of this dissenting elite core. Members of such notable Carolina families as the Fitches, Elliots, Ladsons, Stanyarnes, Mayos, and Waites were among the most prominent early Friends. Many came from Barbados, where in 1680 there were six meetinghouses. Numbering in the hundreds, Barbadian Quakers were harshly persecuted for their criticism of the Anglican church, refusal to swear oaths, nonattendance at militia drills, and efforts to Christianize slaves. A good many began relocating from Barbados to South Carolina in 1675, the year Thomas Tanner Stanyarne and his family landed. Quaker immigration remained fairly steady for at least a decade, but it appears to have reached a high point between 1678 and 1682. It was during this period that a group of English Friends arrived and that a monthly meeting was established in Charleston. In early 1675 Anthony Ashley Cooper commenced negotiations with a group of Quakers in London to settle "a whole Colony of 12000 acres." After finalizing the terms of the agreement he directed Governor West and the council to set aside the land "in such a convenient place as you and they shall pitch on . . . on condition that within five yeares they build a Towne of Thirty houses and 100 inhabitants at the least." Holding Quakers in high regard and "concerned to have perticular care of [them] myself," Ashley envisioned Carolina as a refuge for Friends in America and hoped they would people the colony "in a considerable Number."[115] Jacob Waite and his family were among the first English Friends to settle; other English Quakers included members of the Abbott, Crosse, Ladson, Pye, Samwaye, Strickland, Warren, and, perhaps, Mayo families. Mary (Fisher) Crosse was far and away the most widely known. Venerated as one of the so-called Valiant Sixty, the earliest Quaker disciples who were called to apostleship, "Mother Crosse" (1623–1698) was a pioneering religious leader in her day. In the 1650s she embarked upon a transatlantic missionary tour lasting some six years, preaching and prophecying in England, the West Indies, Massachusetts, and the Ottoman Empire. Arriving in Carolina with her husband John and their family in 1680, Crosse undoubtedly played a leadership role in organizing the Monthly Meeting of Charleston, which in August 1682 sent a letter to George Fox blessing "the favour that the Lord hath given." Fox acknowledged receipt of the letter wherein the colony's Quakers gave him "an account of [their] meeting, and of the country, and of the liberty in that province," and in his reply he encouraged the community to "stand all faithful in truth and righteousness." "My desire, is that you may prize your liberty, both natural and spiritual," he said, "and take heed of abusing that liberty, or losing the savour of the heavenly salt." While Fox expressed a legitimate concern for the future of Quakerism in the colony, memories of persecution among first-generation South Carolina Quakers were too fresh for them to become spiritually complacent in this early period. For example, Jonathan Fitch was repeatedly fined and imprisoned in Barbados for his religious convictions during the 1660s and 1670s. Similarly, Mary Fisher Crosse suffered persecution over and over again and spent many months in jail. On one notable occasion during the 1650s she and another Quaker apostle, Elizabeth Williams, were stripped to the waist and whipped repeatedly by authorities in Cambridge, England.[116] After the Restoration, with the imposition of the Clarendon Code, Quakers suffered even more for their faith.

Religious persecution in Scotland under Charles II, which turned deadly during the infamous "Killing Time" of the 1680s, also led several Scottish Covenanters to settle in Carolina. After two earlier proposals to establish Scottish colonies in the Southeast failed to materialize during the 1670s, a group of Covenanters organized a syndicate called the Carolina Company in 1682, entering into articles of agreement with the Lords Proprietors to establish a Scottish plantation. The company sent out the *James of Irvine* on an exploratory voyage and made extensive plans to advance Scotland's Atlantic national interests, both mercantile and religious. Unfortunately for the undertakers (the Presbyterian nobles, lairds, and merchants who subscribed investments in the syndicate hoping for a return), the reputation of the Carolina Company was tainted with treason when some of the subscribers were accused of being involved in the Rye House Plot to assassinate the Stuarts, foiling the corporate undertaking. With their Scottish American colonizing scheme in disarray, one of the most prominent subscribers, Lord Henry Erskine, 3rd Baron Cardross, secured the company's rights to plant a colony, which for him became something of a Presbyterian mission, a place where Scottish Protestantism might flourish in the New World. Cardross had been imprisoned for his religious convictions and had incurred harsh penalties for attending dissenting religious conventicles in which the forms of the English church were not used. He was also suspected of hosting such nonconformist gatherings at his castle and risked further punishment for his religious convictions. Thus, together with another investor in the Carolina Company, Presbyterian minister William Dunlop, Lord Cardross led a group of Covenanters to found Stuarts Town in 1684. The Port Royal settlers suffered through bad weather, fevers, and leaking ships, and, ultimately, their colony did not last, because in 1686 the Spanish sacked their tiny frontier outpost. Many were killed and Stuarts Town was abandoned. Scottish Presbyterianism exerted a significant influence in seventeenth-century South Carolina nevertheless. A few survivors of the failed colony, including Dunlop and John Stewart, another leader of the Port Royal mission who "deserted the Cuntry of [his] nativity to Enjoy a Safe conscience," fled north to Charleston, introducing a rich tradition of Presbyterian religious practice which increasingly came to center on sacramental revivalism.[117]

Some four years before the founding of Stuarts Town, the first contingent of Huguenot émigrés landed in South Caroliana, carrying a vital culture of French Calvinist worship with them across the Atlantic. Responding to the proprietary recruiting campaign and with financial backing from the Crown, forty-five refugee Huguenots arrived in Charleston aboard the *Richmond* in April 1680. They were followed by three or perhaps four additional and much more substantial groups of religiously minded French and Swiss Protestants who came from 1685 to 1687. Though migration fell off by end of the decade, the number of émigrés may have reached more than five hundred in 1700, or about 15 percent of South Carolina's total white population.[118] The Huguenots, whose special military and political privileges under the Edict of Nantes (1598) were stripped by Cardinal Richelieu in the 1620s and who were thereafter subjected to a variety of persecutions until all forms of Protestant worship were ultimately outlawed by Louis XIV in 1685, greatly strengthened provincial nonconformity during this period. Indeed, as Bertrand Van Ruymbeke has shown, the Huguenots expressed an early determination to found Calvinist churches, enjoyed a strong pastoral presence in the 1680s and 1690s, and successfully introduced ecclesiastical structures modeled on pre-Revocation French Protestantism. In October 1679 a Huguenot leader named Jacob Guérard announced that he was planning to sail to Carolina with several refugee families and that he intended "to found a church thither," and it appears that the first comers organized a Huguenot congregation (or église) in Charleston shortly after their arrival a few months later. The name of a French cleric, Pierre Forestier, appears on one of the *Richmond*'s passenger lists, though it remains unclear whether he ever removed from London with the earliest settlers and actually ministered in Carolina. At least by the fall of 1682, however, a French-speaking clergyman named Laurentius Van den Bosch is known to have been preaching to the refugees. Yet Van den Bosch, an Anglican-ordained Walloon from southern Belgium, quickly proved to be a disappointment, because he sought to exact subscriptions and perquisites with unbecoming zeal and, more significantly, personally represented conformity to the English church. As a result the congregation eventually refused to support him and Van den Bosch was forced to relocate to Boston in 1685. Despite his departure, another French minister, Florent-Philippe Trouillart, landed in the colony about this time with a group of French and Swiss immigrants who came on aboard the *Margaret*, and within the next five years two other ministers, Élie Prioleau and Pierre Robert, arrived, bringing to three the number of settled Huguenot clergy laboring in the colony. Also, apparently under Trouillart's leadership, a number of prominent refugee merchants, planters, and artisans, including Pierre Buretel, Jacques LeSerrurier, and Antoine Boureau, formed a lay consistory (or *consistoire*) to oversee Huguenot church affairs, which was responsible for things such as assisting the poor, constructing and maintaining Huguenot churches, and collecting funds to support ministers.[119]

Together with the other groups who peopled the colony in the last two decades of the seventeenth century, these Atlantic world migrations transformed South Carolina. Barbadians were quickly reduced to a relatively small minority of the population. So, too, were Anglicans, as the vast majority of new immigrants were nonconformists. In fact, organized religion in the colony became overwhelmingly dissenting for over a generation, and it remained permanently and substantially so thereafter. Moreover, the number of people in the province seems to have grown faster during the 1680s than at any other time in the colonial era (except for the founding decade of the 1670s), at an annual compound growth rate of approximately 12.5. Already by 1685 there were more than twice as many inhabitants as there had been five years earlier; within a decade there were well over three times as many, as the total population in 1690 stood at about 3,900. Part of the increase was due to the continuing importation of slaves. In any given year during the South Carolina's first two and a half decades perhaps one quarter to one third of the population was black. Yet until the racial balance started to shift in the late 1690s and early 1700s, white individuals constituted a much higher proportion of the population than Africans and African Americans.[120]

Above all these migrations served to increase Christian activity in the Carolina lowcountry. Formed congregations appeared everywhere, public preaching increased dramatically, and church building proceeded at a prolific pace, thoroughly sacralizing the provincial landscape. In the two decades or so prior to 1701, eleven permanent churches were founded in South Carolina. Significantly only one, St. Philip's, was Anglican. The rest were founded by the colony's growing number of reforming Calvinist and sectarian groups, who now thoroughly dominated the population. During this period Presbyterians and Congregationalists established four churches in the colony; Huguenots established four churches; and Quakers and Baptists each established one church. Though data relevant to the size of these congregations are limited and frequently imprecise, South Carolina suddenly had an extraordinary per capita church ratio, with roughly one church for every five hundred inhabitants, making it among the best churched colonies in English America.[121]

As the population surged and as reform and sectarian Christianity grew, the number of resident clergymen in South Carolina rose substantially. Not counting Quakers, who rejected a formal, "hireling" ministry, at least sixteen nonconforming ministers are known to have settled in the colony by the turn of the eighteenth century, whereas just three or four Anglican ministers are known to have arrived, one of whom, Laurentius Van den Bosch, was appointed by French Calvinists to preach among the Carolina Huguenots.[122] Relations among ministers and between ministers and laity were often conflicted, and clerical competition was sometimes intense. This was especially true when male, female, and lay and ministerial roles overlapped. Joseph Lord, one of four Harvard-trained ministers who immigrated to the colony in the seventeenth century, recalled one experience he had along the Ashley River shortly after he returned to the Carolina lowcountry following a recruiting drive in New England. In 1699 he wrote to Governor Thomas Hinckley of Massachusetts about the intrigues of a Baptist rival who prevailed upon some of the female members of his sect to "enter into the houses" of their neighbors and "lead captive silly women." "When I came to Dorchester, I found that a certain Anabaptist teacher (named Sciven), who came from New England, had taken advantage of my absence to insinuate into some of the people about us, and to endeavour to make proselytes, not by public preaching up his own tenets, nor by disputations, but by employing some of his most efficient and trusty adherents to gain upon such as they had interest in, and thereby to set an example to others that are too apt to be led by anything that is new." Screven had already set a date for receiving two of these women into his congregation "by plunging," but Lord apparently convinced one, a Puritan goodwife, "of the error of that way." He could not be sure about the other. She was the wife of

Thomas Broughton, a prominent West Indian Anglican who later became lieutenant governor.[123]

While some laypersons openly embraced proselytizing, others expressed antipathy toward the Anglican clergy, which often signaled reform tendencies. Atkin Williamson, who arrived in the colony by 1679 and labored "Under the Notion and Character" of an Anglican priest for more than thirty years, soon fell victim to such hostility.[124] Described as a "great Lover of Strong Liquor," Williamson aroused suspicion among many laypeople as to the validity of his episcopal orders, and, as a result, none of them ever "thought fit to take up with him as a settled Minister."[125] Yet no one doubted that Williamson was the target of an impish prank, whereby in 1687 "some Wicked people" got him drunk in a tavern and reportedly induced him to baptize a bear cub. Whether Williamson actually performed the ceremony became the subject of considerable controversy, so much so that Anglican officials investigated the incident twenty years later. Nevertheless, even those who sought to discredit the bear-cub story conceded that "the thing was indeed intended." And in the final analysis, as one dissenting observer put it, that was "the cream of the Jeast."[126]

The context in which this episode took place gave it special meaning to contemporaries, helping to explain why the bear-cub story became "so publickly known that no man doubted the truth of the occasion," why it continued to receive so much attention, as well as why some later sought to debunk it and were "very much offended that such a thing shou'd be mentioned."[127] For the coming of Calvinist reform and sectarian groups not only transformed South Carolina's spiritual environment and created a great stirring of religious expression. It also touched off a furious political struggle for control of the colony's government, one which was given distinctive shape by religious sensibilities.

Determined to break the power of the Barbadians and bring their colony into line, the Carolina proprietors concluded an alliance with English and Scottish dissenters to advance their interests. To encourage nonconformist immigration and actively to cultivate dissenting support, the proprietors revised the Fundamental Constitutions in 1682, significantly liberalizing their policy of religious toleration. First they excised the reference to Anglicanism as "the only true and Orthodox, and the National Religion of all the King's Dominions." Second they included a separate article specifically prohibiting ministers from holding civil offices to prevent ecclesiastical meddling in South Carolina politics. Most important, the proprietors exempted non-Anglican Protestants from paying taxes which might be levied to support the Church of England, granting "every church or congregation of Christians, not of the communion of the Church of Rome," the authority to "lay a tax on its own members."[128]

In addition to the foregoing concessions, the proprietors commissioned the dissenting leader Joseph Morton as governor, suspended several Barbadians from office, and attempted to fix election procedures to give the new immigrants a disproportionate share of power in the legislature. In particular they established three new counties—Berkeley, Craven, and Colleton—with each having proportional representation.[129] Opposition to proprietary reforms immediately mounted. The indefatigable Maurice Mathews, a popish "Jesuit for Designe politick," headed the antiproprietary party, which included most of the West Indians in the province. They became known as "the Goose Creek men" since many of their leaders settled near Goose Creek, a tributary of the Ashley River. Supporting the status quo, members of the antiproprietary party sought to maintain their power and influence and resented what they considered to be outside interference in local affairs. A recurrent argument of the Goose Creek men was that the proprietors did not fully understand conditions in the colony.[130]

The Fundamental Constitutions became the focal point of South Carolina politics during the 1680s. The colonists had never formally approved the document, nor had they ever been instructed to do so. Rather, the proprietors drew up a set of temporary laws to govern the province until the constitutions could be fully implemented. As immigration surged, as the colony continued to develop, and as the strength of the proprietary party grew, however, the prospects for effecting implementation seemed better than ever before. As a consequence the proprietors began pressing the legislature to adopt their "Grand Model."[131] In 1685 Governor Morton asked the legislature to swear allegiance to the Fundamental Constitutions of 1682 as a first step toward realizing this goal. Although proprietary supporters complied, the Goose Creek men balked. Arbitrary changes in the document, they reasoned, were forbidden in the original version, which bound signatories to observe the constitutions as a "Sacred unalterable form and Rule of Government."[132]

The antiproprietary party's refusal to accept the revised Carolina Constitutions produced a political and constitutional crisis, with subsequent efforts to counter their argument proving unsuccessful. After one attempt at compromise, the Goose Creek men moved into ever more resolute opposition. In 1687 they introduced a bill in the legislature declaring the Fundamental Constitutions to be incompatible with the royal charter of 1665. The measure failed, but it had the desired effect, raising serious doubts about the proprietors' motives in repeatedly altering the document, creating confusion among the dissenting supporters of the proprietary party, and strengthening the hand of their Anglican rivals.[133]

In the wake this showdown the situation in the colony increasingly became confused and unsettled. The legislature did not meet in the ensuing three and a half years, and while South Carolinians were quarreling over the charter bill, news of the Glorious Revolution in England and of the outbreak of King William's War (1689–1697) reached the colony through the Atlantic communication network, giving a new sense of urgency to the issues of both provincial loyalty and provincial defense. Alarmed by rumors of a French invasion and the potential for more generalized upheaval, no one could fail to recognize the seriousness of the colony's predicament. Still, political battles grew more intense, with both parties making appeals to voters and vigorously contending for popular support.[134]

An underlying concern of the Goose Creek men was an awareness of the changing character of the population. Reforming Calvinist and sectarian Protestants were continuing to flow into the colony, threatening to weaken their position further. Antiproprietary leaders had been purged from appointive offices and reapportionment had had a negative effect on their legislative influence. Seeing their power slipping away, the Goose Creek men turned, paradoxically, to refugee Huguenots, presenting themselves as their confessional allies and as the true defenders of liberty.[135] Although unanticipated by the proprietors and their provincial supporters, this alliance became a central feature of South Carolina political life, and it enabled Barbadians to continue to exercise powerful influence in local government.

Yet to attack the Fundamental Constitutions was to risk alienating the Huguenots in both a literal and figurative sense. In addition to religious toleration the constitutions provided for a liberal policy of naturalization. The constitutions also granted foreign-born naturalized citizens full political equality.[136] Presbyterian John Stewart, the proprietary party's leading propagandist, seized upon this fact in an effort to expose the Goose Creek men as Machiavellian hypocrites. Attempting to maintain a common front against his provincial foes, Stewart wrote a detailed defense of the Fundamental Constitutions after the protracted charter-bill debate. His pamphlet was translated into French and circulated throughout Huguenot communities in order to awaken the refugees to consequences of the antiproprietary position. "If fundamentals be thrown by," Stewart wrote, driving straight to the heart of the issue, "farewell then Liberty of Conscience [and] Naturalization."[137]

Had it not been for a totally bizarre turn of events Stewart's pamphlet might have tempered the evolving alliance between Huguenots and the antiproprietary party and increased the chances for a political compromise between the proprietary faction and the Goose Creek men. Just after his pamphlet appeared, however, Seth Sothel, who held a share in the Carolina proprietary, was forced to resign as governor of North Carolina under pressure from the Albemarle settlers and decided to travel to Charleston. By the time he arrived Governor James Colleton, Morton's successor as governor, had granted a petition drawn up by Landgrave Thomas Smith to proclaim martial law. Excluded from power, the Goose Creek men boldly invited Sothel to claim the governorship. Sothel readily accepted, and in the summer of 1690 his supporters engineered a bloodless coup which sent a shudder throughout the colony. Not long after, the Goose Creek men proceeded to pass a series of laws to consolidate their position. A naturalization law, transparently partisan, granted full citizenship to French and Swiss refugees, a large number whom had become active supporters of Sothel's dubious administration.[138]

Huguenots paid a heavy price. Appalled by the Goose Creek faction's crude demagoguery, proprietary party leaders pitched upon the refugees as a convenient foil, and it would be hard to exaggerate the bitterness of their response. Never regarded as just another kind of settler, Huguenots became the subject of a virulent campaign designed to brand them as villainous traitors. For dissenter John Stewart and his allies, the French were like having "vipers in our own bowels."[139] King William's War undoubtedly lent credence to rumor and innuendo. While the Goose Creek men primarily viewed the refugees as a way of maintaining their influence in local government, their opponents seized on a two-faced villain. At the first opportunity, they struck with a vengeance.

In 1691 Sothel was replaced by Philip Ludwell as governor. The other proprietors disallowed every law passed during Sothel's tenure, and, in a effort to curb the factionalism that had poisoned the atmosphere of South Carolina politics, temporarily suspended the Fundamental Constitutions. Meanwhile proprietary party stalwarts continued to fan the flames of anti-French hostility. When Quaker proprietor John Archdale arrived in 1695 to assume the governorship he found "all Matters in great Confusion." "Every Faction apply'd themselves to me in hopes of Relief," he wrote. An orgy of Francophobia gripped the colony. The legislature "sat Six Weeks under Civil Broils and Heats" after the council, over the objections of Archdale, introduced a petition to disenfranchise Huguenots by eliminating representation in Craven County, where refugees were most heavily concentrated. Anti-French proprietary representatives were determined to succeed at all costs. The hysteria finally convinced the governor to relent. In order to put "their minds into a cooler Frame of Spirit," Archdale called a new assembly, apportioning thirty seats in the assembly for Berkeley and Colleton Counties and excluding the seats previously allocated to Craven.[140]

With the coming of John Archdale the increasingly bitter and divisive partisanship of the 1670s and 1680s temporarily subsided. At the same time Protestant dissenters came to dominate South Carolina. Led first by Governor Thomas Smith and then (after the tenure of Quaker proprietor John Archdale) by Governor Joseph Blake, nonconformists sought to create a successful, orderly, and godly society in the New World, "a fruitfull Canan, the Wonder and admiration of America." "Good and wholsom laws strictly put in execution," John Stewart wrote of such aspirations, "Tricks and dishonesty Turn'd out of doors, Churches built and charity and maitenance to pious morall teachers allowd will make God love and Bless us and we orselvs will live happy and fortunat."[141]

Commissioned in 1690 on the eve of the Goose Creek coup, Thomas Smith claimed the governorship in the spring of 1693 after the "disturbances and distempers of State that Carolina's Government underwent dureing the time of Mr. Sothwell and Coll Ludwel's govent."[142] He arrived in the colony in 1684 and quickly emerged as one of the largest landowners in the lowcountry. In politics Smith distinguished himself as a leader in the proprietary faction, becoming one of its staunchest supporters. Prior to being commissioned governor, Smith served as a proprietary deputy, councilman, and sheriff of Berkeley County. In John Stewart's estimation he was a "diamond among a thousand pretious stones of great and universall sens, . . . popular honest just Ingenious and Ritch of publick spirit." Given his partisan sensibilities, perhaps this partly explains why Smith was such an effective chief executive. During his tenure South Carolina began to prosper, and the proprietors finally began to realize a return on their investment in colony.[143]

Landgrave Joseph Blake, who accompanied his father Benjamin and other English dissenters to the colony in the early 1680s, succeeded Thomas Smith as governor. Though Blake's was a slightly more moderate political temperament, anti-French sentiment reached fever pitch during his first term in office (1694–1695), contributing to a new flurry of partisan rancor. The "french papisticall Warr" not only posed a direct threat to the colony but aroused nationalistic fervor. As English and Scottish colonists rallied around "King and Country and the Protestant religion," Huguenots' double allegiance caused a xenophobic stir.[144] Their support of the Goose Creek faction only compounded the precariousness of their position. Proprietary party leaders questioned French naturalization, demanded that the refugees declare undivided loyalty to the English king, and sought to curb their political rights. Thus when Governor Archdale arrived in the fall of 1695 he had no choice but to give into the "Enemies of the French."[145]

Lacking Huguenot support, the antiproprietary Goose Creek faction was forced into a position of compromise, and over the course of the following years the "pernicious wheill of politics" yielded to a spirit of bipartisanship. Dissenters came to dominate the provincial government, monopolizing most political offices with proprietary backing and greatly expanding their influence at the end of the seventeenth century.[146] During the brief administration of Quaker proprietor John Archdale (1695–1696), who was sworn into office by affirmation rather than by oath, Charleston Friends enjoyed unprecedented liberty. At the same time they strengthened their ties to the London Yearly Meeting while continuing to remain both active and influential beyond their numbers. In 1696 the Carolina Assembly granted Archdale the power to excuse Quakers from militia duty "upon a conscientious principle of Religion," and the Yearly Meeting of Friends in London could report that "truth spreads and prospers, and the Lord's work goes on, and that there is openness and convincement . . . and divers raised up to bear public testimony for the truth." Also, a substantial number of South Carolina Quakers held political office. For example, Dr. Charles Burham, a prominent Quaker physician who migrated to the province from New England, was elected in 1695 to represent Berkeley County in the South Carolina Commons House of Assembly, and he soon emerged as a leader of the first rank. Although Burnham and several others may have felt called to speak at Quaker meetings, Mary Crosse remained the most visible and authoritative Public Friend in the colony. Exercising her ministerial gift, Crosse delivered inspired gospel messages as a "chosen instrument" of God, and it appears that she continued to preach in Charleston until the time of her death in 1698. A remarkable woman, she was revered as "mother Crosse" even by such non-Quakers as John Stewart.[147]

Like Crosse, many other immigrant women played a leading role in expanding the influence of Protestant dissent in late-seventeenth-century South Carolina. Though she did not preach publicly, Lady Rebecca Axtell, Landgrave Daniel Axtell's widow, was a woman of deep religious feeling who sympathized with the spirit of all sorts of dissenters and was an active instrument of leadership. In the 1690s she supported settlers from both Baptist and Congregational churches in New England, as well as those who arrived with them and were needing ministers. As a result of her patronage and the shifting patterns of Atlantic migration, immigration, and resettlement, Lady Rebecca's country seat at Newington, which was located on the upper reaches of the Ashley River, became a hub of dissenting activity. To the chagrin of the New England Congregationalists who settled there in large numbers, Baptist itinerant William Screven established a vital and expanding religious community in the region.[148] Screven's South Carolina ministry was a long, active, and productive one. A native of the town of Somerton in Somersetshire, England, he migrated to the scattered Puritan communities in Maine around 1668, ultimately settling in Kittery, the oldest town in the province. There he began attending a "Mr. Mowdy's meeting on Lord's days" and was cited for "not frequenting the publique meeting according to the Law."[149] Openly espousing believer's baptism by 1681, Screven, his wife Bridgett (Cutts), and twelve other inhabitants of Kittery joined a congregation of Baptists in Boston. The following year Screven was brought to trial before the General Court of Maine for public preaching and was cited for contempt, "his rash and inconsiderate Words tending to blasphemy":

> Mr. Screven appearing before this court, and being convicted of contempt of his majesty's authority, and refusing to submit himself to the sentence of the court, prohibiting his public preaching; and upon examination before the court, declaring his resolution still to persist therein; the court tendered him the liberty to return home to his family in case he would forbear such turbulent practices, and amend for the future; but he refused, the court sentenced

> him to give *bonds* for his good behaviour, and to forbear such contentious behaviour for the future, and the delinquent stand committed until the judgment of this court be filed.

As punishment for his obstinance, the court ordered Screven to pay a fine of £10, forbade him from holding religious assemblies, and commanded him to attend Sabbath services at the public meetinghouse.

Subsequently Screven and ten other Kittery residents formed a church, the members "having a desire to the service of Christ . . . and the propagating of his glorious gospel of peace and salvation, and eyeing that precious promise in Daniel the 12th, 3d: 'They that turn many to righteousness shall shine as the stars forever.'" Considering their minister's "tribulations" and the fact that there were "many adversaries" in Maine, the congregation of Baptists ultimately decided to emigrate from New England to a colony where settlers were worshiping God in their own way. Prior to their departure, some may have corresponded with family and friends in the Lower South and the West Indies. Bridgett Cutts had relatives in Barbados, for example, and Screven, Humphrey Axtell, and other members of the Kittery church undoubtedly knew or were related to the English dissenters who had recently landed in South Carolina. Whatever the specific connections, the New Englanders found their way into the lowcountry, where they settled the town of Somerton on the banks of the Cooper River. From there Screven preached far and wide, up the Ashley, on the Stono, and in Charleston. By the time he died in 1713 at the age of 84, he had even established a strong Baptist presence at Winyah.[150]

Despite the proprietors' policy of religious toleration, Screven and his co-religionists encountered considerable opposition in the South Carolina lowcountry. Among the Baptists' most outspoken opponents were three Congregationalist ministers: John Cotton, Jr., Hugh Adams, and Joseph Lord. John Cotton, Jr. (1639–1699) was the second son and namesake of the famous Massachusetts divine, the Reverend John Cotton, Sr., minister of the First Church in Boston. Known for his "somewhat hasty and perhaps severe . . . censures upon some persons and things," including Baptists and their doctrines, the younger Cotton assumed the pastorate of Charleston's Independent Meeting House in December 1698.[151] Following in the path of another New England minister, Benjamin Pierpont, who died earlier in the year at the age of thirty-nine, Cotton built an impressive congregation before a yellow-fever epidemic claimed his life in the autumn of 1699. According to a manuscript account of his ministry written by his son Josiah, "there were many Baptised" during his short ministry and "about 25 New members received to full communion," bringing to perhaps 115 the total number of church members.[152] Among the communicants were some of the most prominent merchants and planters in the Carolina colony. These included

Joseph Boone, Robert Fenwick, and Landgrave Joseph Blake. On behalf of himself and "sundry... inhabitants of charlestowne," Fenwick traveled to Plymouth, Massachusetts, to give Cotton a call, offering him a salary of 67£ annually.[153]

That John Cotton, Jr., was a gifted Puritan preacher with proven abilities to win converts is evidenced by his New England preaching career. After graduating from Harvard College in 1657, Cotton assumed the pastorate of the Congregational church in Wethersfield, Connecticut (1660–1663). Subsequently he served as an Indian missionary on Martha's Vineyard (1664–1667). Then, in November 1667, Cotton accepted a call from the congregation at Plymouth, where he preached until 1697. During this period Cotton greatly increased the membership of Plymouth's church. Within a year of assuming the Plymouth pulpit, for example, Cotton increased church membership from twenty-seven to seventy-four, and from 1670 to 1672 some thirty-seven new members were added. Overall, about 178 townspeople made a "Confession of Faith, and a Declaration of their Experiences of a Work of Grace in the Presence of the Congregation" during Cotton's ministry. This was particularly true after Cotton led a covenant renewal ceremony at Plymouth church in 1676.

By this time Cotton had resumed his missionary work among the Native Americans of southeastern New England. In 1670, the same year South Carolina was founded, Cotton began riding on a preaching circuit from Cape Cod, Massachusetts, to Little Compton, Rhode Island, proselytizing among the region's Indians. Meanwhile Cotton maintained his full-time responsibilities as pastor of the Plymouth congregation, which he undertook with fervor and passion.[154] Upon being invited to settle at Plymouth he instituted a series of visitations whereby "the Pastor with the Ruling Elder made it their first special Work together to pass through the whole Town from Family to Family to enquire into the State of Souls, and according as they found the Frames either of the Children of the Church or others, so they applied Counsels, Admonitions, Exhortations and Encouragements; which Service was attended with a Blessing." Following these early revival visitations, Cotton introduced a program of catechizing. He also held fasts "for personal and Family Reformation" and later requested that "the Church Seed who were Heads of Families" join in a question-and-answer exercise. Cotton carried out the activity by distributing to each member "sundry Questions ... to return Answers to out of the Scripture." Like his other revival techniques, this edifying exercise was "not without a Blessing," and the Plymouth church kept it up "for divers Years,"experiencing a kind of cyclic renewal.[155]

Such diverse and successful ministerial experiences obviously help to explain why Cotton enjoyed a fruitful, if attenuated, ministry in Charleston. By experimenting with innovative revival techniques he became an "Instrument of Edifying and Quickening many Saints & Converting many Sinners." According to his son Josiah, in multiplying the membership of the Independent Church Cotton "set up Catechising, Precht a Lecture once a fortnight, Had private meetings, private Fasts alone & with others, Made frequent visits to the Sick, opposed Gainsayers, [and] satisfied the Doubtfull." Diary entries by Cotton for 1698 and 1699, preserved and transcribed by his son, bear this out. On December 11 he preached his first sermon in Carolina (on Matthew 1:21) and "many seemed Affected." On February 21 he wrote, "I catechised 26 Persons[.] Some of the Damsels after Catechising got alone in a chamber & Prayed together having been much affected with what they had heard. The good Lord carry on these Beginnings to a sound Work of conversion. The Eldest of ym was not 13. Some about 10 & under a Good Incouragement to feed Christs Lambs—." On March 15, when the new minister was formally chosen and installed by receiving "the Right hand of Fellowship" from his Carolina congregation, Cotton led a covenant renewal ceremony in which "many were much affected and Blessed God, etc." In New England around this time such covenant renewals were, as Perry Miller once phrased it, "rapidly becoming the focus for the ordering of the spiritual life of the town," thus presaging the First Great Awakening.[156]

Praying that God would make him "a Blessing indeed to many Souls," Cotton literally threw himself into his Carolina ministry. Continuing his conversion work, he began leading a series of church fasts, preaching on salvation, and discoursing with many "about their Soul concerns." "Purchased here by Prayer," the New England minister wrote from Carolina to a friend in Plymouth that he was "well satisfied with ye good Providence of God in bringing Me hither." Cotton's correspondence reveals that by early August his church in Charleston was receiving a number of congregants into full communion.[157] Among the spiritually aroused was Joseph Boone, a leading South Carolina merchant and close ally of Landgrave Thomas Smith. During Cotton's ministry Boone was "propounded for ... chh fellowship."[158] As the church grew, so did charitable contributions. Josiah Cotton noted that his father received "a Considerable sum for his Labours." In addition to his annual salary several church benefactors contributed substantial sums for his ministerial services. The second Landgrave Joseph Morton, a councilmen and judge of the vice-admiralty court, was one such benefactor. In a letter to his son Rowland, Cotton wrote: "I spake the other day to Lantgrave Morton ... who of all the Councill is my most ingenous friend [and] comes to heare me each sabbath he is at towne & always gives me one or 2 visits & though noe subscriber, yet freely gives me divers pounds."[159]

Cotton's letters also reveal that Charleston was a place of intense denominational competition. On one notable occasion Cotton battled with an Anglican minister (presumably Samuel Marshall) for the allegiance of "a Jew professing Christ." Although the rival clergyman was "tampering with him to get him to accept the signe of the cross," the Puritan minister reported to his son on August 8 that "the Jew is come to me this morning lively in his good motions [to be baptized]."[160] The Baptists gave absolutely nothing away to the Anglicans in their efforts to win converts, however, and Cotton was far more concerned about his Baptist than his Anglican rivals. A "living Index to the Bible," Cotton wrote a detailed defense of infant baptism in 1699 and condemned those who were being seduced by the Baptists' message.[161] Still, Charlestonians were assembling in large numbers to hear the preaching of Baptist minister Gilbert Ashley, a justice of the peace who served in the Carolina assembly in 1695 and proved to be a remarkably successful proselytizer. Indeed, Cotton fumed when a sea-faring trader named Cocks abandoned his meeting for Ashley's. "Mr Cocks, who brought me hither," he wrote, "is a rotten Anabaptist [and] never comes to our meeting [but] to heare Gilbert Ashley, little did I thinke he would have prooved soe unworthy a fellow."[162]

This intense denominational rivalry proved short lived. Not long after Cotton penned these words "a great sickness & Mortality" visited South Carolina with catastrophic results. Yellow fever began to invade Charleston in late August 1699 and continued to ravage the town until the middle of November. "Many taken Sick in Town," Cotton wrote in his diary entry for September 4. "It was now a very Sickly dying Time," he noted on the tenth.[163] Rushing around to speak with "divers of ye Ch. To Quicken them to prepare for ye Lords Supper" (some twenty-six in all), the New Englander initially saw the epidemic as an occasion to encourage his congregants to own the church covenant. He began preaching a string of sermons toward this end and "Much of Gods Grace & Glory appeared."[164] But in the midst of this feverish rush of visitations and pulpit preachings he died.

Cotton was not alone. Among the more than 175 people who perished in the 1699 yellow-fever epidemic were at least five South Carolina clergymen, including Gilbert Ashley, John Cotton, Daniel Courtis, Samuel Marshall, and Élie Prioleau. "All ye ministers of ye town are dead," Cotton's youngest son reported to his brother in late October upon hearing the news of their father's death.[165] Hugh Adams, one of Cotton's ministerial colleagues, confirmed the report. On February 23, 1700, he wrote to Samuel Sewell of Massachusetts saying that he had read "a Catalogue of the dead," which included the names of virtually all of the ministers with settled pastorates in Charleston at the time. Adams noted that "Out of Mr. Cotton's church there died himself, September 17th, Mr. John Alexander, Merchant, Mr. Curtice preacher, Mr. Matthew Bee, Schoolmaster, [and] Mr. Henry Spry (besides his Servant man, his youngest child, and an Indian Woman)." Like Gilbert Ashley, Presbyterian preacher Daniel Courtis lost his life "in the beginning of the Mortality." And Adams blamed both his death and Ashley's death on "their peoples contempt of their Gospel Labors." Furthermore, he suggested that the people's refusal to heed the warnings of God's spokesmen in interpreting this ominous sign caused the fever to rage. After the two ministers' demise, Adams said, "the Distemper raged, and the destroying Angel slaughtered so furiously with his revenging Sword of pestilence, that there died . . . 14 in one day, September 28th. And raged as bad all October: So that the dead were carried in carts, being heaped up one upon another."[166]

Before this "terrible Tempest of Mortality" a sprit of confessional rivalry and competition had prevailed. Afterward, however, the mood seems to have been a good deal more catholic. In fact, Adams was busily preparing for the end of the world and appears to have been rather untroubled by all other religious matters. After all, Adams wrote, the Charleston epidemic of 1699 was "worse by far than the great Plague of London, considering the smallness of the Town." "I have Scripture Grounds to fear and expect that some more terrible impending Judgments are hovering over Carolina to be rained down in snares, fire and Brimstone and an horrible Tempest," Adams told Sewell, "as the portion of our cup for the yet tolerated and practised abominations, and Sodom like Sins of this Land." "Dearly beloved Brother," he went on to say, "I intreat you to prepare for the near-approaching of Temptation and Persecution, which Christ will bring upon all the World to try them that dwell upon the earth. When the Lord will search Jerusalem with candles, and punish the men that are settled on their Lees; when Christ will weigh all Professors in the Balance of their Sanctuary. Then wo to them that shall be found out of Christ at that day." While Adams did not know whether he would see Sewall again before the end of the world came, he was hopeful that they might see one another again in God's new creation. "Although we may see one another no more in this world," he wrote, "yet I hope to meet you in Christ with Comfort and Joy at the morning of the Resurrection."[167]

At the time, Hugh Adams (1676–1748) was in the process of organizing two Congregational churches along the Wando River, one at Cainhoy and one at Sewee (Wappetaw), where "many . . . New England Men were planted."[168] Twenty-two years old, Adams began his South Carolina ministerial career in August 1698, which he later wrote about in an autobiographical narrative. Having graduated from Harvard College the previous year, Adams temporarily succeeded Benjamin Pierpont in Charleston before accepting a call in 1699 "to settle at a large parish on both sides of the Wando River, where I preached for two years."[169] Pierpont probably visited the area starting in 1695 or 1696, and it is likely that Cotton urged Adams to accept the call after his arrival. With Courtis acting as Charleston's co-pastor, there was no longer any pressing need for Adams's services there, whereas several other Puritan communities were looking for settled ministers, and Cotton undoubtedly wished to keep up regular services among them. Too, the Wando colonists' offer was an appealing one, as parishioners promised Adams an annual salary of £70 and were making plans to build two meeting houses (one on either side of the river) to accommodate the large but widely scattered number of New Englanders who migrated to the region.[170] A good many appear to have come from Essex County, Massachusetts, from towns and villages such as Ipswich, Salem, and Manchester. In a letter addressed to Governor John Archdale dated June 26, 1696, the Reverend William Hubbard of Ipswich indicated that "a considerable Number of House-holders" in Essex County had resolved "with the Favour of God's Providence ... to Transport themselves into South Carolina," hoping to "reap Recompence as to Temporal Blessings." A few months later several families were dismissed from the Salem church. Puritans from neighboring villages like Manchester also arrived, including Susannah Winborn, whom Hugh Adams married in 1701.[171] A December 9, 1696, memorandum from John Wise, pastor of Chebacco Parish in Ipswich, indicates something of the astonishing scale of Essex County immigration. In his detailed instructions to a party of New England emigrants leaving Massachusetts for South Carolina, he advised them to "take perticular and peculiar account how that place called the Read-Banks is settled, or what condition that neck is in; if it may be sufficient for about one hundred families, more then [*sic*] what may be settled ther already with our friend and neighbor Bennj. Singleterry."[172]

Other Puritan adventurers from northeastern Massachusetts may have settled along the Wando River somewhat earlier. William Hubbard revealed that many Essex townspeople and villagers had been "credibly inform'd" of the fruitfulness of the colony, likely by friends and neighbors who had already removed. Hubbard also revealed that many around Ipswich had "heard the Fame of South Carolina, as it now stands Circumstanced with the honour of a true English Government, with Virtuous and Discreet Men Ministers in it, who now design the promoting of the Gospel for the increase of Virtue amongst the Inhabitants, as well as outward Trade and Business."[173] In his *New Description of that Fertile and Pleasant Province of Carolina* (London, 1707), Governor Archdale alluded to one Puritan congregation that was shipwrecked along the Carolina coast, and it is possible (in accordance with local tradition) that some of the castaways may have planted at Sewee Bay after being rescued. In relating some remarkable events that occurred "quickly after" he assumed the governorship on August 17, 1695, Archdale wrote that "a Vessel coming from New England with 52 Passangers, was Cast-away at Cape Fear." After "four or five of them came to Town," Archdale wrote, "I procured a Vessel to fetch them to Charles Town, which is about 100 Miles from thence, and all came safe but one Child that died."[174] That this group came from Essex County is not improbable, for the adventurers could have landed at Sewee Bay, not Charleston as the governor indicated. But the castaways may also have been part of another important stream of migration, not from Essex but from Middlesex County, and they may have planted elsewhere.

Near the time Wando was settled, a substantial group of English settlers from Middlesex County established a Puritan colony on the Ashley River at Booshoee Creek adjoining Rebecca Axtell's plantation. William Norman, a leading member of the group, had secured a 320-acre tract just above Booshoee Creek in 1684, settling the land with his wife, his son, two servants, and an African American or Native American slave he purchased shortly after his arrival. In 1695 Norman returned to New England and proposed "Ye gathering of A church for ye South Coralina." The heads of several Middlesex families quickly responded, resolving "to goe to South Caralina to settll the gospell there." On October 20 the First Church at Dorchester, Massachusetts, dismissed three of its members—Joseph Lord, William Pratt, and Increase Sumner—for Norman's Carolina venture. Two days later they joined five other men from the neighboring towns of Concord, Reading, and Sudbury to form a church. Four years out of Harvard, Joseph Lord (1672–1748) was ordained pastor. Having studied for the ministry with the Reverend John Danforth while teaching grammar school to support himself, Lord had recently completed his clerical training and apparently welcomed the opportunity to organize a church for the southern frontier of the English mainland colonies. Along with Norman, Pratt, Sumner, and the other Middlesex County pioneers, Lord promptly entered "into a most solem Covenant to sett up the ordinances of Jesus Christ ther if the lord caryed them safely thither accordin to gospell truth withe a very large profeson of ther faithe."[175]

William Pratt kept a journal of the voyage from Boston, recording that nine men set sail aboard the *Friendship* on December 5. They survived stormy winter weather and were at sea fourteen days before coming "in sight of the land of Carolina." The records of the Dorchester church note that "ye othr vessells had a Moneths Passage this by about 14 days," suggesting that an additional ship (or ships) sailed shortly after the *Friendship*. In any event, upon the arrival of the first comers the leaders of the group sought assistance from Governor Joseph Blake and Lady Axtell. Blake encouraged the colonists to settle at New London (later called Willtown) near Landgrave Joseph Morton's plantation, and Joseph Lord went there to survey the site with "som of the church, and others of the church at Charlstoun." In the meantime William Pratt and Increase Sumner traveled up the Ashley to William Norman's and "war kindly resevd and entertained by the Lady Extol." Although "two other men war indevering to get into favior with the ladey and other neighbors and to obtain the land at ashly rever," the Middlesex County group prevailed. In 1696 they secured title to a 1,800-acre tract through a grant to one of their leaders, John Stevens, part of which they quickly divided into 26 lots. Three years later the settlers obtained an additional 2,050-acre tract neighboring the Axtell seat.[176]

The New England colony of Dorchester soon emerged as one of the largest settlements in the South Carolina lowcountry, with a bustling village or "trading town" that by 1708 included about 350 people. It remained the colony's second most populous urban center until George Town was founded in 1729. New Englanders poured into the township and its place of trade in the late 1690s and early 1700s, as friends and family and others associated with the original inhabitants.

Efforts to enlist new settlers began almost immediately. Pratt recorded in his journal for 1696, "the first day of feburary being the last day of the week and the sacriment to be administered and many of us wer to come away on second day morning . . . to com to newingland." On this solemn occasion the Dorchester pioneers "set apart sum time in the afternoun to pray unto god and ther was much of the spirit of god bretheing in that ordinenc and when we touk our leves of our Christian frinds ther was weeping eyes at our departuer and we had many a blesing from them." Sailing on February 8, Prattt and several of the others returned to New England, with Pratt spending nearly a year there. Among some of those they enlisted to settle were William Adams, Michael Bacon, Jonathan Clarke, Abraham Gorton, Peter O'Kelly, Thomas Osgood, John Simmons, Samuel Sumner, Aaron Way, Sr., Aaron Way, Jr., Moses Way, Samuel Way, and William Way. With the exception of O'Kelly, all of these men are known to have occupied lots in early Dorchester, but there were many more. For example, Joseph Sumner, who was born in Dorchester, Massachusetts, in 1674, is not listed as a lot holder, but he immigrated to South Carolina with his father, Increase Sumner, and his uncle, Samuel Sumner, and the large Sumner clan. Other New Englanders set out for Carolina in 1698, after Joseph Lord returned for new recruits (and married Abigail Hinckley Lord, the daughter of the Plymouth colony governor, Thomas Hinckley, at Barstable). One of these newcomers may have been Daniel Axtell of Sudbury. Axtell operated a sawmill and naval-stores business in Dorchester and was likely a kinsman of Lady Rebecca, his business partner. Lord also encouraged John Cotton, Jr., and other Puritans to settle. Cotton mentions several of these New England colonists in his diary entries and Carolina correspondence.[177]

The Dorchester church quickly became a center of community life. Even before the first division of 1,800 acres, settlers were traveling from miles around to attend Sabbath services at William Norman's house. On January 26, 1696, for example, William Pratt recorded in his journal that Joseph Lord preached on Romans 8:1 and "ther was many that came to hear, of the neigbers round about." On February 2 Pratt likewise noted that Lord preached on 1 Peter 3:18 and "most of the neightbors [*sic*] came to hear, all the next neigbrs, and severell parsons came about 10 mils to hear." After this sermon Lord administered the sacrament and the church members chose two deacons. Just as with many other Puritan congregations, this infant church came to include "halfway" members, that is, those who had been baptized but were not admitted into full communion. Pratt accordingly wrote in his journal on March 23, 1697, that "the church and others that wer concarnd did draw loots [lots]," with the "others" undoubtedly being halfway members of the congregation.[178] One of the lots was immediately consecrated for a churchyard, after which construction of a wooden church building began. In 1700 the original wooden structure was replaced by a brick structure that stood until it was destroyed by an earthquake in 1886.

No less than other seventeenth-century churches, the early Dorchester church history reveals important clues to understanding the origins of southern evangelicalism. For a vital part of the process that ultimately gave birth to evangelical movement had begun long before Protestant Christianity entered a tumultuous new era in the 1720s and 1730s. At the turn of the eighteenth century the massive influx of Presbyterians, Congregationalists, French Huguenots, Baptists, Quakers, and other groups meant that an overwhelming majority of South Carolina whites were Protestant dissenters. And by studying these groups closely one can glean deeper insight into the ways in which later attempts at religious renewal evolved out of the early settlement of the colony.

2

True-Blue Protestants

Religious Eclecticism and the Church of England

On the Continent, the Colony of Carolina, was in a fair Way to have been filled with a religious people; until your Society for the Propagation of Religion in foreign Parts, unhappily sent over some of their Missionaries thither; and, I am informed, that with them and from that time, a mighty Torrent of Profaneness and Wickedness carried all before it; and every thing that might be worthy to be called Religion is very much lost in that woful Countrey.

The Reverend Cotton Mather to
Anthony William Boehm, August 6, 1716

On February 28, 1706, the English House of Lords read a petition presented by Charleston merchant Joseph Boone on behalf of himself and several other prominent traders living on both sides of the Atlantic. The petitioners complained of "several proceedings" in the Carolina province and asked the House "to take the deplorable state of the colony into their consideration." In their petition Joseph Boone and the others told of Carolina's "languishing and dangerous condition," declaring that "the ruin of the colony would be to the great disadvantage of the trade of this kingdom . . . and the great benefit of the French, who watch all opportunities to improve their own settlements in those parts of America," and on the basis of these and several other arguments the petitioners made formal application to the House of Lords "to provide such relief as shall seem proper." The specific proceedings to which the petitioners referred involved the passage by the Carolina legislature of two 1704 statutes, an "Act for the Establishment of Religious Worship" (commonly called the Church Act) and an "Act for the more effectual Preservation of the Government" (commonly called the Test Act). Stemming from the growing interconnectedness that developed between early modern Europe and America, these two measures established the Church of England as South Carolina's state church and required that all members of the

Commons House of Assembly receive the sacrament of the Lord's Supper according to the Book of Common Prayer. Significantly, both measures had been signed and sealed by four of the Lords Proprietors, including the Carolina palatine or chief proprietor, John Granville, 1st Baron of Granville. Yet Joseph Boone and the other petitioners objected that the 1704 acts were incompatible with the royal charter issued to the proprietors by Charles II.[1]

Upon reading Joseph Boone's petition, the House of Lords agreed to take the Carolina proceedings under consideration, and after examining witnesses in relation to the passage of the 1704 acts and hearing the proprietors' counsel in defense of the measures, they reached a decision on the afternoon of March 9. First, the House determined that the Church Act, which provided for the creation of a twenty-member lay commission with power to remove South Carolina clergymen, was "not warranted by the charter granted to the proprietors, as being not consonant to reason, repugnant to the laws of this realm, and destructive to the constitution of the Church of England." Second, they determined that the Test Act "was founded upon falsity in matter of fact," as the preamble to the measure "asserted that by the laws and usage of England all members of parliament are obliged to conform to the Church of England by receiving the Sacrament of the Lord's Supper according to the rites of the said church." Furthermore, the House found that the Test Act ran contrary to the royal charter and was "an encouragement to atheism and irreligion, . . . destructive to trade, and tendeth to the depopulating and ruining the said province." As a consequence they moved to present an address to Queen Anne requesting that she deliver the colony "from the arbitrary oppressions under which it lies," along with a copy of Joseph Boone's petition.[2]

Although the findings of the House of Lords are defined with legal precision, they reflect a key religious transformation in early-eighteenth-century South Carolina. In 1704 Anglican officials effected this transformation by barring Protestant dissenters from serving in the assembly and securing legal establishment of the Church of England, which Anglican missionaries had earlier predicted would be virtually impossible because of dissenter opposition. While Queen Anne promptly ordered Lord Granville and the other Carolina proprietors to disallow both of the 1704 acts after receiving a copy of Joseph Boone's petition and the House of Lords' address, the South Carolina assembly quickly passed another Church Act in November 1706.[3] Among other things this second Church Act, which was modeled on the earlier measure, effectively checked the growth of dissenting Protestantism in the Carolina lowcountry. Indeed by the 1720s much more equal numbers of provincial white settlers were attending Anglican and dissenting churches than had been the case in 1700.[4]

For Puritan polymath Cotton Mather, the establishment of the Church of England in South Carolina marked a critical turning point in the history of the

Atlantic Protestant. In reporting on the ecclesiastical state of Britain's New World colonies for Anthony William Boehm, the principal proponent of German Pietism in London and a main instrument in spreading German Pietist influence in America through his correspondence, his scholarship, and his activities in the Society for the Promotion of Christian Knowledge (SPCK) and the Society for the Propagation of the Gospel in Foreign Parts (SPG), Mather singled out South Carolina for special consideration in a letter dated August 6, 1716. In particular, Mather suggested that South Carolina had once been among the most religious societies in America until Anglican church officials "unhappily sent some of their Missionaries thither" and religion fell away to "a mighty Torrent of Profaneness and Wickedness." For Mather, of course, religion meant dissenting Protestantism, specifically New England Puritanism, and to him Anglican missionaries did nothing more than "propagate Impiety" and disorder. In contrast, he said, "dissenters . . . show men the true Methods of living to God, and instruct them in a Religion that shall not wholly consist in lifeless Forms and Ceremonies, Expiations for a vicious Life."[5] It was precisely this sort of vital piety that drew Mather and Boehm together as intimate correspondents in the early 1700s, with both men "embracing the Maxims of the Everlasting Gospel . . . [to] unite the People of God," which they sincerely believed would lead to the destruction of Rome and Christ's return to earth.[6]

While it remains true that most Anglican ministers stressed public Christian ritual over personal religious experience, colonial South Carolina's state church was by no means "merely the low country planter aristocracy at prayer," as historian Donald Mathews once described it. First, as Nicholas M. Beasley has recently shown, Anglicans in South Carolina and the Caribbean colonies created a remarkably rich culture of liturgical worship that was far more robust and spiritually meaningful than historians have tended to recognize. Second, the South Carolina state church grew up radically Protestant, and there is much evidence to suggest that it comprehended a wide range of doctrinal and ecclesiastical opinion, with large numbers of Anglican parishioners being "true blue Protestants in the modern Stamp, or Latitudinarian in Protestantism." Expressing reformed convictions in seemingly every major area of church life—in doctrine, in church government, in liturgy, and in ceremonies—very few actually imagined "much real difference in Principle 'twixt Churchmen & Dissenters of all Denominations." Finally, as Cotton Mather's writings make clear, the rise of the Church of England in South Carolina contributed to growing fears of religious declension among dissenters and stimulated Reformed and sectarian efforts to preach evangelical doctrine.[7]

†

While South Carolinians were distracted by their partisan quarrels in the 1680s and 1690s, Anglican officials in London were undertaking a concerted effort to revitalize and expand England's state churches, an effort that would come to have a major impact on colonial American religious practices. This late-Stuart reform effort centered on evangelism and Christianization, both in England and overseas, and it resulted in the formation of the SPCK, which was founded in 1699 to encourage Christian education and the production and distribution of Christian literature, and the SPG, which was founded in 1701 to send Anglican missionaries to the colonies. The Anglican reform effort also resulted in the appointment of commissaries to represent the bishop of London in America. These officials were charged with clerical oversight as well as the supervision of church affairs. Most important, Anglican reformism resulted in a major push for legal establishment of the Church of England in various quarters of Britain's Atlantic empire, including the colonial lower southern colony of South Carolina.[8]

The Church of England's reform effort coincided with a fundamental change in proprietary policy at the end of the seventeenth century and in the beginning of the eighteenth century. Though the proprietors had reaffirmed their commitment to religious toleration in 1682, they ultimately reneged on their promise that dissenters would not be taxed to support the Anglican church and sought to secure legal establishment for the English church in South Carolina. Presaging a turnaround in transatlantic political allegiance, this policy change ultimately prompted a realignment in provincial party loyalty and set off a rank sectarian conflict that lasted for well over a decade.

On April 9, 1697, William Craven, 1st Earl of Craven, the last surviving member of the original group of men to whom Charles II had granted the territory of Carolina in 1663, died, and John Granville, 1st Earl of Bath, replaced him as Carolina palatine. Craven's death marked a decisive shift in proprietary policy. Unlike his predecessor, Bath was a staunch Anglican partisan who vigorously began pressing the interests of England's state church and, almost immediately, privately attempting to build up a Church party in the colony. Bath was aided in his efforts by Henry Compton, bishop of London from 1675 to 1714, and Thomas Bray, a leading Anglican reformer. At the suggestion of Bray, Bishop Compton recommended that the new Carolina palatine send a promising young missionary named Samuel Marshall to South Carolina to strengthen the Church of England's institutional presence. Lord Bath was quick to respond. In 1698 he instructed Governor Joseph Blake to secure an appropriation to settle a maintenance on Marshall, who was sent to the colony with a parcel of books for the "Laying a foundation for a Good & Public Library."[9]

A leading South Carolina dissenter who contributed £1,000 sterling to the Independent Church in Charleston, Governor Blake had little reason to suspect anything of Bath's motives in sending Marshall or fear that he might try to impose the establishment of the Church of England on the colony. The proprietors had been his strongest supporters, and not only had John Archdale chosen Blake to succeed him as governor, but Archdale had also arranged for Blake to buy a share in the Carolina proprietorship when Blake began his second term as governor.[10] Besides, in 1697 the South Carolina legislature had promulgated an act for religious toleration, providing that "all Christians which are, or hereafter may be in this Province, (Papists only excepted) shall enjoy the full, free, and undisturbed Liberty of their Consciences, so as to be in the Exercise of their Worship, according to the professed Rules of their Religion, without any Lett, Molestation or Hindrance, by any Power either Ecclesiastical or Civil whatsoever." Blake and his allies had collaborated with the Anglican Goose Creek faction in passing the measure, which was packaged together with "An Act for the making of Aliens Free." Since Craven County had lost its representation in the assembly in 1696, the proprietary party no longer saw any immediate need to block all Huguenots from obtaining citizenship when Huguenot leaders petitioned the assembly for the same privileges as those settlers born of English parents. Moreover, religious toleration would apply to all Protestants equally.[11]

Upon receiving his instructions, then, Blake dutifully complied with Bath's request to secure a salary for Marshall and delivered a speech to the assembly "Relating to the Maintaining of a minister of the Church of England Lately Arrived." After resolving that Marshall should have "a Sufficient maintenance," the assembly appointed a committee that drafted a bill providing for a permanent Anglican ministry in Charleston, with funding to be drawn from the public treasury. Though amended several times and thoroughly limited in scope, the measure (commonly called the Ministry Act) carried.[12] Because the act provided for funding through the provincial treasury and was sanctioned by the royal charter, there was apparently little opposition; the likelihood of dissenters ever having to pay directly to support the Church of England was remote. Indeed the assembly even ordered an ad hoc committee to write letters "to ye Lord Bishipp of London and Doctr: Thomas Bray and give them the Thanks of this house for their Pious Care and Paines in Provideing and sending a minister of ye Church of England."[13]

If Marshall's coming gave Governor Blake and other dissenters little cause for concern, Bath's subsequent actions almost certainly led them to question the benefits of certain proprietary policies. On the same day he wrote to Blake with instructions to provide public support for an Anglican ministry in Charleston, the new Carolina palatine oversaw another revision of the Fundamental Constitutions. The 1698 version omitted all of the concessions the proprietors had agreed to under the leadership of William Craven. Gone was the clause prohibiting ministers from holding civil offices; deleted were the provisions giving each

Protestant congregation the power to "to lay a tax on its own members . . . for the maintenance of their public ministers"; and removed were assurances that public maintenance for the Church of England could only "arise out of lands or rents assigned voluntarily, contributions, or such other ways whereby no man shall be chargeable to pay out of his particular Estate that is not conformable to the church as aforesaid." Conspicuously reinserted, however, was language referring to Anglicanism as "the only true and orthodox, and the National Religion of the King's Dominions." Obviously Blake had no incentive to work to secure adoption of the 1698 Fundamental Constitutions even though he himself was a proprietor, and when he introduced the constitutions into the assembly the legislators rejected them out of hand.[14]

Upon the death of Governor Blake in 1700, Bath began organizing a High Church party in the colony with a view to securing legal establishment of the Church of England after the English model. He supported James Moore in a bitter fight for the governor's post to prevent Landgrave Joseph Morton, a dissenter, from claiming the office. A proprietary deputy associated with the high Anglicans in the colony, Moore had taken over leadership of the Goose Creek faction from Maurice Mathews in the wake of the Sothel imbroglio. In predicting this eventuality, Presbyterian John Stewart drew on the Old Testament language of 2 Kings and wrote in 1690 that Moore was destined to become "the next Jehu of the party." Now, with proprietary backing, "the heating Moor" began to effect a shift in transatlantic political allegiance. In opposing Morton's election to succeed Blake as governor, dissenters charged that Moore "acquired and obtained the Government of this Province by fraud, flattery, and trifling exceptions." It was a crucial moment: after Moore was declared governor, partisan strife—which had already been cast in a sectarian mold—quickly reemerged. Although the factional divisions were old, there was a realignment of South Carolina's political parties. In a turnaround that anticipated many future reversals of loyalty, Moore and his allies became proprietary supporters, while their old rivals suddenly found themselves as the party of opposition. Huguenots, whose citizenship and political rights hung in the balance, generally went the way of the Goose Creek men.[15]

The Earl of Bath's death in 1701 temporarily forestalled the drive to create an Anglican state church in South Carolina. However, Bath's younger son and namesake, Sir John, who became Lord Granville in 1703, quickly assumed his father's establishmentarian mantle as Carolina palatine. Meanwhile, the colony was experiencing new political convulsions: "great Debates and Divisions arose, which, like a Flame, grew greater and greater," as John Archdale later put it.[16] Many issues were involved—an attack on St. Augustine, election fraud, and naturalization policy, for instance—which together created such intense partisan hostility as to provoke a week-long riot. Many dissenters were convinced that Governor Moore had from the start "endeavoured . . . to manage all things by base and indirect methods, and crafty projects." In a "Representation and Address" dated June 26, 1703, inhabitants petitioned the proprietors claiming that the governor immediately began scheming and designing and seeking "to engage the Council to his Interest, and to have an Assembly chosen to his liking... to compleat and accomplish his ends & purposes." For example, they claimed that in 1702 there were "several great Abuses made & committed" in an assembly election for Berkeley County, where "much threat'nings, many intreaties, & other unjustifiable actions were made use of, and illegal and unqualify'd votes given in to the Sheriff, & by him receiv'd and return'd." In particular, they charged that "the votes of very many unqualify'd Aliens were taken & enter'd, the votes of several Members of the Council were filed & receiv'd, a great number of Servants & poor & indigent persons voted promiscuously with their Masters & Creditors, as also several free Negroes were receiv'd, & taken for as good Electors as the best Freeholders in the Province." Moreover, when the assembly met and began investigating the alleged voting irregularities in the Berkeley County election, the petitioners stated that Governor Moore, "to prevent such inquiry, did several times prorogue the said Assembly," and, when that failed, purposely sought to divert attention from the election issue "by setting on foot an ill laid design of raising Forces to attaque St. Augustine."[17]

But the most dramatic and sensational charges in the "Representation and Address" involved not allegations of election fraud and obstruction of justice but charges that Governor Moore encouraged and countenanced a riot directed at Protestant dissenters, several of whom were reportedly assaulted, beaten, and abused by Moore's Anglican party adherents with the support of a drunken mob recruited from the Charleston underground. In late February 1703, after the Commons House of Assembly broke up amidst angry discussions involving the St. Augustine expedition, a bill for settling elections, and a much more stringent naturalization proposal, Landgrave Thomas Smith was allegedly "set upon by Lieut. Col. *George Dearsby* [Dearsley], who with his Sword drawn, and the point held at the said Smith's belly, swore he would Kill him, and if he had not been prevented, would have done the said *Smith* some considerable mischief to the endangering of his life." Another principal leader of the dissenters, Massachusetts Puritan John Ash, was similarly set upon in the Charleston street. According to the "Representation," the assembly leader "was assaulted by a rude, drunken, ungovernable rabble, headed, encouraged & abetted by the said *Dearsby, Thomas Dalton, Nicholas Nary,* and other Persons." Furthermore, the petition goes on to say, Ash was followed to a friend's house by the "same armed multitude," which was now headed and encouraged by Lieutenant Colonel William Rhett. The mob then proceeded to lure Ash out of the house and reportedly "drew him by force and violence on board his the said *Rhett's* Ship, reviling & threat'ning of him as they drag'd him along; and having gotten him on board the said *Rhett's* Ship, they sometimes told him they would carry him to *Jamaica;* & at other times threatn'd to hang him, or leave him on some remote Island."[18]

Although the South Carolina petitioners were careful not to implicate Governor Moore in felony charges of assault and battery, they made it clear that the Charleston Riot of 1703 was his riot. On the same day Thomas Smith and John Ash were represented as being criminally abused ("immediately before the Riot began"), it was asserted that the governor "treated a great many of the persons concerned therein, and used such expressions to them, as gave them, next [to] their drink, the greatest encouragements for what they acted." In addition, all those who listened to Moore's speech were "thanked ... for their close adherence to him in all his concerns," including the tumultuous ragtag of Charleston—the "licentious rabble" called out from the ranks of dock workers, common sailors, and day laborers. Also, "after the riot began (of part of which he was an Eye-witness)," Moore, "having first drank with some of them, he withdrew himself out of the way, thereby giving them greater encouragement to proceed in their tumultuous practises, and by [his] example and absence, discouraging the inferior officers from executing their Duty."

If the 150 petitioners are to be believed, what followed was an orgy of sectarian abuse that continued virtually unabated for some "four or five days." On one occasion Landgrave Edmund Bellinger was verbally assaulted by the mob "with all the opprobrious Names they could think of." Afterward, Colonel Rhett "came up to him & struck him over the Head with his cane, and continued beating & striking of him for a considerable time." On another occasion the rioters "beat and abused Mr. *Joseph Boone* & put him in danger and fear of his life." Soon "the riot was at the Church." Being "armed & weaponed to the great terror of the people," the mob later went to the house of a butcher named John Smith; "& there being a Woman big with child in the said House, they with force opened the Door, threw her down, & otherwise misused her, that she brought forth a dead child, with the back and skull broken." John Ash related this same outrageous story in his *Present State of Affairs in Carolina* (London, 1706) and noted that the surgeon who delivered the child was deposed to document the gruesome birth. Other alleged victims of the riotous abuse such as Landgrave Bellinger were also apparently deposed.[19]

Into this highly charged atmosphere stepped Sir Nathaniel Johnson, Moore's successor as governor and the man directly responsible for securing the legal establishment of the Church of England in colonial South Carolina. A Jacobite, former member of Parliament, manager of the English hearth tax, and governor of the Leeward Islands from 1686 to 1689, Sir Nathaniel was recruited and commissioned by Lord Granville to replace Moore, who was given the post of attorney general. An Arminian or High Church Anglican, Johnson had as his primary motivation for assuming the governorship "the Preservation & Establishment of the Church." Other ardent High Church Anglicans who shared Johnson's "care and concern" joined the new administration.[20] They included the governor's son-in-law, Thomas Broughton, and Chief Justice Nicholas Trott, who was deeply religious and a devoted scholar. Trott spent long hours studying the Hebrew text of the Old Testament and firmly believed that the Church of England was the true descendent of the early Christian church. All of the Anglicans in Johnson's government agreed on the need for a strong state church and were inspired by the Church of England's reform effort and the SPG Christianization program. All, too, were unquestionably stimulated into action by the militancy of Protestant Reformed and sectarian proselytizing. In 1699, for example, Thomas Broughton's wife had "set an example to others" by considering whether to join a Baptist congregation "by plunging."[21] Similarly, in 1703 Nicholas Trott wrote to the archbishop of Canterbury, Thomas Tenison, that the colony was "very Much infested, with the Sect of Anabaptists" and asked Tenison to send over literature to persuade several of his co-religionists who were "wavering, as to that point of Infant Baptism."[22]

Yet there was virtually no way Governor Johnson and his Church party could effect legal establishment of the Anglican church through the normal channels of government. Dissenters constituted an overwhelming majority of South Carolina's European population, which was consistently reflected in assembly elections. Moreover, there were always sizable numbers of Anglican assemblymen who sympathized with the dissenters and adhered to a more liberal, moderate version of the faith. These Low Church latitudarians, men such as Stephen Bull, John Barnwell, and Hugh Hext, were led by Thomas Nairne and Robert Stevens and normally supported the dissenter faction. They were devoted to the Church of England but were not uncritical of its form, ritual, or government by bishops. Church party propagandists distinguished them as "half faced Churchmen, who in reality are Dissenters."[23] Finally, while Huguenots tended to side with the Goose Creek men, their voting strength was circumscribed. Gerrymandering and manipulation of naturalization policy following the 1697 alien act limited their influence. In short, there were "so many Dissenters in the Province (many of which have always been in the Government)," as one Anglican missionary reported to London churchmen, it would be "a work of no small difficulty to get an Act to pass in favour of the Church of England clergy... which those who dissent from us violently oppose."[24]

Knowing he could never win under ordinary circumstances, Governor Johnson created an extraordinary situation, relying on the slow pace of communication and travel in the colony to execute a well-planned strategy. In March of 1703 he dissolved the assembly and called for new elections, which dissenters maintained were "managed with greater injustice to the Freemen of this Province than the former." In Berkeley County, they said, "Jews, Strangers, Sailors, Servants,

Negroes, & almost every *French* man in *Craven* & *Berkly* County, came down [to Charleston] to elect, & their Votes were taken, & the Persons by them voted for were returned by the Sheriff, to the manifest wrong & prejudice of other Candidates." After quarreling over this questionable election, while the assembly stood adjourned, Johnson then called a special session of the legislature in the spring of 1704, and before all of the delegates arrived a bare-bones legislature, narrowly dominated by Church party Anglicans, passed by a vote of twelve to eleven an "Act for the more effectual Preservation of the Government" requiring all members of the South Carolina Commons House to conform to Anglican worship and liturgical practice. (A Huguenot from Berkeley County named James LeSerurier may have cast the deciding vote.) Then, having dealt with what in the governor's mind was "the problem" of Protestant dissent, the assembly passed during the next legislative session a bill establishing the Church of England.[25]

Promulgated on May 6, 1704, the Act for the more effectual Preservation of the Government had a preamble boldly announcing that nothing was "more contrary to the profession of the Christian Religion, and particularly to the doctrine of the Church of England, than persecution for conscience only." Yet, as dissenters were quick to point out, it proceeded to make a non obstante argument that was based upon incompatible or inconsistent premises, with the unfortunate transitional term *nevertheless* used to link the opening words of the statute with the contrasting statement which followed, viz. "it hath been found by experience that the admitting of persons of different persuasions and Interest in matters of religion to sitt and vote in the Commons House of Assembly, hath often caused great contentions and animosities in this Province, and hath very much obstructed the publick business."[26] This statement forced defenders of the measure on both sides of the Atlantic to justify its partial construction and ultimately exposed the religious motive behind the law. One of Lord Granville's attorneys, Sir Thomas Powys, summed it up well in the House of Lords in explaining why "there was occasion to require this test of late." A "great part of the assembly withdrew when they were to give supplies," he said rather forthrightly, "which was the occasion of the test."[27]

If it all but completely disregarded liberty of conscience, the preamble to the 1704 Test Act also asserted a factual claim that was "notoriously and manifestly false." In particular, it stated that "by the laws and usage of England, all members of Parliament are obliged to conforme to the Church of England, by receiving the sacrament of the Lord's Supper according to the rites of the said church." Powys had rather less to say about this particular claim, which was beyond his ability to defend. In fact, he was forced to concede that in its preamble the "act mistakes in a recital concerning receiving the sacrament." Another defense attorney, Sir John Hawles, had a more effective rebuttal. He stated that it was "very reasonable to accept of this law, as circumstanced: we [in] England are,

I think, come to alter, and say who shall sit in assembly, as they have done here." "There was a letter prepared against this clause," Hawles went on to note, and "the letter was written three months since." Furthermore, he emphasized, "the proprietors may repeal any laws made, and the proprietors have done what they can to repeal this clause."[28]

As with the falsity in its preamble regarding matter of fact, Hawles showed himself more resourceful than Powys in defending the liturgical and ceremonial provisions of the South Carolina's Test Act. These provisions required every member of the provincial assembly henceforth to prove that he had received the sacrament in an Anglican church according to the prayer-book rite within the course of the preceding one year, or, alternatively, take an oath stipulating in pertinent part: (1) that they were "of the profession of the Church of England," conformed to the church, and regularly attended Anglican public worship services; (2) that they did not "abstain from the Sacrament of the Lord's Supper out of any dislike to the manner and form of the administration thereof, as used by the said Church of England, and as it is prescribed in the communion office in the book of common prayer"; (3) that they had not at any time over the previous twelve months "been . . . in communion with any church or congregation that doth not conform to the said church of England, nor received the Sacrament of the Lord's Supper in such congregation"; and (4) that they would "endeavour the good and welfare of the said Church of England" as a member of the assembly. When questioned about the oath, Sir John Hawles cleverly asserted a moral claim in defense of the measure. "If such a test were established by act here," the quick-thinking counselor said, "I presume it ought to be complied with." "We have a bill for regulating offices," he added, "and [it] ought to be complied with."[29]

The authors of the 1704 Test Act were not simply hypocritical tyrants who could not get their facts straight. Rather they were genuinely zealous Anglicans who were surrounded by a sea of dissenters and who were vitally concerned that there was "as yet but one church in the province."[30] Such anxiousness was intensified by the defection of Anglicans to several other competing denominations comprising a substantial majority of the Christian population in South Carolina. St. Philip's in Charleston remained the colony's only Anglican church, whereas dissenters had formed a substantial number of congregations and were suppling each and every one of them with a fairly steady stream of ministers at their own expense. Moreover, as Sir Thomas Powys revealed, dissenters had absolutely no interest in giving any additional support to Anglican ministers, let alone footing the bill for the construction and maintenance of Anglican places of worship. Vexed and troubled, worried about the safety of the Church of England, Anglican leaders therefore turned to the Test Act to revitalize their faith.

Ultimately it worked. What was in the spring of 1704 already presumed to be the religion officially "establish'd by law" in the colony was, in fact, the religion officially established by law in the autumn, when, on November 4, 1704, An Act for the Establishment of Religious Worship was read three times and ratified in an open session of the South Carolina Commons House of Assembly. Having incapacitated dissenters earlier in the year, Governor Johnson and his religious cohorts moved swiftly to take advantage of the governor's shrewd politicking and to prescribe an Anglican church settlement that proclaimed the Church of England "Settled and Established" in the colony. The 1704 Church Act provided for the creation of six Anglican parishes and the construction of six new churches, five in Berkeley County and one in Colleton County. And, "for the encouragement of faithfull and able ministers labouring in the work of the Gospell, to come and reside in [the] Province," the 1704 law also made provisions for the public maintenance of six parish rectors. These included allocating annual salaries for the prospective Anglican ministers, allotting glebe lands, as well as building messuages or tenements and outbuildings. The 1704 Church Act commanded that this massive undertaking be accomplished with all deliberate speed, rather as if the lawmakers were preparing for a Spanish attack, which most colonists expected to come at any time in retaliation for the 1702 St. Augustine expedition. For example, to build the six new Anglican churches and parsonages the 1704 act empowered church officials to "press bricks or lime, or any other materials, and ... compel bricklayers, carpenters, joyners and all other workmen and labourers, to worke on the said works, as fully and amply to all intents and purposes, and under the same penaltys upon the neglecters and offenders, and the recovering the penaltys imposed, as is given Lieut. Colonel William Rhett, for the building the front wall and other intrenchments and fortifications about Charlestown." Furthermore, the Church Act empowered these same officials to "press any slave or slaves from any person inhabiting within his respective parish and division, to be imployed upon the aforesaid work and building" at two royals per day.[31]

To generate the revenue to pay for this ecclesiastical undertaking, Anglican legislators adopted An Act to Continue an Act entitled an Act for Laying an Imposition on Furrs, & c. (continuing Act No. 204, May 7, 1703), because, in the revealing words of the statute's preamble, "the fortifying of Charlestown, and other unforseen charges for the necessary defence and safety of [the] Colony" meant that South Carolina would "continue and grow more in debt." Two thousand pounds of the money raised by the duty on imports and exports (skins, furs, liquor, and other goods and merchandise) provided for in this measure was appropriated for the building of churches, tenements, and outbuildings, while £450 was appropriated for ministerial salaries.[32] (Under the terms of the 1704 Church Act, each new parish rector was to receive an annual salary of £50 current money, whereas the Ministry Act of 1698 provided that rector of St. Philip's should have an annual salary of £150.) In addition the Church Act authorized each parish vestry to raise up to £100 to pay for parochial expenses by levying a direct tax on "all and every the inhabitants, owners, and occupiers of lands, tenements and hereditaments, or any personal estate, within the severall parishes."[33] This same provision was made to pay for ministerial salaries in the event that there were insufficient funds in the public treasury to cover the expenses.

While Johnson, Trott, and other Arminians favored a high-Anglican church constitution, the governor and his like-minded colleagues had to deal with the strident claims of more moderate, Low Church assemblymen who, as he put reportedly it, "were endeavouring to wrest the Ecclesiastical Jurisdiction of the Province out of the Hands of the . . . the Bishop of London, and out of the Hands of the . . . Governor . . . as Ordinary."[34] Deeply devoted to the Church of England, these Low Church assemblymen represented the views of many Anglicans in the colony and proved to be rather less committed to the episcopal ideal than the Arminian prelacy faction. In their minds the church should not simply be subordinate to the state, or Erastian, as it had been in England since the Reformation. Rather, as the historian S. Charles Bolton has written, government of the church should be "entirely in the hands of the laity," with parishioners having the power to appoint and remove ministers.[35] As a consequence the 1704 Church Act required that the rectors for each parish be chosen by a majority of Anglican parishioners before being officially admitted to their livings. In addition to their annual salaries, fees, and perquisites, such beneficed clergymen were to serve on parish vestries, which, along with church wardens, were also to be chosen annually by parishioners conforming to the Church of England. In turn, parish vestrymen would select a parish register, a clerk, and a sexton, persons who were to serve in their offices at the pleasure of the vestry. More significantly, the 1704 Church Act provided for the creation of a twenty-member board of lay commissioners to administer the provisions of the act and superintend ecclesiastical affairs in the colony.

The powers vested in the board of commissioners were far-reaching. Among other things, the board could take up lands for churches, cemeteries, and glebes. It could direct and appoint the construction of church buildings, tenements, and various outhouses. It could order the enclosing of church yards and glebe lands and the building of pulpits, desks, and pews for the new churches. It could draw out of the public treasury such sums of money as the board thought fit to hire a clerk and pay construction supervisors. It could appoint election days for parish rectors and levy taxes for ministerial salaries. It could hear and determine appeals from parish residents who found or apprehended themselves "grieved or injured . . . by any acts, orders, rules, accounts, or other proceedings of any . . . vestry." Most important, it could remove "all or any of the several rectors or ministers of the several parishes, or . . . translate them from one parish to another." Although Governor Johnson was given a veto to prevent the enactment of a board order to turn out or remove a minister because of the governor's "great zeal and affection to the Church of England as it [was] established by law," this power was to continue only so long as he remained in office, "and no longer."[36] To sum up, the 1704 Church Act established a sort of Presbyterian church government from below.

Of course it was precisely the lay commission's "power, in an arbitrary manner, to remove and turn out any rectors or ministers of the Church of England from their benefices, for any immorality or imprudence, or for incurable prejudices, or dissentions between such rectors or ministers and their people" that proved to be the 1704 Church Act's undoing. In the House of Lords, Sir Thomas Powys attempted to defend the provision by noting that "here we have the bishops to correct the irregular clergy." But in South Carolina, he emphasized, "there is no ecclesiastical government there. These are laymen: there can be no others but one clergyman there. There is none but laymen capable to be in power. The proprietors scrupled at this clause, and were concerned at their ratifying of this clause. There was a letter to have gone along with this return to have this clause repealed. This is not a law, and never to be ratified but by a letter to repeal the clause, and there being so much good by building churches and houses, they thought it requisite to have ratified this (with the letter sent it)."

Sir John Hawles made essentially the same argument, adding that"this law came up as near to the law of England as the nature of the thing would bear at that time." In advancing these claims, both Hawles and Powys drew from a tract entitled *An Account of the Fair and Impartial Proceedings of the Lords Proprietors, Governor and Council of the Colony of South Carolina,* which was put into circulation in the religious literature of the Atlantic by John Granville. The House of Lords would have none of it, however. It found that "establishing a commission for the displacing the rectors or ministers of the churches there" was not warranted by the royal charter granted to the proprietors, as it was unreasonable, opposed to English law, and "destructive to the constitution of the Church of England." As a result the House recommended that Queen Anne secure disallowance of the measure, for to challenge the authority of the bishop of London to rule the American church was, in effect, to challenge the authority of the Supreme Governor of the Church of England itself. After all, the queen appointed bishops and invested them with ecclesiastical power.[37]

Ironically, Carolina dissenters had been making this case for months with backing from their English supporters. To regain their political rights and subsequently to secure disallowance of the Church Act, they sent Joseph Boone to London to succeed Thomas Ash. Ash had presented the dissenters' "Representation and Address" to Lord Granville in the summer of 1703. Failing to obtain any satisfactory redress, he began preparing a sensational pamphlet entitled *The Present State of Affairs in Carolina,* but in the midst of writing this tract he died. Soon thereafter, following the passage of the Test Act, Joseph Boone arrived in

England, and he immediately requested that Granville call a meeting of the proprietors to consider the bill. At the meeting the palatine reportedly said to John Archdale, "Sir, you are of one opinion, I am of another, and our lives may not be long enough to end the controversy."[38] After a vote that pitted Archdale and Granville against one another, a majority of the proprietors approved both 1704 acts, which prompted Boone's appeal to the House of Lords, SPG, and other Anglican officials, as well as the court of public opinion. The great nonconforming novelist Daniel Defoe was retained as part of a sweeping public-relations campaign, and in two widely circulated pamphlets he laid out the dissenters' position. An outgrowth of the charter bill controversy in the 1680s had been a discussion of proprietary authority, provincial liberty, and the politics of conscience. In *Party-Tyranny, or an Occasional Bill in Miniature; as Now Practiced in Carolina* (London, 1705) and *The Case of Protestant Dissenters in Carolina* (London, 1706), Defoe picked up on that discussion. Defoe argued that the royal charter prohibited disenfranchisement under the Test Act while at the same time emphasizing that the subscription measure was politically motivated. Because the Test Act was prohibited by the royal charter, he maintained, its passage represented "a Breach of the express Original Contract between the Proprietors and the People of Carolina."[39] Defoe also linked the Test Act to English politics, as the title of his first pamphlet made abundantly clear. In particular he suggested that the provincial act was tantamount to the ongoing Tory effort to prevent English dissenters from qualifying to serve in Parliament by only occasionally receiving the sacrament according to the prayer-book rite.

Defoe further emphasized that the board of lay commissioners set up by the 1704 Church Act challenged the ecclesiastical authority of the bishop of London. Joseph Boone stated the same point in his petition to the House of Lords:

> The ecclesiastical government of the colony is under the jurisdiction of the Lord Bishop of London; but the governor and his adherents have at last (which the said adherents had often threatened) totally abolished it; for the said assembly has lately passed an act whereby twenty lay persons therein named are made a corporation for the exercise of several exorbitant powers, to the great injury and oppression of the people in general, and for the exercise of all ecclesiastical jurisdiction, with absolute power to deprive any minister of the Church of England of his benefice . . . which the inhabitants of that province take to be a high ecclesiastical commission court, destructive to the very being and essence of the Church of England, and to be had in the utmost detestation and abhorrence by every man that is not an enemy to our constitution in Church and State.[40]

As well, Defoe (and Boone in his petition) stressed that both the Church Act and the Test Act would discourage settlement and economic activity and prevent

South Carolina from developing an extensive imperial trade. Another theme was that French Huguenots were "made tools of & imposed upon, & persuaded by ill-designing Persons . . . to carry on sinister Designs." The dissenting party had particularly objected to Huguenot rights in their "Representation and Address," noting "how easily they [were] drawn into Errors," and when the Church party passed a new naturalization act in 1704 to solidify the Huguenots' support, the English dissenters were furious.[41]

The controversy over the Church and Test Acts reached a crescendo in 1706 when the House of Lords considered the case of the Carolina dissenters and Queen Anne ordered the proprietors to repeal the measures. Undeterred, and with at least tacit support from Lord Granville, Governor Johnson suggested to the South Carolina legislature that it "settle the Church of England in this province by an Act of Assembly so as that it Shall be no way disliked in England," meaning a bill reducing the power of the lay commission. "When the Church is thus Settled," Johnson continued, "I Suppose the Repealing [of] the Act against the dissenters can be no prejudice to us . . . as the Main end of passing the Act against [them] was to Enable us the better to provide ffor the Safety of the Church of England." The legislature accordingly repealed both acts and then passed another Church Act. This 1706 law was modeled on the previous measure but prevented the board of lay commissioners from removing clergymen and drawing unlimited funds from the public treasury to pay construction supervisors. As well, the 1706 Church Act provided for the creation of ten parishes rather than seven: six in Berkeley County besides St. Philip's in Charles Town (Christ Church, St. Thomas, St. John's, St. James Goose Creek, St. Andrews, and St. Dennis), two in Colleton County (St. Paul's and St. Bartholomew), and one in Craven County (St. James Santee). St. Dennis Parish in Berkeley County and St. James Santee Parish in Craven County were created especially for French-speaking settlers. Finally, the 1706 Church Act ordered that one additional church be built in St. Bartholomew Parish in Colleton County, with a churchyard set aside "for the burial of christian people there."[42]

Even before Anglicans secured legal establishment for their church in 1704, the Church of England's transatlantic reform effort and the SPG Christianization program began to effect change in the South Carolina lowcountry. Prior to the arrival of Samuel Marshall in 1698 there had been only two or three Anglican ministers in the colony. By 1702 six or seven turned up, including Samuel Thomas, the first SPG missionary to arrive.[43] Thomas made no bones about the missionary task at hand. Settling at Nathaniel Johnson's plantation on the eastern branch of the Cooper River, he found "many Anabaptists in these parts, there being Preachers of that sort here." Men and women of all religious persuasions opted "to hear them," most notably Anglicans, and scores had already been won over. Knowing of the governor's intention to secure legal establishment for the Church of England, Thomas hoped to found a viable state-supported missionary outpost in the neighborhood "and bring back some." But his message was not encouraging. Within the leavings of his sectarian competitors, there were but "few pious to build up." Many were either spiritually conscientious but theologically unsophisticated (or "ignorant" in contemporary terminology), religiously indifferent, or far from any European church. "I have here a multitude of ignorant persons to instruct," Thomas wrote to the SPG in moment of exasperation, "too many profane to awaken ... and many Negroes, [and] Indians to begin withall."[44] It is important to note that, as Patricia U. Bonomi and Peter R. Eisenstadt have observed, early American clergymen who spoke of religious indifference most often "meant religious impartiality, or a blindness to the fine points of doctrine that differentiated one denomination from another."[45]

At any rate, and despite the enormity of the task, Samuel Thomas and his colleagues helped to raise the public visibility of the Church of England in several quarters of the colony, contributing to the overall sacralization of South Carolina's provincial landscape. In Charleston regular Anglican preaching and worship services officially began with the passage of the Ministry Act in 1698. As elsewhere in the colony, Anglican clergymen quickly enjoyed the patronage of the laity. Affra (Harleston) Coming, who arrived in South Carolina in 1670 with the first fleet, made a "pious and free gift" of seventeen acres of land to Samuel Marshall and his successors.[46] Others contributed to the improvement and furnishing of St. Philip's, which, as Edward Crisp's "Plan of Charles Town" (1704) vividly illustrates, came to dominate everything in sight. Built of black cypress upon a brick foundation, St. Philip's symbolized Anglicanism's sudden resurgence. Even more than other churches at the time, it was an architectural statement that commanded attention to organized Christianity, one that spoke to everyone, even those who might have "any reason to complain or make the least noise" that, like the state-church establishment, it was "an Eye sore to them."[47] This had not been the case a few years earlier. When John Lawson arrived in Charleston in the summer of 1700, for example, he made no mention of St. Philip's, but he did write about the Anglican parsonage and the great number of dissenting churches. "Near the Town is built a fair Parsonage-house, with necessary Offices, and the Minister has a very considerable Allowance from his Parish," Lawson reported in his *A New Voyage to Carolina* (1709). "There is likewise a French Church in Town, of the Reform'd Religion," he went on to say, "and several Meeting-houses for dissenting Congregations, who all enjoy at this Day an entire Toleration, and possess the same Priviledges, so long as they appear to behave themselves peaceably and well: It being the Lords Proprietors Intent, that the Inhabitants of Carolina should be as free from Oppression, as any in the Universe; which doubtless they will, if their own Differences amongst themselves do not occasion the contrary."[48]

Of course, the importance of St. Philip's increased precipitously after Anglican establishment and generally corresponded with the degree of dissenter hostility. State support catapulted the Church of England into the forefront of the battle to win Christian adherents, "to labour heartily in the Cause of God and Religion," as Commissary Gideon Johnston put it when he first arrived in colonial South Carolina as the bishop of London's diocesan agent. Johnston's appointment in 1708 constituted part of the overall effort by England's state church to strengthen its authority and reform its approach to religious activity, which produced the imperial program of Christian proselytizing. For the commissary and the clergy under his charge, no less than their superiors in London, the very "Score of their Mission," evangelism, entitled government sanction.[49]

Yet the mere coupling of church and state in the South Carolina lowcountry did not produce institutional conformity to the English system nor ensure Anglican success. Johnston thus attempted to remedy "many palpable Inconveniences" in the 1706 Church Act in order to bolster the provincial ecclesiastical structure and bring it "nearer the Model of the Church of England" at home.[50] At the same time he insisted that ministers and churchgoers behave "according to the Cannons and Rubrick" of England's state church. His efforts were largely unsuccessful, and they produced both conflict and resentment. Acting through the Commons House of Assembly, the laity exerted extensive control over ecclesiastical matters—even enhancing the power of the board of lay commissioners—thwarting most all of the commissary's "Transactions relating to Public Affairs so far as they concern the Church."[51] The clergy generally enjoyed "full liberty to do as they pleased," and Anglican parishioners balked at Johnston's attempt to impose uniformity of practice in worship or rigid, "Canonical behaviour" in the colony.[52]

Johnston's recurrent theme was that the Church of England's claim to lay adherence was tempered by the presence of the colony's large dissenting population and that ideas derived from Protestant Reformed and sectarian influences weakened the establishment at its base by fomenting religious eclecticism. Anglican ministers were forced by their congregations to abandon the ceremonies and liturgical practices of the state church. Many parishioners demanded that clergymen administer the sacrament to them while they were sitting or standing rather than kneeling; others that they baptize children "without the sign of the cross" and/or without godparents, or even perform immersion baptism. Still other parishioners demanded that they perform marriages in private homes and not use the ring in marriage, and some preferred that Anglican priests minister without vestments or preach and pray extemporaneously like nonconformists. For example, Francis Le Jau of St. James Goose Creek Parish reported to the SPG that "in some parishes where the people have been used to receive the communion in their seats (a custom people introduced for . . . such as are inclined to Presbytery . . .) it is not an easy matter to bring them to the Lord's Table decently upon their knees." More often than not, when Episcopal clergy refused to comply with popular demands, Anglican laypersons simply "threatened to go over to the dissenters." In short the laity had "fallen into such a Comprehensive and Latitudinarian way" that it was "the hardest thing in the World to perswade 'em out of it."[53]

In their efforts to persuade the laity to conform to the regulations of the English state church, Johnston and his colleagues stood in danger of wholly estranging large numbers of Anglican adherents in the colony. Seemingly trivial disputes concerning the reception of the communion or clerical vestments or god parentage were for the commissary and his subordinates matters of obedience, but for many of their parishioners they were matters of conscience. To take communion while kneeling implied to some of them an adoration of the elements of bread and wine and smacked of the Roman Catholic doctrine of transubstantiation; the wearing of the surplice was a symbol of the Roman priesthood, the naming of friends and relatives as godparents a blasphemous tradition invented by the pope. Thus a congregational quarrel over any manner of Anglican ritual and form such as the churching of women or the ritual of baptism could potentially become a point of departure, with communicants choosing to worship in a dissenting church or to have a nonconforming minister perform sacred rites. "In case I cannot have Mr. Whitehead to Cresend my Children at my howes," one layman cautioned Commissary Johnston regarding a clergyman under his charge, "I can have them Cresend by a dissenter Minister." Very much aware of such choice, Francis Le Jau wrote to the SPG, "I have openly declared that I woul'd baptize by dipping when desired." "I find that our Annabaptists have nothing more to say"; he added, "they were strangely deluded."[54]

In a most revealing passage Samuel Thomas of the newly created St. James Goose Creek Parish candidly advised the SPG regarding this "different temper which a Minister in the Province of Carolina will find in the people belonging to his charge," recommending that only "men of true piety, zeal and prudence [be] sent upon this evangelical design." And it helps to explain why, after complaining of the profanity and ignorance of his parishioners just two years earlier, Thomas could report in May 1704 that his "Congregation . . . was so numerous yt the church could not containe them, many stood with out doors [and] the poor people were very attentive." "Among our English inhabitants are many of considerable learning, good judgment and acute parts," Thomas wrote in a detailed report to the society, "and many very ignorant and mean in their attainments, again there are some truly religious and conscientious and others haters of religion and practical Godliness." "Yet further," he continued, "there are some who are heartily in the interest in the Church of England, and understand and approve its constitutions, and there are others who are not positively determined as to their choice who have not actually put themselves under the Conduct of either our Ministers or of those who differ from us, and there are lastly more than a few that do dissent from us and join in communion with the Presbyterians, Independents, and Anabaptists of all which there are considerable numbers in the Country." "This I humbly remark to this ven[era]ble Society," Thomas instructed, "that hereby they may be the more sensible of the necessity there is of their Missionarys being duly qualified to treat with all possible advantage with Persons of this differing temper and profession."[55] Religious diversity and difference and the presence of a dissenting majority were simply facts of provincial South Carolina life.

Commissary Johnston spoke to this same point a few years later, albeit in different terms, famously referring to South Carolina as "a perfect Medley or Hotch potch" of people and religions. What struck Commissary Johnston most, however, was the breadth and scope of Protestant dissent—the large numbers of "Libertines, Sectaries and Enthusiasts of all sorts" in the colony.[56] Charleston in particular was notorious for its cosmopolitan religious diversity, with Baptists, Quakers, and other Protestant dissenters contributing to the city's religious variety. Baptists themselves sustained a large congregation in early Charleston. In 1708 William Screven reported a total membership of "about ninety in all."[57] A letter the same year from William Dunn, rector of St. Paul's Parish in Colleton County, reveals how thoroughly dominant nonconformists were in many rural areas during this period. Dunn estimated that there were some three hundred white adults in St. Paul's. Eighty (or 26 percent) were Anglicans, while the rest were "Dissenters of all Sorts." A dozen or so he could not identify, but the others he identified as follows: 158 Presbyterians and Independents, 40 Baptists, and 10 Quakers.[58]

Other Anglican reports on comparative denominational strength during this time tend to be far less precise and far more suspicious, but even they reveal that dissenters formed a majority of the European inhabitants in most all South Carolina parishes. Robert Stevens reported that nearly all of the fifty or so families living on James Island in 1708 were dissenters, while Samuel Thomas was forced to concede in his detailed "Memorial Relating to the State of the Church of England in the Province of South Carolina" (1705–1706) that only a fraction of those who settled along the Ashley River were "in the interest of the Church of England." "Here are in this parish many Presbyterians and Anabaptists," he wrote, "which contains about 100 families . . . and but 30. families of the profession of the Church of England." Of St. James Goose Greek, "one of the most populous of our Country Parishes containing (as near as I can guess) about 120 familys," Thomas said that "most of the Inhabitants are of the profession of the

Church of England." Yet he suggested that the dissenting population there was unbelievably minuscule: "about five familys of French Protestants who are Calvinists and 3. Familys of Presbyterians and two Anabaptists." Just two years later, however, another minister, Richard Marsden, reported to the SPG that there were much more substantial numbers of nonconformists in Goose Creek and that their numbers were rapidly increasing.[59]

South Carolina's sizable and pluralistic non-Anglican Protestant reform and sectarian population made Commissary Johnston bristle. In 1711 he told SPG officials that he could not decide whether the oft-repeated suggestion that Anglicans made up only a third of the colony's Protestants was "more false or more Impudent," contending that such estimates were simply part of a more generalized disinformation campaign dissenters used to attack the state church. (Daniel Defoe, echoing the view of other nonconformists, asserted that it was "notorious that above two thirds of the People of *Carolina* are Dissenters.") Johnston alluded to some pat election returns so that the society could make "a reasonable Calculation" of the percentages of Anglicans and dissenters. Using his fuzzy data SPG officials may have been tempted to conclude that Anglicans outnumbered dissenters by three or four to one in the colony.[60]

The previous year Thomas Nairne, a moderate Anglican with Presbyterian sympathies who normally supported Protestant dissenters, made a more genuine and perhaps accurate guess. In his *Letter from South Carolina* (1710) he reported on "the Proportions that the several Parties in Religion do bear to the whole, and to each other," noting that Episcopalians constituted 42.5 percent of the population while Presbyterians (45 percent), Baptists (10 percent), and Quakers (2.5) constituted more than 57 percent of the population. Nairne lumped under the Episcopalian rubric two "*French* Protestant Congregations" whose "Ministers [were] lately proselyted to the Church," referring to the Orange Quarter and Santee refugee communities incorporated under the 1706 Church Act as the parishes of St. Dennis and St. James Santee. Under the Presbyterian denominational label Nairne included Charleston's independent Huguenot Church but did not otherwise distinguish between Presbyterians and Independents among South Carolina's non-Anglican Protestant reform groups.[61] Still, there is little evidence to suggest that his estimates were very far off the mark, nor, if Huguenots who vigorously clung to their distinctive style of worship are included as nonconformists, that dissenters were false or impudent as the commissary charged.

If anything, Nairne underestimated nonconformist denominational strength.[62] His census also masked the tenuousness of lay commitment to Anglican worship and practice, the vagaries of ecclesiastical subordination, and deep-seated antagonisms toward the establishment. Just after Nairne compiled his data, French refugee parishioners in St. James Santee and St. Dennis forced their ministers to abandon Anglican liturgy and practice in worship and return to traditional Calvinist services according to "the 'Geneva Way." Commissary Johnston made repeated attempts to suppress such heterodoxy by threatening to suspend the accommodationist clergy. When one, the Reverend John La Pierre, bowed to the pressure and tried to reimpose Anglican ritual at St. Dennis, he provoked an open revolt that took off in a most interesting direction. Several Huguenots opted out of the congregation and formed a popular religious movement. By 1714 they had strayed far from traditional Genevan formulas and apparently attached little significance to them. Indeed the protesters began espousing Sabbatarianism and what La Pierre and other ministers described as Antinomian principles. But what the rebels were really objecting to was the "deadness" of dry-bones Anglican orthodoxy.[63]

The St. Dennis revolt of 1712–1720 was an anticlerical, antiestablishment demonstration against the state-supported Church of England by a group of largely anonymous refugee Huguenots who were searching for a popular alternative to the canons of revealed religion. It strongly suggests that orthodox Anglican and Huguenot religious forms were failing to meet the spiritual needs of the laity. In striking out of St. Dennis the rebels did not simply travel down the Geneva way. They turned to creative experimentation and spiritualism. Johnston, La Pierre, and even Charleston's nonconformist French Huguenot minister Paul L'Escot condemned them. Yet Philippe de Richebourg, the Anglican-ordained minister at St. James Santee, seems to have been rather more sympathetic. After Johnston issued an ultimatum to conform to Anglicanism under threat of suspension, Richebourg complied, but the commissary remained suspicious of him, believing that he was "not with us, but at Geneva or Elsewhere."[64]

For all its peculiarities South Carolina's Anglican establishment began functioning as an important vehicle through which many colonists worshiped institutional Christianity. The number of Anglican churches increased by a factor of ten from 1702 to 1711, and over the next twenty years it nearly doubled, reaching nineteen. What is more, during the first three decades of the eighteenth century the Church of England built with public support more than twice as many churches as dissenters. Whereas dissenting churches outnumbered Anglican churches by ten to one in 1701, exactly one half of the colony's thirty-eight churches in 1731 were Anglican churches.[65] This remarkable growth was reinforced by the arrival of literally scores of Anglican clergymen, most of whom were sent by the SPG. In the twenty-five years following 1706, the year the second colony-wide Church Act was promulgated, some forty-two Anglican ministers landed in the colony, more than six or seven times as many as before, and all but thirteen (or 69 percent) were SPG missionaries.[66]

One of these minsters was William Tredwell Bull, who arrived in 1712 and succeeded Gideon Johnston as commissary of Carolina (1716–1723). Bull witnessed firsthand the dramatic profusion of churches and clergy and was himself a product of the larger transatlantic Anglican renaissance. By the time he resigned as commissary and left South Carolina in 1723, his church dominated provincial Christian practice in many quarters, as census data collected the following year suggests. This 1724 church census, part of the bishop of London's survey of the Church of England in colonial British America, indicates that at least one-half of all white adults in seven of the nine parishes for which ministerial reports were received attended Anglican services on a regular basis. In the parishes of Christ Church and St. John's in Berkeley County, the two exceptions, relatively large audiences still participated in Sabbath services at state churches on any given Sunday, even though sizable numbers of parish residents were dissenters. It was reported that "70 persons"—one-fifth of the total number of white adult parishioners—"constantly" turned out every week for Sunday services in the former parish, while "seldom less 50 or 60" attended weekly services in the latter parish, more than one-quarter of the white adults living in St. John's. Overall, there were some 1,223 regular Anglican churchgoers in 1724, almost two-thirds (or 63 percent) of would-be adherents to the Church of England, representing about 36 percent of the white population in nine parishes. (The total white population stood at about 6,500 in 1720.) This meant that one in three white adults aged sixteen or above "ordinarily" attended an establishment church service every Sunday, a remarkable statistic by any measure, even when accounting for exaggeration, false reporting, and the rounding out of figures.[67]

Not only could some Anglican ministers boast of public worship services wherein the congregations were so large that churchgoers "were forced to stand without the door, and others hang at the windows," as Francis Varnod of St. George's Parish in Colleton County did in 1724.[68] They could also report that a substantial number of their auditors were regular communicants. Evidence from the 1724 Anglican census suggests that an average of approximately 31 percent of the adults who normally attended Anglican public worship services also communicated regularly. Alexander Garden of St. Philip's Parish in Charleston reported the lowest average communication percentage, whereas Brian Hunt of St. John's Parish in Berkeley County reported the highest. Garden estimated that "on Sundays seldom less than 400" worshippers regularly attended St. Philip's and "from 30 to 50" usually took communion each time the sacrament was celebrated (10 percent). In contrast, Hunt reported that "seldom less than 50 or 60" worshippers attended divine services in his rural parish, with 30 adults commonly communicating (55 percent). At Easter, however, a higher percentage of auditors probably communicated. At St. Philip's, for example, Garden reported that 100 worshippers communicated at Easter in his church in 1724, or 25 percent of the usual number of churchgoers in attendance. (Of course, at Easter the auditory could have swelled to possibly 500 people or more.)[69]

As Nicholas M. Beasley has suggested, and as the 1704 Test Act makes clear, the sacrament of the Lord's Supper was highly venerated in South Carolina, and many worshippers abstained from the Sacrament not because they were spiritually lethargic or even indifferent to religion. Rather, they abstained from the taking of the Communion because, in Beasley's words, "the sacrament was dangerous stuff," and some provincial churchgoers felt themselves personally unworthy to consume the elements of bread and wine out of fear of being eternally damned. For example, the 1704 Test Act required all members of the Commons House of Assembly to receive the Sacrament according to the Book of Common Prayer or swear that they had not been in communion with any nonconforming congregation for one year, the exemption being necessary because some Anglican laypeople were so pious that they scrupled "the receiving of the Sacrament . . . by reason they fear they are not rightly fitted and prepared to pertake of that ordinance." Thus, even though the sacrament of the Lord's Supper was administered regularly in South Carolina about four times per year, as it was in England, far fewer numbers of Anglican church worshippers actually communicated (on average) when the Eucharist was celebrated. Besides, at St. Philip's, where the Sacrament was administered monthly and where Alexander Garden reported that only 10 percent of worshippers regularly communicated, the church catered to a substantial number of transient visitors from both sides of the Atlantic, particularly those persons who went down to the sea in ships. Also important, not all of the South Carolina Anglican ministers who reported on the number of communicants in the colony in the 1724 church census adhered to the same standard for admittance. Some comprehended those who preferred sitting or standing to kneeling to receive the elements. Others did not.[70]

One reason why South Carolina Anglican ministers could report such solid gains for their church in the first twenty-five years of the eighteenth century is that the Church of England promoted a religious program just as propitious for slave-owning as for the propagation of Protestant Christianity.[71] While the bishop of London and other church leaders were busy instituting reforms to strengthen and enlarge the sphere of the English state church, South Carolina was being transformed into a full-fledged slave society, where "slavery stood at the center of economic production, and the master-slave relationship provided the model for all social relations: husband and wife, parent and child, employer and employee, teacher and student."[72] Indeed, the successful introduction of rice-planting in the 1690s led to the massive importation of African slaves, whose numbers rose sharply from roughly 2,400 in 1700 to more than 5,000 in 1710, to about 12,000 in 1720, and to at least 20,000 in 1730.[73]

Within ten years after it was founded, the SPG, which was initially organized primarily for the benefit of white individuals, launched a major program to Christianize slaves in response to the explosive growth of the peculiar institution in colonial British America. But even before it was conceived, SPG ministers in the field had encountered intense planter hostility to missionary work among enslaved Africans, especially in South Carolina, where some of the first settlers had been directly involved in a controversy over clerical efforts to baptize slaves. Anglican clergy thereby set out to assuage white opposition to slave conversion in the New World, and in so doing they helped to develop the basis of a new slaveholding ethos, which in effect became a base and prototype for the South's paternalistic ideal.[74]

In a well-known sermon delivered to the SPG in 1711, William Fleetwood, bishop of St. Asaph, sought to alleviate concerns that slavery and Christianity were incompatible in order to facilitate the conversion of slaves, showing how society officials and some other religious leaders back in Europe were reacting to and making plans for the colonies. He identified "three poor Pretences" upon which he thought planters based their resistance to slave proselytization: first, baptism might jeopardize a master's property rights by giving slaves a claim to free status; second, Christian slaves had to be treated "with *less Rigour*" than non-Christian slaves; and, third, conversion would prevent slave owners from selling bondspersons. Fleetwood's response to these "Pretences" is especially important, as he emphasized throughout his discourse an enlightened partriarchalism. In particular Fleetwood emphasized the reciprocal social duties of masters and slaves, the practical benefits of the peculiar institution, and the Christian "obligations" masters had to convert their bondspersons.[75]

In Africa, "a Country where the *Name of Christ* is never heard, or call'd upon," the bishop suggested, blacks were an "unhappy People." Yet God made Africans to be as happy as Europeans, and, "in a Country where Christians govern all," they were "capable of being so . . . , however hard their condition be in this World, with respect to their Captivity and Subjection." According to Fleetwood, what prevented bondspersons from being happy was the un-Christian behavior of masters who inhibited proselytization. Such behavior was not only merciless; it also was damnable. Indeed, Fleetwood said, planters who opposed slave conversion had every "reason to fear God may deny that mercy to themselves, which they deny to others." In fact, they might just as well "throw themselves into the Fire deliberately."[76]

If, as the "Occasion and the Instruments" of bringing slaves from Africa, planters had the duty to Christianize their slaves, and if by such "Munificence" slave owners "would be no losers, and the Servants the greatest gainers in the World," then why were there objections to slave conversion? For Fleetwood, it all boiled down to false pretenses. "*Christ's Command*," the bishop told his audience, was clear with respect to slaveholding and the meaning of liberty. First, it was a mistake to believe that Christianity prohibited planters from owning baptized slaves or from selling Christian slaves "as they do of other Goods and Chattel for Money." Second, "the Liberty of Christianity" was "entirely Spiritual." It bestowed upon people "Freedom from their Sins, Freedom from the Fears of Death, and everlasting Misery, and not from any State of Life," particularly bondage. Third, the Bible dictated "Mercy and Compassion to be shewn to *all the World* alike," including "a *Savage*, and an *Infidel*," whether free or slave.[77]

Bishop Fleetwood was more interested in advancing the Church of England's missionary program than in running the risk of destroying it by attacking the institution of slavery as inimical to "bringing many thousand Souls to Christ." As a result he sought to alleviate concerns that slavery and Christianity were incompatible in order to facilitate the conversion of slaves. This, he believed, would go a long way in changing the more generalized English view of Africans, of those who "only consider these unhappy Wretches, as Creatures that save the Kingdom the Charge of transporting Horses, and Beasts of Carriage, for . . . Service, without reflecting on their Shape and Form, and intellectual Powers, and without looking up to Christ." Once that change occurred, then amelioration might follow. Fleetwood even suggested there was "a *Blessed Medium*" whereby "Slaves, tho' Christians, might be Bought and Sold, and used like Slaves" and "with all the Mercy and good Nature that can well be shown, consistently with their continuing Useful and Laborious Servants." Planterly "Munificence," he argued, would reinforce social bonds and strengthen slave owners' authority, predisposing slaves toward greater contentment, dutifulness, and respect.[78]

The SPG printed thousands of copies of Fleetwood's sermon and distributed it to Anglican missionaries throughout the British colonies in America. In South Carolina, Francis Le Jau, rector of St. James Goose Creek from 1706 to 1717, received "some Number of Copies" in 1715.[79] Having these at his disposal, Le Jau quickly passed the copies of Fleetwood's sermon along to several of his parishioners, hoping that it would have "the Desired Effect," at least among those "Honest & well Dispos'd Masters."[80] Slave conversion was no casual matter in this growing plantation colony, as Le Jau well knew. Ever since his arrival in the colony he had encountered sustained opposition in his efforts to proselytize slaves, which preceded the initiation of the SPG Christianization program and for which he sought the society's advice. Of a similar mind to the bishop of Asaph, he deduced by attending to the "Whispers & Conduct" of his parishioners that slaveholders "wou'd not have me urge of Contributing to the Salvation, Instruction, and human usage of Slaves." The reason: "the Old pretext that Baptism makes the Slaves proud and Undutifull." This contention emerged as "their main Argument," according to Le Jau; and it was pervasive.[81] "The masters of slaves," Gideon Johnston wrote, were "generally of [the] opinion that a slave grows worse by being a Christian; and therefore instead of instructing them in the principles of Christianity which is undoubtedly their duty, they malign and traduce those that attempt it."[82]

Although there were some notable exceptions, a few planters who were "good Christians" and encouraged "wth all their might . . . the Instruction of their Slaves," Anglican ministers continued to find that the opportunities for slave conversion were "neither great nor frequent" in South Carolina. They catalogued their failures in letter after letter to church officials in England, citing the extent to which "the conversion of slaves is thought inconsistent with the planters' secular interest and advantage."[83] Thomas Hassell reported in 1724 that in the parish of St. Thomas and St. Dennis only twelve of the more than nine hundred black persons in his charge had been baptized, a ratio comparable to the one in St. George Dorchester and probably the colony as a whole.[84] "'Tis true . . . that an odd slave here and there may be converted when a minister has leisure and opportunity for so doing, but this seldom happens," Commissary Johnston frankly admitted.[85] Likewise, Richard Ludlam, one of Francis Le Jau's successors at St. James Goose Greek Parish, wrote that because of "the diffidence of owners" it was "almost impractical to convert any but here & there a favorite house slave."[86]

While the Church of England's program to convert slaves failed to move any appreciable numbers of bondspersons to worship in established state churches as formal members, it paved the way for popular evangelism among white individuals and invested slaveholding with spiritual significance.[87] The program mitigated fears that Christianity might "hinder People from being Slaves when they become Christians," fears that Bishop Fleetwood imagined were generated largely out of lay "ignorance." If "these Men ever read the Scriptures," he said, then they would hardly "venture to lay an Impediment in any one's way to Conversion." Moreover, the Church of England supplied early slaveholders with the basis of a paternalistic rationale for African bondage by pressing obligations upon rulers and ruled. It was the masters' spiritual responsibility to "cause their slaves to be Baptized," for "no Man living can assign a better and more justifiable Cause, for God's with-holding the Mercy of a Christian, than that Christian's with-holding the Mercy of Christianity from an Unbeliever." Conversely, it was duty of black people to adhere to the Pauline doctrine that slaves must obey "their masters in all things."[88] Finally, the Anglican program reinforced secular laws regarding slavery.[89] The Fundamental Constitutions of Carolina granted every freeman "absolute Power and Authority over his Negro slaves, of what opinion or Religion soever," and by the turn of the eighteenth century various acts "for the Better Ordering of Slaves" had been passed.[90] These slave codes conspired to strip bondspersons of almost all legal protections traditionally afforded servants and bestowed despotic patriarchal power upon slaveholders. Anglicans ignominiously accepted the import of the South Carolina slave codes while at the same time providing powerful new theoretical and practical support for the status and behavior of slave owners. Every assertion of reciprocal obligation simply highlighted the power of those who owned slaves.

By 1724, then, the Church of England could report solid gains for its program of evangelization and Christianization in South Carolina. After a quarter of a century it had secured legal establishment in the colony and, with public support, erected sixteen new churches. About one in three white adults regularly attended Anglican services, and there was striking increase in the number of officially ordained ministers. Some twenty to twenty-five Anglican priests (most of whom were SPG missionaries) served eleven parishes at various times during the decade in which the bishop of London conducted his survey. Additionally, Commissaries Johnston and Bull helped strengthen the establishment by superintending church affairs with rigor and determination. Indeed, when William Bull resigned after eleven years of service in the colony, the state church was reportedly in "a flourishing condition."[91]

There was from its inception in 1704 intense hostility toward the Anglican establishment in South Carolina. For years dissenters protested against the church while repeatedly calling for disestablishment. Charleston merchant Joseph Boone, employed by many principal inhabitants and traders of the colony as the dissenting party's agent abroad, spearheaded the effort to disestablish South Carolina's state church in England. Boone's Carolina allies included "four Chief Men" of the province. This group comprised Thomas and George Smith, Joseph Morton, and Edmund Bellinger. Other wealthy dissenters such as Lady Rebecca Axtell and her daughter Elizabeth (Axtell) Blake also advocated for disestablishment, as did a number of dissenting clergymen.[92] Presbyterian minister Archibald Stobo, a survivor of the second Scottish expedition to the Isthmus of Darien (1699–1700) who preached at the Independent Church in Charleston, was among the Church of England's most outspoken critics. Stobo and several "Country preachers" in Colleton County were described by an Anglican writer as men "who on all occasions foment and stir up the people to ffaction and Sedition." Common people took an active role in opposing the Church of England, "insulting" Anglican ministers and prominent Anglican laypeople "with Mobbs and Riots and Tumults." Dissenting party leaders were as skillful as agitators as Governor Moore had been.[93] Many Anglican observers feared that they would succeed through sheer determination: "they are never to be satisfyed till they can compass the downfall of this Infant Church," one reported. "We guess that they wou'd have the whole province to themselves," said another.[94]

One of the main arguments South Carolina's dissenters used to dispute the legitimacy of an Anglican establishment was based on the Act of Union between England and Scotland (1707). Dissenters stressed that provincial legislation was inconsistent with the act, which recognized Presbyterianism, and therefore should either be disallowed or expanded to provide for a multiple establishment, whereby both Presbyterians and Anglicans would be privileged by government sanction and support. "With this View it is that they wou'd have their Ministers provided for in all respects equally with us," Commissary Johnston wrote.[95] Dissenters focused their attention on Anglican disestablishment, but they employed the multiple establishment claim to good advantage through the 1720s.

At first they seized upon this argument as a justification for refusing to pay taxes to support the Church of England. Joseph Boone and some of the dissenting "Chief Men" and women encouraged open defiance. Dr. George Smith informed St. Philip's Parish tax collectors that the Church Act was "only fit to wipe his A—se with."[96] Axtell and her daughter Elizabeth were "so extreamly factious and seditious" that some Anglicans "wished that they cou'd be banished as common Plagues and Nusances out of the Country."[97] Opposition was steadfast. By 1710 the Anglican-dominated assembly was forced to amend earlier legislative enactments. Since the method of raising revenue to pay for parochial expenses had been "found inconvenient, dilatory and troublesome," and because "factious persons have given out that the acts of 1706 and 1707 are not lawful," legislators decided to secure funds for parish maintenance from the general treasury.[98] Import and export duties were thereby used to help defray the total cost of the state church for the rest of the colonial period. As Thomas J. Curry has observed, no other English colony had such an establishment provision.[99]

Dissenters were hardly satisfied. Francis Le Jau reported to the SPG that there was "a dangerous party of Men here that give to understand they have a design to destroy our establish't Churches, break our Acts & introduce ways like those of New England."[100] Toward these ends Thomas Smith encouraged his coreligionists to withdraw from the Commons House of Assembly in a coordinated act of defiance against the Anglican establishment, a strategy designed to deprive the house of a quorum. "Never was there a pack of more unreasonable Dissenters than we have here" was the usual refrain; "they are so strangely wild, and Malicious, as to the generality of them." Gideon Johnston found it impossible "to begin or Continue a friendly Correspondence with them." "I well know that many of them hate me," he said. The feeling was mutual. Johnston and his successors viewed their Protestant Reformed and sectarian rivals with disdain. They looked down every avenue to find "the shortest way with the Dissenters," that is, how to suppress dissent.[101]

In 1712 Charles Craven arrived to assume the governorship, and in his inaugural address to the legislature on March 2 he expressed his belief that Anglicans and dissenters could "live amicably together" in peace and tranquility because of constitutional guarantees of religious freedom. Remarkably tolerant of different faiths, Craven promised "to show the greatest Tenderness to those who are under the misfortune of dissenting" from the Church of England "and to do nothing that may seem to endanger them that liberty."[102] Yet at about the same time the Anglican clergy began holding a series of meetings in another quarter of Charleston and laying "open their grievances to one another." One grievance against Baptist "Mecahnicks" and other dissenters suggested that they were no more in favor of religious toleration than the pope. Another grievance was that South Carolinians were calling the bishop of London a pope, "nay worse than the Pope," as it was widely known that the Anglican hierarchy wanted to establish an American bishopric in order to bolster its institutional strength. The colony's ministers favored the idea, but they dared not do so too openly. While their authority was "Extreemly deprest if not almost quite sunk," the laity was strongly opposed to the idea of settling a bishop in colonial British America.[103]

A sincere Arminian, Commissary Johnston firmly believed that episcopacy was divine in origin, that "wherever Christianity was planted there was a Bp Settled in Apostolocal and primitive times." He also believed that since the provincial clergy was "thus Neglected in this respect, It is but reason that we should do Justice to our Selves." Yet he thought London officials' plans for an American episcopate, which crystalized during the last years of Queen Anne's reign, were rather premature given the "new Schemes of Church Government Erected in the Transmarine parts," particularly the colonial lower southern colony of South Carolina. Here the ecclesiastical framework of the church was "contrary to the Scriptures [and] the Cannons and Rubrick and the Lords Proprietors Charter," and until it was fixed any effort to establish an American episcopate would be futile. "In vain therefore it is to think of Sending Bishops abroad," he observed while visiting England in 1713, "till they are forced to it by one General Law here at home." "When this is done," Johnston added, "then Episcopacy will of Course take place of all those wild and rambling Scheems of Church Government which are but so many senseless Satyrs upon our Constitution at home."[104]

However much Johnston complained about colonial South Carolina's scheme of church government; however much Anglican ministers desired an American bishop; and however much Arminian church officials wished to suppress religious dissent and enforce conformity to the canons and rubrics of the Church of England, the clergy's problems were ones far more deeply rooted—and not simply in the eclectic "Principles and busy restless tempers" of the provincial laity, most of whom tended to be Low Church moderates, Puritan sympathizers, or outright nonconformists whose consciences led them to reject all manner of

Anglican theology, form, and ritual. For the history of the established clergy during these years was in many ways the history of anticlericalism. The Church of England was highly venerated but its ministers were not.[105]

First, the reputation of the Anglican ministry suffered because of its worldliness. Many parishioners believed that clergymen were more interested in their livings and perquisites than in being spiritual mentors and guides. And they had some grounds for their beliefs. At least one out of every nine of the twenty-six to twenty-eight ministers who labored in the colony from 1696 to 1719 (or 11.1 percent) was accused of putting worldly above pastoral concerns; in the 1720s the percentage seems to have risen even higher. During the former period William Dunn of Goose Creek Parish openly admitted to profiteering, while Richard Marsden, who ministered first at St. Philip's and then at Christ Church, lived ostentatiously and accumulated a sizable debt before fleeing the colony. In another instance Ebenezer Taylor, rector of St. Andrew's, became embroiled in a conflict with the parish vestry over his income. This prompted his parishioners to send a petition to the SPG explaining why he "Should Be No Longer Suffered to Officiate in the Said Parish." Later, Brian Hunt of St. John's Berkeley Parish aroused resentment for conducting a "Collusive & Clandestine" marriage simply to make money, and Thomas Moritt, who officiated in Prince George's, Winyaw, and in Prince Frederick Parish, was charged with engaging in secular pursuits and neglecting his ministerial duties.[106]

These are obvious examples, but even those ministers whose life and work might otherwise be considered exemplary (and there were many) were commonly perceived as being worldly by the South Carolina laity. Low clerical salaries were a source of constant complaint, and Anglican clergymen such as Samuel Thomas dilated upon the subject at length, encouraging local officials to "make such further provision as shall capacitate their clergy to live comfortably" while pleading with the SPG to make "some augmentations to [their] salarys," either by raising missionaries' wages or advancing "sums to stock . . . Glebes with negros."[107] In almost all cases low wages forced ministers to rely much more heavily on perquisites, particularly during periods of high inflation when the value of local currency decreased. Commissary Johnston informed the SPG of a particular grievance regarding church fees during one such period that illustrates the problem: "They have by Law, vested the Church and Church yard in the [parish] Clerk, he having the fee the Minister should have for breaking up the ground in either place, it is well known that all Churches & their Yards being Legally dedicated and set apart for Religious uses, are in a more peculiar Manner the Ministers ffreehold and in right of these they are qualified to vote tho' they have no personage houses of Glebes to intitle them to it." Johnston apparently convinced his parishioners that he was in fact entitled to the privilege of collecting the burial fee, at least in theory, but they refused to allow him to collect it nevertheless. "They say, it was by a mistake or oversight in the church Act, that the Clerk had that perquisite and consequently the Church and Churchyard vested in him," he wrote. Most important, by quarreling with the laity over the issue—partly to assert ecclesiastical authority but partly, too, out of financial necessity—the commissary undoubtedly diminished the reputation of the clergy.[108]

Aside from seeking financial gain and focusing too zealously on the business of their careers, South Carolina Anglican ministers often engaged in conduct unbecoming the church and, sometimes, even worse abuses. Such abuses lowered the prestige of the clergy even further. The records of the SPG, which was responsible for sponsoring the large majority of ministers who labored in the colony before mid-century and which was increasingly held responsible for sending loose-living and unsavory missionaries abroad, are chock full of examples of bad behavior. These ranged from habitual drunkenness to forgery, horse stealing, and criminal impersonation. Indeed, scandalous ministers constituted a high percentage of the total number of Anglican clergy in colony in every decade prior to 1750, at least 15 percent.[109] And the whoremongering, performance of incestuous marriages, exploitive sexual relationships with parishioners, adultery—all these undermined clerical authority and the ability of Anglican ministers to command respect.

Anticlericalism persisted in the late proprietary period, but it increased rather dramatically during the early royal era. Conflicts between Anglicans and dissenters also grew during this time. The violent Yamasee War of 1715 and the subsequent revolt in 1719 against proprietary rule ("by reason of the ILL-GOVERNMENT and MALE ADMINISTRATION of the Proprietors" in general and their "inability and incapacity . . . to protect or defend" the colony in particular) plunged South Carolina into an unprecedented crisis.[110] By the time Crown officials completed negotiations with the Lords Proprietors in 1729 for the purchase of South Carolina and plans for recovery had been made, this crisis reached a critical juncture. Rice exports expanded steadily and white planters and merchants continued to import thousands of African slaves in order to sustain production of the lucrative staple. Still, the interceding years were mostly ones of divisive and unsettling turmoil. The land office closed, the naval-stores industry fell into rapid decline, and the issue of paper money led to mob action under the leadership of Congregationalist stalwart Thomas Smith. The provincial government ultimately collapsed in 1728 under the weight of internal conflict. Then, yellow fever visited horrific "putrefaction" on the inhabitants of Charleston, while a hurricane wrought havoc on an otherwise drought-stricken harvest.[111]

Distracted, distressed, confused—these were the words that contemporaries used to describe the situation. Anglican minister Brian Hunt wrote that "Carolina is now in a distracted condition: government despised: property invaded: justice perverted: malice, villainous calumny defended; tricking in trade is universal."[112] A committee of the Commons House of Assembly added that the colony was "in a very distressed and calamitous condition occasioned by the great losses which the Inhabitants in general have sustained by the late dreadful hurricane and storms, by the great mortality among them and their slaves, by the large and growing Debts of the Province, the scarcity of money, and the decay of public credit."[113] In sum, not only was "the whole Province Complaining of want of Government," as Sir Alexander Cuming observed at the end of 1729, but "Every Person did what he himself thought fitt, which threw the Country into Such Confusion, that no Person had any Security either for Life or Property."[114]

These were especially troubling and unsettled times for the Anglican clergy. During the Revolution of 1719, the bloodless revolt that made South Carolina a royal colony, the clergy remained loyal to Governor Robert Johnson and rejected allegiance to James Moore, Jr., who was appointed governor by a revolutionary convention after Johnson refused an offer to take over the government on behalf of King George I.[115] This set them at odds with a majority of their parishioners. "Ye people in genl have Entertained an Extraordinary prejudice against ye Clergy," wrote the minister of St. Andrew's Parish, William Guy.[116] The rebellion had placed the clergy in a dilemma, and by choosing to remain loyal to the proprietors they thoroughly alienated the respect and affection of their parishioners.

Adding intensity to this increasing popular resentment, Governor Moore ordered Anglican ministers to stop performing marriages without his permission in the spring of 1720. Robert Johnson contravened Moore's order, and the entire clergy chose to obey him. Being "coldly looked upon by ye . . . Government," the assembly threatened to stop paying their salaries and "send ym out of ye Country to get a better Sett of Clergy." Rumors and insults flew, yet scarcely had this conflict begun when the "Evil eye" of the colonists grew even more intense. After a months-long dry spell, Governor Moore proclaimed July 20, 1720, a day of fasting and prayer, but Johnson, in another attempt to reassert his authority, designated July 22 a day of fasting and prayer, prompting ministers to observe this date. Commissary Bull reported that the churches were well attended that day. Yet he was fully aware that popular regard for the clergy had reached a new low.[117]

Given their status, it is not surprising that the clergy welcomed the arrival of Sir Francis Nicholson in 1721. A professional soldier and experienced executive who served as South Carolina's first royal governor, Nicholson was a leading Anglican reformer and SPG charter member. When it came to supporting the Church of England, Nicholson spared "neither his purse nor person," and during his tenure as governor he held the clergy "up by the chin," securing salary increases, funds to support the building and improvement of parish churches, and a commitment from London to send forth additional missionaries.[118] To the delight of many Anglicans, Nicholson also spearheaded a campaign against the colony's dissenters, exacerbating religious conflict and hatred. Shortly after he assumed the governorship, the clergy presented Nicholson with a petition asking him to stop issuing marriage licenses to "dissenting Teachers," complaining that they "have invaded the rights of the Church by Publishing the Banns of Marriage in their Meetings & joyning people in Marriage contrary to the prescribed form."[119] William Tredwell Bull claimed that the practice ran contrary to provincial law and was "a Dishonour to ye Church & an injury to the Clergy." The clergy maintained that they had "the undoubted Right & Priviledge of Marriage" because the "Established Church hath every where been vested by ye Civil Authority with the Sole power of Marriage & its Bishops with the sole Jurisdiction as to the Lawfulness of ye Same, ever since the days of ye first Christian Emperours."[120] That the clergy based its petition on demands for conformity is revealing. Nicholson's ready acceptance of it is too. For his goal was their goal: the suppression of Protestant dissent.

Completely devoted to the state church, Nicholson was exceedingly zealous in his efforts to suppress nonconformity and almost seemed to revel in the matter. Even before he responded to the petition to stop issuing marriage licenses to dissenters, he insisted that representatives in the Commons House of Assembly lay their hands on the Bible when taking their oath of office, knowing full well that some members' "Consciences will not Suffer them to take an Oath but according to the fform of their profession." At first dissenters simply ignored the governor, but when he continued to press the issue both the Commons House and the council urged him to back off. In the meantime the Presbyterian Archibald Stobo drew up another petition calling for joint establishment as part of an effort to push back on the issue of marriage licenses, which forced Nicholson to give in and allow dissenters to marry people. With the clergy's effort thwarted, Francis Varnod of St. George's Parish lamented the "want of such laws as those of Barbados, Jamaica, and Virginia, to hinder our Dissenters from christening, marrying and burying," revealing one of the many peculiarities of South Carolina's state church.[121] Having won the battle over marriage licenses, dissenters turned to the issue of oath taking. In 1724 the Commons House presented an address to the governor calling on him to "grant that necessary indulgence" to members of the assembly in "Qualifying themselves ... without Swearing on the holy Evangelist." Yet on this issue Nicholson refused to budge.[122]

As the Crown's chief executive following the Revolution of 1719, the governor ultimately had the upper hand. The assembly was leery of challenging his authority and thereby prejudicing their case against proprietary rule with government officials in London.[123] Too, Nicholson's administration had done much to restore order in an especially turbulent era, giving the colonists a greater sense of peace and security than they had had in years. But the governor's uncompromising High Church stance, his intolerance, and his unfair treatment of dissenters proved highly offensive to many. Indeed he aroused deep resentment, a resentment that carried over into the tenure of his successor, Arthur Middleton, a wealthy rice planter who served as interim governor after Nicholson's departure in 1725.[124]

During Middleton's years, South Carolina's economy slid into depression. After Parliament refused to subsidize colonial naval stores that did not meet the standards set by the Royal Navy, this once-thriving forest industry fell into rapid decline, devastating smaller farmers and provoking calls for more paper money and tax and debt relief. Discontent quickly led to armed protests, a series of tangled events involving the leading supporter of the farmers, Congregationalist planter Thomas Smith, and, finally, the complete breakdown of colony's government in 1728. As "daily affronting Royal Authority and his Representative and Ministers" became ever more common, Governor Middleton exclaimed, "I know not where will be the end of these things."[125]

Neither Middleton nor anyone else knew where things might end, not until news reached the colony that the Carolina proprietors had agreed to relinquish control of South Carolina and Robert Johnson had been appointed governor. Governor Johnson was a popular, respected politician with remarkable abilities and extensive kin connections. An Anglican of high social station, he was a good deal more tolerant in religious matters than either his father, Sir Nathaniel, or Governor Nicholson. He also had executive experience, having held the governorship for two years prior to the Revolution of 1719.[126] In addition, Johnson was a native of South Carolina—"not a stranger"—with whom many gentry could identify.[127]

Most significantly, however, Governor Johnson had an ambitious plan designed to alleviate the South Carolina crisis by providing greater security for the colony. The plan called for the creation of eleven frontier townships to protect against Indian, Spanish, or French attack, besides the possibility of a massive slave uprising. These frontier parishes would be inhabited by Protestant immigrants enticed to settle in the colony through land concessions and generous offers of material aid. The prospective colonists would not only provide a first line of defense in the event of a foreign attack, but they would also help augment the white population.

Governor Johnson's township plan ultimately transformed the face of Protestant Christianity in South Carolina and extended the Atlantic circumference of religious pluralism in the Lower South region of colonial British America. While the townships never attracted as many immigrants as authorities had hoped, there was a considerable influx of European settlers in the 1730s and 1740s.

Contributing to an ever-widening stream of pluralistic Christian expression, this new influx brought with it remarkable ethnic and religious variety—Swiss, German, French, and Dutch Reformed immigrants, German Lutherans, Continental sectarians such as Illuminists, as well as a substantial number of Welsh Baptists and Scottish and Scots-Irish Presbyterians. Furthermore, it engendered an important shift in the ecclesiastical balance of the colony and contributed powerfully to the development of a new religious synthesis during the era of the Great Awakening.

3

A Party of Seekers

The Origins of Southern Evangelicalism

And, that thus, we are threatened, with the last and greatest Plague, wherewith the Church of GOD, is to be infested, in the latter days. . . . The latter times [I say] are perilous times, 2 Tim. 3.1 Why? From what sort of Men, will the dangers arise? not, so much, from the Popish Antichristian party—this is a party of Seekers, looking for new discoveries, holding nothing certain in Religion, ever learning, and never coming to the knowledge of the truth, ver. 7.

The Reverend Hugh Fisher, *A Preservative from Damnable Errors, in the Unction of the Holy One* (1730)

A "party of Seekers" took shape in colonial South Carolina in the 1720s. Like many other clergymen at the time, Presbyterian minister Hugh Fisher, Joseph Lord's successor at the Dorchester church, was deeply concerned. Among Presbyterians and Congregationalists, the Seekers had started a vicious street fight over religious truth, and their "mistaken notions" were beginning to "infect others." In *A Preservative from Damnable Errors, in the Unction of the Holy One,* a sermon first preached at a clerical gathering in Charleston around 1727 and published a few years later, Fisher proclaimed that "as matters now stand, we have no choice." Either the ministers could meet the religious challenge of the Seekers in their "own way," or "like false friends to Truth, suffer it to fall in the Street, without putting an hand to support it; and stand by, and see her head broke, without stepping in, to ward off the blow." Fisher was no false friend. Indeed his sermon to vindicate commonly accepted knowledge claims proved to be among the most important religious writings to appear in print in the decades leading up to the Great Awakening of 1740.[1]

It was a crucial moment in the history of the Atlantic Protestant world. Beginning in the 1720s and continuing through the 1730s, there were outbreaks of bizarre enthusiasm, combative pulpit preachings, remarkable spiritual outpourings, and separatist movements of all sorts in the South Carolina lowcountry. Some Protestants came to believe that they were God's chosen people, others that the Kingdom of Heaven was at hand. Many concluded by the 1730s that only a divine outpouring of the Spirit could effect a religious awakening and save the frontier settlement on the British mainland from certain destruction, a theme George Whitefield swiftly picked up on in his *Three Letters from the Reverend Mr. G. Whitefield*, which he penned shortly after embarking on his famous preaching tour of the American colonies.[2]

With expectations rising and emotions running high, the period saw a great stirring of religious expression that, having no certain outcome, took off in all directions. In the early 1720s a small group of French refugees in the parish of St. Dennis embraced some "wild and frantic Notions" and committed murder under what they perceived to be orders from God; in the late 1720s a nasty subscription controversy split both Presbyterians and Congregationalists; and in 1736 a storm of controversy occasioned a bitter religious schism in the Baptist community, resulting in the Ashley River Baptist Revival. During these same years immigrants from Switzerland, Germany, the British Isles, and the Middle Colonies settled the inland frontier, bringing with them an eclectic mix of beliefs and worship practices as well as strong traditions of revivalism.

For all their obscurities, for all the uncertainties and fear they engendered, and for all their ambiguities and contradictions, these scattered awakenings formed an original movement for religious reform that eventually captured "the soul of the South" in the nineteenth century.[3] Anyone seeking to understand the history of southern religion must take them seriously, as they reveal a nuanced, sophisticated, and complex story of the origins of evangelicalism in South Carolina—and ultimately the Lower South in general—during the 1720s and 1730s. They also demonstrate the utter implausibility of the conventional wisdom suggesting that Protestant evangelicalism was of no vital importance in the South before the Revolutionary era.

Alexander Garden, rector of Saint Philip's Church in Charleston from 1720 to 1753 and commissary for the Carolinas and the Bahamas from 1728 to 1748, was vitally interested in furthering the cause of Anglicanism in eighteenth-century British America, and like his two predecessors, Gideon Johnston and William Tredwell Bull, he believed that the Church of England should be settled, protected, and maintained by the colonial state. Deploring both the minority position of Anglicans in the lower southern colonies and the reluctance of colonial authorities to provide adequate salaries for parish clergy, Garden sought to strengthen the established order in the region by bringing it into greater conformity with traditional European practice. The commissary was particularly worried about the Church of England's continuing dependence on the SPG for financial assistance. Despite legal establishment, English settlers obstinately refused to bear all the costs of provincial maintenance, even after tensions stemming from the early-eighteenth-century debates over Anglican establishment began to subside. As a result Anglican religious development in the lower southern colonies remained heavily dependent on the SPG, forcing the society to direct a significant amount of its resources to the Carolinas and Georgia.[4]

In a 1733 letter to Bishop Edmund Gibson, Commissary Garden outlined a clever plan to free South Carolina's state church from its continuing dependence on the SPG in order to settle the colony's church on a firmer footing. Hoping that the provincial assembly would assume responsibility for paying the full salaries of resident clergy, he secretly told Bishop Gibson that the legislature might show a greater inclination to maintain the Anglican ministry if the SPG simultaneously cut clerical stipends for new ministers from £50 to £40 sterling and demanded local pay increases. In setting forth "these two Hints," Garden recommended that the SPG call attention to the colony's increasing wealth and prosperity, for he knew that provincial authorities could not deny the profitability of South Carolina's slave-based plantation economy—or the ability of taxpayers to bear all the costs of provincial maintenance.[5] Intrigued by these machinations, SPG officials decided to carry out the commissary's secret plan, and in early 1735 they wrote to the unsuspecting royal governor, Robert Johnson, in accordance with Garden's suggestions. No sooner had Johnson received the SPG's letter than the governor agreed to lobby the provincial legislature on behalf of full support for the parish clergy, telling Garden that he was certain that "the assembly wou'd make such Provision in 2 or 3 years."[6] Garden must have been well pleased, that is until his scheme failed. Governor Johnson died late in the spring and, furthermore, Johnson's successor, Lieutenant Governor Thomas Broughton, quickly became embroiled in a conflict with the South Carolina legislature over freedom of debate in the assembly, specifically executive attempts to influence laws before they were passed.[7]

Of all the South Carolina Anglican officials who wrote home to England during these years, Alexander Garden must have been among the most thoroughly disingenuous. Not simply because his secret plan was so calculating but also because it was formulated in the context of a religious development that was changing the face of Protestant Christianity in the colony—the evolution of Protestant evangelical dissent. Commissary Garden was very much aware of what was happening when he concocted his scheme, having seen firsthand how this "enthusiastick Turn . . . set Men's Heads thus a Roving and Wandering, till finally they wandered into all the Errors, Distractions, and Misery, that 'tis possible for Men to wander into."[8]

First arriving in South Carolina in 1720, Garden had been concerned about all the Protestant dissenters in his midst for some considerable time. He joined with other Anglican clergy in protesting the practice of allowing dissenters to perform marriages with licenses from the governor and believed that they had entirely too many "Liberties and Privileges" in the colony. He witnessed the Presbyterian minister Archibald Stobo issue a direct challenge to the Church of England with a bold petition openly avowing joint establishment and public maintenance.[9] He commiserated with Sir Francis Nicholson, South Carolina's first royal governor, a High Church Anglican who shared his view of nonconformists and could only suppose "under what Denominations they pretend to be Dissenters"; thought he could "Prove that all . . . are of Common Wealth Principles both in Church and State and would be Independent to the Crown of Great Brittain if it were in their Power"; and labored under the conviction that they generally "Infuse Ante Monarchical Principles in to the people."[10] Yet Alexander Garden also saw the nature of Protestant dissent change, as it entered a new, iconoclastic phase in the 1720s and 1730s.

The commissary reacted predictably to the rise of Protestant evangelicalism. He endeavored to fortify the establishment as his predecessors had done. This was no small task. Again, most everyone recognized, as the Commons House of Assembly did in 1724, that Protestant dissenters formed the "great part of ye Body of this Province."[11] This very fact illuminated an element of puritanism with a lowercase *p* in the Church of England, prejudiced lay adherence and Protestant Christian worship and practice, and impeded attempts to bolster the Anglican ecclesiastical structure. It also created an atmosphere of hostility and discontent. The bitter struggle over Anglican establishment left a lasting legacy of resentment and grief.

Given what dissenting Protestant leaders knew of that struggle, the "persecuting Spirit" that reigned, and their subsequent history in the colony, they had every reason to complain.[12] Many nonconformists were defecting to establishment church services, with several becoming formal communicants. Protestant dissenters groped for a response. The Presbyterian Archibald Stobo's petition for joint establishment, drafted against the background of new harassments under Sir Francis Nicholson and the obsequious clergy he so fervently supported, reveals something of the extent of their frustration and angst. A quite different sort of response is reflected in the actions of refugee Huguenot laypeople in the parish of St. Dennis, including those families involved in the infamous incident that became known as the Dutartre affair.[13]

In 1724, as part of his regular duties as rector of St. Philip's, Alexander Garden visited five men in Charleston who had been convicted of murdering a provincial magistrate and condemned to death. John Dutartre, two of his four sons (Daniel and John, Jr.), Dutartre's son-in-law Peter Rombert, and a man named Michael

Boineau, a member of the Dutartre household or a neighbor, were Huguenots who said they committed the murder under orders from God. The Dutartre affair was the talk of the town, and Garden attended the men "with more than ordinary Pains and Diligence."[14] He had little patience with their mystical beliefs, but it appears that he listened carefully as these men told their story, endeavoring to disabuse them of their errant notions and enthusiastic ways after they had finished.

John Dutartre was the head of a large family in the parish of St. Dennis, a family that included his wife and their eight children. As many as one-third of the parish's 565 or so white members were of refugee extraction, and a substantial number had been involved in the St. Dennis revolt of 1712–1720.[15] In the early 1720s the Dutartres and their neighbors embraced some "wild and fantastick Notions" after reading the works of the great Lutheran mystic Jacob Boehme and "other Authors of the same Stamp." These included writings on London's notorious French Prophets, who created a stir throughout the Atlantic world from 1705 to the early 1710s by preaching their ability to raise believers from the dead and the imminent end of the world. It is also entirely possible that, as Garden claimed, the Dutartres had been influenced by the preachings and prophecyings of a "strolling Moravian, Dutch, or Swiss Enthusiast." At any rate the Dutartres came to know God through the facts of experience, through divine impulses and tokens, and they subsequently withdrew from the world. Speculative mysticism led the Dutartres to "open Visions and Revelations" whereby "God raised up a Prophet unto them from among themselves." Peter Rombert, the husband of John Dutartre's widowed daughter, prophesied that God intended to destroy humankind through some cataclysmic event ("as in the days of Noah") and preserve the Dutartres to people the earth "pure and undefiled." In order to prepare for the cataclysm Rombert married his sister-in-law Judith, because he foretold the resurrection of his official wife's first husband. Judith Dutartre was a young woman and a virgin, and Rombert said that she had been chosen by God to carry the family's "holy Seed." John Dutartre readily approved of Rombert's marriage to his virgin daughter after seeing a sign that appeared to confirm the spiritual truth of Rombert's prophecy.[16]

Eschewing all earthly authority and embracing pacifism, the Dutartre family restlessly awaited the cataclysmal moment in what they imagined were the last days. After some time they learned that the local constable was preparing to serve multiple warrants on the men for failing to comply with provincial laws requiring militia service and road maintenance, as well as a warrant executed against Judith Dutartre for carrying a bastard child. Consulting their seer Rombert, they reportedly learned "that God commanded them to arm and defend *themselves* and their *Substance* from the *Persecution* and *Robberies* of the Men of the *Earth*, and that no *Weapon formed against them should prosper*." With this enthusiastic call to arms the Dutartres engaged the local constable upon his arrival, along with two or three of his deputies, forcing a call for help. Justice Symmons, the magistrate who issued the warrants and the neighborhood militia captain, hurried to the scene with about a dozen soldiers. Another armed struggle ensued, leaving two dead and several wounded.[17]

For Garden, the Dutartre affair became more than a story about fanatical mysticism and murder. It became an object lesson in the dangers of religious emotionalism, the dogma of experience. "How amazing a Delusion prevailed over them!" he wrote. "They had the *Spirit* of God . . . leading them into all Truth. They were *sure* of it, they *knew* it, they *felt* it." The Dutartres' truth was at the opposite pole from Garden's belief in the supremacy of reason in understanding scriptural revelation. He did not believe that people could come to know God as the Dutartres did. Truth discovered through emotional experience was no truth at all, for human emotions were perverse, arbitrary, and utterly fallible. Yet the Dutartres had a different view. In expostulating the teachings of the Church of England, Garden noted, "when I came to *reason* with them, they treated me with great Disdain!"[18]

Alexander Garden did not set out to write about Dutartre affair. He penned his account sixteen years later, when many others began espousing a similar sort of religious enthusiasm. Yet the incident no doubt alerted him to the subtle resonances of ideological currents that were spilling over into his tiny corner of the Atlantic world and giving shape to indigenous developments.[19] At the doctrinal level there was obviously a concern over the growing influence of rationalism, which had many expressions. Among them were fears of the spread of deism. As commissary, Alexander Garden was sufficiently concerned about the movement to initiate a full-blown antideist campaign in 1731, putting the Anglican clergy on alert and recommending that they consult such works as Charles Leslie's *A Short and Easy Method with the Deists* (London, 1723) to counter deistical arguments. The following year, when Thomas Whitmarsh began publishing the *South Carolina Gazette*, he expressed in rhymed prose a regard for religious views that raised additional suspicions:

> Cool Reason I bow to, wheresoever 'tis found,
> And rejoice when found Learning with Favour is crown'd,
> To no Party a Slave, in no Squabbles I join
> Nor damn the Opinion, that differs from mine.

A disciple of Benjamin Franklin, Whitmarsh vowed to "sift Truth from all Rubbish" in the pages of the *South Carolina Gazette*. In May 1732 he decided to start taking subscriptions to reprint a controversial visitation sermon preached by the English vicar William Bowman entitled *The Traditions of the clergy destructive of Religion* (London, 1731), which raised additional fears that deism was gaining in popularity in the early modern overseas Anglophone Atlantic world. The decision sparked a lively debate extending over a period of several months.[20]

Deism was a particularly touchy subject in the Church of England. The church's moderate confessional stance was broader and more humane than the rigidity of the dissenters' position. Yet its stress on the reasonableness of Christian doctrine opened it up to charges of hypocrisy. Garden's eagerness to declare war on deism probably derived as much from his desire to disarm the Church of England's critics as from the reality of the danger that outright deism posed in the colony, though as the historian John Walsh has noted, deist works were circulating in South Carolina and other British American colonies. In addition, Whitmarsh was an Anglican, at least nominally, and it goes without saying that the established clergy resented his decision to proceed with the publication of Vicar Bowman's sermon. Some even viewed the sermon as "a Libel against the Church of England and her Ministers."[21] Worse still, in the newspaper controversy that followed, Anglican ministers endured all sorts of abuse. One theme of the attacks was that parish clergy sanctioned immoral behavior by turning a blind eye to pride and dissoluteness. Another theme involved issues of religious tolerance and intolerance. Established clergymen were upbraided as religious bigots whose religious dogmatism enjoyed government support, bringing into question not only their privileged position but their stand against Protestant dissenters as well.[22]

Unnerved by the dreadful specter of deism, facing new pressures for a more enlightened policy of toleration, and alarmed by popular outbreaks of religious enthusiasm, Garden set out to strengthen the church and effect ecclesiastical reform. In the 1720s and 1730s he focused his attention squarely on clerical discipline, for his experience had shown him how "one disorderly Brother" could "easily . . . break down whatever the rest shall be able build up." For Garden deviance from orthodox doctrine, ritual, and form proved an especially sore spot, and the commissary threatened to punish irregular clergy with the full "Force of Ecclesiastical Laws."[23]

Nevertheless, Francis Guichard, the Anglican rector of the Huguenot Church in Charleston from 1732 to 1752, presented Garden with an especially difficult problem. Guichard used "one or the other Liturgy as the People were minded & . . . thought the matter of no consequence," yet Garden could do little to discipline him. First, Guichard drew his income from a nonconformist church, not from the Church of England. In addition Guichard began officiating at the Huguenot Church just as liberty of conscience emerged as a subject of heated debate in the first issues of the *South Carolina Gazette*, when Garden was called "a furious Zealot" for his intolerance of dissenting religious views. Finally, if the commissary acted to discipline Guichard, Garden knew that Carolina's French settlers "wou'd be apt to make much ado about it, take up Much Prejudice agt the Chh upon it, & run it into a Party Quarrel."[24]

While his hands were tied with respect to Guichard, Garden nonetheless refused to tolerate any dissent from the liturgy prescribed in the Book of Common Prayer from other clergy. He was a strict disciplinarian as well. After being commissioned as commissary of Carolina by the bishop of London in 1728, Garden initiated yearly visitations and enjoined ministers to "behave in every Instance of their Duty, as the ministry May in Nothing be blamed." But his directive was poorly obeyed. Indeed clerical behavior proved to be Garden's bane.[25] Early on the commissary witnessed "an incredible deal of mischief," a series of high-profile episodes involving badly behaved clergy that gave "great Scandal & offence" to churchgoers and fueled anticlerical sentiment.[26] By the late 1720s the reputation of the clergy reached another new low. This put the Church of England on the defensive against "her open enemies," namely Protestant "Sectaries of all kinds." Dissenters not only seemed "more implacable" than ever before—they seemed to "swarm."[27] "The ill behavior or fault of any one Clergyman seldom misses of being improved into a Scandal & Prejudice agt Religion, the Church & the whole order of the Clergy by their enemies," South Carolina ministers wrote to the SPG.[28]

South Carolina's dissenting community underwent a change of great and lasting consequence in the 1720s and 1730s, helping to explain why Anglican ministers discerned a swarming. This change began with the murderous Dutartre affair, which had direct links to the St. Dennis revolt of 1713–1720 and developments in Atlantic world Protestantism more generally. This "tragical Scene of Enthusiasm" was not simply an aberration.[29] Nor was it geographically limited. On both sides of the Atlantic there were many others who were seeking a new definition of the Christian life, and sudden, seemingly disconnected episodes of religious enthusiasm arose contemporaneously throughout various Protestant regions in both Europe and America. In describing these many ecstatic outbreaks clergymen commonly invoked caricatures of past spirit-filled events in condemning them, powerful images that survived in living memory. For example, Alexander Garden linked the Dutartre episode to the Munster Anabaptists of the sixteenth century, the radicalism of English Civil War and Commonwealth period, and the spiritual enthusiasm of London's French Prophets.[30]

Furthermore, there were many others who, like the Dutartres, were convinced that they were living in "the last age of the World" and that the moral turpitude of the present would inevitably lead God to destroy humankind if Christians did not forsake "the Evil of their Ways." In 1707 the Quaker proprietor John Archdale admonished South Carolinians (and by example, other British Protestants) in his *New Description of Carolina,* excoriating them on their general "Disobedience and Neglect of God's Laws." "God had some peculiar Love for the Children of

Israel," he wrote, "yet they held their Land of Canaan on Terms and Conditions." After God "brought various Corporeal Punishments upon them to alarm them to Repentance," and "when His Chastising Hand did not prevail," Archdale emphasized, then "their Utter Destruction immediately ensued." Citing a litany of what he thought were divine judgments brought against the colony (for example, disease, the threat of foreign invasion, internecine political quarrels, and religious persecution), the proprietor warned South Carolinians of the "dangerous Prognostick" for their American Canaan, believing that if colonists did not repent, then "more severe Judgment will follow." He reminded them that Christ's death was purchased after the Fall of Man for the absolution of human sin. "The Act of Consideration is in the Soul's power," he concluded, "whereby a Capacity comes to be awaken'd in us, to choose the Good and refuse the Evil."[31]

Archdale's Quaker beliefs could be disputed by other Protestants, and they no doubt were. But his view of time and how God worked in history was widely shared, by Cotton Mather and other American Puritans such as Hugh Adams. And Archdale's view was taken very seriously. For him, as for others, it was in "this last Age" that "the Mysteries of the Kingdom of God are to be unsealed" and "the Earth . . . filled with the Knowledge of God, as the Waters covers the Seas."[32] Should Protestants refrain from totally forsaking God, then they might look forward to a great outpouring of the Holy Spirit and the rapid, worldwide spread of the Christian gospel. Yet the prognosis for such a future was not encouraging in the 1710s and 1720s, especially among dissenters living in the South Carolina lowcountry.

Indeed South Carolina could boast of no significant Presbyterian or Congregational growth during this period. Church-building proceeded lethargically—in the turbulent 1720s not at all—and the eight to ten Reformed ministers laboring in the colony in 1710 had not increased by 1730. Sectarians were suffering their own problems. Baptists had a much better record than all other dissenting Protestant groups, but Quakers did not fare well. In 1740 there remained only one Quaker meetinghouse in the colony. Furthermore, the number of Friends who attended the Charleston Quaker meetinghouse for worship was probably not too much larger in 1740 than it had been at the turn of the century, particularly in relative terms. Elsewhere, the Edisto meeting for worship, a branch or offshoot of the Charleston Monthly Meeting that had been established when several Quaker immigrants settled in Colleton County, may have disbanded altogether by this time.[33]

Of course Quakerism never commanded a large following in South Carolina, but, as the fate of the Edisto meeting would suggest, the movement lost its early vitality and fell into decline after about 1700. In 1710 Thomas Nairne estimated that Quakers accounted for only about 2.5 percent of the colony's white population, which meant that they could claim no more than about 125 adherents.[34]

When the traveling preacher Thomas Chalkley visited Charleston three years later he recorded that"there are but few Friends in this province; yet I had several Meetings in the Country." As Jo Anne McCormick has suggested, Chalkley's visit no doubt helped to sustain South Carolina Quakerism during these otherwise listless years, and, at least to some extent, it may have even helped to revitalize the movement. ("The longer I stayed there, the larger our Meetings were," Chalkley wrote.) Yet outmigration following Anglican establishment, the death of other early immigrants who remained, and the disloyalty of Quaker children to the Quaker faith led to the almost total collapse of the movement in the 1710s.[35] A London Friend, William Piggott, recounted the breakdown. In writing an introduction to a Charleston Monthly Meeting minute book commencing in 1719, he recorded, "In this province of South Carolina . . . the Lord had formerly a tender peopel, who were by Scorn called Quakers, but by reason of some goeing out of the Country; the death of Most of the Aintiants, togather with the Unfaithfulness of many of their Off Spring; the Number of those who walkt in the Law of the Lord became verey Small." At one point Piggott added that "by the best Acco'tt we now have, it appears that for Some Considerable time [there] was no meeting for worship; and for 20 years and upwards no meeting for business."[36]

In the early 1700s several South Carolina Quakers renounced the faith of their parents. Some Friends became Baptists; others converted to Anglicanism, as did Jonathan Fitch, Jr., who served as a militia captain from 1706 to 1711. "I have baptized several Quakers," Francis Le Jau reported from Goose Creek Parish in 1708, "and one who was a dying [and] sent to be prayed for in our Church . . . is now better and will soon receive the Blessed Sacrament with us." Four years later Le Jau wrote that "there has been nothing of Moment transacted of late in this Parish but the Baptizeing of 3 Adults coming Originally from Quakers and very much tempted by the Anabaptists about the time the Divine Providence Inspired the Society to Send Clergymen here." In addition to the outright defection of Quakers, the South Carolina Society of Friends failed to sustain itself through marriage and family growth. A substantial number of Quaker descendants were born or married outside of the faith, which further contributed to an overall decline in the total number of colonists who could claim "to have made a profession of the truth."[37]

In some important respects the history of South Carolina Quakerism paralleled the history of South Carolina dissent. There was a revitalization of the Charleston Meeting around 1718 or 1719, when lowcountry Quakers reestablished regular gatherings for worship and business, started making repairs to the Charleston meetinghouse, and began corresponding with their co-religionists in England and America to maintain currency in the Atlantic Quaker community. Even so, South Carolina Quakerism still seemed to lack genuine vitality. In mid-October 1723 Quaker missionaries John Fothergill and Lawrence King landed in the colony and spent about two weeks preaching both in Charleston and in "other parts of the Country," and journal entries by Fothergill several times imply a lack of religious vitality. According to Fothergill, the missionaries preached to Friends and "some moderate people." "Divers of the People, and some of these the chief in the Place, were also very loving," Fothergill reported, "but many seemed much above the true *Christian* Simplicity." By and large the missionaries found that everywhere they went in Carolina "the Lord opened freely in his Power and Wisdom, to declare the Way of Life and Salvation to the People," and in Charleston the preachers noted some good success, especially among Quakers. Although there were "but a few Friends there-away," Fothergill wrote on behalf of himself and Lawrence King, "yet there were some with who we were comforted, and to whom our Visit was of service." In relating their two-week Carolina visit to the ministers gathered at the 1724 London Yearly Meeting, Fothergill stated that he and his Atlantic traveling companion had "laboured there some time in the Service of the Gospel, having Meetings with the few Friends there, and among other People: The Lord our God was with us to our Comfort and Help, tho' the generality of the People seemed but cold and very indifferent about true Religion." "There are but few Friends in these parts," Fothergill went on to say, "and but very few who seem to love Truth in Uprightness; yet there are some there who thus love it, and retain the Simplicity thereof in a good degree."[38]

Like the history of early-eighteenth-century South Carolina dissent in general, the Quaker movement's enervation and seeming listlessness was set over and against the late Stuart / early Hanoverian Anglican renaissance in both the Old World and the New. With the growth of the Church of England in the lowcountry from 1704 to 1724, it appeared to many South Carolina dissenting ministers that their Reformed and sectarian movements were in total disarray, if not utter "decline." Indeed the late-seventeenth and early-eighteenth century bespoke to many religious observers throughout the Atlantic Protestant world a major crisis in Christian practice. By the 1720s and early 1730s the sense of anxiety became notably acute, suffused as it was with chiliastic expectations and fears stemming from the growing influence of Enlightenment rationalism. Over and over ministers in America and abroad spoke of decay, decline, and spiritual deadness while at the same time emphasizing the need for renewal, revival, and reform. The theme was generalized. It was the subject of sermons, correspondence, and religious tracts, and it was discussed by word of mouth, too, even on the margins of refugee Huguenot societies. As Susan O'Brien has shown, there was a far-reaching, very crowded transatlantic communications network that strung Protestants together and spread news and ideas. Ministers in Europe and America regularly interacted with one another through a variety of channels, including "human intelligence" (that is, personal interaction with others) as well as through written words. An increasingly common theme of this religious discourse concerned what was perceived to be a state of spiritual deadness on both sides of the Atlantic. Many Protestants in both the Old World and the New expressed dismay at the decline of religion and worried about society's departure from a virtuous past—a mythical Golden Age that had supposedly prevailed in the late 1500s and early 1600s.[39]

Josiah Smith, pastor of the Independent Church in Charleston, was thoroughly familiar with this transatlantic dialogue, which spanned great distances and played a direct role in stimulating efforts at religious renewal and revival in Britain and America, as well as in Germany, Holland, and Switzerland. Born on December 25, 1704, Josiah Smith was the grandson of the first Landgrave Thomas Smith (1648–1694), governor of the Carolina colony from 1693 to 1694, and the second son of Dr. George Smith (1674–1753), a prominent physician who was locally renowned for his outspoken opposition to the legal establishment of the Church of England.[40] Although Josiah Smith always considered South Carolina his "own Country," at some point (probably in the mid-1710s) he traveled with his parents to St. George's, Bermuda, as his father, who held a degree from the University of Edinburgh, "found there a comfortable provision & support for his Family on temporal accounts."[41] This early experience holds an important place in the evolution of Josiah Smith's ministry. Once dominant, Presbyterians and Congregationalists were by the early decades of the eighteenth century only a small struggling minority in Bermuda, and upon moving to the island George Smith immediately discovered that "the bread of life (the means of Grace) for his own & the Souls of his household was sadly wanting." Not only was Bermuda's dissenting community without a settled minister, but the moribund "remains of a Flock in the Island" had been unsuccessful in attracting a suitable candidate. Yet, as he had done earlier in South Carolina, George Smith promptly assumed a leadership role among Bermuda's dissenters. According to one contemporary account, he "minister'd to the Souls of his Neighbours, as well as to those of his own house." What is more, Smith sailed to Boston around 1720 to secure a regular minister for the island. "Mr. Smith fail'd of his Expectation . . . at this time & returned without a Minister." Shortly thereafter, however, another dissenting clergyman, James Paul, "a Minister from Great Britain . . . who was bound to some other part of America," arrived to serve the Bermuda congregation.[42]

Despite James Paul's coming, George Smith decided to prepare his gifted young son for the ministry, taking special care of his education. In 1721 he enrolled Josiah in the grammar school at Cambridge, Massachusetts, in preparation for Harvard College. Advanced to the college "within the space of a Year," Josiah Smith "follow'd his Studies with such diligence & industry" that he quickly won the attention of the Harvard faculty. In 1723 he "had a *year* given him" by the college for his outstanding work. Graduating with the class of 1725, he returned with his father to Bermuda as "a *Master* in the Gift & Art of preaching; a kind of finish'd *Preacher.*" Following a twelve-month probationary period in the pulpit of the church at St. George's, Smith sailed back to Boston, where on July 11, 1726 he was ordained by Benjamin Colman, Cotton Mather, and other leading ministers as co-pastor of the Bermuda congregation . "No one has risen among us & gone from us, so suddenly, with like esteem, affection & applause, as Mr. *Smith* has done," Benjamin Colman remarked of the young Harvard graduate. "It is an honour to our *College* to have such a Son to boast of from among the *Islands.*"[43]

Delivered at a unique and early stage of his long and extraordinarily successful ministerial career, the two sermons Smith preached at Boston in 1726 attracted widespread attention. The first of these, *A Sermon Preached in Boston, July 10th, 1726* (Boston, 1727), focused attention on the workings of the Holy Spirit, which, as the historian Thomas S. Kidd has suggested, helped to distinguish early evangelicalism from other Protestant movements in the early modern Atlantic world.[44] Taking his text from Paul's letter to the early Christian church of the Thessalonians (1 Thessalonians 5:19), "Quench not the Spirit," Smith compared the Spirit of God to a holy fire in order to make three general observations on the nature and character of Christian grace. The comparison reveals the extent to which early evangelicals placed new emphasis on the person of the Holy Spirit in their revival sermons. It also helps to explain why, in one of the key documents of the First Great Awakening, Smith wrote of George Whitefield's visit to Charles Town in early 1740: "I was not displeas'd to hear a Gentlemen of the Establishment delivering some of the same Tenets, which I had so long before adopted into my own Creed and System, especially when he could support them so well from Scripture, Experience, and the Articles of his own Church."[45]

A Sermon Preached in Boston opens with an important discussion of the essential characteristics of the Spirit. Like fire, Smith said, the essence of the Holy Spirit was mysterious. "I never could yet find, with my small Enquiries into *Philosophy,* any stated definition of *Fire;* any fix'd rational Account of its Nature; such an one I mean, as leaves no room for future debates." Despite the mysterious nature of fire, Smith emphasized, its effects, like those of the Holy Spirit, could be felt. "The *effects* of the Spirit we *feel,* and so of Fire; but the *way* of the Spirit in its efficiency we know not." Furthermore, the Spirit, no less than fire, worked instantaneously, "just as the spark dropping from the Steel *instantly* fires the Tinder." Once that spark of God's grace dropped from above, Smith preached, "it penetrates far into our secret parts, by its special Operations; puts a Byass upon the most retired Spots, and affects the remotest Dispositions of the Soul," searching "every part of our whole Man" in a certain, instantaneous moment of time. However, the Holy Spirit or saving grace had "a *different* effect on *different* Natures." Indeed, just as one could "observe the fire to *soften Wax* and *harden Clay,*" Smith proclaimed, "as great a difference is observable in the frame and temper of Men's Hearts." In some instances the holy fire produced a quick, powerful sensation.

In others it could "gradually arise to a greater and greater appearance." In still others it could be "swallowed up by the flames of lust and passion." Nevertheless, Smith said, fire and grace both gave light, and as much did "Grace *illuminate* the Mind as fire [did] the World." Both agreed in their mixture of light and heat as well: "But this I may venture to say, that where there is Light, there is generally some degree of Heat; and so *vice versa.* And in this mixture fire resembles *Grace,* which is light in the Mind, and heat in the Heart. No sooner is a spiritual Light sprung up in the Christian's Head, but it conveys a warmth down to the *Affections,* till the Passions are fired with *zeal* and *devotion.*" Next Smith underscored the extent to which the Spirit of God wrought in Christians "a qualitative change upon every Faculty," whereby those touched by the Spirit were made "like itself" and "created anew in Christ Jesus to holiness and good works" (Ephesians 2:10). He also underscored the extent to which saving grace resembled fire in a communicative sense. Indeed, "one Christian with his gracious sanctified Knowledge improves another," because his "experimental acquaintance with the methods of Grace . . . clears up the doubts of his brother."[46]

After discoursing on the Spirit of God as a holy fire, Smith turned to his second and third observations on 1 Thessalonians 5:19, "Quench not the Spirit." Here he outlined six different ways in which the fire of the Holy Spirit could be extinguished, offering up specific reasons why Protestant sinners and saints should use the utmost caution lest they "abate the special light and warmth of the Spirit." Of course Smith emphasized throughout *A Sermon Preached in Boston* that he was speaking in a figurative sense, that the Spirit of God was too powerful to be quenched in a literal sense. Moreover, when speaking of the elect he made it clear that he firmly adhered to traditional Calvinist doctrine regarding the final perseverance of the saints (that is, those who received God's special grace could never fall from God's special grace). Still, Smith said, the fire of the Spirit could in fact be extinguished, and it could be extinguished in a whole variety of ways: in neglecting religious exercises such as public worship, private devotion, and prophecying; in performing religious duties "in a careless perfunctory way, with a lifeless frame and inactivity of Soul"; in forbearing meditation; in expressing a malicious inclination to revenge; in permitting a spirit of worldliness to gain ascendancy in the mind; and, perhaps most important, in being carried away by "the fire of Lust" and other unclean practices. Cautioning saints to heed Paul's advice in 1 Thessalonians, Smith declared: "By quenching the Spirit we dishonour God, *wrong* our Souls, and *injure* our Neighbour." Sinners had to be equally cautious. By heedlessly quenching the spirit, they forfeited any hope of receiving God's special grace, stood personally responsible for the irreparable loss of their souls, and provoked God's resentment so that their "condition will be more intolerable in the day of Judgment than that of *Sodom* and *Gomorrah.*" Echoing revival ministers throughout the Atlantic Protestant world, Smith concluded his sermon by saying that "*we have too much ground to suspect, that many the greater part of the World quench the Spirit.*"[47]

Written for the solemn occasion of his ordination, *A Discourse Delivered at Boston, on July 11, 1726* (Boston, 1726) was entirely different in character, tone, and substance from the sermon Smith preached the day before. In this unique discourse Smith presented a meditation on Canticles 5:16, "His Mouth is most Sweet," contemplating the unsearchable excellencies of Christ. He quickly came to focus on Christ's prophetic office. In particular he sought to prove the doctrine that "*Christ is a* PROPHET *truly Excellent, and altogether Lovely.*" To illustrate this doctrine Smith considered the person of Christ invested with the office of divine prophet, the excellency of the doctrines he taught, and the excellent manner of his teaching. Immediately after illustrating these three proofs, Smith closed with sincere, heartfelt reflections on the excellency of Christ's prophetic office, and in doing so he sought to "draw some instructive Lessons from it . . . in a more immediate Application of them to *myself.*" It was here, in drawing lessons from his meditation, that Smith devoted himself to the work of translatlantic religious revival, proclaiming:

> Christ must be my pattern. I must as far as I am able to imitate, preach and live as he did. I must not confine my work to the Pulpit, but on all occasions go about doing good; *being instant in season, and out of season;* consider the necessities of the people under my Charge, and make suitable applications to them. I must teach them *fully* without any secret reserves from sinister views, not acted by the inferiour motives of favour and respect; but regarding their Souls more than their Persons. My Discourses must not be framed for applause, to gain repute from men of parts and distinction. My stile must be as free, simple and easy as the nature of my subject will allow: Endeavouring a free access to men's Consciences, rather than touch their fancies, and gratify their humours. I must be unweariedly diligent in repeating and enforcing the principles of Religion, and essentials of the Gospel; as delighting in the work. My Sermons must carry an affection with them. I must preach as for *Eternity,* and make nothing so much the subject of my joy as the success of my Ministry.

"You need not be told the importance and difficulty of this Work," Smith said in addressing the powerful New England ministers assembled before him. "I need therefore all your interest in Heaven to be improved for me, for strength equal to my burthen." "Let Christ but *touch my lip and heart with a live coal of his Altar,* and then make the Enquiry, *Whom shall we send? And who will go for us?* I will chearfullly answer, *Here am I, send me.*"[48]

Following this moving close Smith was formally ordained by the synodical gathering, and he set out once again for Bermuda, but within a few months disaster struck. Two powerful storms rocked the island and Smith and his parents fled to Charleston. Soon thereafter, the twenty-two-year-old minister accepted a call to serve the Cainhoy church. Located on the upper reaches of the Wando River roughly ten miles from its mouth, the church had a long history in the colony, as it was originally organized by Hugh Adams in 1699. Yet though it had a distinctive Congregationalist tone from the beginning, the Cainhoy church trended toward Presbyterianism over time, as was the case with some other low-country Puritan churches that were composed of both Presbyterians and Congregationalists. This was mainly due to the influence of Scottish Presbyterian ministers who settled in the colony, especially including Archibald Stobo.[49] Yet it was also partly due to the death or departure of some New England–born ministers who were trained at Harvard. For example, Hugh Adams, who preached at Cainhoy, Wappetaw, and later at "A Neighbourhood On South Edistoe River, about 50 Miles from Charles Town," quit the colony after the establishment of the Church of England.[50]

Perhaps in part because the church had become Presbyterianized but mostly for other reasons, Smith found Cainhoy's spirituality waning, and like revival-minded ministers on both sides of the Atlantic he was alarmed by what appeared to him to be a transoceanic withering of Protestant dissent. Writing of religious decline throughout "the greater part of the World," Smith was taken aback by the "Reigning Vices of my own Country," and he feared that God's wrath would soon be visited against "the Place of my Birth and Baptism." Sinfulness in Carolina seemed to be growing to biblical proportions. The secular crisis in the wake of the Yamasee War and the Revolution of 1719 no doubt added intensity to Smith's concern for the "Dreadful Province." Equally alarming, and perhaps far more disturbing, was the terrible earthquake that struck New England in October 1727. The historic earthquake was the worst colonial New Englanders had ever experienced, and Smith was afraid that "a Providence of that nature . . . would be liable to a double Misconstruction." Not only might some represent it in a "False and Disadvantageous Light" and "improve it to Eclipse the glory of New-England," but they might also be more prone to "harden themselves in their own Impieties." Determined to set the record straight, Smith preached *The Greatest Sufferers Not always the Greatest Sinners* in February 1728. Written in language that is direct and plain and profoundly meaningful, this sermon represents a bold defense of the colonial New England colonies and argues for "the Excellency of their Constitution" in a circum-Atlantic comparative perspective, in which the earthquake is used as a means to arraign "the Vices of Carolina."[51]

With *The Greatest Sufferers* Smith issued a clarion call for repentance and began a ministerial career that quickly won him international recognition. Having determined that an "Evangelical Ministry is a Work Originated in Christ," he started to formulate "a design" for religious reform and, at last, spiritual renewal.

At the Cainhoy church he "found the Dissenting Interest declining; the Pious Aged but few, and the Youth, tho' numerous, generally ignorant, and neglected, and in a fair way to become vicious, and corrupt in their Morals." Reflective of a transforming demographic change in the South Carolina's dissenting population, there was a large number of young people in Smith's congregation. Yet church membership was in marked decline, and the outlook at Cainhoy seemed grim, as a majority of the young people appeared to be turning away from the righteousness of their parents. "I could think of no Remedy so likely under GOD, to reform, and Strengthen the things, which remained, and were ready to dye," he wrote, "as to preach, and press the duty of Parents to their Children." Smith descanted upon the theme in 1727 in a string of sermons, but to no good or lasting effect, because he found that the impressions of his discourses quickly wore off "and, that it very much arose from the temptations of the Tavern with some, and the infection of Evil Company, with others."[52] Tempted by the local nightlife and the wickedness of their worldly neighbors, Cainhoy's Puritan children were utterly sunk in sin. So with a great "pungency of Expression" Smith adopted a slightly different tact, of equanimity. "Religion is the proper business of every Man's life," he declared. Both parents and children had to be exhorted regarding temperance and the pernicious effects of keeping company with ungodly companions. As a result, in 1729 Smith preached two sermons on the Proverbs of King Solomon (Proverbs 1–10 and Proverbs 23:31–32), *The Young Man Warned; or Solomon's Counsel to his Son* (Boston, 1730) and *Solomon's Caution Against the Cup* (Boston, 1730).[53]

"After such repeated endeavours" this approach worked little better. The passage of time appeared "not only to erase the impression, but to bury the remembrance of such Subjects," Smith said. Utterly dismayed, he searched for another means of religious reformation, deciding in the meantime to publish his "three continued discourses" from 1727, which were collected together as *The Duty of Parents to Instruct their Children* (Boston, 1730). In an ironic nuance so subtle as to belie its incongruity and significance, he wrote: "I can think of no way now to revive them, but the Press." Suddenly Smith began invoking the language of religious revival—at the same time he was reaching the conclusion that the divine "affects and seals" of the Holy Spirit were missing from his ministrations. Equally important, the congregation at Cainhoy was not Smith's only concern. Rather he was thinking much more broadly. He dedicated *The Duty of Parents* not just to South Carolinians but also to "the late People of my Charge in Bermuda, and to all others, in the same circumstances."[54]

Around 1727 Smith and seven other ministers gathered together in Charleston and "sat in presbytery," constituting the first separate, independent presbytery in the prerevolutionary South, variously called the South Carolina Presbytery and the Charleston Presbytery. An heir to the tradition of such gatherings in the British Isles, the South Carolina Presbytery was established to strengthen the Presbyterian and Congregational churches in the colony. The regional gathering enabled the ministers to share information, engage in scriptural study and symposia discussion for intellectual stimulation, and contemplate closer cooperation. It also provided a forum in which they could discuss ecclesiastical oversight and disciplinary matters, as well as a program of reformation. Also important was the fact that individual congregations might look to the presbytery for guidance in securing ministers and evaluating their credentials.[55]

Among the ministers who attended the South Carolina Presbytery meeting were five or six mostly older, more traditional Presbyterian clergymen trained in Scotland. These included Archibald Stobo, a Darien-colony survivor who first arrived in the colony in 1700, and Hugh Fisher, pastor of the church at Dorchester. Another presbytery minister was Nathan Bassett, a Harvard graduate who served as pastor of the Independent Church of Charleston from 1725 to 1738. While none of the ministers at the presbytery meeting ever intended it, scarcely had they gathered together when the presbyters found themselves heaping abuse on each other, hopelessly split into factions. The central issue was one of authority. Some time before March 1728 a Scottish minister proposed that the presbyters subscribe to the *Westminster Confession of Faith* (1648). This confession had originally been adopted by the Westminster Assembly during the English Revolution, and it was later endorsed by the General Assembly of Scotland, the Synod of Ireland, and a synod of churches in New England. Smith flatly refused to subscribe to the *Westminster Confession* because of his strict biblicism, besides his belief that the subscription proposal was an infringement on liberty of conscience. He was joined by two other presbyters, Nathan Bassett and William Porter, the latter one of the older Scottish clergymen who served as pastor of the church at Wappataw.[56]

The subscription controversy spilled "upon the publick Stage" in one of the bitterest and most important pamphlet wars in both colonial southern history and in the religious history of the British-Atlantic world.[57] The principal antagonists were Hugh Fisher and Josiah Smith, though Nathan Bassett contributed to pamphlet war too. In *Humane Impositions Proved Unscriptural, or, the Divine Right of Private Judgement* (Boston, 1729), Smith argued against blind subscription to an inherited creed and asserted the right of nonsubscribers to search the Bible for themselves to discover the vital elements of Christian faith, claiming that his opponents presumed "an infallible Knowledge of what are really [its] Fundamentals and Essentials." He did not disbelieve any of the basic tenets of the confession, and he openly professed his devotion to the document, three "non-essential Articles only excepted."[58] Nor did he espouse a theology at variance with it at all, and by no means did he reject any and all forms of ecclesiastical hierarchy. In fact he took pains to "honour Synods and Councils" while highlighting their "vast service in the Illustration of Scripture." (And, of course, Smith was ordained by a presbytery in 1726.) Rather what Smith was objecting to was the subscribers' presumptuous "Power of Imposing," which arose from their knowledge claims and denied "a Liberty in People to judge [Scripture] for themselves, and . . . to believe as they see reason." He insisted on the right of individuals to make the Bible the "only rule of Faith and Practice," because for him it was "the immutable standard of Truth and Orthodoxy."[59]

The subscription proposal was most likely introduced by Fisher, and behind it was an obvious effort to assert the South Carolina Presbytery's authority in the face of what some believed was dangerous heresy. By signing the Westminster articles ministers tacitly consented to the presbytery's power to govern—its sovereignty—ultimately binding themselves to its decisions involving ministerial qualifications, orthodoxy, and discipline. In doing so they surrendered what Smith considered sacrosanct: liberty of conscience. Most important for him, this included discovering God's will in his written word, his mind in hardening people's hearts, and interpreting scriptural prophecies "*in these last days.*" Of particular interest were manifestations of God's Spirit. In vindicating the right of private judgment, Smith chose passages from the Bible "shewing, that when *Holy Men of* GOD *spake, they spake as they were moved by the Holy Ghost:* Not *of themselves,*" suggesting here and in another instance that he was taking not just a principled stance but an inspired one. He also emphasized that "the same Spirit" that descended upon St. Paul "should descend to all his Successors" and affirmed that "the SPIRIT Applies and Seals" God's grace. "It puts a life into every Promise . . . But inconceivable terror into the Threatenings" of God, Smith proclaimed.[60]

"These angry Fits of Zeal, do but awaken the disorderly Passions of Men," said Hugh Fisher. In his eyes Josiah Smith "vented horrid opinions" subversive of all true scriptural doctrines "in the cry of Enthusiasm." Consequently, in response to the appearance of *Humane Impositions Proved Unscriptural,* Fisher published a scathing reply, *A Preservative from Damnable Errors, in the Unction of the Holy One* (1730). Smith was obviously too important to be ignored, and Bassett and Porter's opposition to subscription meant that Fisher could not simply play down the controversy as one errant minister's personal attack on the "Friends of Creeds, and Church Authority." "Such defection, of some who had once a name among Christians; and perhaps had shone as stars, with a peculiar lustre in the firmament of the Church," Fisher wrote, "was apt to raise sad thoughts of heart, in many serious Christians, all abiding in the truth." The "gainsayers must be stopped," he decided, rushing to press with his sermon, attached to a fifty-three-page appendix. For the subscription controversy had "disturb'd and inflam'd several Churches," stirring up subterranean forces that, even in the rural town of

Dorchester, Fisher could feel shaking the whole church's "superstructure rear'd upon the foundation ... of important Gospel Doctrines."[61]

Well before either his or Smith's sermon was preached, and months prior to the time either was published (more on this below), Fisher faced an open challenge to his Calvinist convictions when the two men entered into an epistolatory exchange following a presbyterial gathering. It involved a passage in a one of Fisher's sermons wherein he expressed his views on the liberty of judging Scripture "*common to Men*" and permitted by Christian divines. According to Fisher, Smith wrote to him and said that "he took this to be my opinion; because, he supposed, I would not take it well, not to be thought Orthodox." Smith supposed rightly. Apparently both ministers delivered short extemporaneous address on the topic at a subsequent presbytery. Then, with "debates on that Subject, continuing; and rather growing warmer," Fisher prepared a formal discourse, with Smith doing the same in response.[62]

At least by this point Fisher began thinking in stark chiliastic terms, discerning an ominous sign in the subscription struggle: "we are threatened, with the last and greatest Plague, wherewith the Church of GOD, is to be infested, in the latter days," he prophesied. To better understand the nature of the plague, Fisher consulted the best "Heresiology's" and turned to the works of Puritan authorities who considered last things.[63] He also turned to scripture. Gravely concerned that Smith's "party of Seekers" might infect the godly with false teachings, Fisher found encouragement and assurance in 1 John 2:20, "But, ye have an unction of the holy one, and ye know all things," the text he ultimately chose to preach upon.[64] All God's elect are illuminated by the Holy Spirit, Fisher emphasized, which gradually leads them to knowledge of the truth, providing an antidote to those who might deceive God's chosen people.

However, the real significance of *A Preservative from Damnable Errors* is not so much what Fisher said in his sermon (though Smith maintained that the printed sermon was a materially altered version of the one delivered at the presbytery meeting in Charleston, to which he responded from memory in *Humane Impositions*) but what he wrote in the appendix.[65] The heart of the piece was that Smith's right of private judgment led directly to religious skepticism and favored "Atheists in their Atheism" and "unaccountably caress'd" all others, including "Arians, Socinians, Arminians &c. in regard to their Heresies." Smith had not "plainly defin'd the Right of private Judgment," leaving himself open to an argument that he would find difficult to refute. Fisher lunged, exposing Smith's fondness for "the Modern Principles of Liberty," meaning the principles of Francis Bacon and John Locke. These principles led to the growth and spread of infidelity in the Atlantic Protestant world. "What makes ... Non-subscribing Principles most terrible," Fisher wrote, "is, that they are founded, in this miserable Skepticism; whereby, Christianity it self, is pluckt up by the roots."[66]

Both Josiah Smith and Nathan Bassett responded, Smith penning *The Divine Right of Private Judgment Vindicated* (Boston, 1730) and *No New Thing to be Slander'd* (Boston, 1730). The first of these is sourly punctilious. "I only pleaded for a general Liberty in People, to declare their Sentiments upon the Truth," Smith said defensively. As to Fisher's more basic challenge, it was "only a Chimera of his Brain." Besides, Smith said ironically, Fisher could not prove that the spread of infidelity was caused "by the *modern* Principles of Liberty," it might just very well "arise from some *other* Cause." Here Smith implied that creed-bound orthodoxy was to blame. Also he said that in order for subscribers to prove that they had the authority to impose their sentiments upon others they "must first make it Evident, either that Ministers have the infallible Conduct of the Spirit, in all that they *esteem* Fundamental; or else, that the Conduct of the Spirit is not necessary, to make them infallible, in things of that nature."[67]

Shortly thereafter, in October 1730, Smith wrote to his mentor Benjamin Colman in Boston, enclosing a copy of *No New Thing to be Slander'd,* summarizing recent events, and offering a penitent explanation of his actions:

> I am not only censured as an Heretick in General, and opposing the Doctrines of the *Westminster Confession,* but charged with the particular opinions of Arius and Arminius.... For these Reasons I lately Preached the Sermon that is herewith sent to the Press. I observe in your last Letter a Friendly Reproof for Engaging in a Controversy, which indeed has been a Wasp's Nest all over the World where it has come, and as You justly observ'd to Me, has no mercy upon Names, Families, Serviceableness, nor nothing else. But had you been here upon the Spot, and seen what our *Scotch Brethren* were aiming at, Had you heard the Sermon which Mr. Fisher Preached (in the room of which he has plainly published another), and did you know the long Consultation of my own Mind and the previous advice of some judicious Friends upon which I acted, I believe I should not appear so sudden in conduct as you are ready to think.[68]

Smith was being forced to prostrate himself. In refusing to subscribe to the *Westminster Confession* he did not anticipate the backlash, let alone that he would be charged in "a Conspiracy against the Church of God." His concern in meeting with his colleagues of the colonial South Carolina Presbytery had been to "cultivate their Friendship" so that they could collectively "improve themselves, know the Condition of their respective Charges, and better consult the common Interest of their Churches." Now, with the presbytery split, these "natural fruits" of association were dead on the vine, the ministers and churches divided in loyalty.[69] Smith read a declaration of his adherence to the confession's articles of faith and practice to the ministers assembled in the South Carolina Presbytery, making "a publick Appeal ... to their Judgment." But members of the subscribing party refused to render a majority opinion unless he further declared his "free Assent to seven or eight Articles of their own drawing up," forcing him to explain why he would not subscribe to these.[70]

Things went from bad to worse. Fisher continued to press his main argument, publishing a reply to Smith's rejoinder and Bassett's concurrent salvo. In *The Divine Right of Private Judgment, Set In a True Light* (Boston, 1731), he expounded upon the meaning of "liberty" and "slavery." "True liberty," he said, "has bounds set to it, and these limits are its perfection." Civil liberty was confined by the law and tradition; Christian liberty was framed by God's revelation. Smith's right of private judgment was a license for Christians "to throw themselves into bondage, and give themselves up, to the guidance of a blind heart." It was sin, "the opposite of liberty"; it was slavery, "a liberty to err from the real mind of God in Scripture."[71]

As the subscription controversy continued, complex realignments occurred. Bassett's church in Charleston fractured under the stress of incipient evangelical forces. Lay supporters of Fisher's party bolted from their less traditional coreligionists, founding the First Presbyterian Church in 1731. They secured the services of Hugh Stewart, a Scottish subscriber. Contemporaries revealingly called the newly built church edifice, which was erected in 1734, the Scotch Church. The Wappataw and Dorchester congregations tended to move in the opposite direction, embracing their Congregationalist roots and circum-Atlantic religious revivalism. When William Porter died in 1733, Job Parker, a New Englander, succeeded him; likewise, after Hugh Fisher's death in 1734 the Dorchester laity settled a Harvard-trained South Carolina native, John Osgood. Conversely, the Cainhoy church chose a Presbyterian minister trained in Scotland to replace Josiah Smith, who accepted a call to be Bassett's assistant just as the Scotch Church was nearing completion.[72]

Josiah Smith assessed the situation from Charleston. "There is at present a Suspension of ye Controversy Among Us, and no *Paper Contests,*" he wrote to Colman in November 1735, "But doubt [not], My Antagonists are *privately* endeavoring to Supplant Me." As to Smith's party, John Osgood was "made choice of to Succeed Mr. Fisher" at Dorchester, and he and Bassett were ensconced in Charleston at the Independent Meeting House. Job Parker, however, had died suddenly and unexpectedly the previous month. His Wappetaw congregation had written to the president of Harvard for a replacement. In his letter to Colman, Smith added curiously, in regard to the application, "because I can't Question, I need not Ask, *Your* good offices and concurrence in it." Then he begged the question with an equivocal phrase. "I hope your candidates will Consider, That the Welfare of *two* Societies depends on Their Complyance."[73]

Two societies? The gravity of the provincial situation called for verbal gymnastics. Congregationalists were splitting into Old Lights and New Lights,

Presbyterians were splitting into Old Side and New Side. The center folded. Josiah Smith watched as it began to give way during the 1720s and 1730s, and he actively encouraged it. Despite contentious controversy and repeated charges of heresy, he remained skeptical of conventional wisdom. Received traditions, Smith thought, were equally problematic and promising. They had to be examined critically. They could not be adapted to contemporary South Carolina life in a wholesale manner. Change seemed to him, if not inevitable, at least necessary, a change that demanded new solutions for practical problems. In light of this view the young evangelist looked to the future, watching developments at home and abroad, continuing to publish, and maintaining a transatlantic posture. English dissenters, including Isaac Watts, commented on his "pious and learned character" while news of events elsewhere in the Atlantic Protestant world started to arouse Smith's expectations of divine intervention and an impending religious revival. By 1739 he had made a firm commitment to a new evangelical doctrine that would eventually come to dominate southern religion.[74]

Religious controversy and conflict stalked nearly every dissenting group in colonial South Carolina in the 1720s and 1730s, even recent arrivals, some of whom were seeking asylum from intense persecution in the Old World. After decades of stagnation European immigration to the province began to pick up during this period in response to new promotional and recruiting efforts. Especially noteworthy was Governor Robert Johnson's township plan, which was formally adopted by the provincial legislature in 1731 and designed for defense against the French, the Spanish, and multiple Indian peoples, as well as in response to the growing danger of slave revolt in the longer-settled tidewater region. Providing for the establishment of eleven twenty-thousand-acre townships, Johnson's settlement plan quickly began to transform the southern frontier of the British North American empire. After only five years nine of the eleven townships had been surveyed, and within a decade or so all but two of them—Amelia and Fredericksburg—had attracted a substantial number of new settlers from Europe and America. These newcomers added precipitously to South Carolina's ethnic and religious pluralism and complexity.[75] From the early 1730s there was a rapid expansion of Swiss and German Reformed groups throughout the western townships—Purrysburg, Orangeburg, New Windsor, Saxe-Gotha, and, to a lesser extent, Amelia—and of Ulster-Scot Presbyterians in two of the eastern townships, Williamsburg and Kingston. Among the latter arrivals were many "of the sort that followed field-meetings." Meanwhile, Welsh Baptists from New Castle County, Pennsylvania, settled through the northeastern sections of Queensboro and up the Pee Dee River, with the heaviest concentration of Baptists at the river's so-called Welsh Neck. There were significant handfuls of Lutherans at Purrysburg, a few in Orangeburg and elsewhere, and small pockets of Continental sects all over the west. Christian Gottlieb Priber, a radical religious seeker who had been forced out of Saxony because of his provocative sectarian beliefs, came to South Carolina expressing an interest in establishing a communitarian Utopia.[76]

This bewildering pluralism was displayed in the diversity of worship practices and organized religious services of the new townships and helps to explain how contemporaneous evangelical revivals occurred in several of these immigrant communities in the mid-1700s.[77] There was a rapid entry into South Carolina of many variations of Atlantic Protestantism. While the eastern townships quickly emerged as Baptist and Presbyterian revival centers, Continental Protestants transformed the western frontier. More than 1,200 Swiss and Germans landed in the colony before 1740. Some remained in Charleston, but the vast majority settled the townships. Most were French- and German-speaking Reformed Calvinists. About three-quarters of the new arrivals came from Switzerland; the rest were largely German Palatines.[78] When they departed Europe and crossed the Atlantic, these immigrants carried with them controversies that had been raging within Continental Protestantism as a result of the Pietist Reformation, and a surprising number of the immigrants were, like Priber, exiles from persecution. Hans Ulrich Hagenbucher, one of the German-speaking Swiss who arrived with his wife Barbara and their three children, left his home in 1737 because of his "enthusiastic" religious views, having "been severely punished at Kyburg the previous Spring for blasphemous speeches."[79] Likewise, seventy-seven-year-old Pietist John Ulrich Giessendanner ran afoul of both religious and secular authorities on several occasions before he landed in Charleston. On one occasion he was banished from Zurich after the town council heard testimony concerning his activities on the estate of a wealthy patron. According to one eyewitness account, Giessendanner's followers "fell into ecstasy, threw their arms back and forth, distorted their eyes, and spoke in the Spirit, without any notion of what they were saying." Their mystically inclined leader "himself often received inspirations . . . of the Holy Spirit," stirring prophecies that ultimately provoked the town councilors to drive Giessendanner away.[80]

From the beginning the flames that these conflicts engendered flared up furiously within Swiss and German communities in South Carolina. John Tobler, a prominent leader among the Appenzeller Swiss who settled at New Windsor, spoke to their seeming innateness as a layman who favored Reformed traditionalism and orthodoxy when he first came to the colony. "You . . . who have a desire to come in here," he wrote to his friends and relatives in Switzerland shortly after his arrival, "guard against all kinds of people whom you do not know." "Should people be with you whom you call Pietists," he continued, "test them well, for all is not gold that glitters." Tobler failed to provide much guidance in performing his proposed litmus test, however. Pietists "are not all to be shunned," he said.

Even those separatists "who cannot endure the church and the ministry" would make good neighbors; "and here in this place they can hold publicly their teachings and meetings." "We also like them well if they, like others, help to found churches and schools," Tobler admitted, as long as they "live according to the word of God as much as possible, do not scorn the pastor when he teaches according to God's word, also do not always rail in their teachings only against the church and declaim passionately against the people who go in it."[81]

These and similar comments foreshadowed some of the difficulties that lay ahead. Many of the controversies within Swiss and German state churches had been smothered by authorities who forced Pietist dissent underground, where it survived in conventicles and often intermingled with Anabaptism and mysticism and religious radicalism of all sorts; it emerged from that context and quickly surfaced even before settlers reached South Carolina, where it continued to rage. "We had people in our ship who were as maliciously angry at all the Appenzellers as I have seen in my whole life," Tobler wrote of the journey across the Atlantic with a group of sectarian Pietists, "and nothing else [was] to be expected than that they would continue it." Bartholomew Zouberbuhler, Sr., a Swiss Reformed minister trained in the scholastic tradition who traveled with Tobler, was the focus of separatist antipathy and religious scorn, but "the quarrel and strife" knew no bounds.[82] Conflicts among the laity and between laypeople and ministers were common, perhaps as common as those between ordained ministers.[83]

Such conflicts were in many ways inherent in South Carolina's expanding frontier, where the spiritual environment was hotly contested by various groups of newcomers. When a group of Moravian missionaries arrived in 1738, they immediately aroused suspicions among Lutheran and other clergy because of their enthusiastic religious views, which stressed rebirth and experiential piety; and they soon encountered considerable lay opposition in their efforts to promote slave Christianization. Led by Peter Bohler and his assistant Georg Schulius, the Moravians settled at Purrysburg and established a church school, which initially won them favor from local residents and facilitated the commencement of a novel program to convert slaves to Protestant evangelicalism. In addition to white children, who were taught separately, the missionaries instructed a small number of black individuals, hoping someday to effect the wholesale conversion of South Carolina's extraordinary large African slave population. Bohler and Schulius also visited surrounding plantations and made two trips to Charleston, preaching, teaching, and witnessing along the way. Within just a few months, however, white hostility to the Moravians' slave mission mounted. There were rumors of a slave conspiracy on one plantation they visited, and Purrysburgers openly confronted the missionaries shortly thereafter. Reports surfaced that Bohler and Schulius were preparing to baptize large numbers of enslaved Africans without proper religious instruction, exciting fears and anxiety. Having no more than equivocal backing, fewer and fewer residents were willing to uphold their mission. It quickly languished and then collapsed, as Bohler very unwisely decided to close the white school after Schulius fell ill and died.[84]

Still, the Moravian mission contributed to an important stirring of pietistic religious expression in the South Carolina lowcountry, no less important because of its short duration and not unlike the brief ministry of John Giessendanner, who also bequeathed an experiential legacy to the colony. Born the son of a bureaucrat in Lichtensteig, Switzerland, in 1660, Giessendanner became a goldsmith and local politician, sitting at one time on the City Council.[85] As Pietism spread from Germany into the Reformed Church of his native land in the late seventeenth century, Giessendanner embarked upon a new life. Reborn in his faith, he moved to Marburg, Germany, in 1714.[86] There he turned openly to Illuminism, which led him on a wayfaring mystical journey. For years he lived by traveling from place to place, peddling his religious views, preaching, holding private meetings, and spreading the influence of mystical Pietism far and wide, from one town to the next as he was constantly forced to move on by local authorities. On Sunday, June 28, 1716, a Swiss minister named Peter Ringgli attended one of his gatherings on the estate of wealthy patron in Engstringen, and Ringgli's eyewitness account of Giessendanner's radical religious activities helps to explain why Continental authorities opposed his ministry. When he arrived about two o'clock in the afternoon, Ringgli found a small congregation gathered together in the landowner's house.

> In the room writing implements were already on hand, and on the table lay a paper which had been headed, "Pronouncement of Hans Ulrich Giezendanner." Then Giezendanner knelt in prayer, until a soft southwind, which seemed to him suspicious . . . ended his praying. Then he became still. Gradually some movement—shuddering, and twitching of the mouth and head—came over him and he began to speak, sometimes slowly, sometimes more rapidly, but always in broken snatches, at the same time he moved around in the room, his eyes closed. Then he sat down for a quarter of an hour. When he stood up again he picked up his speaking at the exact point where he had broken off, while his whole body trembled. This happened about four times.

The prophet assigned others to record his shudderings, twitchings, and snatches, instructing them "not to edit the style of his utterances," because he intended "correct the 'Inspiration' later." As a result, Ringgli could not say what the edited expression foretold. Yet he knew enough about Giessendanner's inspiration to testify that he "addressed himself to the cities of Zurich and Bern and had interpreted the animals found on their coasts of arms," pronouncing judgment against both cities.[87]

The peripatetic lay prophet moved on. After traveling through Germany, he found his way back to Toggenburg, where he participated in a series of ecstatic revivals during the mid-1730s, calling forth another crackdown. Knowing of the "spiritual and physical freedom" in South Carolina, Giessendanner followed a crooked path to the colony. In 1736 he landed in Charleston, separated from the group he was with, and advertized as a metal worker. In the spring of the following year he wrote to a friend in Basel, saying "I . . . will remain here in peace with my family until I know where the dear God will have me or what use he will put to me." Informing his friend that he rented a room and planted a garden, Giessendanner continued, "I support myself by my profession. The crops we sowed seven weeks ago are already nice and high. Flax, hemp, peas, etc. But because of the godless life here the land will be made unfruitful. The poor Moors are very severely treated as slaves by the Christians. And unfortunately, the Christians usually give great offense to those savages who lead an honest and quiet life, through greed, usury, etc." Such an outlook informed Giessendanner's subsequent ministry. Considering yet another move, the goldsmith from Toggenburg wrote that he had been invited to settle in Orangeburg. "There are 80 German families here, and also Orangeburghers, among them many poor people, who, since they have no regular minister at hand, have suggested to me that I stay with them and hold spiritual exercises with them every Sunday." "I want to see what God ordains in this matter," he added.[88]

Shortly thereafter, Martin Boltzius, one of the Lutheran ministers at Ebenezer, Georgia, noted that "Giessendanner, a coppersmith and seal engraver who came with the last colony of Swiss to Carolina wrote me . . . a letter from Orangeburgh, in which he reported that he had been called by the people there as their regular preacher, that he had accepted the call and was now attending to the duties of his office by preaching the word of God and administering the holy sacraments. His congregation is much scattered and he is spending much time in visitation."[89] Hans Trachsler, another member of the same colony of Swiss that landed with Giessendanner, remarked that "he preaches every Sunday in the open air, next to his little hut," which Trachsler described as a small "pole house" plastered with clay. "The people bring children to him for baptism," he observed, "and they come a distance of forty miles to hear his sermons." Giessendanner must have felt at home when he died in the summer of 1738. Although his ministry was short-lived, he engraved a deep impression in the area's historical memory. Peter Rowe, a descendent of the earliest settlers, recalled much later (in the nineteenth century) that the "old church was of wood and clay." Still living near Orangeburg, Rowe was 103.[90]

†

Whether or not he was aware of it, Rowe in his skeletal reminiscence hearkened back to the initial forming of a new religious synthesis in prerevolutionary southern society, one that pietistic German-speaking immigrants such as Giessendanner and others helped to formulate. The Ashley River Baptists were similarly archetypical.[91] Originally a branch of the Charleston Baptist Church, the first permanent Baptist church in the American South, the Ashley River Baptist Church was organized in 1727 when a small wooden meeting house was built on a six-acre lot conveyed by Richard and Sarah Butler. Located on the public road about fourteen miles from Charleston, it remained part of the mother church until a storm of controversy occasioned a bitter religious schism. After protracted and "diverse Debates" with their Charleston brethren, the Ashley River Baptists agreed to disagree with and separate from them. In the spring of 1736 they withdrew and established an independent "gospel Church" under the leadership of their minister, the Reverend Isaac Chanler.[92]

The nature of the controversy that precipitated the secession centered on matters of both doctrine and ritual, and it reveals quite clearly how southern evangelicalism originated, much like the Presbyterian subscription contest and the spiritual saga of frontier expansion. Around 1733 sharp disagreements suggestive of the new religious mood began to develop. These disagreements eventually resulted in the emergence of two denominational factions. One faction, later termed the Particular Baptists, was led by Isaac Chanler. By and large, supporters of this party were rigidly Calvinistic, upholding all of the five points of Calvinism. The other faction, the so-called General Baptists, was led by Robert Ingram. This group was but mildly Calvinistic and tended to espouse what is commonly referred to as an Arminian or free-will version of the faith. However, in the early and middle 1730s it is perhaps more accurate to understand the General Baptists' position as one that implied a greater degree of human agency, not "Arminianism" in classic sense but a sort of diluted Calvinism. The Particulars regarded such an implication as a rationalistic error, and they associated it with Socinian heresy, because Socinians viewed reason as having absolute power in judging and determining religious truth, whereas they emphatically did not.[93] Another important element of the disagreement involved the use, application, and efficacy of religious rites, particularly the Baptist ritual of the laying on of hands with prayer for all baptized believers. Chanler practiced the religious rite and maintained that it was vitally important to the spiritual life of the church, not only to sanctify the newly baptized but also "as a means to obtain fresh & further Supplys of the holy Spirit of grace."[94]

The ritual controversy and the doctrinal dispute were interrelated. First, both centered on a sharp debate over the ways in which spiritual knowledge was principally to be achieved, with each side intimating a different approach. Second, both demonstrate that the names given to the two factions, which apparently came into use in South Carolina only in the 1740s, are rather unavailing in these early years. General or Six Principle Baptists had traditionally held to the rite of the laying on of hands with prayer; the Particulars did not. Similarly, the specific doctrinal point used to distinguish the groups (that is, general versus particular atonement) was not the major theological issue involved; spiritual enlightenment was.[95]

Nevertheless, these disputes ultimately fractured the Charleston church and left it divided and enfeebled. Under Ingram, nearly all of the General Baptists formed an independent church at Stono, another branch of the Charleston church first organized in 1728. Under Chanler, the Particulars constituted an independent church on the Ashley River, though some, along with few General Baptists, remained in Charleston with Thomas Simmons, the beleaguered minister of the mother church. Simmons had overseen a remarkable period of church growth during his thirteen-year ministry, which began in 1723. He was a self-proclaimed and committed Calvinist, but his theological outlook was much more moderately Particular. (Alexander Garden even came to praise him for his humble and modest spiritual temperament.)[96] Unfortunately, such an outlook set him at a disadvantage in the combative atmosphere of the mid-1730s, for in rejecting Chanler's rigidity and attempting to humor the General Baptists' theological mood, Simmons found himself in an untenable position. After the 1736 split, attendance at the Charleston Baptist Church declined dramatically according to one contemporary report, and few apparently turned to Simmons to administer the sacraments of baptism and the Lord's Supper. Eventually a majority in Simmons' congregation suspended him, causing yet another split.[97]

In the meantime the Ashley River Baptist Church flourished. Drafting a special covenant shortly after constituting themselves into a distinct congregation, the Ashley River Baptists began to add a substantial number of new members to their church, with Chanler baptizing "Such as Shall be Saved." Within three years (June 19–20, 1736, to March 17–18, 1739) about twenty adults made a public profession of faith at quarterly communion celebrations and were admitted into fellowship, bringing to about fifty the total number of church members. On two occasions in the spring and summer of 1737 several new converts were baptized together in the wake of impressive spiritual awakenings. During the same period "Divers others," including at least twenty-one members, "submitted to the holy ordinance of Laying on of hands with prayer, for ye obtaining of fresh Supplys of ye holy Spirit of grace." Ashley River's members came from all ranks of society, with men and women present in roughly equal numbers. Susannah Baker represents one end of the social spectrum. A wealthy elite, she was one of the most prominent rice planters in the South Carolina lowcountry. In 1726 she owned sixty-one slaves and employed several servants, making hers among the seven largest households in St. George's Parish. Arrayed conversely in the social order were the "Ethiopian members" at Ashley River, such as a slave named Elsy who was one of the first to submit "unto ye [holy] ordinances of laying on of hands with prayer."[98]

Though Isaac Chanler thought of it in terms of a supernatural outpouring, the Ashley River Baptist revival was at least partly due to his efforts. Born in Bristol, England, in 1701, Chanler arrived in South Carolina with his family sometime around 1733. He immediately began preaching and stirring up excitement and controversy. He also started building up a comfortable estate, which at the time of his death in 1749 included a plantation on the Ashley River, several slaves, two three-hundred-acre tracts in Craven County, and an impressive library. Chanler's secular pursuits did not prevent him from remaining active in the church.[99] Fired by an insatiable desire to bring the Kingdom of God to earth, he was, as eighteenth-century Baptist historian Morgan Edwards put it, "very laborious in the ministry." More than any other single individual, Isaac Chanler gave the Ashley River Baptist Church its "Particular manner."[100]

As the records of the Ashley River Baptist Church indicate, and as his numerous publications make abundantly clear, Isaac Chanler was an unbending Calvinist who found much to criticize as he surveyed colonial South Carolina's religious landscape. Obviously he did not like his fellow Baptists' ritual practice. Nor did he like Thomas Simmons's willingness to compromise in the face of what he considered heretical error.[101] About his early religious life very little is known, but by the time he came to South Carolina in the 1730s he was espousing a pattern of vital sentiment that generally came to define Protestant evangelicalism in the eighteenth-century Atlantic world.[102] Chanler, like John Ulrich Giessendanner and other Pietists, was instrumental in cultivating this peculiar religious mood in the colony, which through a sort of religious empiricism (apprehending God through touching, feeling, experiencing) provided adherents with a certain sovereignty of self and a sense of exaltation and righteousness, as well as a certain and continuing spirituality.

Such introverted masterlessness required "a good degree of honour & great boldness in the faith which is in Christ Jesus," the basic rationale for the Ashley River Baptists' strict code of forbearance. Among other things, members were called on to account for drunkenness, adultery, profanity, lying, inattendance at church, and quarreling. All members—black and white—were held to the same moral oversight and together they submitted to agreed-upon rules of behavior. Lapses from prescribed moral conduct were punished by admonition and suspension, and, if persisted in, by excommunication. Signs of repentance had to be real to be considered adequate for restoration. According to Chanler, "Church discipline is certainly highly needfull to be kept up in a gospel Church both for the honor of the gospel & ye good of professors both for keeping them watchful & bringing them to a Sense of their folly when they go astray."[103]

While church discipline was in one sense punitive, it was primarily intended to edify. This helped to legitimize palpably the fragile nature of the evangelical Baptists' authority over individuals who, in almost all cases, voluntarily consented to reproof, censure, or suspension when found guilty of a disorderly or sinful offense. That authority, which did occasionally come under open challenge, was of course greatly enhanced by each member's spiritual conversion and baptism into fellowship. It was further enhanced by concerns about the possibility of being publicly humiliated through communal admonition, not to mention the deep-seated fears of being suspended from communion. The sacrament of the Lord's Supper was highly venerated at the Ashley River church. James Coffin, for instance, "begged to be restored to his place & privilege in the Church" after being admonished and suspended from the Lord's Supper in early 1740. Yet the church's authority also seems to have been enhanced by the conspicuously few number of occasions disciplinary proceedings were actually undertaken, especially in relation to the ever-growing pool of members. The Ashley River Baptists only considered an average of slightly more than one case every other year in the prerevolutionary era, and church members worked tirelessly in their efforts to bring about repentance. They appointed and sent messengers "in token of their Love & Care" to encourage and advise wayward congregants. They endeavored "Amicably & Justly to accommodate matters of Difference & variance" in domestic disputes and interpersonal relations. And in all cases they practiced "Lenity towards" their godly brothers and sisters.[104]

Almost all deviants agreed to confess their sinfulness, humbling themselves with "hearty sorrow." But on occasion individuals "obstinately Refused to obey the Churches Authority" and were formally excommunicated.[105] Such ostracism restored order by putting the offender outside of the church, as in the sensational case of Will, one of the African American members of the biracial congregation and the "servant of Susannah Baker." At a church meeting on December 11, 1738, Will was "charged being present with unhandsom carriage to the Church." For reasons not altogether clear, "when Treating with him about his disorders particularly with Respect to his useing unjustifiable severity towards his wife in Beating of her," Will remained "Contumacious under Discipline." Consequently he was "suspended untill he shall manifest Such Repentance as Shall be Satisfactory to the Church." Nine months passed. Will remained unmoved, even "after due measures were used in order to bring him to repentance." Then, in the middle of September 1739, a "Complaint was made . . . against madam Bakers Will for unlawfully Seeking after another wife, While his Lawfull one was yet Living[,] wc. matter the Church . . . did conclude that the Said Will Should be Excommunicated or cutt off from being a member." The ritual of detestation, carried out in "an open and Publick manner" only after it was determined that Will was "unreclaimable," was designed to bring "destruction to the spirit of the flesh," thereby restoring order to this fledgling evangelical community.[106]

Will's case was the exception, not the rule. Over the course of the next thirty years only one other member of the congregation at Ashley River was purged from fellowship in an open public ritual. What is more, Will was the sole black member disciplined, and the records of the Ashley River church tend to confirm the general observation that in southern biracial churches "blacks were not disciplined out of proportion to their numbers; on the whole, they were charged with infractions similar to those of whites and they were held to the same moral expectations as whites."[107]

This observation is especially important to bear in mind when considering Will's case in the context of what was taking place during the 1720s and 1730s—the sudden and remarkable upsurge of "a party of Seekers" in lowcountry South Carolina. Although relatively few slaves embraced evangelicalism before 1760, early evangelical attempts at slave conversion engendered a vitally important new beginning in African American religious history. During the second half of the eighteenth century and at the beginning of the nineteenth century, massive numbers of captive Africans and their descendants would convert to evangelical Christianity, fusing traditional West and Central African beliefs with Christian forms to create a dynamic new Afro-Christian faith. A reciprocal process involving negotiation, contestation, and syncretic blending, the beginnings of this great religious transformation emerged almost imperceptibly in the years leading up to 1740, as the Ashley River Baptist Church records clearly show, setting in motion the African American slave journey to Christianity.[108]

4

A Hammer and a Fire

George Whitefield and the First Great Awakening

I am sorry I had so little discourse with you . . . when you was here with me last; being very desirous to know, if it has pleased God to bless your frequent sicknesses last winter to you. As for me I have learned by happy experience that it was good for me that I have been afflicted, and must own that I had wrong notions of religion 'till lately. Had any one told me before that illness, that we were to be born again of God, and feel the power of God in our hearts, convincing us that we were the children of God, and making so intire a change in us, as to make us new creatures, and to be so entirely altered, not only in our outward actions, but in our thoughts, words, and desires, as to endeavour to make them all tend to God's glory, or else, that we were not in a state of salvation, I should have thought it very strange, and what could not be true; but I am now as much convinced of it, as that I am now writing. Indeed we may feel the spirit of God in our hearts, and be as sure of it, as that we feel any thing we have in our hands. Be not surprised that I tell you so, for I have experienced it.

Catherine (Barnwell) Bryan to her sister, October 1739

Even before George Whitefield arrived in South Carolina on New Year's Day in 1740, his influence was beginning to be felt in the colony through the transatlantic communication network linking Europe and the Americas, as the experience of Catherine (Barnwell) Bryan vividly illustrates. Born to a prominent family on the Lower South frontier, Catherine Bryan was the third wife of Hugh Bryan, a wealthy slave-owning planter who served on the vestry of St. Helena's Parish. A deeply devout Anglican and constant churchgoer, Catherine Bryan was suddenly awakened during an illness she suffered in 1739, when she was "seized with great fear." Not fully cognizant that she had discovered "a living faith in Christ," Bryan began reading "Mr. *Whitefield's* sermons . . . and likewise his *Journals*." From these she "received great advantage," finding many things in Whitefield's writings that she had experienced during her affliction. Most important, Catherine Bryan discovered that she had had a mystical experience (had been "born again of God"), and in a letter to her sister she began describing that moment of religious ecstasy in the common language of eighteenth-century Protestant evangelicalism, as "a ray of light and joy unto my soul." It was as "if an angel had been sent to tell me of it," she said.[1]

Catherine Bryan's religious conversion was one of many on both sides of the Atlantic during the First Great Awakening. So, too, was her husband's. Hugh Bryan had felt secure in his notions of religion as a member of the Church of England until Catherine "was born of the spirit." But afterward he was stricken with doubt, vexed by the mystery of his wife's new birth. No sooner had Whitefield arrived in Savannah after his two-month preaching tour of the Middle Colonies in the spring of 1740 than Hugh and Catherine Bryan and their niece went to hear him preach. A few days later Hugh determined to seek God "in the holy sacrament of the Lord's supper." His existential moment came shortly thereafter, as he prepared for the sacrament through secret prayer, meditation, and self-examination: "my heart [was] enlarged with a ray of light that darted into my soul," Bryan recalled. Using "the light of [the] Spirit to search the scriptures," he became convinced that "the light of your own reason can never understand them effectually."[2]

The Bryans were part of a great stirring of religious expression that had many international tributaries, including Anglo-American Puritanism, Scotch-Irish Presbyterianism, and Continental Pietism. This stirring coalesced in the years 1739 to 1742 and was touched off and led by George Whitefield, who visited South Carolina on six separate occasions in 1740 and early 1741. In all, Whitefield spent some fifty-eight days in the Carolina colony and preached at least seventy-five sermons (in addition to those he delivered in Georgia, where the Bryans and many other South Carolinians traveled to hear him preach). Whitefield also led public prayers, initiated a series of Wednesday-evening lectures designed to further "the good Work of Grace begun," and held countless private meetings with colonists in the lowcountry.[3] By the end of 1739 he completed nearly three-quarters of the sixty-three sermons collected in his official works, and these were widely circulated and read throughout the Atlantic world, as were his journals. Though Alexander Garden was quick to criticize Whitefield's "manner of Journalizing both Persons and Things," he was forced to acknowledge openly "the outward visible Effects of his Preaching, viz the Crouds attending it, and the Numbers proselyted to his Doctrines."[4] Indeed almost everywhere Whitefield preached in South Carolina "the Word . . . came like a hammer and a fire," striking testimony to his ability to win adherents and the nature and extent of his support, as well as the predisposition of many settlers to embrace the Great Awakening. "People seemed to come from all parts," Whitefield wrote on one occasion after preaching an outdoor sermon at the Ashley River.[5]

✣

George Whitefield arrived in the northeasternmost corner of South Carolina about midday on Tuesday, January 1, 1740. Bound for Savannah, where he had spent several months in 1738 and began making plans to establish an orphanage, he was on his second and best-known trip to America. This trip extended from October 30, 1739, to January 24, 1741, and was accompanied by great outbursts of emotional religion.[6] Whitefield's present journey took him first to the Middle Colonies, then on through Maryland, Virginia, and North Carolina. Although he had already spent two months preaching in the British mainland colonies by the end of 1739, the Great Awakening did not begin in earnest until Whitefield reached the Lower South, where he remained for the next four months before embarking upon a Mid-Atlantic preaching tour. Indeed while Whitefield preached to much larger crowds in Philadelphia the previous year—perhaps as many as ten thousand people—it was in the Carolinas and Georgia that he first sparked the Great Awakening, which, as Frank Lambert has written, involved a process whereby "revivalists themselves wove their own web of meaning which convinced them and thousands of others that they were participating in a glorious 'Work of God.'"[7]

Traveling from the Carolina dividing line toward Charleston on New Year's Day, Whitefield "immediately perceived the people were more polite than those we generally met with." At a tavern he found "several of the neighbors . . . met together to divert themselves by dancing country dances," and he immediately determined to confront them. His description of the encounter reveals a touchstone of the Awakening in the colonial South:

> I went in amongst them whilst a woman was dancing a jig. At my first entrance I endeavored to shew the folly of such entertainments, and to convince her how well pleased the devil was at every step she took. For some time she endeavoured to outbrave me . . . but at last she gave over. . . . It would have made any one smile to see how the rest of the company, one by one attacked me . . . to support their wantonness; but Christ triumphed over Satan. All were soon put to silence, and were, for some time, so overawed, that after I had discoursed with them on the nature of baptism and the necessity of being born again, in order to enjoy the Kingdom of Heaven, I baptised, at their entreaty, one of their children, and prayed afterwards.

Whitefield was no doubt correct in believing that many of the celebrants regretted his coming "to be their guest that night," but his willingness to attack openly their convivial behavior and arousing "wantonness," his efforts to awaken them to a sense of sin—their total depravity—and his emphasis on the need to experience an instantaneous new birth in Christ to escape that fallen state proved to be central themes of the Great Awakening.[8]

Whitefield's subsequent journal entry exposes another significant factor that gave shape to the revival in the Lower South. Intending "to call at a gentleman's house" on the night of January 2, his small party rode there, "but the moon being totally eclipsed," Whitefield recalled, "we missed the path that turned out of the road." He continued:

> We had not gone far when we saw a light. Two of my friends went up to it, and found a hut full of negroes; they enquired after the gentleman's house... but the negroes seemed surprised, and said they knew no such man, and that they were new comers. From these circumstances, one of my friends inferred, that these negroes might be some of those who lately had made an insurrection..., and had run away from their master. When he returned, we were all of his mind, and, therefore, thought it best to mend our pace.

After encountering another "nest of such negroes" and "expecting to find negroes in every place," it is little wonder that the travelers thought that their lives were "in great peril," particularly following the Stono Rebellion of 1739, the single largest slave rebellion in the southern British mainland colonies and one of the most important slave revolts in American history. Although the bloody uprising at Stono ultimately failed, it cast fear throughout the lowcountry and had religious consequences that were profoundly meaningful. Many Carolinians believed that God had uttered a terrible judgment against them for their sinfulness and saw in their own worldliness and spiritual complacency an explanation for the revolt. That the Stono Rebellion came on the heels of a prolonged drought and two deadly epidemics only added fuel to such thinking.[9]

On Saturday morning Whitefield arrived in Charleston, a bustling port city whose population numbered some six to seven thousand. The "largeness of the place" and the "neatness of the buildings" had already impressed him, for he had briefly occasioned the city on his first trip to America in 1738. "The church is very beautiful," he wrote of St. Philip's at the time, "and the inhabitants seemed to be excellently well settled," adding, "God's judgments have been lately abroad amongst them by the spreading of the small-pox." "I hope they will learn righteousness," Whitefield said.[10] In the fourteen months or so that passed between this and his second visit to South Carolina, such divine visitations seemed to intensify, and Whitefield decided to incorporate this theme into a Sunday sermon.

While negative reports of Whitefield's itinerant ministry had already reached South Carolina, most Charlestonians, including "several gentlemen of the town," welcomed the opportunity to hear him preach. His reputation as a spellbinding minister preceded him, and the townspeople generally greeted his arrival with both anticipation and excitement. Even after Whitefield discovered that Alexander Garden was out of town and the commissary's assistant could not "lend [him] the pulpit," they were, by his account, "eager to hear" him. So he preached in the pulpit of a dissenting church, drawing from his observations and experiences in the colony and picking up on the theme of God's judgments against the men and women of Carolina. Whitefield suggested that his listeners adhered to a variety of different faiths. He also implied that the congregation included a disproportionately large number of elites. "The auditory was large, but very polite," he said, questioning "whether the court-end of London could exceed them in affected finery, gaiety of dress, and a deportment ill-becoming persons who have had such Divine judgments lately sent amongst them." "I reminded them of this in my sermon," he wrote, "but I seemed to them as one that mocked."[11]

Josiah Smith and other Protestant evangelical clergy had already begun developing a more "severe and searching ministry," endeavoring to "honour the names of those ministers in the church, who have been *Sons of thunder*, and whose sermons have been like pointed arrows, in the consciences of their hearers."[12] But Whitefield's mockery, his open defiance, his rhetorical challenge to South Carolina's polite society—all this represented a new departure. Nevertheless he was utterly dismayed by his listeners' response. He found "little concern" among them, despite repeated visitations by an angry God, and he concluded that their unwillingness to reform was a clear sign that their hearts had been "hardened."[13]

Whitefield redoubled his efforts the following day when he was invited to preach "at the French church" by Francis Guichard, who became a firm supporter. He hinted that his listeners included a broader range of men and women in Charleston society and that the crowd was very large. He also noted his success. ("I saw a glorious alteration in the audience, which was so great that many stood without the door," Whitefield wrote.) What he said, what he changed, whether or not he seemed inspired, how and when he raised and lowered his voice for dramatic effect, what gestures and biblical metaphors he might have used—all this is lost to view. "I felt much more freedom than I did yesterday," Whitefield noted revealingly, and "many were melted into tears." Whatever he said or however he said it differently seemed this day to resonate with the crowd: "Instead of the people going out (as they did yesterday) in a light, unthinking manner, a visible concern was in most of their faces."[14]

Of course Whitefield attributed his success to divine inspiration ("God strengthened me to speak, I trust, as I ought to speak," he wrote in his January 7, 1740, journal entry), but Alexander Garden saw it differently. Accusing him of journalistic artifice, the commissary wrote, "if he perceives his Audience to keep their Countenances, and that none of them will commence [a] Scene of *Contrition;*—then he's full of Trouble for them;—Cries out, 'Where's your *Contrition*!

Where your *Tears*! No Body *weep*! No *Meltings* amongst you! Come, my Friends, I will *weep* with you and for you';—And so falls a howling himself, till the *Handkerchiefs* begin to move, and then there's *Conversion-Work, Power,* and *Success;* and all as it should be fitted for the *Journal.*" Garden came to know Whitefield well, and he dedicated long hours to writing a thirty-three-page preface to one of his best-known sermons, *Take Heed How Ye Hear* (preached in 1740), attempting to discredit the revivalist's journal, which he argued was "partly *defective,* partly *false, warped* and *mangled* throughout." Here and elsewhere the commissary also sought to debunk the notion that Whitefield's ministry was somehow moved by the "Aids, Influences, and Operations of [God's] *holy Spirit.*" To him, the secret of Whitefield's success was no secret at all. It was his "*Talent of Delivery,* or Voice and Vehemence in Speaking, adapted to take the Ear and excite the Passions of his Hearers." In other words there was a natural and perfectly rational explanation.[15]

This sort of homiletical style, which Garden was one of the first to analyze and critique in print, proved to be a topic of great interest in the polemical battles that raged in the 1740s, because it spoke to the very nature of regeneration, the central fault line separating pro- and anti-revivalists. No one questioned its efficacy though. Even Garden, who charged that Whitefield was too prone "to fish for some Expression or other . . . in his *Favour* or *Applause,* and then, with a little more favourable Turn, [write it] down . . . in the *Journal*"—even he himself did not deny the persuasive power and force of evangelical preaching. And of course Whitefield, who probably did more than any other single individual to invent and model this style of revivalistic rhetoric, frequently commented on its effects, partly because of his firm conviction that they were divine "*Seals* to his ministry." He noted how "one of the town, most remarkabley gay, was observed to weep" during his stirring sermon at the Huguenot church, for instance. He also wrote that after a weekday sermon several men and women in the audience pleaded with him "for help in the way to salvation" and asked him to pray for their souls. "Many of the inhabitants, with full hearts, entreated me to give them one more sermon," he said, having to delay his departure to oblige them: "Notice was immediately given, and in about half an hour, a large congregation was assembled in the meeting-house, where I preached yesterday, because it was the largest place."[16]

Whitefield embarked for Savannah the following morning. He had been in South Carolina less than eight days, in Charleston less than three. By no means was the colony yet ablaze with a generalized religious awakening, but the young Anglican itinerant left a lasting impress on its inhabitants during his short tenure, departing "full of joy at the prospect of a good work having begun" and making plans to return again soon. In the meantime he had business to attend to in Savannah, which involved reaching out to the poor, the dispossessed, and the enslaved. "Set out for Georgia in an open canoe (having five negroes to row and steer us)," Whitefield noted. "The poor slaves were very civil, diligent, and laborious," he added, contrasting these Creole seamen with the African slaves he had encountered northeast of Georgetown. Stopping at Beaufort, another growing urban port like Georgetown, Whitefield visited with Anglican minister Lewis Jones, rector of Saint Helena's Parish in Port Royal from 1726 to 1744. Jones was a sympathizer who treated the party "with great civility." Taking leave the next day, January 9, Whitefield recorded that his party stopped at a plantation and then, after sunset, they "made a fire on the shore, and slept round it for about four hours." A "little after midnight," he said, "we prayed with the negroes."[17]

Arriving in Georgia the following day, Whitefield spent the next two months carrying out his plans to establish an orphanage. While there, he continued to preach and to stir controversy, composing two religious tracts that became the subject of intense debate, especially in the lower southern colony of South Carolina.[18] Dated January 18 and January 23 respectively, these texts are particularly important, for not only do they illustrate the revivalist's commitment to principle, courage, and piety; they also illustrate the development of his thinking as the Great Awakening unfolded. Both are sharply critical of the Church of England, and both show how the teachings of John Calvin increasingly informed Whitefield's preachings. In addition, both tracts reflect in different ways Whitefield's conviction that God had a peculiar quarrel with the colonial South, where the Church of England was most firmly established and where African slavery fostered immense human suffering.

The first text was written as a letter to "a friend in London" concerning Archbishop Tillotson, the archbishop of Canterbury under William and Mary. In this text Whitefield declared war on "all the natural Men" who thought well of the prelate's works, meaning those who preached rational Christianity. Writing the letter to vindicate his belief that the archbishop "*knew no more of true Christianity than* Mahaomet," an assertion that he repeated throughout the text and one that he avowed in pulpits on both sides of the Atlantic, Whitefield argued that the Church of England had abandoned basic Protestant doctrine in emphasizing Arminian free-will principles.[19] In developing his argument, Whitefield first attempted to defend his attack on Tillotson by pointing out that he did not coin the expression that the archbishop "knew no more of true Christianity than Mahaomet." Rather he was merely repeating what John Wesley once said. To prove his assertion, however, and to mount his assault on natural religion, Whitefield sought to use the seventeenth-century archbishop's own words, citing passages from several sermons he had written on the nature and necessity of regeneration. By reading these, Whitefield maintained, "any spiritual Man" could plainly see not only that Tillotson "knew no other than a bare historical Faith," but that he also preached "Deism refined." Worse than simply denying revealed Christianity, which at least was a consistent belief, Archbishop Tillotson, according to Whitefield, espoused a most dangerous heterodoxy. He "pretends to own Christ, and yet puts our Righteousness in the Place of his," Whitefield said.[20]

As an aside, but important for the evolution of the Great Awakening in the months ahead, Whitefield felt compelled to "tax the Dissenters with acting very partially." Tillotson had been a chief architect of the 1689 Toleration Act, and because he was friendly with dissenters and "behaved with much Moderation towards them whilst he lived," they failed to speak out against him even though they knew he preached doctrine that was contrary "to the Truth of the Gospel." Here the revivalist implied that nonconformists were guilty of indulging rational Christianity too. Finally, Whitefield encouraged consultation of John Edwards's *The Preacher: a discourse, shewing, what are the particular offices and employments of those of that character in the church* (1705). He had been told that Edwards "treated the Archbishop with much more Severity" than either he or John Wesley. Furthermore, Whitefield knew Edwards as a "noble Champion for the Doctrines of Grace" as well as "a Man of Letters, . . . Piety [and] a Presbyter of the Church of *England*."[21]

In a subsequent letter on the topic Whitefield sought to bolster his initial attack before extending and broadening it in a scathing discourse on Anglican churchman Richard Allestree's *The Whole Duty of Man*, a popular and influential devotional work that stressed the importance of religion in sustaining an ordered community. In March, after securing a copy of Edwards's book during his second visit to Charleston, Whitefield wrote against Archbishop Tillotson again, proclaiming that "the Mystery of Iniquity, wrappp'd up in the Writings of our late celebrated Author, has been hid long enough—'Tis Time now to reveal it to the World." Carefully selecting extracts from *The Preacher* to expose the prelate's Arminian views (quotes concerning Tillotson's opinions on the scriptures, the eternity and torments of hell, and idle conversation, for instance), Whitefield rested his case, feeling confident that he had, with Edwards's backing, proved "again and again how stark blind the Archbishop was, in the fundamental Points of the Christian Religion."[22]

In his letters concerning Tillotson, both of which were intended to combat the growing influence of rationalism, Whitefield hinted at an underlying belief that he made explicit in the third of his trilogy of letters from Georgia, *A Letter . . . to a Friend in London, shewing the Fundamental Error of a Book, Entitled The Whole Duty of Man* (Charleston, 1740). "I have frequently thought," he wrote, that "next to the falling away of the Clergy from the Principles of the Reformation, the Books which are in our Church founded on the *Arminian* Scheme, have been the chief Cause why so many of our own Communion in particular, have built their Hopes of Salvation on a false Bottom." Through his literary expositions, therefore, Whitefield hoped to awaken the reading public to what he saw as the Arminian apostasy, "to open People's Eyes" and "shew them that the Writings which for some Years past, have been so much admired, are directly contrary to the Gospel of *Jesus Christ.*" While the overall theme and import of Whitefield's testimony against *The Whole Duty of Man* was much the same as his previous letters, there are two important differences. First, whereas the two attacks on Tillotson were aimed at works consumed by "the more learned and polite," this attack targeted a book "read by the more common sort . . . of People." Also, Whitefield did much more in this piece to assert an openly Calvinistic stance on two theological doctrines to combat the Arminianism he saw all around him. In particular he staked out a purely Calvinist position on both unconditional election and total depravity in attacking the popular devotional.[23]

The other tract written just after Whitefield's first visit to Charleston in January 1740, *Letter to the Inhabitants of Maryland, Virginia, North and South-Carolina, concerning their Negroes,* seems on the surface to be an entirely different species of text, because it focuses on the topic of slave treatment in the colonial South. Yet close analysis reveals some subtle and deep-lying connections between this and Whitefield's other letters from Georgia. For example, all represent an effort to draw a sharp distinction between the "civilizing and christianizing" aspects of Protestant teaching; all reflect a belief that the "Cause of all the Evils and Miseries Mankind" suffered (as well as "all the Vices" in individuals to be found) resulted from the failure of the clergy to preach the true "Gospel of Christ"; and all emphasize doctrines such as original sin and justification by faith alone, doctrines that ran against the currents of modern Western thought. And while one had as its focus a regionally specific colonial audience, all four letters suggest that George Whitefield believed that God had a peculiar quarrel with eighteenth-century southerners.[24]

Of course, Whitefield wrote his letters from Savannah, and he spent five of the first seven months of 1740 in the Lower South.[25] On his initial journey there he was eager to carry out his plan to establish an orphan house, having a land deed and some £1,000 to proceed with the construction of a residence hall. As a result, he stopped "as little as possible on the Road." Still, Whitefield sensed a generalized and particularly pronounced "Deadness as to divine Things, and . . . a general Prophaneness . . . both in Pastors and People" on his trip through the Chesapeake and the Carolinas, which led him to Annapolis, Williamsburg, and New Bern, and then on to Charleston and Savannah. Here, in the Anglican colonial South, the writings of Tillotson were "as much admired and read" as anywhere, and *The Whole Duty of Man* "led the People Captive" in large numbers. A "Man whom I reproved lately on the Road for Gaming in the Christmas Holy-Days . . . told me the Whole Duty of Man said he might do so," Whitefield noted in bearing "a publick Testimony" against that book and referring presumably to a Carolinian.[26] Summarizing his observations in his *Letter to the Inhabitants of Maryland, Virginia, North and South-Carolina,* he wrote:

> Most of your are without any [Anglican] teaching Priest.—And whatever Quantity of Rum there may be, yet I fear but very few Bibles are annually imported into your different Provinces.—God has already begun to visit for this as well as other wicked Things.—For near this two Years last past, he has been in a remarkable Manner contending with the People of *South-Carolina.* Their Houses have been depopulated with the Small Pox and [Yellow] Fever, and their own Slaves have rose up in Arms against them.—These Judgments are undoubtedly sent abroad not only that the Inhabitants of that, but of other Provinces, should learn righteousness. And unless you all repent, you all must in like Manner expect to perish.

Though characteristic of all four letters from Georgia, "a Fellow-Feeling for the Miseries of the poor Negroes" informed such strong and impassioned language. Having been "sensible touched" by the plight of enslaved Africans and African Americans, Whitefield wrote intently to southern slave owners: "I think God has a Quarrel with you for your Abuse . . . and Cruelty."[27]

In making his case for amelioration, Whitefield chose not to consider the question of "whether it be lawful for Christians to buy slaves," but he was certain that God was contending with the South because of the "inhumane Usage of cruel Task Masters." Considering slaveholders' treatment of bondspersons, Whitefield wondered why there had not been "more Instances of Self-Murder among the Negroes," wondered why "they have not more frequently rose up in Arms against their Owners." "*Virginia* has once, and *Charlestown* more than once been threatened in this Way," he wrote. With this, Whitefield focused his readers' attention on the future, on what they could expect in the years ahead. He offered a chilling vision for the slave colonies by citing 2 Samuel 21:1. The lesson he taught was that God sent a plague on the Israelites "many Years after the Injury . . . was committed." So for southerners, the worst was yet to come. The God of justice did not "disregard the Cry of the meanest Negroes!" Whitefield exclaimed, nor did he ignore the plight of bondspersons: "The Blood of them spilt for these many Years in your respective Provinces, will ascend up to Heaven against you."[28]

Like Bishop William Fleetwood almost thirty years before, Whitefield emphasized that, "comparatively speaking," slave mistreatment was "an inconsiderable Evil." But he went several steps further in advancing the notion of slavery as a positive good, primarily because of his Calvinist beliefs. He told slave owners that their "present and past bad Usage" of slaves, "however ill-designed, may thus far do them good, as to break their Wills, increase the Sense of their natural Misery, and consequently better dispose their Minds to accept Redemption." Also like Fleetwood, the revivalist excoriated masters for holding to "the general Pretence" that biblical instruction made slaves "proud, and consequently unwilling to submit to Slavery"—these and other such "blasphemous Notions" reflected but poorly on the Christian faith. Still, and again like Bishop Fleetwood in 1711, Whitefield sought to assure slave owners that the basic "Precepts of Christianity" required servants "to be Subject, in all lawful Things, to their Masters." "Do you find any one Command in the Gospel, that has the least Tendency to make People forget their relative Duties?" he asked. Lastly, to those who might "be so bold perhaps as to reply, *That a few of the negroes have been taught Christianity, and, notwithstanding, have been remarkably worse than others,*" Whitefield posed a simple question, drawing another direct connection between this and his other letters from Georgia: "what Christianity were they taught?"[29]

While George Whitefield was busy composing his first two letters from Georgia, a heated controversy over the peripatetic young evangelist erupted in pages of the *South Carolina Gazette.* The morning after the revivalist left Charleston, Josiah Smith wrote a letter to Benjamin Colman in Boston assessing Whitefield's character and preaching, which was published in the newspaper just ten days later. Dated January 9, 1740, it proved to be one of the key documents in the First Great Awakening. First of all, Smith's letter was widely circulated and read, and it shaped the reception Whitefield met with in New England later in the year, raising expectations, opening pulpits, and predisposing many northern colonists to embrace him. In addition Smith was able through his account of Whitefield's character and preaching to validate his own efforts to promote religious revivalism, his actions during the subscription controversy, and his subsequent decision to preach evangelical doctrine. Furthermore, Smith's letter sparked one of the earliest and most significant "Party Disputes in Divinity" anywhere in colonial British America, which set the stage for Whitefield's second visit to South Carolina in March.[30]

Smith's first audience was with colonial New Englanders, particularly the "eminent Ministers of Boston, and adjacent Towns." And although he was later forced to admit that some of the analogical language he used to describe Whitefield's preaching went beyond his "usual Stile," there is no reason to believe that he was anything other than sincere when he wrote that he had not formed a fixed opinion of the transatlantic revivalist before he arrived in the colony.[31] Whether Whitefield was a bona fide Calvinist remained an open question; additionally, many critics had charged that he stood ready to "deceiveth the People" with a new brand of Antinomian fanaticism. Having had the opportunity to observe him preach and to converse with him privately, however, Smith offered his honest assessment, knowing his own reputation was at stake. "I confess, his Composures seem'd not so much calculated to acquire the Reputation of a Man of Letters," he reported to Colman. "The Beauties and Ornaments of Language were not so much consider'd in them, but the Decencies of Action in his Deportment and Gesture, the Modulations of his Voice . . . join'd with the Zeal, Pathos, and Fire of his Expressions, would embellish any Sermon of the lowest Rate." Likening Whitefield to the Prophet Isaiah, to a seraph, and to St. Paul, Smith opened himself up to charges of blasphemy, and in a moment of rhetorical flourish he even went so far as to write that "the Pulpit seem'd almost to be the Tribunal, and the preacher himself, if the Comparison may be pardon'd, the Great Judge, cloathed in Flames, and adjudging a guilty World to penal Fire."[32]

These particular "Figures of Speech," Smith later confessed to Alexander Garden, were written while his imagination was "a little heated," while the thunder of Whitefield's preachings was still reverberating in his ears. Yet they were not uncommon on extraordinary occasions, he said in his own defense, citing examples from both secular and sacred writings. More important, only those with "a *Dulness* of Apprehension" could miss the larger point he was making in his account. Whitefield was not only a master pulpit orator, but he preached with intense fervor and earnestness and seemed to be divinely inspired.[33] "If he drops any Expressions, which seem to border upon what is call'd Enthusiasm," Smith told Colman, "a small Degree of Charity will attribute it to the sudden Excursions of his divine Warmth and Zeal." This same holy disposition, Smith also suggested, might excuse "some harsh and damnatory Expressions" Whitefield used in his sermons, such as those he used in attacking the ideas of Arius and Socinus (and hence Unitarianism). Finally, Smith was happy to report that Whitefield espoused doctrines that were wholly consistent with the five points of Calvinism, especially the doctrine of original sin. "There is perfect Harmony and concurrence in our Principles," he told Colman, noting with exultant validation that he was "not displeas'd to hear a Gentlemen of the Establishment delivering some of the same Tenets, which I had so long before adopted into my own Creed and System, especially when he could support them so well from Scripture, Experience, and the Articles of his own Church."[34]

Together with a subsequent communication, Smith's letter of January 9 formed the basis of his best-known sermon, *The Character, Preaching, & c. of the Reverend Mr. Geo. Whitefield, Impartially represented and supported* (Philadelphia, 1740), which he preached in late March following the revivalist's second visit to the colony. Circulated widely throughout the Atlantic world, these writings carried extraordinarily heavy weight with the New England Standing Order. After Whitefield's tour of New England in the fall, Smith received "several obliging Letters" from ministers there showing with "what sort of Reception" he met. One minister wrote: "You rais'd our Expectations of him very much . . . but we all own now we have seen and heard him, that our Expectations are all answer'd and exceeded." Another minister, who "conceived very highly" of Whitefield from Smith's letters and the sermon he "preached by way of Apology, &c," confessed that Smith had "not gone high eno' in his tho'ts of him." Colman, who gave over his pulpit to Whitefield as soon as Whitefield landed in Boston and knew that Smith was "impatient to know, what Manner of Entring" the revivalist had had in New England, summarized the gist of the ministerial correspondence. "*We* (*Ministers, Rulers and People*) generally received him as an *Angel* of God, or as *Elias*, or *John the Baptist* risen from the Dead." "We are abundantly convinc'd that you spake the Words of TRUTH and SOBERNESS."[35]

Of course Alexander Garden thought differently about Smith's truthfulness and sobriety. After the publication of Smith's letter of January 9, Garden issued a seven-thousand-word reply, which was carried in three separate issues of the *South Carolina Gazette* under the pseudonym Arminius.[36] On balance, Garden's response was much more of an attack on Smith and the larger cause he espoused than on Whitefield, thus representing the drawing of a party line between pro- and anti-revivalists in the colony. Smith certainly read it that way. He began preparing an answer to Arminius as soon as the commissary's first installment appeared, asking Peter Timothy for permission to "fill up the first Vacancy" in the paper after his "Nameless Correspondent" had finished his calumnious charges. Ultimately he filled up several vacancies, some eight in all, with each piece running from 1,400 to 1,800 words.[37]

The thesis of Garden's reply is clear. Smith and his Calvinist party held Whitefield up "as something more than Human" and triumphantly celebrated "his performances . . . as inimitable" only because of the "old and exploded doctrines" the charismatic young preacher espoused in a new, more popular manner. Smith had not represented Whitefield impartially, nor had he even attempted to do so. Rather he set out to "give as bright and shining a Character of Mr. Whitefield as possibly he could" merely on account of his speaking ability and the evangelical principles he maintained. Charging Smith with using "almost blasphemous" imagery in his letter, Garden alleged that his opponent knowingly committed an "unpardonable Fault" by comparing Whitefield to Jesus Christ. Consequently he could only suppose that Smith had "something in him bordering on Enthusiasm."[38]

Moreover, Garden said, if Smith was bordering on such emotional fervor, then Whitefield was beyond the pale. "Did he not affirm he felt the Spirit of God sensibly moving within him, that all who have the Spirit must feel it, as sensibly as one, who perceives the Sun shining in his Face, and that whoever have not this Sense and Certainty of the Spirit of God moving within them are not new-born nor in a State of Salvation?" How could Smith simply dismiss such an unnatural affirmation? Whitefield was a conceited, presumptuous young man who claimed he owned God's Spirit and taught that an experiential new birth was the sole source of religious truth and assurance, and Garden was determined not to let Smith pass off his "enthusiastick Expressions" so easily, not without admitting that he, too, shared similar sentiments. Even "the utmost Charity can attribute them to nothing better than to human *Weakness, Ignorance, & Rashness,*" Garden said. Further, there was no rational evidence to suggest that they stemmed from "sudden Excursions" of divine inspiration, only that "the Doctrine of the Necessity of a full Assurance" was "a standing and established Article of *Methodism.*" In the final analysis, Garden contended, "the Source of all the Gentleman's Pleasure, the Grounds of his Panegyrick, [and] the Foundation of his Charity" stemmed from the fact that Smith shared "*some of the same Tenets*" as Whitefield.[39]

Of course Smith addressed each of the commissary's charges, focusing most of his attention on defending the doctrine of original sin, which Garden said Whitefield supported "but very poorly" and which all three men recognized as being so closely "interwoven with all the *five famous Points in Dispute.*" Garden's position was untenable without denying the total depravity of humankind. However, in perhaps the most revealing passage of the whole Garden–Smith exchange, Smith drove straight to the heart of debate, the central essence of the party divide that was emerging. Writing that Garden, "in *imitation* of some Moderns of the same Stamp," represented him as a Deist or Socinian would, he said:

> A *rational Religion* is what they affect and triumph in; a *cold* Religion, not animated with Warmth and Zeal. . . . A Religion that shuts out every sacred *Passion* and Emotion. This is *Their* Religion, and the *colder,* the more *rational.* Upon this Scheme, all Appearance of Devotion, every Sign of Reverence and ardent Respect to the *Deity,* which rises out of, and is an essential Ingredient in the Religion of *Nature,* is pronounc'd *irrational,* censur'd as *Enthusiastick,* and fit for *old Women.* If a Man in Prayer rises a Degree above the *Pathos* of a *Parrot,* or speaks of eternal Themes, with any feeling *Concern,* 'tis *Enthusiasm,* beneath Man's *Reason* and Powers of Intelligence. Mention the Name of *Christ,* 'tis a *Charm;* speak of *feeling the Spirit,* 'tis the Spirit and Quintessence of *Quakerism,* the discriminating *Shibboleth* of Enthusiasts.

Here in the pages of the *South Carolina Gazette* the great debate of 1740 began to solidify. How could anyone be "so angry at *feeling* the SPIRIT!" Smith exclaimed. "Is not *God* a Spirit? Did he not inspire our Souls? And shall we deny him *access* to them? Is there any Thing, in one Spirit's acting upon another, repugnant to any one Principle of *Reason*?" Writing in the "yes and no" tradition of medieval intellectuals, Smith described how spirits "'apprehended one another, as our *Senses* do material Objects,'" maintained that "'Our out-ward Senses are too-gross to apprehend God,'" and attempted to show why such apprehension came solely as a "feeling," often instantaneously. To do so Smith turned to the authority of

Joseph Addison, one of the great literary oracles of the Augustan Age, believing that Addison, unlike Isaac Watts or other authorities, might "be less liable to Exception, and of more Weight with the Gentlemen of such Principles, as are now under Censure."[40]

For months Garden seems to have simply asserted an agnostic position when confronted with these enthusiastic arguments. But as scores of lowcountry parishioners were by his account "carried away with so strange a *Wind of Doctrine*, as persuades to the Belief and Expectation of a certain happy *Moment*, when, by the *sole* and *specifick* Work of the Holy *Spirit*, [they would] at once (as 'twere by *Magic* Charm) be metamorphosed," he was forced to defend his agnosticism and address the new birth of which Smith and his New Light party spoke. So the commissary preached two sermons on the topic, which he later collected and had printed at the end of November as *Regeneration and Testimony of the Spirit* (Charleston, 1740). Like Garden's other religious writings, this piece was devoured by antirevivalists across the Atlantic littoral, and it quickly assumed a prominent place in the literature on the Great Awakening in America. Designed to "guard . . . against the Puzzle and Perplexity of some crude *Enthusiastick* Notions, which so much prevailed about the same *Period* of the last *Century*, and are now revived and propagated by Mr. *Whitefield* and his Brethren *Methodists*," Commissary Garden first defined religious enthusiasm and then stated how these new Puritan radicals conceived of spiritual regeneration. "Enthusiasm," he wrote, substituted in the place of reason and God's word one's "own *Conceits* of *immediate* Revelations, by certain *Impulses*, *Motions*, or *Impressions* of the Holy Spirit" on the mind "without any rational objective Evidence, or clear and sufficient Proof," such as the ability to raise the dead or give sight to the blind. Further, enthusiasts believed that regeneration was instantaneous and that it suddenly transformed the human will "from Evil to Good, from being corrupt and vicious, to being pure, virtuous and holy." In addition, Garden said, enthusiasts believed that men and women were wholly passive in the work of regeneration and claimed that the soul-ravishing new birth was a physical presence, "as plainly and distinctly *felt* and known, as those of the *Wind*, or other material Thing, outwardly on our *Bodies* are."[41]

Throughout, Garden emphasized that these doctrines were not new. They were left over from the Puritan Revolution and "explained and taught in a *new* and *better* Manner." "Look back to the *Oliverian* Days," he pleaded with his parishioners, "what Ruin and Desolation *such* [*spiritual*] *Pretenders* brought upon the Kingdom! How did they swarm throughout the Nation! A *Parliament*—; even an *Army* all Saints, Preachers, spiritual and regenerate Men!" Should the whole realm again be "*divided* and *subdivided by the Spirit* into a 1000 Sects, Sorts and Divisions," he warned, another cloud of darkness and confusion would reign. Thus Garden endeavored to explicate an entirely different formulation of regeneration and spiritual testimony. Regeneration was not any sort of physical presence, nor was it "the Work of a *Moment.*" Rather it was a moral change wrought throughout one's life, "a *gradual* and co-operative Work of the *Holy Spirit,* joining in with our *Understandings,* and leading us on by *Reason* and *Persuasion,* from one Degree to another, of Faith, good Dispositions, Acts, and Habits of Piety." What is more, spiritual testimony meant "*walking, abiding, living, and being led* in or by the *Gospel*" with the aid of God's spirit, which was evidenced by its "*Fruits and Effects,*" namely "Faith, Repentance, good Dispositions of the Heart, and good Works of the Hands." Every true Christian, Garden insisted, must be conscious of or "feel" this testimony—nothing more.[42]

By the time Garden penned his two sermons on regeneration he openly admitted that he felt dejected. Religious enthusiasm was the worst of all "*Religious* Maladies," the "most desperate and hardest to be subdued." Fundamentally different than Catholicism, Islam, and Judaism, as well as atheism, paganism, and deism, the disease was beyond "the Reach of all the Arguments and Conclusions of Reason and Revelation." Hence, there was literally no way to persuade religious enthusiasts. Indeed, these new Puritan radicals simply claimed for themselves an infallible knowledge of religious truth and labeled all those who disagreed with them as unregenerate Christians. Worse still, the religious radicals had been "throwing out their Opinions with Sybilline Rage and Fury" in colonial South Carolina for several months–preaching their opinions fervently in pulpits throughout the colony–"*running a Muck* . . . on Mankind with them, and cramming them down their Throats with Anathema's, Hell and Damnation at the End of them, on all that will not implicitly receive them."[43] Garden became a lightning rod for this New Light insurgency, the symbol of an unconverted ministry. Yet one of Garden's supporters, speaking he said on behalf of all the established clergy, believed him to be a most "able . . . Advocate on their behalf." Presuming to advise Josiah Smith as "a Friend of his" in an editorial letter appearing in the October 30 issue of the *South Carolina Gazette,* he suggested that Anglican ministers thought "that thrusting themselves into the Debate" might actually offend the commissary. But he warned Smith and his revival party that "they might deem it not so fair and honourable to engage a single Enemy with Numbers."[44]

Far more dejecting to Garden was the spell Whitefield had cast over his flock, particularly "all the *Passion* and *Prejudice,* that prevailed 'mong *some* . . . in his favor, against them and everything else that opposed him." Indeed he took to lecturing his congregation on their "tumultuous Assemblies, Preacher, and Doctrines" in a scathingly contemptuous tone.[45] Whitefield's "Mobb-Preachings" had become all too common; "the Danger to Religion," and "the Peace and Happiness of Society [had] but too plainly appeared." Still, there was a "Multitude after the Preacher." Thousands attended Whitefied's sermons, and scores had been converted. Everywhere they were "building up one another in Conceit of their being righteous," men and women from all segments of South Carolina society.[46]

Although Whitefield addressed large audiences in January of 1740, the mob preachings to which Garden referred began in mid-March during Whitefield's second visit to the South Carolina lowcounty. On this occasion he spent nearly a full week in Charleston, arriving on the thirteenth and departing on the sixteenth. During his second visit Whitefield delivered what the *South Carolina Gazette* described as "*nine* excellent Discourses, upon very important Subjects," and the revivalist made "a deep Impression upon many People."[47] Whitefield's arrival was widely anticipated, with scores of men and women flocking to hear him and daily coming "to town more and more from their plantations." These ever larger crowds now knew Whitefield not only as a stirring orator but as a man at the center of an intense provincial party controversy. No sooner had he landed than Whitefield and Garden confronted one another. At the same time the long running Garden–Smith newspaper debate continued to rage. Equally important, Whitefield's first two letters from Georgia made bold headlines. When Peter Timothy announced that Whitefield's other two letters were being printed, the *South Carolina Gazette* carried a notice showing how wildly popular such religious works had suddenly become: "Sermons, which used to be the greatest drug, are now the only Books in Demand."[48]

The *South Carolina Gazette* also noted the size of many of Whitefield's audiences during his March preaching tour. On Friday, March 14, the revivalist preached in the Independent Church "to a large Audience." On Sunday morning, when he visited the Presbyterian church, the sanctuary was packed and "the Yard . . . was also very full." On Sunday evening "the Crowd was so great at Mr. Smith's Meeting . . . that the Gallery crack'd, and frighten'd the Congregation." In this instance Whitefield moved the service out-of-doors and began speaking from a makeshift platform, using it again the following day.[49] The *South Carolina Gazette* passed over in silence the size of the crowd at the First Baptist Church, where Whitefield preached on Saturday, but his sermon caused a great stirring, helping to explain the appearance of *Some Queries, concerning the Operation of the Holy Spirit, Answered* (Philadelphia, 1740).[50] For his part Whitefield noted that he preached on the "the utter inability of man to save himself, and [the] absolute necessity of his dependence on the rich mercies and free grace of God in Christ Jesus for his restoration." He also noted that "some . . . were put under concern; and most seemed willing to know whether these things were so."[51]

Using voice inflection and dramatic gesture, Whitefield hammered upon his evangelical Protestant message during his springtime tour of Charleston, emphasizing the nature and necessity of the new-birth experience. That he did so while raising money for his Bethesda orphanage and visiting the sick helped to insulate him from his opponents' charges that he preached with Antinomian license. So, too, did Josiah Smith's newspaper commentary on the "Notion of *Charity*," wherein he emphasized the importance of Christian love toward humanity and expressed his opinion that Whitefield gave "the most shining Proofs of it."[52] In summarizing the revivalist's second visit to the colony, for instance, the *South Carolina Gazette* noted that Whitefield "insisted much upon Original Sin, the proper Divinity of Christ, and Justification by Faith alone, while at the same Time he guarded against a licentious Abuse of that Doctrine, and shewed how necessary it was, that they, which believe, should be careful to maintain good Works."[53]

Another theme Whitefield hammered upon was class specific, and in doing so he drew attention to both elite culture and clerical responsibility, stirring even more controversy. No less than during his first visit, the itinerant condemned "the polite Diversions of the Province," which the *South Carolina Gazette* also noted. In fact he said that he was "more explicit than ever" in witnessing against these diversions, continuing to link them to God's angry judgments in order to arouse a great spiritual awakening.[54] In his letter to Benjamin Colman, Josiah Smith took pains to comment on "Mr. WHITEFIELD's publick and repeated Censures upon our BALLS and MID-NIGHT ASSEMBLIES; especially in the present Situation of our Province." And it is likely that Smith authored an editorial piece shortly after Whitefield's first visit in response to a newspaper advertisement for an upcoming ball. "Good God," the editorialist wrote, "what can the Advertizor mean! To make Stocks and Epicures of us? . . . Is the Small Pox, is the Fatal Fever, is the Sword, etc. so soon forgot! or if we are called upon to praise God for our distinguishing Deliverance, can it only be done in Dance! Must it be done in the Theatre, before the Church. But I relieved myself a little with this. Sure said I, the Clergy at least, will be alarmed at the Impiety, and the Artillery of Heaven must play from every Pulpit in the Town."[55] Alexander Garden saw no great danger in these diversions. And his refusal to sound an alarm ultimately led Whitefield to "exclaim against" him in a high-profile confrontation in Garden's home that both men subsequently wrote about in an exchange of charges and countercharges.[56]

The confrontation began when Whitefield went to see the commissary on Friday, March 14, the morning after Whitefield landed in Charleston on his second visit to the South Carolina lowcountry. At issue were the accusations Whitefield leveled against the Anglican clergy. "After I had been there a little while, I told him I was informed he had some questions to propose to me, and that I had now come to give him all the satisfaction I could in answering them," Whitefield wrote. (According to Garden, the church bells were ringing for morning prayer, but Whitefield insisted on charging the clergy with preaching false doctrine, hypocrisy, and negligence right then and there.) Subsequently, Whitefield said, the commissary "charged me with enthusiasm and pride, for speaking against the generality of the clergy, and desired I would make my charge good." Claiming that he had already done so but was prepared to do still more, Whitefield suggested that Garden pressed the issue. So it seems that at this point Whitefield reiterated his accusation that the clergy did not preach justification by faith alone. Precisely "what passed on the subject" the revivalist omitted from his journal, as Garden was quick to point out in his retelling of the episode. But as the two men debated the matter Whitefield determined that among the Anglican parish priests in eighteenth-century America "the Commissary . . . was as ignorant as the rest," insinuating that he too was spiritually unregenerate and had no real knowledge of religious truth.[57]

Next the commissary accused Whitefield of breaking his "Cannons and Ordination vow" for not using the Book of Common Prayer in dissenting churches and threatened to suspend him if he preached in any Anglican church in South Carolina. Whitefield replied that he was officially ordained by the bishop of London. He also claimed that the canon applied only to public worship in Anglican churches and defiantly told Garden that he would regard his threat of suspension "as much . . . as a Pope's bull." The confrontation reached crescendo when Whitefield asked, "Have you delivered your soul by exclaiming against the assemblies and balls here?"[58] With this, Garden turned Whitefield out of his house, whereupon both men proceeded to make their way to St. Philip's for public prayers.[59]

Thus began Whitefield's second visit to South Carolina. On the whole it was much more controversial than his first, did more to shape the overall course of the Great Awakening in the colony, and had a deeper, more lasting effect. Like the revivalist did when the commissary challenged him to defend his charges against the Anglican clergy, Garden sought to make good on his threat of suspension—which he did in July—and he also began speaking out against Whitefield in church. As David T. Morgan has observed, "Whitefield's insolence prompted Garden to take the offensive. . . . On March 17, 1740, he publicly called in question the evangelist's doctrine and censorious utterances."[60] Specifically, Garden preached a sermon against Whitefield and represented him "under the character of the Pharisee, who came to the temple, saying, God I thank Thee that I am not as other men are." Then he penned a letter to the popular evangelist on the subject of justification, which he later published as one of his *Six letters to the Rev. Mr. George Whitefield* (Charleston, 1740), a collection which was widely circulated throughout the Atlantic world.[61]

"I have perused your *Sermon,* entitled, *What think ye of Christ,*" Garden wrote in his March 17, 1740, letter to Whitefield, "to which you were pleased to refer me t'other Day, in support of your Charge, or rather railing Accusation against the *Clergy* of the *Church of England* in general, and the present *Bishop of London* in particular, of their teaching false Doctrine, contrary to the *Gospel,* and the Articles of the Church, in explaining that of *Justification by Faith alone,* in such a Manner, as including good Works a necessary *Condition.*" Having perused the sermon and having made several observations upon it, Garden noted that on page 18 Whitefield had written of Article 12 of the Anglican church "Observe my dear Brethren the Words of the Article, *good Works are the Fruits of Faith, and follow after Justification.* How then can they precede, or be any Ways the Cause of it? No, our Persons must be justified, before our Performances are accepted." Garden contended that, "after setting down the Article at large in the next preceding Page," Whitefield had explained it in such a way as to contradict his own doctrine, "As if good Works which are *the Fruits of Faith* and pleasing to God, did not precede *Justification,* but follow after it only." He went on to say:

> For as a true and *lively* Faith, you admit must *precede* Justification; so *good Works,* teaches the latter Part of this Article, *do spring necessarily out of a true and lively Faith.* Now, if good Works do *necessarily spring* out of a true and *lively* Faith, and a true and *lively* Faith *necessarily precedes* Justification, the Consequence is plain, that good Works must *not only follow after,* but *precede* Justification also. And therefore your explaining the Article so, as to separate a true and lively Faith from good Works, admitting the one to go before, and the other only to follow after *Justification,* is explaining the Article into a Contradiction to your own Doctrine.

Garden concluded his letter with a bold challenge, asking Whitefield to "untie this Knot, if you can." But the revivalist chose to evade the issue. "Your Letter more and more confirms me, that my Charge against the Clergy is just and reasonable," he wrote on March 18. "It would be endless to enter into such a private Debate, as you, Rev. Sir, seem desirous of. You have read my Sermon; be pleased to read it again. And if there be any Thing contrary to sound Doctrine, or the Articles of the Church of *England,* be pleased to let the Publick know it from the Press." As he indicated in the second of his *Six letters to the Rev. Mr. George Whitefield,* Garden found Whitefield's reply totally unacceptable, and he went on to reiterate his belief that "*good Works* do as necessarily spring from and accompany a true and *lively* Faith, whether *before or after* Justification, as Light and Heat do the Sun."[62]

In the meantime Whitefield preached to more and larger audiences, even on week days, as men and women flocked from all around to hear him in Charleston. "Many sent me little presents, as tokens of their love, and earnestly entreated that I would come amongst them again," he wrote as he prepared to leave South Carolina on March 19, noting that "invitations were given me from some of the adjacent villages; and people daily came to town . . . to hear the Word." In this colonial lower southern mission field, moreover, Whitefield counted among the crowds some of the wealthiest men and women in America.[63] Though Alexander

Garden reported to the SPG in April that "only the multitude ran to hear him and the ears of passions, not the understandings, of the lower sort, especially dissenters, were taken," and though he assured Anglican officials that those of "tolerate capacities regard him only as a weak and wild visionary youth, whose head is filled with a jumble of Antinomian and Quaker notions, and turned with the populace, every where running to hear him," there is much evidence suggesting that by this time Whitefield's followers included substantial numbers of wealthy elite planters and merchants who had grown rich on rice.[64]

†

From Charleston, Whitefield proceeded again to Georgia, where he laid the cornerstone of the Bethesda orphanage and began making preparations to travel to Philadelphia. South Carolinians expected him to return in six weeks and "preach at the several Places in the Province to which he has been invited," but Whitefield did not return to the colony until July. During the spring the revivalist embarked upon an extended preaching tour of the Middle Colonies, where "Great and visible effects follow'd his Preaching."[65] In early June he returned to Savannah, knowing, as he put it, that "Charleston people were in expectations of seeing me, before I went to the North, and that God had been pleased to work by my ministry among them."[66] Whitefield arrived in South Carolina just as news reached the colony that James Oglethorpe's expedition against the Spanish at St. Augustine had ended in failure. In outlining God's quarrel with the South, Whitefield had predicted this eventuality. In his letter to southern slave owners, he warned: "A Foreign Enemy is now threatening . . . you, and nothing will more provoke God, to give you up as a Prey into their Teeth, than Impertinence and Unbelief,— Let the cause be removed, and the Sons of Violence shall not be able to hurt you." "God first generally corrects us with Whips," he said; "if that will not do, he must chastize us with Scorpions."[67]

Landing at Beaufort on July 1, Whitefield visited with Anglican minister Lewis Jones. Although Jones thought the evangelist went "too far in condemning Archbishop Tillotson" and placed undo emphasis on "*free justification,*" Jones remained supportive—"candid," "courteous," and "more noble than his brethren."[68] Jones's congregation was consuming the plain-style revival message, swelling in numbers, often "throng'd every evening with . . . inhabitants," as St. Helena's parishioner Hugh Bryan observed. And, despite knowing he was "in danger of incurring the commissary's displeasure," Jones invited the revivalist to officiate in his church.[69]

In defending his decision, Jones suggested not only that Whitefield enjoyed broad popular support but also that his ministry actually benefitted the Church of England. In August he explained his decision to Garden. Jones noted that he personally "looked upon it to be a matter of Discretion, And thought myself at Liberty to Comply with what I found to be the general Desire of my Congregation." In a subsequent letter Jones informed the SPG that he would "have incurr'd the displeasure of most of my Parishioners, And put it out of my power of being any further useful here" had he not invited Whitefield to preach. In both instances Jones emphasized that he acted not out of any "Contempt to Authority" but based his decision on the people's will. Further, he admitted that he did not "find any ill Consequence" arising from it. In fact, he said, the "uncommon Success that attended" Whitefield's preaching "induc'd me to think That I sh'd have done Greater disservice by opposing than by complying with my Parishioners."[70]

Whitefield struck out from Beaufort and stopped off at Hugh Bryan's plantation as well as at the Bethel Presbyterian Church on his way to Charleston, where he arrived on Thursday, July 3.[71] Over the next three weeks he preached some 34 sermons, ranging far and wide throughout the lowcountry, as a great religious revival shook South Carolina. In addition to his sermons at "the usual Place in . . . Town," where "Great numbers stood without the doors" to hear him, Whitefield visited eight country churches and exhorted large crowds at several lowcountry plantations. On one occasion he simply preached at an appointed time near Pon Pon "under a great tree."[72] Of his third and longest visit of the year, which extended from July 1 to July 25, the *South Carolina Gazette* reported that Whitefield's preaching met with "very general Acceptance." Indeed both Anglicans and dissenters flocked to hear him, and, as before, he preached to both the rich and to the poor.[73]

During his stay Whitefield worshiped at St. Philip's every Sunday, normally preaching at the Independent Meeting House both before and after divine service. On week days he traveled from Charleston to the rural towns and settlements where he had standing invitations to preach. He visited Ashley Ferry, Dorchester, Christ's Church, and John's Island during the week of July 6; James Island during the week of July 13; and Pon Pon and "Hoospanah" (read Huspah) during the week of July 21. Followed by a large entourage, Whitefield usually preached twice each day, sometimes at the same location. In Dorchester, for instance, he "preached twice to a large audience in Mr. Osgood's meeting-house" on July 8, and at St. John's in Colleton County ("where there was a great congregation" gathered at the parish church) he read prayers and delivered two sermons on July 12. At Ashley Ferry, Whitefield preached on three separate occasions. Initially, on July 7, he "preached to the conviction of some, and the comfort of others," a clear indication that the fires of evangelical revivalism had burned through the Baptist congregation well before his arrival. Still, he stopped by again two days later, and people "from all parts" crowded into the church, forcing Whitefield "to preach under a tree near Mr. C[hanler]'s meeting house, . . . it being now too small to contain the congregation." On this and on a subsequent occasion a couple of weeks later, when Whitefield read prayers and preached to another great crowd at Ashley Ferry, there was a generalized spiritual outpouring throughout the neighborhood, as "the Word came with convincing power."[74]

In these rural communities Whitefield's congregants were no less diverse than they were in Charleston. He visited as many Anglican as dissenting churches, and elites regularly sent him invitations to preach. On July 12, for example, Whitefield noted that he "went this morning to John's Island . . . whither I was invited by Colonel G . . . . s." Upon his arrival, he and his associates were "received . . . most hospitably," and after the itinerant read prayers and preached at the parish church they "returned to the Colonel's," as he hosted a late-afternoon religious gathering for his friends and neighbors. "I was enabled to give a warm and close exhortation to the rich that sat about me," Whitefield wrote later that night, adding that "a lasting impression, I am persuaded, is made on many hearts; and God, I believe, will yet shew that He hath much people in Charleston, and the countries round about."[75]

A similar scene unfolded on James Island, where less than a week later, on Thursday, Whitefield "was called upon . . . to preach at the house of Madame W . . . . . d." In his journal entry of Saturday, July 19, he noted:

> This gentlewoman, as she informed me herself, was at one time much prejudiced against me, insomuch that she thought it dangerous to come and hear me; but, having read my sermons, she changed her mind, and coming both to town, and to St. John's Island to hear me preach, was, with her daughter and another gentlewoman, much melted down. Being given to hospitality, she provided food sufficient for a great multitude. People came from town and the neighbouring places. Her barn was put into proper order, and I read prayers and preached in it. A lovely melting was visible in several parts of the auditory. After sermon, God enabled me to speak many Gospel truths amidst a polite set of people.[76]

This was truly a new kind of elite gathering, a form of spiritual treating whereby evangelical and polite cultures began to resonate. That Whitefield took pains to note the gentlewoman's earlier opposition to his preachings is significant, for in doing so he not only sought to highlight the ways in which new converts suddenly came under conviction, but he also sought to highlight the significance of what had happened at his ecclesiastical trial in Charleston, which had ended earlier that same day.[77]

After Whitefield preached at St. Helena's on the first of the month, Alexander Garden brought judicial proceedings against him. On July 7 the commissary issued a writ citing Whitefield to appear at St. Philip's the following week to answer charges that he had broken canon law and his ordination vows by failing to use the Book of Common Prayer in dissenting churches. During his meeting with

Garden in mid-April, Whitefield had answered these charges: he argued that he had neither violated canon law nor broken his ordination vows because canon law required Anglican ministers to use the Book of Common Prayer only when officiating in Anglican churches, not in dissenting churches. However, the commissary interpreted the law differently, believing that every Anglican minister was required to use the Book of Common Prayer whenever and wherever he preached. Consequently, Garden threatened to suspend Whitefield if he preached in any Anglican church in South Carolina.[78]

Despite his having arranged to preach at Ashley Ferry and Pon Pon, and despite declaring in April that he would regard Garden's threat of suspension no more seriously than he would a papal bull, Whitefield appeared at St. Philip's at nine o'clock on July 15. According to the *South Carolina Gazette*, the sanctuary was thronged, as "many attended to know the Issue of the Tryal."[79] Surrounded by four other members of the Anglican clergy—William Guy, Timothy Millechamp, William Orr, and Stephen Roe—the commissary began the proceedings by calling on Whitefield to answer the charges against him. Whitefield immediately challenged the authority of the court by questioning its ecclesiastical jurisdiction, and he refused to answer any charges until this issue had been settled. After considerable debate, Garden finally agreed to postpone the proceedings to establish the court's jurisdiction.

The next day Whitefield executed a clever legal maneuver with the help of a prominent attorney, Andrew Rutledge, attempting to make an end run around Garden's charges against him. Rather than challenging the jurisdictional authority of the court, or Garden's right to interpret and apply canon law, Whitefield challenged the commissary's integrity. In dramatic fashion he entered a *recusatio judicis* plea, which brought into question Garden's ability to render an unbiased decision. As evidence of the commissary's prejudice against him, Whitefield cited a sermon Garden had preached at St. Philip's the previous Sunday, *Take Heed How Ye Hear*, and he suggested that the matter be decided by a panel of six independent arbitrators, three of his own choosing.[80]

Naming "two Independents and one french Calvinist and all of them his zealous Admirers," Whitefield pressed his plea in front of the crowded audience, asking Garden to choose three names as well. Clearly on the defensive, the commissary refused. While Garden fully realized that he could not prevail against the revivalist through arbitration, he apparently overlooked the fact that two of men Whitefield named to determine whether he should recuse himself did not have any official standing in his ecclesiastical court, as neither were Anglican ministers. At any rate Garden ultimately rejected the recusation plea. So on the advice of Rutledge, Whitefield appealed the decision to the English High Court of Chancery the following day, promising to prosecute his appeal within one year and posting a surety bond.[81]

⁜

In some ways Whitefield's trial encapsulized the tenuous position of the Church of England in the South Carolina lowcountry; in others it marked a turning point in the First Great Awakening. Although he failed in his secret attempt to make the established church independent of SPG subsidies in the 1730s, Alexander Garden did much to shore up its authority during his twelve-year tenure as commissary—disciplining immoral clergy and seeking to win influence with the provincial laity by making concessions relative to parish government, for example.[82] Yet that authority was weak and did not extend to a majority of colonists. Despite the commissary's efforts, anticlerical sentiment remained strong, and puritanical nonconformity within the Church of England continued as before, a disposition which Garden was no more willing to tolerate than his predecessors had been, especially among parish clergy. Further, most men and women worshiped outside of South Carolina's established church; Protestant dissenters tainted it with an air of illegitimacy; and Anglican laypeople tended to favor a broader policy of toleration than their ministers, being notably pluralistic and latitudarian in their religious behavior.[83]

In one sense, then, Whitefield's trial was an example of a continuing problem with South Carolina's established state church, reflecting the tenuousness of its position and the fragility of its authority. Yet in exercising that authority Commissary Garden exacerbated the problem and badly damaged the Church of England, while at the same time emboldening Whitefield and his supporters. On the night after the judicial proceedings, Garden and Whitefield met one another and walked along a Charleston green near St. Philip's. During the course of their conversation the commissary explained why he had brought the charges against Whitefield and implied that Whitefield knew "in his Conscience I was but doing my bounden Duty." Indeed, carefully following his official instructions on how to proceed against irregular clergy, Garden first admonished Whitefield in private, then censured him from the pulpit, and then brought him up for trial. Claiming to be duty-bound, he knew that there were grave risks involved.[84]

First, Garden knew that he stood on shaky legal ground. Whitefield was licensed to preach in Georgia, technically outside of Garden's jurisdiction, and just a few years before Garden had written about a similar case involving an Anglican chaplain garrisoned at Port Royal, noting that he had been prevented by his commission from taking legal action against the badly behaved cleric. Second, the commissary realized that clerical support for his actions was soft. Presumably, he could count votes, that is, he could count on the support of his assistant, William Orr, a former Presbyterian, and the other three judicial assessors who sat with him at the trial. But opposition to the revivalist was by no means universal. Among the Anglican clergy were some who were sympathetic to Whitefield. Lewis

Jones reportedly "disapproved entirely of the Commissary's treatment" of Whitefield. In addition Whitefield noted that Thomas Thompson of St. Bartholomew's Parish "refused to preach or sit in judgment against me." It is unlikely that Jones and Thompson were alone. There were some twelve or thirteen Anglican ministers in the colony in 1740, and two were former Huguenots while another, Orr, had been a Presbyterian. Still another, Francis Guichard, the French Calvinist to whom Whitefield referred in his recusation plea, had taken Anglican orders but preached in a nonconformist church.[85] More important, and third, Commissary Garden was fully aware that he risked alienating lay opinion by proceeding with the trial. In several of his published sermons he acknowledged that Whitefield enjoyed broad popular support, maintaining that his popularity stemmed from his oratorical talents and his ability to excite emotion, not unlike "Mahomet, Muncer, Fox, Nailor, and Muggleton . . . who carried on, not the Work of God, but of the Devil plainly."[86]

Also important, Garden took the risk of martyring Whitefield by enabling him to raise the specter of persecution, despite knowing he was so fervently desirous of it. Earlier, in April, Garden wrote on the topic in a piece that was later published in his *Six letters to the Rev. Mr. George Whitefield,* in effect anticipating what would happen should he turn to ecclesiastical coercion. Calling on Whitefield to retract the slanderous and defamatory charges he had leveled against the Anglican clergy, Garden concluded his third letter to the itinerant by saying:

> You boast indeed, in your *Journals,* that you have kindled a Fire which all the Devils in Hell shall not be able to extinguish! Alas (Sir) the Fire you have kindled is that of Slander and Defamation. . . . You and your Brethren cry out Persecution! 'Tis true, Persecution there is in the Case; but are not you the Persecutors? Is it not you that falsely accuse the Brethren; disturb the Peace off the Church;—trample on her Laws and Canons, (tho' solemnly engaged to obey them) and despise her Authority? But still Persecution you cry out;—for Want of it you mean: For Ours is no persecuting Country for Religion; every Man may enjoy his own Way in Peace and Safety; but as you may regard the being persecuted as something essential to a true Christian, and necessary to keep up the Spirit of Christianity, you seem to be in Quest or Pursuit of it;—please only to step into a Neighbouring Country, *Spain* or *Portugal,* and you'll bid fair, I dare say, to find it.

The only reason Whitefield could claim for being persecuted, Garden argued in his April 8 letter, was that he had been excluded from "*Church of England* Pulpits. . . . for the trifling Cause of accusing the Clergy, openly and avowedly accusing them in general, for Apostates from Christianity, and ignorant of it as *Mahomet;*—for blind Guides, false Teachers, and leading the People to the Gates of Hell."[87]

But Alexander Garden chose to give Whitefield yet another reason to cry out persecution. And just as he suspected, Whitefield reacted predictably, which infuriated the commissary nevertheless. In recounting their posttrial meeting of July 19, Garden noted that he made it a point to tell Whitefield that he particularly "objected . . . that his *Behaviour,* ever since he had been cited to appear before me, had been very *base* and insidious, in *haranguing* the Populace every Day, to *excite their Passions* against me as a *Persecutor.*" Arousing people's emotions to awaken them to a sense of sin was one thing, but stirring passion so they might cry out persecution against the commissary was quite another, as his personal authority stood publicly challenged.[88] This challenge had been building privately for some time, of course, and it was played out most openly and perhaps most dramatically in the St. Philip's court proceedings. For his part Garden sought to meet it with a challenge of his own, which ultimately played into Whitefield's hands. The day before he officially cited the renegade cleric to appear in court, he preached a sermon on justification in preparation for the sacrament, which, according to Garden, was "contained Word for Word in the Third of the Six Letters." According to Whitefield, the commissary "preach[ed] as virulent, unorthodox, and inconsistent a discourse as ever I heard in my life." "His heart seemed full of choler and resentment; and, out of the abundance thereof, he poured forth so many bitter words against the Methodists (as he called them) in general and me in particular, that several, who intended to receive the Sacrament at his hands, withdrew." When the commissary sent Whitefield a message indicating that he too should abstain from the sacrament until the two of them had had a chance to meet (apparently to discuss the pending citation), Whitefield reveled in the appearance of persecution. He did the same the following Sunday when Garden preached his infamous sermon, *Take Heed How Ye Hear.* "I think, if ever, then was the time that all manner of evil was spoken against me falsely for Christ's sake," Whitefield wrote, explaining that "the Commissary seemed to ransack church history for instances of enthusiasm and abused grace [and] drew a parallel between me and all the Oliverians, Ranters, Quakers, and French Prophets, till he came down to a family of Dutarts, who lived, not many years ago, in South Carolina, and were guilty of the most notorious incests and murders." Comparing Garden to "the persecutor Saul," Whitefield cited this sermon to support his recusation plea, representing it in such a way that the commissary was later forced to print it in his own defense.[89]

Given their personal animus, it is somewhat surprising that these two men met following Whitefield's trial. However, it is not surprising that they "parted" after their walk together. Whitefield proclaimed Garden "*an unregenerate man*" and began encouraging his own followers to boycott worship services at St. Philip's, "since the Gospel was not preached in the church." His public preachings became intensely personal and abusive, even violent, so much so that "he sometimes feared" that the crowds "would be too hot against the Commissary." Whitefield claimed that at one point he "endeavoured to stop their resentment, as much as possible." Garden claimed that he behaved in this respect "just as *Mark Anthony* behaved towards the Conspirators, in the Case of *Julius Caesar.*" He continued to preach against the revivalist and, according to Whitefield, "condemned all that followed me, and gave *all* hopes of Heaven who adhered to him and the Church."[90]

As Whitefield prepared to leave Charleston then, the Great Awakening grew in both intensity and strength, reaching fuller development. "Numbers are seeking after Jesus," Whitefield wrote after preaching his farewell sermon; "the fields here . . . are white, ready to harvest." Traveling to Ashley Ferry, he made his way to Pon Pon, proceeding with his inland preaching tour as he had planned to do before his trial. At Pon Pon, Whitefield was hosted again by Thomas Buer, an elder in the Bethel Presbyterian Church. Whitefield also met with "two Scots' Presbyterian ministers," Hugh Stewart and Archibald Stobo, as well as with Thomas Thompson, rector of St. Bartholomew's Parish, and then he delivered a shade-tree sermon around noon. Whitefield subsequently headed back to Georgia, stopping to preach at Huspah Chapel as well as St. Helena's. On the former occasion he noted that "several followed hoping I would preach again in the evening," a sentiment shared by a great number of men and women living in the Lower South.[91]

Whitefield spent most of the next four weeks in Savannah, where South Carolinians were continually drawn to hear him throughout the year, particularly from adjacent communities. In mid-August, for example, one of Lewis Jones's parishioners traveled to the city after having been awakened during the Whitefield's second visit to Port Royal. Upon hearing a particularly stirring sermon, she began "confessing her sins and crying out, 'What shall I do to be saved?'" Earlier in the month other St. Helena's parishioners had had similar experiences. On August 3 Jones arrived with his wife and several other members of his congregation, including Jonathan Bryan and Stephen Bull. The charismatic revivalist lay ill in bed, but when he learned that the group had come with the expectation of hearing him preach, he promised them he would try. While Jones read from the prayer book, Whitefield said he became so sick that he asked William Tilly, a Baptist minister visiting from Euhaw, South Carolina, to preach in his stead. When Tilly declined, Whitefield commenced praying. Suddenly Bull "dropped down, as though shot with a gun" and after a few minutes "got up, and sat attentively to hear the sermon." "The influence spread," Whitefield wrote, so that the "greatest part of the congregation were under great concern." Indeed when Whitefield called on his visitors the next day, he found Bryan laboring "under . . . strong convictions of sin," his wife in tears, and her brother, Stephen Bull, "groaning in bitterness of soul."[92]

These dramatic scenes were repeated time and again in the year 1740. In the South Carolina lowcountry they were repeated quite vividly when Whitefield passed through the colony on his way to preach in New England. Landing at Charleston on August 22, Whitefield began his fourth visit to the city, which was similar in duration to his first visit in January, as it lasted just three days, but there were important differences that separated the two visits. In August the crowds who assembled to hear the young preacher were much larger, and Whitefield said that he preached "with greater success" than ever before. "I scarce know the time, wherein I did not see a considerable melting in some part of the congregation, and often it spreads over the whole of it," he wrote. Carried away by spiritual yearning, some of the awakened "were esteemed mad by their relations." Whitefield described how one guilt-stricken woman was turned out by her family. He wrote about another seeker who "in an extraordinary manner . . . burnt near forty pounds' worth of books written by such authors as Chubb, Foster, etc." News of the book-burning episode spread quickly throughout the Atlantic world, and Whitefield clearly recognized the importance of such newsworthy events. In less than two weeks the *South Carolina Gazette* carried a list of the revivalist's recommended readings, which included works by Ebenezer and John Erskine, Gilbert Tennent, and Jacob Boehm.[93]

By August, moreover, the party line separating pro- and anti-revivalist factions had hardened considerably. At the same time new religious practices were arising that would help solidify and expand the Great Awakening. With several other Anglicans opposed to Alexander Garden's preaching, for instance, Whitefield began worshiping in Charleston's dissenting churches, thrice administering the sacrament in a private house. "What was best," he wrote of one these sacramental occasions, "Baptists, Church folks, and Presbyterians, all joined together, and received according to the Church of England, except two, who desired to have it sitting."[94] Meanwhile, the newspaper controversy that started at the beginning of the year continued to rage, growing ever more participatory and antagonistic. One Anglican correspondent wrote on the question of denominational allegiance, revealing something of the nature of the controversy as well as the complexity of the factional conflict involving George Whitefield and the First Great Awakening:

> It greatly misbecomes such a Profession and Character to countenance and encourage a Person, by attending his irregular Motions. I am sensible the Reasons here offered affect me only as a Member of the Church of England, and one who thinks himself happy in continuing so. But such Reasons will be so far from discouraging those of a different Way of thinking, that they

have gained him the Bulk of the Hearers, and if I mistake not, will continue to do so. All who are not steady Members of that Church upon sound Reasons, and Christian Principles, all who dissent from or oppose it, will for those very Reasons hear and encourage him.[95]

As such contrasted ways of thinking continued to develop, the religious struggle in the South Carolina lowcountry grew and intensified, so much so that it attracted the attention of religious leaders throughout the whole of colonial British America.

In August, for example, Alexander Garden brought out his *Six letters to the Rev. Mr. George Whitefield,* prompting Andrew Croswell, a radical New Light pastor in Groton, Connecticut, to issue an immediate reply, which he completed by mid-December. In *An Answer to the Rev. Mr. Garden's Three First Letters to the Rev. Mr. Whitefield. With an Appendix Concerning Mr. Garden's Treatment of Mr. Whitefield, & c.* (Boston, 1741), Croswell set out to refute Garden's contention that Whitefield was guilty of contradicting himself in his sermon entitled *What think ye of Christ,* asserting that Whitefield held that faith and justification were coexistent, not that the former must precede the latter. At the same time Croswell sought to show that a majority of the Anglican clergy "had run away from their own Articles, leaving them to the Dissenters to keep for them: And more particularly that of *Justification by Faith only,* crying up *dead Works* in Lieu of it." In this way he made the debate a contest between Anglicans and dissenters, revealing, as William Howland Kenney III has pointed out, "the satisfaction which colonial dissenters took in Whitefield's battles with the Anglican hierarchy." Like Whitefield, Croswell contended that the Anglican clergy had generally "turn'd their Backs upon their own Articles, and [had] embrac'd, and propagated the Errors of *Arminius,*" with only a few Anglican ministers actually adhering to "the Doctrines of the Reformation." Furthermore, he said, "ministers of a worldly Spirit, have in all Ages affected worldly *Dominion* and *Authority,*" which "rais'd their Pride, and made them Worldly, nourished their spiteful Passions, ruined their humble Character; and given them a dreadful Scope to wreak their Malice and Revenge, on those beneath them." Such was the case with Alexander Garden, Croswell wrote. Indeed, because he was born of the flesh and not of the spirit, and because he was a clergyman "*invested with worldly Dominion and Authority,*" and because Whitefield adhered to "the Holy Scriptures, as well as the Articles and Homilies of the Church of England, in the great Point of Justification by Faith in Christ," the Carolina commissary "Persecuted *Mr. Whitefield* . . . as *Ishmael* Persecuted *Isaac.*"[96]

Just as the Great Awakening in the South Carolina lowcountry sparked bitter controversy and division, so the outpouring inspired new religious activities, provided new opportunities for cross-confessional cooperation, and gave rise to new institutions that helped lay out the terms by which enslaved Africans and African Americans would turn to Christianity in subsequent decades. In August Whitefield took pains to note that South Carolina Protestants of many denominational backgrounds were joining together to receive the sacrament. Also in August, several New Light ministers began participating in a Wednesday-evening lecture series set up for the newly awakened, which was initiated at Whitefield's suggestion. In a letter to Boston's William Cooper, for instance, Josiah Smith reported on the success of Whiteifeld's ministry in Charleston and noted that "the *Baptist Ministers* have joined *us* in a stated Weekly Lecture, to which the People shew a surprising Disposition and Affection; and I sometimes shed Tears of Joy in my Retirements." Cooper in turn wrote a preface to the first lecture, Isaac Chanler's *New Converts Exhorted to Cleave to the Lord* (Boston, 1740), which Smith sent along for publication. In it Cooper celebrated the "spiritual evangelical Truths" that Chanler espoused and recommended the sermon "to all such as have *tasted that the Lord is gracious,* & desire *Establishment in Grace.*" Chief among these spiritual truths was Chanler's exhortation to "write after the bright and fair Copy" of George Whitefield, "both in Regard of *Soundness* in the Faith, and *Holiness* of *Life.*" "Let our Love like his be *catholick,*" Chanler preached, "breathing in a *free* and *open Air,* abstracted from all *Bigotry* and *party Zeal,* loving the Image of GOD on whomsoever we may see it impressed [among] all the regenerate Sons and Daughters of GOD, howsoever they may be distinguished by different Denominations among Men."

Cooper was overjoyed by the "successful Progress of the Gospel of CHRIST... and its saving Efficacy on the Hearts of Men," and he held up Chanler's sermon as an example of an emergent ecumenical evangelicalism in the Atlantic Protestant world. "The Increase of *the Household of Faith* is acceptable to all that already belong to it," he wrote, "And how much is their divine Master honour'd and pleas'd, when the *Members* of this his Family live united in the Bonds of Love and Charity; and, if they can't be one in Judgment in every *lesser Matter,* are yet one in Disposition and Affection, in Aim and Design.—More especially is the Unity of *Ministers* the Beauty and Strength of the *Church.*" Chanler in turn held up George Whitefield as "a *sincere, true,* and *faithful* Servant of the living God, sent forth to preach the everlasting Gospel to poor Sinners." Not only was he "giving new Life to Religion in so many Parts of the World, both in Europe and America," he was promoting cooperation and unity among Protestant evangelicals. In fact, Chanler pointed out again and again that it was by Whitefield's "pious Advice, That a Weekly Lecture shoul'd be set up, and carried on in a united Manner, by several dissenting Ministers of different Denominations," which to him was prima facie testimony of Whitefield's spiritual commitment to primitive Christianity and the forming of the church universal. That Chanler preached this unique catholic quality in religious matters was highly significant, especially because his sermon was intended "for the Benefit of young Converts, newly inlisted into the LORD's Service."[97]

One obvious reason why Chanler's preaching was significant was that some of the new converts he spoke to were beginning to respond to Whitefield's exhortations regarding slave instruction. Near the end of his July visit Whitefield noted that African and African American slaves often attended his sermons, adding that "many of the owners, who have been awakened, have resolved to teach them Christianity." Whitefield also noted that he hoped to institutionalize slave instruction. "Had I time and proper schoolmasters," he wrote, "I might immediately erect a negro school in South Carolina, as well as in Pennsylvania." After discussing his intentions with several slave owners, the Bryan family committed themselves to the idea. In late August, Catherine Bryan and her brother-in-law Jonathan, now "much established" in God's grace, traveled to Charleston to report the news to Whitefield, informing him that they had already made arrangements to employ a teacher for a plantation school.[98]

Like the Bryans, hundreds of men and women flocked to see and hear George Whitefield in Charleston before he left South Carolina in August, knowing he would "be absent from them for a long season." When he preached his farewell sermon at the Independent Church, a great crowd gathered: "it was supposed, that not less than four thousand were in and about the meeting-house," Whitefield said. Whatever the precise number, here and in subsequent sermons Whitefield spoke more and more in terms of a new evangelical crusade, encouraging the awakened to "take up their daily crosses, if they would follow Jesus Christ." For by late August Whitefield was not simply preaching as he had preached in January or March—although he continued to do just that—but rather as he had preached near the end of July, when he first began boasting of "the conversion of many souls."[99]

5

The Kingdom of Heaven

Continuing the Great Awakening Tradition

I was led by extraordinary impressions to compute the Numbers of Daniel and John, who are both beloved prophets, and the Counterparts to each other: They contain the beginning and end of all the great confusion, which sin has brought in the works of ALEIM JEHOVAH.

Richard Clarke, *The Prophetic Numbers of Daniel and John Calculated: In Order to Show the Time, when the Day of Judgment . . . is to be Expected* (1759)

In the mid-1750s some of South Carolina's wealthiest and most influential planters, merchants, and professionals joined together to form a religious and literary society in Charleston. They met regularly with several of the city's clerics, including Richard Clarke, rector of St. Philip's Church, and William Hutson, pastor of the Independent Meeting House.[1] One can only imagine what the group talked about, or whether their discussions gave any final shape to the enthusiastic convictions of Richard Clarke, who in early 1759 articulated a stirring apocalyptic prediction. In a report to the Board of Trade dated the first day of September of that same year, Governor William Henry Lyttelton described what happened: "In the month of February last the Reverend Mr. Clarke . . . preached some sermons in which he asserted that the world wou'd very soon be at an end, and that in this month of September some great calamity wou'd befall this province." Lyttelton continued: "At length this enthusiasm rose to such a height that he let his beard grow and ran about the streets crying, Repent, Repent for the Kingdom of Heaven is at hand, but on the 25th of March he resigned his Benefice and embarked for England."[2]

Today such apocalyptic preaching might seem rather bizarre, but for a few tense months in the year 1759 many South Carolinians seriously wondered whether Clarke had gotten it right—whether a cataclysmic event such as a colony-wide slave rebellion would usher in Christ's return to earth.[3] And though his initial prediction missed the mark, Clarke continued to prophecy and people everywhere in the Atlantic Protestant world continued to pay close attention to his millennial speculations. What is more, Clarke was so highly regarded in South Carolina that several influential colonists sent their children to a school he opened outside of London. Among them were such well-known social figures as Henry Laurens and Benjamin Smith, two of the constituent members of the religious club in Charleston.[4]

In many ways the history of Richard Clarke's ministry at St. Philip's from 1753 to 1759 reflected the tenor of religious revivalism in the South Carolina lowcountry from 1740 through the outbreak of the Seven Years' War, when Protestant evangelicalism came to predominate in a majority of congregations in the colony. A brilliant student of the great Anglican theologian William Law (1686–1761), Clarke steeped himself in cabalistic mysticism, feeling, like Law, that the Church of England had grown spiritually barren. As rector of St. Philip's, he became well known by contemporaries for his piety and fervor as much as for his "great learning," and his friendship with dissenters and evangelical clergy caused him to be respected by Anglicans and nonconformists alike. He was a strong supporter of religious revivalism in the Church of England, and during his six-year pastorate at St. Philip's many men and women flocked to hear his eloquent preaching.[5] Around the same time Clarke "declared in one of his Sermons, 'that he was directed by the Spirit of God, to acquaint Mankind, that the Day of Judgement was to happen in less than five Years,'" Charles Martin reported to SPG officials from St. Andrew's Parish that Clarke's "abilities as a Divine were so great, and his piety so strict, that he gained over many to the Church of England, and even induced many averse to Religion in general to become hearty espousers of it."[6] Joining with Protestant dissenters, Clarke testified against ostentatious displays of wealth as well as against the polite diversions of South Carolina's planter-merchant aristocracy, building upon a common theme of evangelical sermons in the 1740s and 1750s. He also began a weekday lecture series for his followers and encouraged cross-confessional cooperation and interchange.

Oliver Hart, who succeeded to the pastoral charge of Charleston's First Baptist Church in 1749, was one contemporary who remarked on Clarke's "Catholic Spirit." Like Clarke, Hart lamented the "little outward Differences" that prevented Protestants from realizing "a greater Harmony between persons of all persuasions," and he worked together with other evangelical clergy to facilitate ecumenical unity and cooperative evangelism in the spirit of the Great Awakening. Also like Clarke, Hart witnessed a revival in his church in the mid-1750s, raising the possibility of yet another great outburst of emotional religion and, perhaps, the beginning of the millennium. Indeed the interdenominational harmony that came to prevail as well as the awakenings occurring across the Atlantic sphere suggested to many Carolinians that the Kingdom of Heaven might be close at hand. So too did the outbreak of war with Catholic France, which helped open up "a vision of prophesy" for Clarke and resulted in the publication of his *The Prophetic Numbers of Daniel and John Calculated* in 1759. Laboring under "extraordinary impressions," Clarke predicted that Christ's Second Coming would occur between 1758 and 1765, giving his preachings an entirely new sense of urgency.[7]

Like other Americans, both lay and clerical, many eighteenth-century South Carolinians thought that they were living near the advent of the millennial age. In 1724 John Dutartre and members of his household committed murder because they thought that God was preparing to destroy humankind, having been influenced by London's French Prophets who preached the end of the world. Five years later Hugh Fisher interpreted the Presbyterian subscription controversy as a token of the last days. Millennialist rhetoric flourished during periods of crisis in colonial British American society, with fires, epidemics, and other dramatic episodes conjuring up visions of Christ's Second Coming and his thousand-year reign on earth. The Great Awakening nurtured these visionary speculations. Although he pretended "to no Spirit of *Prophecy*," Josiah Smith ventured to "make some humble and faint Conjectures at the Times" in early 1740. In fact, he cast the conclusion of his best-known sermon, *The Character, Preaching, & c. of the Reverend Mr. Geo. Whitefield*, in a millennialist framework, attempting to divine the sacred meaning of God's raising up young revival preachers such as Whitefield to revive the "primitive *Spirit* of Christianity" throughout the Atlantic world. To Smith it looked "as if some happy Period were opening, to bless the World with *another* Reformation." "Some great Things seem to be upon the anvil," he exclaimed, "some big Prophecy *at the Birth:* God give it Strength to bring forth!"[8]

Biblical prophecies were "usually too dark and Mystic to be fully understood," of course, and scriptural seals were "seldom broken, until the several Periods of Accomplishment." Thus, Smith said, the passage of time was "the best and surest expositor." Yet seers who possessed special knowledge and skill could decipher God's will and render oracular pronouncements. From his inspired calculations, for example, Richard Clarke discerned that sacred writings foretold the Protestant Reformation with chilling accuracy. By his reckoning it was set to unfold in 1522, "nearly the time" it did. But this was "only the *opening* or partial *redemption* of the Church," Clarke emphasized. Dark, mystical references to much greater promises were scattered throughout the Bible.[9]

That the Great Awakening presaged a second, more generalized reformation preparatory to the messianic age was a conviction shared by many eighteenth-century evangelical Christians. It informed their efforts to promote revivalism throughout the 1740s and 1750s and frequently found expression in their sermons. When George Whitefield returned to the South Carolina lowcountry in early December 1740 he discovered that a catastrophic fire had broken out in Charleston on November 18, destroying more than three hundred houses and other buildings and consuming an estimated £250,000 in merchandise. Considering the fire against the backdrop of the Stono Rebellion and outbreaks of smallpox and yellow fever in 1738 and 1739, he used the occasion to build on one of the major themes of his previous sermons, noting in his journal that he cataloged the sins of the inhabitants and explained how these sins provoked God to rain down his fire among them. In addition he noted that he made "an application suitable" to the great disaster in his pulpit preachings, urging his listeners to righteousness. Josiah Smith's *The Burning of Sodom* (Boston, 1741) sheds light on the nature of Whitefield's application, as it was delivered around the same time and in a rather similar spirit.[10]

Composing his sermon "amidst a thousand Confusions, and Strifes of Passion," Smith chose, like Whitefield, to focus mostly on the moral causes of the fire, drawing from the same biblical texts and endeavoring to show why God pointed his vengeful finger at Charleston (pride, wantonness, idleness, lust). Also like Whitefield, in his sermon Smith at base called for repentance: "it becomes us now to put on *Sack-Cloth,*" he said. Nevertheless, Smith evoked visions of the millennium throughout *The Burning of Sodom,* and in the conclusion of his sermon he even suggested that the Kingdom of Heaven was near. In building his main thesis Smith emphasized not only that the burning of Sodom and Gomorrah represented the "strongest *Image* of the *last inextinguishable Fire,* of any on the Records of past Ages," but also that it was set forth as an example of the Last Judgment for subsequent generations—particularly his own stiff-necked generation. Similarly, Smith wrote that the Charleston fire "represented something of *the Terrible Day of the Lord,* which shall burn as an Oven." Further, he warned that Sodom's destruction came suddenly and unexpectedly, just as the late fire, and that Christ would "*come in a Day and Hour, when we think not.*"[11]

It was to this last point that Smith turned in the final section of *The Burning of Sodom,* as he made an explicit attempt to locate the Charleston fire in sacred time. Lowcountry South Carolinians had been repeatedly warned away from worldliness and religious complacency, he instructed, "but they said with the *modern Scoffers:* where is *Promise of his Coming?*" So it was when God breathed out his fire and destroyed the colony's capital, Smith preached—and "so shall the coming of the *Son of Man* be." Urging holiness, he announced that all ought to be "*looking for and hasting unto the Coming of the Day of God.*" For Charleston's burning was not simply another divine warning to repent. It provided ostensive evidence of the approaching messianic age, "when *the great Day of the Wrath of the Lamb is come,* and not a *Town,* a *Province,* a *Nation,* but the *whole World,* shall be *burnt up*—when every Eye shall behold CHRIST coming with *Clouds and Flames*, and every Tongue, that would not *confess* him, shall wail because of him!"[12] In embracing a prophetic spirit Smith picked up on and fleshed out a theme he and other revival ministers preached throughout 1740 when they bore public testimony against sinfulness. Comparing himself to Lot, who foretold Sodom's destruction "yet seem'd . . . as one that mock'd," Smith dwelled on Old Testament prophets who decried wickedness and evildoing just as he had and said that he had long expected a great calamity to befall the colony. Moreover, he noted that the evening assemblies Whitefield and his supporters condemned were scheduled to begin on November 18—"But Heaven beheld the Impiety, and spoke in Fire and Thunder against them, because the Warnings of GOD's Ministers were ineffectual." Finally, Smith enthusiastically boasted, "Now we know that a Prophet has been among Us: One, that would not, through servile Fear, be drawn into a Conformity to the Vices of the Age, to countenance them; but had Zeal and Courage enough to strike at the Root of our Pride, and to pronounce the Judgments of Heaven upon it."[13]

Here Smith spoke to one of the most important controversies of the Great Awakening. Too many ministers failed to "*set up a Standard*" in their own lives and sanctioned provincial vices by refusing to "*lift up their Voices against them like a Trumpet.*" Some were simply "too supine and indolent," others just "too cowardly and timorous," even those of exemplary character, and Smith warned against their "censorious *mistaken Comments* upon this fiery Judgment." With George Whitefield's assistance, Hugh Bryan took such criticism of the ministry considerably further. On November 20 he wrote an incendiary letter charging unregenerate ministers with gross negligence and sent the letter to his brother Jonathan. Jonathan asked Whitefield to revise his brother's letter for publication when he traveled to Georgia to invite the revivalist to preach at Port Royal. Intending to set sail for England from Charleston in early 1741, Whitefield accepted Bryan's invitation, readily agreeing "to correct . . . and make some alterations" to Hugh's letter, which was written in bold millennialist language.[14]

As he had the previous year, Whitefield arrived in the South Carolina lowcountry on New Year's Day, landing at Port Royal in the company of Jonathan Bryan and few other impassioned followers. In the afternoon he preached at Jonathan Bryan's house to several neighbors, and that evening Hugh Bryan arrived to meet with Whitefield. Less than one week later Hugh Bryan's letter was published in a special postscript to the *South Carolina Gazette* (January 8), only five days after Whitefield and the Bryan brothers had made their way to Charleston. In his printed letter Hugh Bryan declared that those "who do the Work of the Lord negligently, and speak leasingly [falsehood], and cry *Peace, Peace, when there is no Peace*" were guilty of "deceiving precious Souls and causing them to sleep in their Sins to Damnation." "Many, too many such are crept into Christ's visible

Church," he said, explaining why so many colonial men and women failed "to seek unto the Hand that hath smitten us," why more had not experienced faith after God had scourged them "by Drought; by repeated Diseases . . . ; by Insurrections of our Slaves, and lately by Battling shamefully our Enterprize against our Enemy." Bryan spoke in terms of both the Old Testament book of Daniel and the New Testament book of Revelation. He prayed that the Charleston fire might finally awaken lowcountry Carolinians to a sense of their own sinfulness as God intended, but he expressed grave doubts about whether the fire would have its intended effect. "How many poor careless souls have we in every Parish that stand in Need of being informed of their Danger, and of the absolute Necessity of being born again of God, and having Christ's personal Righteousness imputed to them, before they can have any well-grounded Hope of being finally saved! How many within a few Miles of their Teachers die in their Sins, without being warned or exhorted to come to CHRIST by Faith!" Over and over Bryan emphasized that the "Blood of such will be required at their Teacher's Hands." He also emphasized that their unrighteousness would "eat them as doth Fire, at the glorious Appearance of our Lord, when he shall call them to an Account!"[15]

Bryan fully expected God to pour out "more terrible Vials of his Wrath" if the colonists did not repent, which would soon lead him to make "sundry enthusiastic Prophesies of the Destruction of Charles-Town, and the Deliverance of the Negroes from their Servitude."[16] In the meantime he had more immediate concerns. Just after his letter appeared in the *South Carolina Gazette*, Bryan, Whitefield, and Peter Timothy were arrested on charges of libeling the Church of England. While Bryan's printed letter was carefully couched in fairly general terms, it was clear that the accusations were aimed at the Anglican clergy. At one point Bryan even implied that parish priests "break their Cannons daily." Alexander Garden read Bryan's printed letter as an effort to "slander and defame the Clergy of this Province, and thereby prejudice their People against them, and defeat their Labours in their respective Parishes." He told the bishop of London that "the Libel is chiefly aimed at the Clergy of this Province, & more particularly at me," suggesting that the commissary was responsible for instigating the legal action that resulted in the arrests. For his part Whitefield openly admitted that he corrected the letter for press. Like Hugh Bryan and Peter Timothy, he was promptly bound over for trial.[17]

Although nothing ever came of the charges, Whitefield made the most of his arrest. "My soul rejoices in it," he wrote after posting bail; "I think this may be called persecution." As he had after his trial the previous July, Whitefield incorporated this theme into his sermons, fanning the flames of anti-Anglican sentiment by directing his message "to *men in authority*" and emphasizing the "heinous sin of *abusing the power* which God had put into their hands." Preaching twice each day, Whitefield, the *South Carolina Gazette* reported, delivered twenty-two sermons by January 15, the day before he boarded the *Minerva* in order to set sail for England. In addition the newspaper reported that the "congregations were numerous" during this two week- period and noted that the charismatic preacher "likewise exhorted great Companies of People almost every Night at his Lodgings." Also important, Whitefield continued to preach while waiting for his ship to set sail. "The winds being contrary, many friends came from Charleston," he wrote, for example, on January 18; "I preached, and the Lord was with me."[18]

George Whitefield's preaching tour left colonial South Carolina ablaze in a spirit of revivalism. The transatlantic itinerant made five more trips to America (1744–1748, 1751–1752, 1754–1755, 1763–1765, and 1769–1770) and, following his departure in January 1741, he visited the Carolina colony on several different occasions during the middle decades of the eighteenth century. In advance of those visits the Great Awakening continued to reverberate throughout the lowcountry, shaking the foundations of the Church of England and revitalizing the area's dissenting Protestant majority. As revival ministers attempted to solidify and expand their base of religious support, Alexander Garden made every effort to "to apprize well measuring People of the real Intention of these Enthusiasts." After Hugh Bryan published his thinly veiled attack on the Anglican clergy, the commissary suggested (among other things) that Whitefield's followers preached "a *Community of Goods,* as was practiced by the *Primitive Christians.*" He also maintained that evangelicals were conspiring to disestablish the state church, insinuating that they believed it to be "the Scarlet Whore, prophesied of in the Revelations; and there will be no true Christianity as long as that Church subsists."[19] Josiah Smith and Isaac Chanler joined the debate over religious enthusiasm, defending the emotional experiences of the awakened against the commissary's charges of Antinomian radicalism. Too, they carried forth the challenge to the established church, albeit more cautiously than Bryan.

No sooner had Garden's charges appeared in the *South Carolina Gazette* than revival propagandists offered new evidence in support of Whitefield and the Great Awakening. In late January, Josiah Smith published extracts from several personal letters he had recently received from his colleagues in New England. The extracts were carefully chosen for publication in an effort to blunt the force of Garden's charges as well as to marginalize his opposition. One of Smith's correspondents wrote that Whitefield enjoyed support among a broad range of men and women in New England society, "old and young, high and low." These included Massachusetts's governor, who accorded Whitefield "the highest Respects; Carried him in his Coach from Place to Place; [and] could not help following him Fifty Miles out of Town." "*His own received him not,*" one of Smith's correspondents said, referring to the Anglican clergy. Another correspondent reported on "the good Effects of his preaching"; yet another wrote that opposition to Whitefield was limited to a "small Set of Gentlemen." Knowing full well of Garden's outspoken opposition against Whitefield and the Great Awakening, this last writer maintained that "whoever goes to lessen Mr. *Whitefield's* Reputation, is in Danger of *losing* his own." Skillfully using the extracts, then, Smith made an obvious attempt not only to answer but also to marginalize the commissary's antirevivalist strictures, as well as to refute his oft-repeated charges that the spiritually awakened threatened to turn the world upside down (a charge that had been leveled against Smith in the Presbyterian subscription controversy in the late 1720s and early 1730s).[20]

Garden responded with his own New England letter extracts, though he did so anonymously, exposing himself to charges that he manufactured the extracts merely to attack "the greatest Zealot among the *Whitefieldeans,*" Josiah Smith. "But alas! Sir," one of Garden's correspondents reported from Boston in the spring of 1741, "a fanatick Turn of Mind over sets all." Whitefield had "sowed *Discord* and *Madness* and *Fury,*" he said, "strip'd us of all Peace and Order," and "left us a visionary extatick Religion, void of all good Principles." Garden's correspondents outdid themselves in describing the frenzy. Neither the severest winter in memory nor the Charleston fire the previous November were "half so bad as [the] sectarian enthusiastic Madness" that gripped New England, one correspondent wrote in a letter dated April 15. People everywhere were "terrified, bewilder'd, distracted," the Anglican clergy "*cursed, damned, double-damned, the Generality stiled unregenerate, proud, Hypocrites, rotten-hearted, old Sinners, and Devils, and worse than Devils.*" Awakening ministers and converts threatened to "fill the Country up with *Antinomian* Reveries," he warned, echoing Garden's own expressions earlier in the year.[21]

Writing under the pseudonym Philalethes, Smith was quick to respond to these "*defamatory* Extracts," questioning their authenticity and ascribing their production "to a certain ECCLESIASTICK among us." He particularly objected to the suggestion that revival ministers criminally excited human passions and that the newborn were dangerous Bedlamite radicals, a recurrent theme of the Garden's ministerial informants. The Great Awakening was "*Musick* in the Ear of every sincere Minister of *Jesus Christ,*" Smith said, continuing to press the charge against unregenerate clergymen, especially including those with an "establish'd Salary."[22] Isaac Chanler, styling himself "ZEALOT THE SECOND," built upon this charge. Significantly, he suggested that Garden used his government salary "to support Calumny" in publishing the antirevivalist letter extracts. More generally, all of his publications cost the public "a good round Fee."[23]

As the newspaper controversy raged in the spring and summer of 1741, Chanler emerged as the commissary's main antagonist, and in a long vituperative postscript in the *South Carolina Gazette* he heaped abuse on his adversary. Garden's reputation did "not grow quite so fast as his *Belly,*" he wrote, "but dwindles every Day in the Esteem of all . . . of a serious and *truly* religious Character." His merit now lay "chiefly in the *Glare* of his *Dress,*" while his continuing opposition to the Great Awakening indicated that he was a man "who *can't* understand the Things of the *Spirit of God,*" namely the "*spiritual of new-Birth.*" Chanler dilated upon this indictment to explain why Garden opposed and vilified the extraordinary events occurring throughout the Atlantic Protestant world, why he could "be found to fight against God." Meanwhile the commissary busied himself writing a lengthy reply.[24]

Throughout these important debates Garden and his opponents exhibited contrasting views in their basic approaches to the acquisition of saving knowledge and, in discussing religious enthusiasm and the spiritual new birth, they revealed that they held fundamentally differing perspectives on ethical matters. Garden believed that spiritual insight came through revelation and rational reflection. He accused revivalists of shamelessly exciting perverse emotions, which prevented evangelical converts from using reason to control their wills. His view had clear moral implications. Smith and Chanler, in contrast, rejected the notion that spiritual insight simply derived from human reason. For them the essential nature of saving knowledge arose from the experience of conversion, as did virtuous dispositions of character. Smith elaborated on this point at slightly greater length in a sermon entitled *A Zeal of* GOD *Encourag'd and Guarded* (Boston, 1745), but even in the newspaper controversies of 1741 pro- and anti-revivalists debated it. For example, one of Garden's Boston correspondents reported that emotionally stirred "Boys and Girls from 6 Years and upwards take upon them to meet together for religious Exercises, and to go the Rounds, praying, conferring and exhorting," sparking an interesting exchange over such youths.[25]

Smith began the exchange. "What serious consistent *Clergyman,* who has any Reverence for a Gown or Band, and would preserve the Honours of the *Priesthood,*" he asked, "could represent Children[']s meeting together for religious Exercises, Prayer and pious Conferences . . . as a *criminal* Thing, of ill Report, and dangerous Consequence?" As a rationalist, Garden shot right back, questioning "what religious Exercises, what Prayers, and above all what *pious Conferences,* which must be the Result of, and flow from Reason and reflection cou'd such Children possibly be capable of?"[26] Chanler then inquired, "But are Children of these Years without Reflection?" Further, he asked, "may they not, under the Influences of the blessed Spirit confer upon Religion as well as any Thing else, tho' not with all the Accuracy and Exactness of riper Years?"[27] Insisting that their saving knowledge endowed them with a virtuous disposition, Chanler set Garden to wondering how anyone could "with Patience endure to hear their Teachers and Guides talk against Reason; and not only so, but they pay them a greater Submission and Veneration for it." "One would think this but an odd Way to gain

Authority over the Minds of Men," he continued (quoting Locke on enthusiasm and Archbishop Tillotson), "but some skillful and designing Men have found by Experience, that it is a very good Way to recommend them to the Ignorant, as Nurses use to endear themselves to Children, by perpetual Noise and Nonsense."[28]

A similar exchange involved another antirevivalist charge that evangelical "women forgot the Tenderness and Delicy of their Sex" and acted immorally.[29] At one point Garden claimed that women's evangelical zeal turned them "into *great Sluts*" and sent them to "worship before the *Deity* in Garbs, they ought to be asham'd to pay a common Visit in to their Fellow Mortals." Chanler inveighed against this attempt to "asperse the Daughters of our *Zion*, who have been taught not to place Religion in *Ornaments, Chains, Bracelets, Ear rings,* and many *changeable Suits of Apparel;* the outward adorning of *platting* the Hair and wearing of Gold." In doing so he revealed a quite distinctive perspective.

> Forasmuch as we are the Off spring of God, we ought not to think that the God head is like unto Gold or Silver or Stone graven by Art or Man's Device, or is pleas'd with these. No: God is a *Spirit,* and seeketh such to worship him, as worship in *Spirit* and *Truth.* Let Women be but cloath'd with *Humility,* with the Ornament of a *meek* and *quiet Spirit.* This will commend them to *God* beyond all the Riches and Gaieties of Dress . . . Whatever this Writer may think, this is a better Character than to have it said of *any Lady* Together lie her Prayer-book and Paint, At once improve the Sinner and the Saint.[30]

Garden's morality assumed a social order in which women wore clothing "such as is suitable to their Circumstances, Rank, and Station." He recommended that lowcountry women consult an essay on dress in the *Ladies Library* rather than listen to the "crude and sexless Jargon" of Chanler, Smith, and other Awakening ministers, who in his view preyed upon women's "ductile and pliant Fancies." Admitting that "negligence as well as Affection in Dress is an Error," Garden said "that Virtue itself is disagreeable in a Sliven." One of his main arguments was "that Women may have as much Pride in Callcoes as in Brocade." And to him, even "to think there is any Merit in rejecting all Gaiety and Expence in Apparel is . . . dangerous."[31]

Sophia Wigington Hume (1702–1774), who embraced the Great Awakening and renounced her "splendid Apparel" during the revival, was thoroughly familiar with Garden's charges. A member of the Church of England, Hume was a fixture in Charleston's polite society before she was "born again in Christ" around the year 1741. After her conversion she moved to London and joined the Society of Friends, returning to the colony to "take up the cross" in the Quaker ministry. Shortly thereafter she published *An Exhortation to the Inhabitants of the Province of South-Carolina* (Philadelphia, 1748), in which she addressed virtually every one of antirevivalists' claims concerning women's fashion, including those advanced by Commissary Garden. "One Argument some have made Use of to support the Vanity of gay and costly Clothes," she wrote, was "that the Pride was not in the Clothes, but in the Heart." Another, Hume said, was "*that costly and splendid Apparel, &c. is necessary to make and support a proper Distinction between Persons of high and low Degree.*" To the former claim Hume responded that women were "not so ignorant, as not to be sensible that they are respected and courted according to the Appearance they make in the World." Also she eschewed any "Pride and Arrogancy of Heart" in exclaiming against gaiety of dress and maintained that both scriptural injunction and the facts of her own experience confirmed her belief that the wearing of fine clothes nourished a "proud, vain Desire" among lowcountry women. Respecting the latter claim, Hume thought the argument was especially "weak, and unworthy to be offer'd by a Christian, as I am of Opinion, every reasonable Person will grant, that Piety and Virtue (not Gold and Tinsel Ornaments) ought to distinguish and render truly honorable the higher Rank of People." Agreeing with Isaac Chanler's position, she rejected the notion that "a Person can be both a Sinner and a Saint, at the same Moment of Time."[32]

To opponents of the Great Awakening Hume stood as a prime example of the Antinomian excesses to which early American evangelicals were prone, as her emotional new birth experience "naturally led, in some Degree, to what is called Quakerism." Among the most radical and zealous of the newly awakened, Hume challenged social conventions by publicly bearing witness to the workings of God's Spirit in her soul as well as warning the colonists of the need for repentance. Her arrival in Charleston was deeply shocking to her acquaintances and friends, most notably Carolina Anglicans of high social standing. When "I beheld the Faces of many of the Inhabitants whom I have been known to, some Years," she wrote, "the Meanness of my Appearance . . . render'd me despicable in [their] Eyes." Some "not only profess'd a Dislike, but a Concern that I should appear in so contemptible a Manner, and so different from what I usually had done," she went on to say. Even more shocking was Hume's decision to enter the Quaker ministry. A woman's preaching was certainly "a novel and uncommon Occasion," and many were no doubt "induced to consider such an One under some unaccountable Delusion, or affected with religious Madness." Beyond her pioneering break with traditional gender roles, the Quakerism that Hume espoused (dramatically symbolized by her "Self-denying Life") was perhaps most shocking. She seemed to exalt religious experience above all external authority and also placed much emphasis on the establishment of the Kingdom of Heaven on earth, beseeching the colonists to "fly from the Wrath to come." Thinking that Christ's return was imminent, Hume expressed great concern for her "native Country" and an ardent sense of urgency underwrote her errand to redeem the Carolina colonists.[33]

If *An Exhortation to the Inhabitants of the Province of South-Carolina* reveals the ubiquity of millennialist propositions in eighteenth-century revival tracts, it also exposes a major source of Hume's fervor and passion. As a mark of her faith Hume felt called to embark upon a transatlantic ministry to prepare colonial South Carolina society for Christ's Second Coming, helping to explain why she "appeared thus publickly in Print." Significantly, Hume's concerns were Hugh Bryan's. Just as Hume's *Exhortation* was seen by many of her contemporaries as "the Production of a distemper'd and enthusiastick Brain," so Bryan's letter attacking the Anglican ministry was described by antirevivalists as the work of an overstimulated religious eccentric.[34] Like Hume, Bryan became increasingly engaged in religious life after his conversion. Also like Hume, he stressed the importance of postconversion behavior and was sincerely committed to reforming lowcountry society in anticipation of the millennium. Together with his brother Jonathan and several of their neighbors in St. Helena's Parish, including William Gilbert and Robert Ogle, Bryan devoted himself to converting slaves to evangelical Christianity. In August 1740 George Whitefield reported on the Bryan brothers' religious commitment, saying that "by my advice, they have resolved to begin a negro school." "A young stage player [William Hutson], who was convinced when I was at New York last, and providentially came to Georgia, when Mr. Jonathan B. was there," Whitefield continued, "is to be their first master."[35]

In mid-1741 Whitefield learned through the Atlantic communication network that there was a great religious awakening under way among the enslaved Africans and African Americans living in the Parish of St. Helena's. But as news of the religious frenzy spread, provincial authorities grew increasingly alarmed, for it appeared to many lowcountry slaveholders that William Hutson, the Bryans, and other white citizens who adopted Awakening ideals were threatening to undermine the region's racial hierarchy. Indeed the "frequent and great Assemblies of Negroes" southwest of Charleston seemed only to foment active resistance. As a result the South Carolina Commons House of Assembly began an investigation of the religious commotion in February 1742. After making their initial inquiry, the assembly concluded that, "however commendable it may be for any Master, or other Person having Care of Slaves, to instruct them in the Principle of Religion or Morality, in their own Plantations; it may prove of the most dangerous Consequence . . . if great Numbers of Negroes should be encouraged to meet together from different Plantations." They further concluded that white persons "who shall be so important as to excite, encourage or countenance them to meet and assemble, in [the] manner aforesaid, may be justly deemed guilty of a public Nuisance." As a consequence the Commons House called on Lieutenant Governor William Bull, Sr., to take action to stop the interplantation gatherings of slaves in St. Helena's. Before Governor Bull could follow through on their request, however, the assembly was presented with a "Book or Paper signed by

Hugh Bryan," which Bryan had sent to the Speaker of the House out of a "sincere Regard for [the] Country's welfare." The Grand Jury of South Carolina later described the manuscript as containing "sundry enthusiastic Prophecies of the destruction of Charles-Town, and Deliverance of the Negroes from their Servitude." Quickly realizing the "the great Danger" that might arise should these prophesies "be published amongst the People," the Commons House of Assembly immediately called for Bryan's arrest.[36]

Telling lowcountry settlers "to prepare for death and judgment," Bryan had not only warned South Carolinians against trusting in the deceptive teachings of unregenerate clergy but also that Christ's return would occur "at a time when they expect not." Following the spectacular Charleston fire, Bryan predicted that God was preparing to visit a great destruction on the land. "His Drought hath spoken; His Diseases inflicted on us . . . have spoken; the Insurrections of our Slaves have spoken; our Augustine Expedition hath spoken; the Faithful of CHRIST's Ministers have lately, in a remarkable Manner, been speaking; and the yet later dreadful Fire of Charles-Town hath spoken Terror," he explained in January 1741. Convinced that the colony would be "utterly consumed," Bryan came to understand himself more and more as God's mouthpiece, and he began prophecying and performing signs while continuing to preach to slaves. Eliza Pinckney wrote that "he came to working miracles and lived in the woods barefoot and alone for several days with his pen and Ink to write down his prophecies," saying Bryan predicted that "Charles Town and the Country as farr as Ponpon Bridge should be destroyed by fire and the sword, to be executed by the Negroes." Bryan attempted to warn local officials of his "prophetick Predictions" on several different occasions, but his dire prophesies foretelling that slaves would revolt and win their freedom were ignored. Thus he ultimately sent his journal to the Commons House of Assembly, knowing full well that he did so "at the Risque of suffering for it." At last Bryan "went with a wan[d] to divide the waters" of a river in a sensational episode that seemed only to vindicate the opinion of Alexander Garden.[37]

Bryan quickly attempted to account for his spiritual misadventure. In a letter dated March 1, 1742, he wrote "with Shame, intermix'd with Joy" to the Commons House of Assembly, explaining:

> I find that I have presumed in my Zeal for God's Glory beyond his Will, and that he has suffered me to fall into a Delusion of Satan. Particularly in adhering to the Impressions of my Mind.—Though not to my knowledge in my Reflections and other Occurrences of my Journal. This Delusion I did not discover 'till three Days past, when after many Days intimate Converse with an invisible Spirit, whose Precepts seem'd to be wise and tending to the Advancement of Religion in general, and of my own spiritual Welfare

> in particular, I found my Teacher to be a Liar, and the Father of Lies, which brought me into a Sense of my Error, and has much abased my Soul with bitter Reflections on the Dishonour I've done to God, as well as the Disquiet which I may have occasioned to my Country.

Conscious of this spiritual "Delusion" as well as "the Ill that may attend it," Bryan felt obliged to address the assembly "to prevent the Uneasiness which my Journal may create to the Government." Yet he never disclaimed the contents of his journal, as Harvey H. Jackson and other historians have observed. Rather Bryan sought in his apology to reassure colonial officials that his recent behavior in no way confirmed allegations that he was nefariously engaged in "SECRET DESIGNS" to promote a slave uprising. For example, he pointed out that in sending his journal to the assembly and in writing his letter he acted "with a conscientious Regard to discharge my Trust truly to God and my Country." Furthermore, Bryan repeatedly emphasized his patriotism, concluding his letter by writing, "I beg Leave only to add, that God's Favour is our Country's Safety, and our sincere Obedience to his Commands is our wisest Method to obtain it."[38]

A few weeks after Bryan wrote to the Commons House of Assembly, the Grand Jury of South Carolina issued a presentment against him at the general sessions court. Having considered his journal and the information that reached them from St. Helena's Parish, they found that under Bryan's influence "great Bodies of Negroes [had] assembled together, on Pretence of religious Worship, contrary to Law, and destructive to the Peace and Safety of the Inhabitants of this Province." The Grand Jury therefore recommended that the general sessions court take "effectual and speedy Measures . . . to prevent and suppress the same." In particular they recommended that Hugh and Jonathan Bryan, William Gilbert, Robert Ogle, and any other instigators of the marshaling of enslaved Africans and African Americans living in St. Helena's Parish be brought to justice. Yet no sooner had the Grand Jury issued its presentment than Joseph Moody, a deacon in Josiah Smith's church, started stirring up additional alarm by preaching to "cabals of Negroes" in Charleston, prompting Chief Justice Benjamin Whitaker to write an article on Moody's dangerous activities. Quickly placed under arrest, Moody refused to post bond and was soon brought before the Royal Council, whose members inquired if Moody knew just "how much the lives of his Majesty's subjects might be endangered if great Body's of Negroes, were encouraged, or permitted to assemble together."[39]

Against this backdrop Josiah Smith and his colleague James Parker coauthored a public letter in defense of efforts to convert slaves to evangelical Christianity, particularly efforts by those "Families . . . who sustain the same Character and Denomination with *Us*." Smith and Parker saw the first generation of colonial South Carolina evangelicalism as being imperiled by antirevivalists' protests against Hugh Bryan's visionary ecstatic experiences and at the same time perceived growing white sentiment against evangelical attempts at slave Christianization. Appearing in the April 17, 1742, issue of the *South Carolina Gazette,* Smith and Parker's letter appealed, paradoxically, to the authority of Bishop Edmund Gibson, who had written on the subject of colonial slave proselytization in an important series of pastoral letters, which were eventually assembled as *Three Addresses on the Instruction of the Negroes* (London, 1727). After noting that Bishop Gibson had lamented the lack of progress being made in Anglican proselytizing attempts among colonial slaves, Smith and Parker contended that the failure of the Anglican slave-Christianization program provided sufficient grounds to carry out new attempts at slave conversion in British America. They even went so far as to suggest that official efforts to stop "ATTEMPTS of this nature" amounted to an infringement on liberty of conscience. Not surprisingly, Alexander Garden immediately responded. In an unsigned letter published in the next issue of the *South Carolina Gazette,* he maintained that under such false pretense "every idle or designing Person that pleases, shall be at Liberty to pursue ATTEMPTS not of *this,* but *another* and most dangerous *nature;* viz. Gathering *Cabals* of *Negro's* about him... [and] filling their Heads with a Parcel of *Cant-Phrases, Trances, Dreams, Visions,* and *Revilations,* and something still *worse,* which Prudence forbids to name."[40]

With the issues of slave proselytization and religious freedom being openly debated in the public arena, and with one of the leading members of his congregation locked up in jail, and, additionally, in the wake of the St. Helena's affair, Josiah Smith preached another thundering sermon, *Jesus Persecuted in His Disciples,* which was printed in Boston three years later. Taking his text from Acts 9:4, Smith spoke on the conversion of the apostle Paul, considering the circumstances surrounding Paul's conversion and focusing on "what he was *before.*" In doing so Smith sought to explain why "Rage and Spite were levelled against the Propagation of the *Gospel.*" He also sought to demonstrate that the "Spirit of Persecution has nothing to plead in its own Defence."[41]

First, Smith said that the men and women Saul set out to persecute were neither "Enemies to *Church* or *State.*" Rather they were noble, well-intentioned Christians who were "most friendly to *Government,* and beneficial to *Society.*" Yet Saul "did not enquire ... whether they were *for* or *against* CAESAR, but [only] whether they professed *the Way,* which he then called *Heresy,*" and it was for this reason—a matter concerning individual conscience and one's "Conduct in *religious Life*"—that he sought to persecute them. In discussing the meaning of his text Smith emphasized that Saul was extraordinarily officious in his efforts, no less than contemporary authorities. He secured "a *Commission* and *Letters* from the HIGH PRIEST, and cover'd his own Spleen with a Shew of *Authority.*" Still, Saul could not hide his true motive, which stemmed from a desire to persecute Christ's followers because of their beliefs. The circumstances might have changed, Smith suggested, but the lesson of Saul remained, "tho' policy may lead us to varnish it over with a different Name, to give it some fine Palliative, and make it carry the Face and Countenance of legal Prosecution."[42]

Just as understanding recent attempts to "pursue and hunt, bind and imprison" lowcountry evangelicals was important, so also was explaining efforts to "slander and traduce them, to the Injury of their Reputation." Yet Smith's primary goal in *Jesus Persecuted in His Disciples* was to show how impossible it was for "*Persecutors* . . . to exculpate themselves." He premised his argument on the claim that evangelical Christian precepts were "all *Love* and *Purity*." "Their Endeavours are to reform *Mankind*, and to restore the Beauty and Order of *every Relation;* to make better *Christians*, better *Subjects*, better *Masters*, and better *Servants*, that *Superiors* and *Inferiors* may know their Place, and act in their own Sphere and Character." He also claimed that no "Laws of Equity and natural Justice . . . gave one Man a Right and Sovereignty over the *Understanding* of another." Further, Smith asserted, persecution was altogether contrary to reason and presupposed infallibility. "Pray, what can I propose," he preached, "when I *persecute* a Man for differing from me, in *his Scheme* of Religion, or any other Points of Speculation? Certainly I go upon the Presumption, that I am infallibly right my self, and his Opinion is founded in Error and Heterodoxy; agreeably to which, my *Design* must be to reclaim and *correct* his Sentiments—But is *Persecution* the Way to accomplish this? Do *Persecutors* understand *human Nature*, and the make of a reasonable Being? Are *Imprisonments, Pillories, Scourgings, Faggots*, or any *pecuniary Fines*, &c. proper *Syllogisms* to work upon our *Reason*, & to convince that Faculty, which we call the *Understanding*?" Finally, Smith claimed, persecution "frequently produces . . . quite *contrary* Effects," because it tends to harden the resolve of the persecuted—"the Blood of *Martyrs* has ever been the *Seed* of the *Church*," he observed.[43]

Despite the context in which he wrote, there was no anger or despair in Smith's message, only hope. He cautioned against "venting . . . personal Revenge" in the face of persecution and reminded his congregation that when they suffered, they suffered with and for Christ. "'Tis an *Honour* for us to be crucified *with Christ*," he said, "for we have *his* Presence with us in all our Tribulations—in *Distress*, in *Persecution*, in *Famine*, in *Nakedness*, in *Prison;*—in all these Things we are more than *Conquerors* thro' him.—The Presence of our Lord turns *Prisons* into *Palaces*, and gives a *Glory* to the *Cross*."[44]

Amid the anxieties and tensions generated by the First Great Awakening, conversion-centered revivals persisted in Charleston and throughout the South Carolina lowcountry in the 1740s and 1750s. Together with earlier outbursts these revivals shepherd in the rise of evangelical Christianity in the early South, and in these decades they were undergirded once again by a belief that God's kingdom was drawing near. So exalted was Josiah Smith's vision of Christ's return to earth that on a visit to the Bethesda orphanage in 1743, he likened a communion celebration there to "eating Bread in the Kingdom of Heaven."[45] Fully aware from his earlier experiences that "Great Opposition demands great Zeal to counterbalance it," Smith insisted on full and free liberty of conscience in the face of renewed opposition. What is more, he became increasingly convinced that the time was ripe for renewed spiritual outpourings in the South Carolina lowcountry and the Atlantic world. In fact he spoke on this theme in *A Zeal of GOD Encourag'd and Guarded* (Boston, 1745), declaring: "Zeal, like other Things, is most beautiful in its Season—And there are some particular Seasons, wherein our Zeal is call'd upon, and ought to exert itself." Now was such a time, Smith proclaimed. "When Providence opens a Prospect and great Probability of Success—when a considerable and extensive Reformation is going on in the World, we are requir'd to shew our Zeal for it; to let the World know our Sentiment and hearty Concurrence—to strike, as we say, when the Iron is hot."[46]

As *A Zeal of GOD Encourag'd and Guarded* makes clear, the fight against religious enthusiasm had not dampened Smith's passion for the evangelical cause nor his optimism about its eventual success. As an early leader of the revival movement, he continued to preach the centrality of the conversion experience, as well as to defend and encourage emotion-laden awakenings across the Carolina colony. Smith also remained steadfast in his support for George Whitefield. When the charismatic revivalist visited Charleston on his third trip to America (August 1744–June 1748), for example, Smith hosted Whitefield at the Independent Meeting House on a number of different occasions, reporting that Whitefield spoke to extremely large and enthusiastic crowds. Smith greeted each of Whitefield's visits as evidence that a new reformation was unfolding, and, as before, sought to "clench the Nails that this great master of Assemblies . . . fastened."[47] A gifted pulpit orator in his own right, Smith continued to impress his listeners with his fiery sermonizing, including the sea captains and sailors who typically filled his church on their way to or from Europe, Africa, or other New World colonies. John Newton (1725–1807), a slave trader who later became an Anglican priest, hymn-writer, and abolitionist, wrote of the "excellent and powerful" preaching of Smith during an Atlantic voyage he made aboard the slave ship *Browlow* in 1748 and 1749. During the voyage Newton experienced a spiritual conversion and embraced evangelical Christianity.[48]

Tragically, Smith suffered a severe stroke in 1749 that left him partially paralyzed and unable "to articulate distinctly."[49] Although his health prevented him from carrying out his regular ministerial responsibilities as before, he persevered through the affliction and remained a strong supporter of evangelicalism in the South Carolina lowcountry. Smith became well known for his pastoral care, maintained regular correspondence with clergy elsewhere, and played an active role in church business. Moreover, he wrote and published numerous "gospel sermons," led prayers, and even officiated at the Charleston church on occasion.[50] After seeking the advice of George Whitefield, who visited Charleston again during his fourth trip to America (October 1751–May 1752), Smith, too, helped to secure an evangelical Presbyterian minister, James Edmonds, as one of his successors at the Independent Meeting House.

Apparently Edmonds had some initial reservations about ministering to a congregation that was composed of both Congregationalists and Presbyterians, and there may have been some question among a few leading members of the church about whether he was an appropriate fit for the job. But Whitefield, after having "some close talk with Mr. L——, and several of Mr. S[mith]'s congregation concerning him," assured Edmonds that "all seemed unanimous to give you a call." "I need only observe," Whitefield added, "in the congregation there are many dear children of God. . . . And . . . I hope you will be an happy instrument of . . . adding to the church such as shall be saved." Equally attractive in Whitefield's mind was the fact that there were "several pious ministers of other denominations, who will be glad to keep up a Christian correspondence with you, and strengthen your hands." Whatever initial reservations Edmonds may have had quickly proved unwarranted. After accepting the call from the Charleston congregation, he soon found himself gaining in popularity, so much so that the meeting house had to be enlarged to accommodate the large numbers who flocked to the church during his ministry.[51]

Other Presbyterian and Congregationalist ministers such as William Hutson were equally successful in their efforts at religious revival. Hutson was converted by Whitefield in 1740 and afterwards began to preach on the Bryan family estate, where he was employed as a teacher at the family's slave school. While his name is not among those of the ones indicted by the Grand Jury of South Carolina for unlawfully preaching to blacks, he undoubtedly played a key role in fomenting the religious awakening among the enslaved Africans and African Americans living in St. Helena's Parish. Subsequent to his efforts there (or possibly because of them), Hutson moved to Georgia and became a licentiate at the Bethesda orphanage; but he soon abandoned that mission and accepted a call to become the pastor of the Stoney Creek Independent (Presbyterian) Church. Located on a tributary of the Pocataligo River in an area of St. Helena's Parish referred to by contemporaries as the Indian Land, the church at Stoney Creek was founded by the Bryans and several of their neighbors who had experienced a spiritual conversion during the First Great Awakening.[52] After he accepted the church's call, Hutson was formally ordained by Josiah Smith and John Osgood of the Dorchester Independent Church, and a "Day was set apart by the Church for Fasting and Prayer, to settle matters about and to organize the Church." Accordingly, Hutson drafted a church covenant and a confession of faith.[53]

By signing the covenant, members of the Stoney Creek church committed themselves to evangelical Christian fellowship, showing how the awakenings of the 1740s and 1750s evolved in remote parts of the South Carolina lowcountry. For example, subscribers agreed to "openly without reserve" give themselves over to "Christ the complete Savior of Sinners in Church Fellowship & Communion, Resolving & Promising in his Strength, to Believe his Promises, [and] Live by Faith on him." They also committed themselves to obey God's "Precepts, Hearken to the Voice of his Providence, serve him and each other According to all the Laws,—Statutes & Ordinances of his House, taking the written word for our Rule, aiming in all at the Glory of Christ . . . each others Edification . . . the Increase of Christ's Kingdom, & the good of all mankind." Furthermore, Stoney Creek church members dedicated themselves to the "Special Direction & Assistance of the spirit of the Lord."[54]

William Hutson remained at Stoney Creek until 1756, during which time the church's membership grew rapidly, with substantial numbers of black and white individuals joining the congregation. Hutson then removed to Charleston to join James Edmonds as co-pastor of the Independent Meeting House, where he preached until his death five years later. During his ministry in Charleston, Hutson did much to advance the revivalist movement in the South Carolina lowcountry and abroad. After the death of his wife Mary (Woodward) in 1757, he published a collection of her letters and diary extracts to preserve her memory and promote the evangelical cause. In 1760 he arranged to have the collection reprinted in England along with Hugh Bryan's memoirs. This volume, published as *Living Christianity, delineated* (London, 1760), had great international appeal and became one of a growing number of widely read revival tracts circulating in the Atlantic Protestant world. Also during his five-year ministry in Charleston, Hutson helped to maintain the Independent Church as a leading center of revival activity in the Lower South, working closely with his colleagues Edmonds and Smith. Too, Hutson regularly visited and preached at numerous Congregational, Presbyterian, and Baptist churches across the South Carolina lowcountry.[55]

Hutson's successor at Stoney Creek, Archibald Simpson, emerged as yet another evangelical voice in the South Carolina lowcountry during the mid-1700s. Simpson was born in Glasgow, Scotland, in 1734 and was awakened as a teenager after hearing multiple "action sermons" in Glasgow and the nearby village of Cambuslang. Following his conversion experience, Simpson was admitted to Glasgow College, where he graduated in 1752. Shortly thereafter he accepted an invitation from George Whitefield to manage the Bethesda orphanage and sailed for British North America. After spending a few months in Georgia, Simpson became dissatisfied with his new position. As a result he moved to South Carolina in the spring of 1754 and was employed as a probationer at the Wilton Presbyterian Church in Colleton County. In mid-June of that same year, while visiting a neighboring planter, Whitefield confronted the young Scot. "He accused me of Ingratitude and falsyfying all my engagements to him," Simpson said.[56]

In writing about the confrontation in his journal, Simpson claimed that Whitefield had assured him "more than once or twice" that if he "was ever dissatisfied or saw ground to be discontented" at Bethesda then he "was free from that moment to go when [he] pleased." He also claimed that "no offer nor considerations could have drawn me from his service without his allowance." Yet Whitefield insisted on charging Simpson with "Spiritual pride, hypocrisy, Self Conceit, forwardness, love of popularity and the like." He even went so far as to insinuate that Simpson was guilty of some sort sexual "mis-step" at the orphanage. "He accused me of sending for my wife so soon after I came as proceeding from vile [and] base ends," Simpson wrote, and "said that He would pass over all (as He called it) if he could do it honourably."[57]

Less than a week later Whitefield apologized to Simpson "for having spoke of the irregular step of [his] marriage" and "said he would see how things could be made up." Smoothing over their differences, the two ministers "parted in a peaceable way," with the poverty-stricken probationer agreeing to "repay . . . the expenses he was at about me." Whitefield continued to visit Simpson, renewing "his professions of friendship" and "paying him a great deal of respect in both public and private," though one can sense some lingering bitterness on Simpson's part. Nevertheless, Simpson remained a loyal supporter of the itinerant and his "evangelical preaching." During one of Whitefield's subsequent visits to South Carolina, for instance, Simpson reported that he met with three Presbyterian ministers in Charleston and was "not greatly pleased nor edified with this night's conversation, it being mostly against Mr. Whitefield and ministers of his stamp." "As I felt myself pointed at," Simpson continued, "I thought it my duty to speak freely, and stand up for the preaching warmly and zealously the doctrines of grace, the necessity of regeneration, the Catholic practice of preaching in all pulpits, employing pious ministers of every denomination, and holding occasional communion with all sound Protestants, with all Christians who held of the glorious Head, and both lay and ministerial communion."[58] Attacks on Whitefield, in other words, were attacks on Simpson and the increasing number of other evangelical ministers in the colony.

By the time Simpson penned these remarks, he, like many other revivalists of Whitefield's stripe, had become a fixture in the South Carolina landscape. Originally licensed by the South Carolina Presbytery as a probationer, he was formally ordained in 1755 following the customary trial period. Simpson preached at Wilton for just over one year before accepting a call (as a Presbyterian minister) from the church at Stoney Creek, where he remained until his departure from the colony in 1772. Judging from the references in his journal and by the number of families said to have been connected with his churches, Simpson had considerable success during his ministerial career.[59] At his first sermon at Wilton in May 1754, for example, he found a "numerous and attentive Auditory both of white people and negroes." The following Sunday he "saw severals melted down into tears and much affected." A month later, after telling his congregation of what he himself had "known, felt, and experienced about the Soul[']s being under clouds and darkness," Simpson was able to report that the "Lord [drew] Some Souls to himself" in a "downpouring of his Spirit Amongst us." By the first of November there "seemed to be a time of glorious power to many Souls for their [*sic*] was Much kindly and affectionate weeping."[60]

In addition to his revival labor at the Wilton and Stoney Creek churches, Simpson traveled throughout many parts of the South Carolina lowcountry to preach. Even as a probationer at Wilton the young minister was facilitating "Awakenings of Conscienceness" in a fifteen-mile radius; thereafter he extended his ministerial work. In fact, from 1754 to 1772 Simpson preached in many different churches in South Carolina and Georgia.[61] For the most part Simpson seems to have focused his itinerant efforts on organized churches that were "vacant" (that is, without a regular minister), but he also helped to organize a few congregations.[62] Of course vacancies among lowcountry churches were not unusual because malignant diseases were able to thrive in the area. Frequent, early, and widespread death among ministers was commonplace.[63] In contrast to the lowcountry, vacancies in the Carolina backcountry were primarily the result of the rapid spread and disparate pattern of settlement in the second half of the eighteenth century. Early on, though, the problem also seemed to lie—at least in part—in the consuming nature of the mosquito-infested lowcountry; for oftentimes when a minister was sent into the backcountry, he ended up accepting a call from a vacant church in the lowcountry, considering "the temporals better."[64]

Nevertheless, ministerial activity was increasing in the backcountry in the 1750s and early 1760s, and Presbyterian ministers began to locate there. Among them was William Richardson. Richardson was born in Egremont, England, in 1729, the youngest son of a comfortable middling family. After attending the University of Glasgow, where he befriended Archibald Simpson, Richardson immigrated to Philadelphia in 1750. Traveling south, he visited Simpson at the Stoney Creek settlement in April 1759. Richardson informed Simpson that he had been ordained by the Hanover Presbytery of Virginia and "had gone some months ago on a mission to the Cherokees" but had "laid down his mission [and] accepted of a call from a people at the Wa[x]as about 200 miles beyond Charlestown." The two friends spent the better part of a week together in "pleasant conversation," and after preaching at both Pon Pon and Stoney Creek, Richardson quickly showed himself to be "a great gospel minister." Knowing that there were several lowcountry congregations in need of ministers, Simpson encouraged Richardson to stay, but he conceded that if his colleague was willing to settle at the Waxhaws he would be an "eminent blessing in the parts where the Lord has called him to labour."[65]

As Simpson's remarks suggest, Richardson's talents were well suited to the Waxhaw settlement, a rapidly expanding community in the lower Catawba River valley comprising mostly Scots-Irish immigrants from Virginia and Pennsylvania. After applying for membership in the South Carolina Presbytery, Richardson was formally installed at the Waxhaw church in the fall of 1759, and under his guidance and leadership the congregation flourished. So, too, did several neighboring congregations of Scottish and Scots-Irish immigrants. Tapping the explosive religious proclivities of these clusters of early backcountry settlement, Richardson quickly began preaching to and helping to gather churches in a number of adjacent communities in the Catawba and the Broad River valleys. By 1763 he had extended his ministerial work out from the Waxhaw church to the Presbyterian churches at Brown's Creek, Bull Run, Fairforest, Fishing Creek, and Rocky Creek. By the end of the decade he was even laboring as far away as the Long Cane and Little River valleys. Of course Richardson did not labor alone in the frontier environment of the Lower South region of colonial British America, nor was he the only Presbyterian minister to locate in the backcountry. Presbyteries to the north continued to send ministers to preach in settlements across the region, and the South Carolina Presbytery arranged for visits to backcountry communities as well, recruiting ministers from within its own ranks and seeking clergyman through Scottish presbyteries. Following William Richardson's lead, some of these ministers joined the South Carolina Presbytery and were installed in churches on the Carolina frontier.[66]

In pursuing their ministerial work Richardson, Simpson, and other leading Presbyterian and Congregationalist clergymen helped to expand the reach of evangelical revivalism in colonial South Carolina in the 1740s and 1750s, when religious revivals steadily transformed and reinvigorated organized Christian expression throughout the colony and at the same time opened up bright prospects for the years ahead. In these decades evangelical Christianity was firmly established at several Independent and Presbyterian churches southwest of Charleston, as well as at a few Presbyterian churches in Prince Frederick's Parish. Among them were the Presbyterian churches in Beaufort and Wilton, the Congregational or "Independent" church at Stoney Creek, and the Presbyterian congregations at Edisto, Pon Pon, and Satlketcher Creek. The Presbyterian churches at Williamsburg and Black Mingo Creek also developed strong evangelical followings. As the revival movement grew and spread from 1740 to 1760, Archibald Simpson alluded to the remarkable progress evangelical religion had made in the colony, offering an ecstatic vision of the potential for future expansion. Shortly after Richardson's departure in 1759, he noted that by God's providence religious renewal had brought lowcountry settlers "to discover a greater desire for the gospel . . . and put it on a better footing that ever it has yet been." Believing that most of his co-religionists had "gospel religion among them," he wrote that "the Lord . . . seems to be opening a more effectual Door for the gospel in this place than ever."[67]

In addition to Presbyterian and Congregationalist settlers, many German and Swiss groups who settled in Amelia, Orangeburg, Purrysburg, Saxe-Gotha, and near the confluence of the Saluda and Broad Rivers during the mid-1700s also sustained, as Evangelical Lutheran observers in Germany commonly referred to it, *seligmachenden Bibel Glauben* (living Bible faith). About one-quarter to one-third of these European settlers, numbering more than 3,500 in 1760 and constituting roughly 10 percent of colonial South Carolina's white population, were Reformed, while roughly two-thirds to three-quarters were Lutherans, most of whom were evangelical Pietists rather than *rechtglaubig* (orthodox). After an initial phase of settlement in the 1730s and early 1740s, there was an important shift in the overall pattern of immigration from the European continent. Prior to 1750 or so, a majority of immigrants from the European continent were Swiss, but beginning in the mid- to late-1740s Swiss immigration fell off and more and more German men and women (mostly palatines from the Rhineland, Baden, and Württemberg) began to arrive, so that by the 1760s Germans outnumbered Swiss in the colony by at least two to one.[68]

Religious differences of a broad range were manifest among German and Swiss groups from the start, not only between Lutheran and Reformed immigrants but also among Pietists and orthodox, furnishing a major source of religious intolerance and often causing "much strife."[69] Yet these differences in religious belief and practice also underwrote attempts at religious renewal and facilitated the growth of syncretic pietist expression. Indeed, as Protestant evangelicalism emerged as a predominant force in South Carolina religious life during the 1740s and 1750s, many German and Swiss settlers followed in the path of John Tobler of New Windsor. When he first arrived in the 1730s, Tobler disavowed evangelical Pietism, but during the 1740s he underwent a remarkable transformation and embraced spiritual rebirth, trusting more in "the mission of the Holy Spirit" than "in human powers or works." In fact, by 1754 Tobler began to identify himself "with the doctrine of the Pietists" and wished that there were more ministers in the province "who proclaim the word of God purely and sincerely." Among these, Tobler reported revealingly, "one can justifiably include Mr. Whitefield, an English preacher."[70]

Though many German-speaking settlers emphasized *Erleuchtung* (illumination or enlightenment of the Holy Spirit), *Empfindung* (feeling or sensation of faith), *Gnadendurchbruch* (piercing through of grace), *Wiedergebut* (new birth), and *Frommigkeit* (piety), Lutheran and Reformed settlers generally tended to shun German-speaking "sect people." For example, John Tobler reported that a family of German Seventh Day Baptists came from Pennsylvania and settled in New Windsor township in 1752. "The man had supported himself [and his family] for almost two years in the woods, with hunting," Tobler wrote. "But he grew tired of this life and tried to settle somewhere." "I let him and his numerous family . . . stay in one of my houses," Tobler went on to say, "but because he, as a Seventh-Day Baptist, wanted to celebrate Saturday and work on Sunday, I could not stand to have him for long at my place because of this offensive behavior. Otherwise he came also to our worship service, was a devout man and a particularly good singer."[71]

Only a few years later, the activities of a group of radical German-speaking sectarians known as Weberites greatly exacerbated such tensions, especially when they brutally murdered two of their own members during an enthusiastic religious frenzy. Jacob Weber, a native of the Swiss canton of Zürich, was brought up and educated in the Reformed church. As a fourteen-year-old boy he left his parents and immigrated with his brother to South Carolina, settling in the German and Swiss communities of Saxe-Gotha and Dutch Fork. Scarcely had Weber arrived when he experienced the traumatic loss of his brother. Overwhelmed by feelings of loneliness and guilt, the young Swiss became despondent. Ultimately he embraced an emotional, individualistic religion and turned to God. In a letter to his children dated April 16, 1761, the year he was condemned to death for murder, Weber described these religious experiences while he was awaiting his execution in Charleston. Recalling the painful emotions he experienced after his brother's death, he wrote:

> Thus I was forsaken of man, and without father or mother. But God had compassion on me amid much trouble and sorrow. He planted the fear of the Lord in my heart, so that I had more pleasure in the Lord, in godliness, and the Word of God, than in the world. I was often troubled about my own salvation when I reflected how strict an account God would require, that I must enter into judgment, and know not how it would result. . . . Through such exercises of the heart I arrived at a knowledge of my sins, and learned how the human race had fallen from God, and how low all mankind, without exception, are sunken in depravity. As soon as I experienced this, I earnestly besought God day and night for forgiveness, for the Holy Spirit, for a pure heart, and for saving faith, and I felt the necessity of retirement to restrain my thoughts, and to prevent the Divine work from being hindered in me. In this retirement I forgot the turmoil of the world. In this light I regarded all vain desires and thoughts and all human works as by nature damnable in the sight of God. Fear and sorrow now seized upon my poor soul, and

> I thought, what shall I do to be saved? It was shown me that nothing would suffice but being born again of water and of Spirit.

Feeling utterly helpless and lost, Weber finally determined to cast himself "entirely upon the mercy of God." "I lay at the feet of Jesus with all my heart in submission," he later recalled, "sighing and praying night and day for his grace, until I had passed from death unto life." "Then all my sins were forgiven me, and I was full of the Holy Ghost, and rejoiced with a joy unspeakably great."[72]

Having joined a group of worshipers in the lower Saluda River valley, which was thought to have been started by John George Smithpeter (a.k.a. Peter Schmidt or Schmidt Peter), Weber and several of his neighbors were converted to a religion eerily similar to that of the Dutartres some two decades before. It was a visionary ecstatic religion that affirmed converts' highly individual and unique life experiences, regardless of race, class, or gender. John Smithpeter and Jacob and Hannah Weber, as well as "a colored preacher" named Dauber, were the leaders. They espoused the equality of believers irrespective of all concerns other than faith. Aided by singing, Bible study, and prayer, the Weberites came to "despise the joy of the world, and disregard its reproach." According to the Lutheran minster Henry Melchior Muhlenberg, "numbers of both sexes went about uncovered and naked, and practiced the most abominable wantonness." In the weeks, months, and years following his conversion in early 1756, Weber and his companions endured through various vicissitudes until at last there "followed the great misery and awful fall into sin." Worked up into an enthusiastic frenzy, Weber, Smithpeter, and Dauber exalted themselves as God the Father, the Son, and the Holy Spirit.[73]

In 1761 Weber's cohort self-destructed. Borrowing a phrase from the book of Revelation, Weber and Smithpeter charged Dauber with being "neither hot nor cold but lukewarm" in his spiritual beliefs, and they and their followers brutally smothered him to death. Then Weber came to believe that Smithpeter was the devil. Another violent murder ensued. The Weberites chained Smithpeter to a tree and "struck him with their fists, and beat him and trampled upon his throat until he was dead." When news of these activities reached authorities the Weberites were brought to justice. Jacob and Hannah Weber and two others, John Geiger and Jacob Burghart, were tried, convicted of murder, and sentenced to death. Lieutenant Governor Bull pardoned Hannah Weber, John Geiger, and Jacob Burghart, but Jacob Weber was sent to the gallows.[74]

Lutherans and Reformed ministers understandably went to great lengths to distance themselves from this "pernicious sect," sternly denouncing the Weberites while applauding authorities' swift action against them. And in the years that followed the "Weber Heresy" was continually cited as an example of the abhorrent excesses to which sectarian enthusiasts were prone.[75] Yet Weber's case is significant because it points up the extent to which evangelical Christian revivalism was powerfully altering eighteenth-century South Carolina society and encouraging the growth of radical religious groups in the colony in the 1740s and 1750s. It also points up the liberating implications of the spread of evangelicalism, showing how the revival movement was crossing racial and gender lines. Women, like enslaved Africans and African Americans, were becoming increasingly attracted to and engaged in the revival movement throughout the Atlantic world, and the conversion experience gave them the power to assert themselves in new and sometimes provocative ways. From the point view of the continually evolving configuration of religious practices among women, free black persons, and slaves in both American history and the history of the South, the violent Weber episode thus proved significant.

The Weberites emerged from a complex religious environment in which lay proselytizing was commonplace in a variety of religious communities across the South Carolina lowcountry. As in other parts of colony, popular efforts at sustaining religious worship and practice among the German-speaking communities of the township settlements stood at the center of mid-eighteenth-century German and Swiss spiritual life and at the fulcrum of an evolving culture of Protestant evangelical religion on the southern frontier of the British colonial mainland. Nevertheless, German-speaking laypeople expressed great interest in securing permanent ministers, and they looked to Lutheran and Reformed churchmen on both sides of the Atlantic in their efforts to attract suitable candidates. John Tobler, who was himself a lay minister, lamented the "great lack of true preachers here in the province" and "fervently . . . wished that sincere preachers might decide to come here and make the most of their talents." Additionally, Tobler and other prominent laymen appealed to their German-speaking correspondents in Europe and America for guidance in summoning pastors. While there were four or five Reformed ministers laboring among the Carolina colony's German and Swiss communities at any given time during the 1740s and 1750s, the shortage of clergymen meant that most congregations remained without settled ministers. The first German Luther minister, John George Friedrichs, did not arrive in the colony until around 1755. Even so, immigrants from the European continent sustained strong piety and fervor by maintaining regular public worship services under lay leadership at several different locations in the South Carolina lowcountry, including such places as New Windsor, Four Hole Creek, Cattle Creek, Indian Field Swamp, and Twelvemile Creek. Furthermore, several German Reformed and Lutheran ministers took up settled ministries with congregations of German and Swiss. John Ulrich Giessendanner II (d. 1761), nephew and namesake of Pietist reformer John Ulrich Giessendanner (1660–1738), served two congregations at Amelia and Orangeburg during his twenty-three year ministerial career. Christian Theus, a native of the Swiss canton of Graubünden, occupied the pulpit of

St. John's, Congaree, in Saxe-Gothe from 1739 to 1791. After organizing St. John's Church in Charleston in the late 1750s, George Friedrichs received an invitation to the pastorate of St. Mathew's, Amelia, where he served for more than fifteen years. John Tobler's son-in-law, John Joachim Zubly, also served in Amelia township before accepting a call from the Wappetaw Independent Church in 1753. Later renowned for his opposition to American independence as pastor of Savannah's Independent Meeting House, Zubly was an acknowledged leader of the revival movement in the Lower South, and like other German-speaking settlers he played an important role in shepherding in the rise of evangelical Christianity in the South Carolina lowcountry.[76]

Baptists spearheaded efforts at religious revival in the South Carolina lowcountry in the decades after the religious excitement of the Great Awakening, experiencing explosive growth. As a result Baptists began to rival Presbyterians as the single largest dissenting denomination in the colony by 1760. While evangelical Presbyterians and other groups saw remarkable gains during these years, Baptist church membership more than doubled in each of the two decades after 1740. What is more, the number of formally organized Baptist churches rose by 157 percent from 1740 to 1760, increasing from seven to eighteen. At the same time major new centers of Baptist revival activity appeared in the lowcountry from the Pee Dee River to the Savannah, and the number of evangelical Baptist clergymen also increased dramatically.[77]

The Baptist minister Isaac Chanler continued to assume a leadership role in expanding the reach of evangelical religion in the South Carolina lowcountry in the 1740s, defending religious emotionalism against charges of enthusiasm, baptizing new converts, and helping to gather new churches. In 1744 Chanler published a 445-page revival manifesto, *The Doctrines of Glorious Grace Unfolded, defended, and practically Improved,* in which he denounced Arminian theology and defended Calvinist revivalism. In May and June of the same year he began baptizing converts in Prince George Winyaw Parish and organizing the Black River Baptist Church, a branch of the Ashley River congregation. In addition Chanler continued to preach regularly in Charleston, where another one of Whitefield's associates, Jonathan Barber, a Rhode Islander who superintended the Bethesda orphanage, settled in 1746.[78]

Also important, Chanler remained extraordinarily active among a group of Welsh Baptists from Newcastle County, Pennsylvania, who had recently secured and settled a large tract in Queensborough Township on the Big Pee Dee River. In early 1743, after several visits to the so-called Welsh Neck settlement, Chanler ordained Philip James, a member of the group who was widely known for his "great spirituality." Soon thereafter Chanler began keeping an "An Account of Persons who I Baptized at the Welch Tract and at Mr. Kolbs in the way thither." (One entry includes the names of twelve men and women.)[79] John Fordyce, the SPG missionary in Prince Frederick Parish, reported to Anglican officials in London that Pee Dee Baptists had "suffered themselves to be imposed on by the wretch whom they call their teacher, as ignorant as themselves, not knowing any other language than English and Welsh, yet they are so enthusiastical as even think him inspired, so ignorant are they!" Two years later, in 1745, Fordyce said that Baptists in the region were "so possessed of the spirit of enthusiasm that there are about as many ignorant preachers as there were in Oliver's camp, that one can scarce beat a bush, but out comes a preacher."[80]

Beyond his efforts elsewhere, Chanler started preaching at Euhaw, which was located along the High Road leading from Charleston to Purrysburg on an estuary of Port Royal Sound. Here and at both Edisto and Hilton Head, William Tilly, another early supporter of Whitefield and the Great Awakening, had been laboring since the early 1730s. With Tilly's death in 1744, Chanler took up ministering in the area, speaking of a church both "*Militant* and *Triumphant.*" In 1746 he oversaw the organization of a congregation at Euhaw (which became a branch of the Charleston church). He also oversaw the ministerial work of two young Baptist pastors, William Elbert and Francis Pelot, who were licensed to preach in the region when the Euhaw church was organized. Pelot was a young Swiss Calvinist whom Chanler had converted, and following his ministerial apprenticeship Pelot quickly emerged as the leader of revival activity in lowcountry South Carolina.[81]

After Chanler's unexpected death in late November 1749, Oliver Hart became the most influential Baptist leader in the South Carolina lowcountry. Hart (1723–1795), a native of Southampton, Pennsylvania, embraced evangelical religion during George Whitefield's tour of the Middle Colonies and was baptized in the Philadelphia area in 1741. Licensed to preach by the Southampton Baptist Church five years later, he was ordained "to the great work of the Ministry" in October 1749, just before he set sail to succeed Jonathan Barber as pastor of the First Baptist Church in Charleston, where he arrived on December 2, the day of Chanler's burial.[82]

No sooner had Hart landed than he embarked on a campaign to establish the Charleston Baptist Association to promote Baptist unity, ministerial labor, and clerical education. After the Charleston church formally ordained him as pastor in February 1750, Hart quickly began cultivating relationships with ministers, deacons, and elders in Baptist congregations across the South Carolina lowcountry, enabling him to garner support for the founding of a centralized church organization similar to the Philadelphia Baptist Association (est. 1707). He had been settled at the Charleston church hardly more than a year and a half before he had arranged to meet representatives from the Ashley River, Euhaw, and Welsh Neck churches to establish the Charleston association. Although delegates from the Euhaw church proved unable to attend the first meeting of the association in October 1751, they resolved to join the organization the following year, agreeing to convene annually on the Saturday before the second Sunday of each November. Before delegates to the Charleston Baptist Association "Met on Business" each year, they spent two days in public worship and prayer. Business meetings, which typically lasted from Monday through Thursday, usually involved answering queries from constituent congregations on a variety of theological and social questions, advising them on worship and disciplinary practices, and consulting with individual Baptist churches in choosing ministers.[83]

Under Hart's vigorous religious leadership, the Charleston Baptist Association emerged as an increasingly powerful institutional force for sustaining and expanding Baptist growth in the Lower South. During the 1750s, 1760s, and 1770s, the association continually grew in both size and influence, extending its membership to include churches in both North and South Carolina. Early on, it focused its efforts mostly on missionary work and clerical training. Beginning in 1754, for instance, the "great meeting," as Hart called it, sponsored John Gano on two separate preaching tours through the Carolina backcountry. Gano, a native of Hopewell, New Jersey, was a young minister with a connection to the Philadelphia Baptist Association who preached mainly in the Yadkin River settlements in North Carolina. On his first trip to the Carolinas, Gano noted in his journal that he preached a sermon in Charleston "to a numerous and brilliant audience, among whom were twelve ministers and one of whom was Mr. Whitfield." At Ashley River, he wrote that he preached "to a large congregation of negroes." On his subsequent missionary tour Gano noted that he endeavored to "proclaim free grace wherever I went." In addition to sponsoring proselytizing, the Charleston Baptist Association raised money to train young converts for the ministry. In 1756 member churches contributed £133 to finance the training of youths. The celebrated Baptist minister Samuel Stillman, one of Hart's converts who later became pastor of the First Baptist Church in Boston, was one of the earliest recipients of these funds. Evan Pugh, a Yankin River settler whom Gano recommended as a candidate in 1759, was another early beneficiary.[84]

Quite apart from his leadership role in establishing the Charleston Baptist Association, Oliver Hart engaged in a wide range of activities to promote religious revival in both Carolina and Georgia Baptist churches. During the course of his ministerial career, he traveled throughout South Carolina and Georgia to preach, helped to gather a number of new churches, and frequently assisted in ordaining Baptist ministers, deacons, and elders. Shortly after his arrival in Charleston, moreover, he began delivering a series of evening lectures to supplement his Sabbath-day sermons, and also set to work catechizing children. Many young people and others enquiring about their faith visited him and sought his advice, including Samuel Stillman. Through his inspired guidance, Hart brought many of these people to religious conviction in a "Revival of Religion." "The remarkable Revival in our Church began in August 1754," he wrote. The strong presence of young people in the revival sent Hart's spirits soaring, as did the revival's spread from the Charleston church to nearby James Island, where Hart baptized ten new converts at the Baptist deacon William Screven's house in early October. "Many of them are very young," Hart noted of this new cohort, "and will be Expos'd to many Temptations; most are of the female Sex; and therefore their Case is perhaps more Dangerous; take them O Lord; take them into thy peculiar Care and keep them as ye Apple of thine Eye." As the revival spread to James Island, Hart benefitted from cross-confessional cooperation and interchange. He shared his pulpit with such pastors as William Hutson and John Joachim Zubly, who in turn lent their unhesitating support to Hart's energetic revival work. Hart also cooperated with Hutson and Zubly in testifying against "stage plays," as did Richard Clarke, who sought Hart out to preach a funeral sermon in his stead at St. Philip's after he unexpectedly fell ill. In commenting on the occasion Hart wrote that Clarke gave "gave me free Liberty to speak in my Own way; which Discovered a Catholick Spirit." "Oh that all Bigotry was rooted out of the Earth," Hart opined; "it is Indeed a pity that our little outward Differences Should cause Such a Shyness between us."[85]

Another Baptist leader, John Stephens, who succeeded Isaac Chanler as minister at Ashley River, conceived of the "visible Church of Christ" in similar terms, and he too enjoyed notable successes in winning converts. A native of Staten Island, New York, Stephens responded warmly to George Whitefield's preaching during the First Great Awakening, experiencing a spiritual conversion and accepting the doctrines of evangelical Christianity. Following his ordination in 1747, Stephens traveled to New England and settled at Horseneck, Connecticut, where he gathered a small church. Three years later Stephens was invited to become pastor of the Ashley River church. After his arrival there in 1750 Stephens became well known as a revival minister, and church membership skyrocketed because of his evangelical zeal. In fact, by 1755 Stephens had baptized some forty-three adults at the Ashley River and Black River churches, helping to broaden and extend the Baptist presence in the South Carolina lowcountry.[86]

To the south, Francis Pelot was building a new nucleus of revivalism around the Baptist church at Euhaw, preaching at both the Edisto and Hilton Head Baptist churches. Whitefield often visited Pelot's congregation, undoubtedly attracting large audiences and contributing to the evangelical movement's success in the area. Hart considered Pelot his dearest friend and counselor, and the two men worked regularly together for more than twenty years to promote revivalism. Hart wrote that Pelot "had a fine Turn for introducing Religion, and spiritualizing most Occurrences in Life." "As to his Preaching," Hart wrote that Pelot did not "content with delivering a little dry Morality, but unfolded and applied the great and glorious Doctrines of the Gospel." "His principles were truly evangelical," Hart thought, "and his knowledge of the Truth was extensive, clear, and judicious."[87]

Scarcely had Pelot's Euhaw church emerged as a new center of revivalism when a group of Baptists emigrated en masse from Lynches Creek in the Pee Dee River region to the upper reaches of the Coosawhatchie River, just twenty-five to thirty miles to the north. Several of these Pee Dee settlers, along with some members of the Euhaw congregation, immediately began holding biweekly worship meetings. In 1759 a church was formally constituted by Hart, Pelot, and James Smart, a Virginian who had recently arrived in the colony. Under the ministry of Smart, the Coosawhatchie church grew steadily. Only four or five years after its initial founding, a branch of the Coosawhatchie church was established on Pipe Creek, where Baptist ministers such as Evan Pugh traveled to preach. Pugh was one of John Gano's converts who was baptized in North Carolina. After his conversion to Baptist principles in 1754, Pugh, per Gano's arrangement, studied for the ministry with Hart, Pelot, and other pastors under the sponsorship of the Charleston Baptist Association.[88]

In many ways the founding of the Coosawhatchie church testifies to the powerful influence exerted by the Welsh Neck church in the development of evangelicalism in the Lower South during the mid-eighteenth century. Originally founded in 1738, the Welsh Neck church grew steadily during the 1740s and 1750s, and by 1760 at least six branch congregations has sprouted up: one, Cape Fear, in North Carolina; and five, Catfish, First Church on Lynches Creek, Cashaway, Mars Bluff, and Cheraw Hill, in South Carolina. Three of the latter congregations became particularly important revival nuclei in the 1750s. The first, Catfish, was formally constituted as a separate church in 1752; the second, First Church on Lynches Creek, was formally constituted in 1755; and the third, Cashaway, was formally constituted in 1756. All three of these separated churches quickly established branches of their own and greatly expanded the reach of the evangelical Baptist movement in the South Carolina lowcountry.[89]

Much of this Pee Dee vigor and dynamism resulted from the energy and enthusiasm of a zealous corps of Baptist ministers and licentiates such as Philip James, John Brown, Joshua Edwards, and Evan Pugh, some of whom gave voice to visions and prophetic dreams. Following the death of one of his children, for example, Welsh Neck minister Philip James volunteered that he had a spiritual vision concerning the dead child, writing: "as my soul quitted my body the resemblance of a man in black made towards me, and . . . took me towards the sun which filled me with fear; as I was ascending a bright figure interposed and my black conductor was pushed off; the bright man took me by the hand and said, we go this way, pointing to the north; and as we ascended, I saw a company of angels and my child among them (cloathed in white and in the full stature of a man) sing with them as the company passed by us; whereupon my bright conductor said, I am one of that company and must join them; and as he quitted me I found myself sinking fast till I came to my body." According to the contemporary Baptist historian Morgan Edwards, Philip James was a popular minister and "an excellent man." "After this vison," Edwards wrote, "the old man minded no worldly thing but was full of heavenly joy, and attentive only to spiritual concerns." Another Baptist minister, John Brown, also articulated a provocative vision that transfixed the Welsh Neck congregation. In 1747 he preached a chiliastic sermon advancing "some curious speculations" about the resurrection of the dead, the final judgment, and the "degrees of glory in heaven, etc." Emanating from a visionary-dream culture, the sermon positively inflamed the passions of the Welsh Neck church and apparently facilitated a great outpouring of emotion, "but when the sense of [the] Philadelphia association, and that of other ministers were obtained both parties perceived that they were only making much ado about nothing."[90]

"Much ado"—Brown's speculative notions reveal valuable insights into the breadth of Christian expression in the South Carolina lowcountry and point up once again just how seriously eighteenth-century Americans took religious ideas predicting Christ's return to earth, helping to explain why Richard Clarke's millennialist preachings were so popular among his parishioners at St. Philip's. As elsewhere in the Atlantic world, Christian millennialism and visionary apocalyptic thinking helped fuel the spread of Protestant evangelical revivalism in the Lower South, especially between the Great Awakening of 1740 and the French and Indian War of 1754–1763, when a growing number of Carolinians, both white and black, were brought into the evangelical fold. In an intriguing epistolatory exchange with the German Moravian pastor John Ettwein of the Bethabarba congregation in North Carolina, Henry Laurens grappled with some of the intricate consequences of this eighteenth-century religious transformation, most notably evangelical emphasis on spiritual equality and postconversion behavior. Underpinning this interesting exchange were such issues as those involving religious tolerance and intolerance, slavery, and the return of Christ.

In January 1761, while on a recruiting mission in North Carolina during the Cherokee War, Laurens befriended Ettwein at a visit to Bethabarba, where he reportedly told the German elders of the settlement "that he had not come out of mere curiosity, but that he had heard much about us and wished to know us." Laurens had apparently undergone a spiritual conversion. As the Moravian Brethren told it, "It appeared that he and others had been awakened by Whit[e] field, and had formed a religious association or club." "He modestly asked many questions about our doctrine and mode of life," they added, "and seemed well pleased with all."[91]

After his return to Charleston following the Cherokee Indian campaign, Laurens maintained a keen interest in the religious life of the Bethabarba settlers, and Ettwein became one of his frequent correspondents. "I am delighted with your truly catholic sentiment," he told Ettwein in April 1762. "Christs Church upon earth I believe is invisible, made up of Members of various outward denominations & professions amongst Christians all Led by the same Spirit & hungring & thirsting after the same Bread & Fountain of Life." Convinced that Laurens was a true "Lover of Christ & a Friend to practical Religion," Ettwein expressed similar ecumenical convictions: "Christ has but one Body, Whereof He is the Head, His Church is invisible, in the English, Lutheran, Presbyterian, Brethrens & other Christian Churches, all Believers in Christ." Significantly, Laurens was eager not only to learn about the religious tenets of the Moravians but also to share his own views and principles. He was particularly eager for Ettwein to read and comment upon two of Richard Clarke's works, as well as on three tracts by the Anglican churchman William Law, which he sent to Bethabarba with copies of some recently published newspapers.[92] Ettwein had nothing but good things to say about Law's writings, though he admitted that he was "quite a novice to mystic language." As for Clarke, Ettwein wished that "he had remain'd a Preacher of Jesus Christ," thinking that "he would thereby have more wrought in the Vineyard of the Lord, than by his Writings." Expressing concern for Laurens's spiritual mentor and friend, the Moravian pastor wrote that he was familiar with "several blessed Servants of God, who have lost themselves in the Revelation & Daniel." "If one has a call to open up what others were to seal up," he added, "he must do it, but if he had no Call he would do better to keep it a profound Secret." "Watch and pray for you know not when the Son of Man shall come, is argument enough for any Man to be prepared for the coming of the Lord," Ettwein instructed. Finally, Ettwein warned, "I am afraid there will come a worse Anti Christ, perhaps from among the Protestants; than any one has been yet."[93]

In the spring of 1763, after Ettwein visited Laurens in Charleston, the two correspondents struck up another tantalizing exchange. Reporting on his return trip through the German and Swiss settlements of the interior, the Moravian pastor wrote that he was dismayed by the moral influence of slavery on German-speaking children, writing that he was fearful for their future because "the Negroes have too much Influence upon them." "I have observ'd that often where a Man has Slaves his Children become lazy & indolent & c.," he told Laurens. Meanwhile Ettwein expressed interest in proselytizing among African and Native Americans. "What I saw & heard of the Negroes made me very uneasy . . . ; If some care was taken of their Souls their Servitude might be a Blessing unto them," he said, adding that "to propagate the Gospel amongst the Heathens is one of our Plans in this World & I consider myself as a Centinel to watch the Opening of the Door to the Indians for Messengers of the Peace of God, [and] as you will know from Time to Time how matters stand amongst the Cherokees or Creeks I hope you will aprize me of it, when you think that such Message could have Access without giving much Umbrage." Laurens responded positively to Ettwein's desire to undertake missionary work among the Lower South's native population, promising to send along "good intelligence" once it became available. He also believed that Ettwein's observations concerning the moral effects of slavery were "but too justly founded." "I have often reflected with much concern on the same subject & wished that our oeconomy & government differ'd from the present system," he wrote, "but alass—since our constitution is as it is, what can individuals do?" "Each can act only in his single & disunited capacity," Laurens went on to say, "because the sanction of Laws gives the stamp of rectitude to the Actions of the bulk of any community."[94]

Laurens continued to struggle with the problem of slavery, expressing his thoughts on the prospects for proselytizing work among the black population. "If it was to happen that every body or even a considerable majority of people were to change their sentiments with respect to slavery & that they should seriously think the saving of Souls a more profitable event than adding House to House & laying Field to Field," he wrote, then "those laws which now authorize the custom would be instantly abrogated or die of themselves," thereby facilitating evangelization. Yet while slave laws remained in force and colonial merchants continued promoting the African slave trade, "the difficulties, which a few who would wish to deal with those servants as with brethren in a state of subordination meet with, are almost insurmountable." Furthermore, there were "bad precepts & worse examples daily & hourly set before" African American converts by others, both black and white. Despite these "discouraging circumstances," Laurens nevertheless remained sympathetic to efforts at evangelizing slaves, and he was "perswaded that there are some few who will not be defeated in their strife & who think if they gain but one Soul in their whole life time that they are happy instruments & as such are amply rewarded for their trouble." For Laurens, the best rule to follow was "that which our Saviour laid down to us," namely "'By their fruits you shall know them.'" Along with his friend Ettwein, he prayed, "Thy Kingdom come, Thy Will be done O Lord!"[95]

6

Wrestling with God

Protestant Evangelicalism in the Lowcountry and Beyond

Have these days been in a heavenly humble frame of soul trusting in the Lord my God and having all my dependence upon him alone. And yet have been uneasy with many fears, doubts, and troubles of various sorts. Have been much concerned because of the melancholy times. Sin abounding prodigiously, professing of the gospel amazingly lost in profanity, deadness, and carnality; little success or rather none at all attending the gospel with respect to the conviction and conversion of sinners. And very little power attending it to believers themselves.

The Reverend Archibald Simpson,
journal entry for Saturday, July 10, 1756

On July 10, 1756, the introspective Presbyterian pastor Archibald Simpson entered into an unusually revealing spiritual dialogue with "his book," or journal. Having recently accepted a call from the Stoney Creek church in Colleton County, the young Scottish minister suddenly became "much concerned because of the melancholy times." Sinfulness appeared to him to be "abounding prodigiously, professing of the gospel amazingly lost in profanity, deadness, and carnality." These conditions obviously did not bode well for organized Christianity, nor for the growth and spread of evangelical religion in the colonial lower southern colonies of North America.[1] A talented preacher with a proven track record of multiplying the membership of the Presbyterian congregation at Wilton, where he began his colonial South Carolina ministry in 1754, Simpson had lamented his lack of progress in spreading the evangelical gospel on previous occasions, of course. One such occasion occurred in the spring of 1755. Following several notable accomplishments—the baptism of "a Married Lady among . . . the best rank in the Congregation who had been brought up among the Anabaptists," for example—Simpson became deeply distraught, feeling himself to be "such a worthless, vile, carnal [and] Slothful Sinner" that he could "hardly look for, expect, or even plead for success." There had been "a revel of drinking, Swearing, & fighting . . . in the Neigborhood," a flagrant scene that Simpson thought was altogether "too common in this country on . . . Muster days and other public occasions." The muster-day festivities utterly discouraged him—especially since several members of the Wilton congregation had been "too much concerned" in them. Reflecting on his pastoral work in the lowcountry, Simpson wrote the following entry for April 19: "Have these passed days been very Melancholy and much grieved in my mind and that not only for so much on account of the daily struggling of corruption in my own soul as on account of my congregation and the abounding of iniquity and profanity so much about this part I live in both among my people and others."[2]

Yet though he had written about melancholy times before, Archibald Simpson's diary entry for July 10, 1756, was different from the earlier entries in his journal, for on this occasion he began writing about a more generalized spiritual "deadness," not simply in his own congregation or even in the neighborhood of Stoney Creek but "thro' all the churches at home and abroad." What had caused such a perverse state to descend upon the Atlantic Protestant world was God's "withholding of the Divine Spirit." In other words there were increasing signs that Protestants had been cast out of God's favor and were being visited with a "spiritual plague."

For Simpson, this plague was evidenced by news of recent international events: by "the falling off of some Protestant Princes of the Empire"; by the "growing of popery, Deism, and Immorality in all the Protestant Churches"; and, no less important, by the fact that colonial South Carolina was being "threatened with a bloody French and Indian War." The war had already wrought "dreadful havoc to the Northward," Simpson wrote, and in the summer of 1756 it seemed ready to strike the Southeast. Equally disconcerting, there was "a French War and Invasion expected at home" in the British Isles, which had "already affected trade" and was "bringing on hard times" in the British American colonies. All this was deeply troubling, "but that's nothing," Simpson noted, "to the concern of my Soul for the Interest of Christ, which Suffers amazingly."[3]

Later, in the autumn of 1756, Simpson revealed much more about his perceptual universe and the ways in which it was given distinctive shape by the international news he received, news that conditioned his response to "the dismal appearances of publick Affairs" and informed his efforts to awaken "a very Sinful people sadened with Iniquity." "All seems against us," he wrote in October, "both at home and in America. Our fleet put to flight in the Mediteranian, as is thought not so much thro' the cowardice as the treachery of our Admiral or the Ministry, for we are ruined by an Intestine enemy, a vile Jacobite party within ourselves. The strong Garrison of St. Philips on the Island of Minorca taken from us by the French, several of our ships taken. The fort of Oswego in North America also taken by the French and finally our men often cut off and the back Settlements in Northward provinces dreadfully harassed."[4] As the bad news continued to filter in, Simpson's "weighty concern . . . for the melancholy situation" mounted, and he continued to stand firm in his belief that an angry God had visited a spiritual plague on the Atlantic Protestant world. Then, in late November, after hearing from some of his correspondents in Scotland, Simpson preached to his lowcountry congregation "with a design to Engage them to join in a day of prayer that is resolved to be kept the first friday of every Month by Most of the Dissenters on the Continent." This design marked the beginning of a transatlantic effort to revive the Stoney Creek church. "In the forenoon laid before them the evil of the times from Timothy 3:1.; and in the afternoon endeavoured to show them the unreasonableness of security midst Such . . . dangers as we are surrounded with." Exhorting the congregation to prayer "by showing them how far even we professing Christians are out done . . . by the zeal of heathens on worshiping their idols," Simpson preached later in the day from Jonah 1:6: "The captain came and said to him, 'What are you doing sound asleep?'"[5]

In the weeks leading up to his decision to join the Stoney Creek church with congregations of other Atlantic regions in an international day of humiliation and prayer, as he corresponded with other ministers in Europe and America and as his concerns over evangelical Christian interests grew increasingly weighty, Simpson recorded a great flurry of religious activity. At one point he noted that there "was a great stirring among the waters of the Sanctuary" during a Sabbath sermon, which he memorialized in his journal as "a day never to be forgotten." Such days brought renewed hope. After baptizing another "Married Lady whose parents never had any of their Children Baptized," for instance, the young minister began to have "reason to believe the Lord is blessing his Word in this place."[6] When the appointed international day of prayer finally arrived on January 17—that is, when the "Wrestling with God" for spiritual relief began—Simpson gave "a short account of the Judgements that [were] hanging over the Northward Provinces and indeed over all Europe." Then the Stoney Creek congregation prayed and sang. Simpson sermonized. The congregation prayed and sang some more. By the afternoon "there was a great time of melting among Severals," and Simpson baptized two African American women who were "greatly revived by the power of God in the Gospels." "O it is so pleasant to see Souls flocking to Christ and a particular pleasure to sea [*sic*] the poor Ethiopian slaves stretching out their hands to the Redeemer," he wrote.[7]

Thereafter the "times of reviving and quickening for the down pouring of the Spirit to carry on reformation and conversion work" continued. The monthly transatlantic prayer vigils did, too, as did "the supplication and weeping," the "remarkable convictions . . . of some worldly and covetous creatures," and Simpson's relentless preachings and pleadings. By April 1757 "the number of Communicants was by far larger than was ever seen in this place," he wrote, and the "Gospel was blessed . . . both to old and young, especially the better sort," with many "young persons . . . joining fellowship publickly." The late spring brought more news and ideas, other innovative suggestions from abroad. "Received a pamphlet intitled a Call to Prayer designed to excite people of all denominations to that most necessary duty especially at this time of publick calamity," Simpson wrote, "and was able to be very faithful and very pressing with people about family religion, especially family worship." Here Simpson was not simply referring to his own congregation. When he preached to a "very crowded auditory" at the Anglican church on Huspah Neck on June 12, for example, he "read from the pulpit the call for prayer."[8]

Eventually, as spring and summer gave way to fall, the prayer days "were obliged to be laid aside for want of people to attend them," as "vast numbers black and white were every where daily taken down." The "universal sickness and Mortality" of 1757 made it the sickliest fever season in living memory. Simpson himself grew ill and did not recover for months. When he did finally recover, after he was able to preach "in a more endeavouring Manner," Simpson immediately began thinking about how he "might promote . . . Gospel conversation" as well as "improve afflictions and trials for the glory of God." For Simpson could "not help looking . . . in this Wilderness." "Our Popish Enemies still prevail," he noted. "The Lord seems to have a Controversy with all Protestant Countries and especially with Britain and its Provinces." Simpson and the Stoney Creek congregation continued to wrestle with God for relief. And more and more South Carolina men and women were joining them, as they did on May 17, 1758, a day Governor William Henry Lyttelton "appointed . . . as a publick fast." Once again Simpson used the occasion to "convince the people that Our Sins are the cause of the Lord's with-drawing so awfully from us."[9]

Archibald Simpson's diary entries not only hearken back to the earliest origins of Protestant evangelicalism in the colonial South but also look forward to future developments, both in the South Carolina lowcountry and beyond. With a strong tradition of dissenting Protestantism and a remarkably comprehensive Anglican establishment, a feeling of crisis not unlike the one Simpson expressed had arisen in the colony in the early decades of the eighteenth century—at a time when all substantial evidence suggests that South Carolina's white population was highly churched. Throughout the 1720s and 1730s there was a decided turn toward inward, experiential faith as a heterogeneous medley of English-, French-, and German-speaking religious enthusiasts invoked the power of the Holy Spirit to combat what was frequently thought to be a "deadness" plaguing the Atlantic Protestant world, giving rise to the formation of a new religious synthesis and sowing the seeds for the Great Awakening. As the historian John B. Boles has written, "before a powerful religious revival can occur, several prerequisite conditions have to be met." "There must be in place a network of churches and ministers, there must be a shared community of belief about how God works in history, and there must be a shared sense of religious and social-cultural crisis so intense that many believe only divine intervention can set things aright."[10]

Like South Carolina's earliest evangelical revivalists, Simpson gave voice to a belief that God was punishing Protestants because they had abandoned old values and were everywhere forsaking religion, which prompted the young Presbyterian minister to join the Stoney Creek church with a chorus of other congregations in Europe and America to pray for an outpouring of the Holy Spirit. Hope lay in understanding the cause of God's controversy with people living "in all Protestant Countries" and in seeking forgiveness, for there was no escaping divine judgment. To awakening ministers and converts, to be in right relationship with God meant being "born again of God" and discovering a "living faith in Christ."[11] To those men and women who embraced evangelical religion, it also meant continually striving to "cleave unto the Lord" by living a life of faith.[12] For Archibald Simpson, as for South Carolina revivalists of an older generation (pastors such as Isaac Chanler, John Giessendanner, and Josiah Smith), such striving was impossible without fresh and further spiritual supplies from God.

Cut short by sickness and death, the Stoney Creek revival of 1757 did not last, but it resulted in an impressive spate of emotional-filled conversions, with Simpson recording a substantial increase in the number of churchgoers and communicants—black and white, high and low, young and old. Remarkably, he sought to "excite people of all denominations" after receiving a pamphlet from his ministerial correspondents in Scotland, underscoring the transatlantic character of Protestant evangelicalism while at the same time pointing to its ecumenical thrust. When Simpson later sought to defend George Whitefield and "ministers of his stamp" at a meeting of the South Carolina Presbytery, he stood up for "the Catholic practice of preaching in all pulpits, employing pious ministers of every denomination, and holding occasional communion with all sound Protestants."[13] Born in the spirit of 1740, this cooperative ideal was one of the distinguishing marks of the eighteenth-century evangelical movement.

Also remarkably, Simpson continued calling for an outpouring of the Spirit of God even as he chronicled an impressive number of "stirrings," "meltings," and professions of faith in this period, a religious paradox that led directly and causatively to future seasons of religious revival in the South Carolina lowcountry and beyond. In the winter of 1757–1758 Protestants remained on the defensive against their Catholic rivals, and on both sides of the Atlantic there seemed to be universal deadness and decay. Deism seemed to be on the rise; atheism seemed ready to engulf the British Empire; and profaneness and decadence seemed all too commonplace.[14] As Simpson corresponded with ministers at home and abroad, his concern for the state of religion grew, evoking new calls for God to provide spiritual relief. Richard Clarke's concern over religion increased just as Simpson's did. Observing international events at this same time, he interpreted the outbreak of the French and Indian War as evidence that the millennial age was at hand.

No less than Hugh Bryan's radical prophecies a generation earlier, Clarke's enthusiastic predictions created a great stirring in colonial South Carolina and immediately attracted attention throughout the North Atlantic. That they came at a time when Protestant evangelicalism was expanding its reach in the southern colonies is relatively well known. But in the pluralistic colonies of the Lower South this late colonial expansion can be rightly understood only by closer study of religious developments in the prerevolutionary era in general and the thirty to forty years prior to 1760 in particular. Here there was no sudden late-flowering burst of evangelical practice and activity as there was in Virginia and the Chesapeake Bay region, no exotic upsurge that set Protestant Christianity on a new and prosperous course. There was rather a significantly different pattern of revivalism and evangelicalism that was fueled by both indigenous and transatlantic dynamics. This prerevolutionary process began with the early settlement of South Carolina, the economic and cultural center of the Lower South, and it was directly shaped by the resurgence of the Church of England.

Prior to the 1740s and 1750s, the Church of England played a central role in the cultural life of South Carolina. Although Protestant dissenters remained a "great part of ye Body" of the province throughout the 1710s, 1720s, and 1730s, Anglican legal establishment resulted in rapid institutional expansion and significantly advanced the church as major cultural force in provincial society.[15] Beginning in 1704, there was a dramatic increase in the number of Anglican churches; clergymen were hired by the dozens; and the Church of England came to hold a position of power and influence. In fact, by the mid-1720s Anglican ministers reported that a substantial plurality of white residents were worshiping in state-supported churches. Yet nonconformity struck deep roots among the South Carolina laity, so parish clergymen were forced to make concessions to popular religious opinion, which encouraged the growth of a dynamic religious culture from which evangelicals and their followers later discovered large fields for preaching the gospel of the new birth. Most Anglican worshipers showed themselves to be decidedly "low" church and maintained only half-hearted commitment to Anglican forms. In several lowcountry parishes they even upheld Reformed and sectarian principles while occasioning Anglican worship services. In 1742 SPG missionary William Orr reported that St. Paul's Parish "was at first settled by Baptists & Quakers, so their descendants (tho' they come to church now

& then) . . . still retain, & are more or less under the influence of their Father's Principles."[16]

Twenty-five years later the Anglican itinerant Charles Woodmason wrote about how such spiritual eclecticism had "quite inverted the Nature of Things." Settling in the vast reaches of St. Mark's Parish, he found that the Anglican chapel on the Congaree River had "No Pews, Font, Communion Table, or any thing resembling a Place of Worship, saving [the] Pulpit." He also discovered that the former rector of the Congaree church "would dispense with the Ring in Marriage—[to] prevent tender Consciences from running to unknown Magistrates, to get Married." Woodmason preached at length about this unknown but otherwise "Pious, Just, Upright, and Holy Man."

> Mr. Rowand . . . retrenched the Service—omitted 2 or 3 Repetitions of the Lords Prayer—Gave an Extempore Prayer before Sermon—Preach'd Extempore—Wore no Surplice—Officiated in a Coat—Put his Band in his Pocket—Wore a Blue instead of a Black Coat—Never call'd for God fathers or God Mothers:—Nor us'd the Sign of the Cross excepted desir'd—Or read the Nicene or Athanasian Creeds, but by desire—Left it to People to receive Standing, or Kneeling at receiving the Communion—Varied several Passage in the different Offices, and endeavored to make himself All Things to All Men.[17]

Remarkably, Woodmason began acquitting himself in a comparable fashion at a very early stage of his itinerant career, despite his ecclesiastical temperament. As he ranged here and there to preach among the parishioners of St. Mark's, he came to see himself as being "exactly in the same situation with the Clergy of the primitive Church," preaching and praying extemporaneously and using "no book but the Bible." After preaching to one congregation he even boasted, "My discourse pleas'd so well, they said I was inspired."[18]

Woodmason was in St. Mark's at a time when the South Carolina backcountry was rapidly filling up with people. Already by 1770 the population of the region had grown to about thirty-six thousand people, as "a mix'd Medly from all Countries" settled the inland frontier.[19] Along the fringes of these new frontier settlements, Protestant evangelicalism began to exert a strong influence from the 1730s and 1740s, just as it had from a slightly earlier date in the longer settled areas to the south and east. Moreover, white evangelical ministers and their followers were undertaking significant new efforts to convert African American slaves to evangelical Christianity. In speaking about efforts to baptize and convert slaves in British America, John Tobler reported in 1754 that "in Carolina, many of them can be found who are baptized, and also a few among them who demonstrate their Christianity in their lives." Immediately after making this important distinction, Tobler drew attention to his son's routine catechizings in New Windsor by noting that "my older son, when he is here (for he is often traveling), instructs the Negroes in Christianity every Sunday." (Tobler was presumably referring to his son-in-law, Pastor John Joachim Zubly of the Wappetaw Church, who married Ann Tobler in 1746.)[20]

Much like Archibald Simpson and other revivalists, Tobler celebrated the advance of Protestant evangelicalism among African American slaves, great numbers of whom embraced evangelical Christianity in subsequent decades. Also like Simpson, Tobler expressed much concern over the state of religion in colonial British America. Along the frontiers of settlement in the lower southern region, only a few ministers preached "the birth, passion, death, resurrection and ascension of Christ and the mission of the Holy Spirit," and everywhere there were too many people "who, to all appearances, have no religion at all." "The golden image of Nebuchadnezzar still has many worshippers," Tobler reported in 1754, "and the belly is also not forgotten." "In addition to these," he said, "there are also people who have denied God and who believe neither in God nor in hell and the devil." Despite these concerns, Tobler remained "hopeful that things would get better than they are now," supposing that if God raised up "many righteous preachers" in the Carolinas and Georgia they would reap "an abundant harvest."[21]

Around the same time that Tobler penned his account, a group of Seventh Day Baptists from the Conococheague Valley region of Pennsylvania, began organizing the Broad River Baptist Church, constituting the first Baptist church congregation in the South Carolina backcountry. They were the vanguard of a surging tide of Atlantic-world migration that brought thousands of people to the area in the years leading up to the American Revolution. During the 1750s and 1760s migrants from Pennsylvania and Virginia continually poured into the piedmont, including large numbers of German and Scotch-Irish settlers, while others migrated from Charleston and the older maritime settlements along the coast. Reformed and sectarian Protestantism experienced phenomenal growth as a direct result of this influx, with Presbyterians, Baptists, Lutherans, Quakers and a variety of other groups multiplying in great numbers. Very quickly a new wave of spiritual enthusiasm arose throughout the region. A letter by John Pearson of the Broad River Baptist Church dated May 5, 1764, is suggestive of dissenter activity in this period. Writing of "a great meeting" scheduled to be held in the Congarees later in the month, Pearson urged his son Philip to come up to the three-day event with his grandmother, his aunt Patience and uncle Moses, and some other family members who had not yet experienced conversion "so God may make Use of some of our Ministers as a little Clay to Open there [sic] Eyes that they may Desire Spiritual Things." "Itt may be for there Eternal Wellfare," Pearson stressed, "for itt is Good to be where Jesus is passing by as poor blind Bartemus found to his Eternal Happiness."[22]

As Continental Pietists, evangelical Presbyterians, and New Light Baptists converged in the South Carolina backcountry, then, Protestant evangelicalism quickly gained new ground in the colonial lower southern colonies. In 1772 German Seventh Day and Dunker Baptists alone counted four South Carolina churches (Broad River, Beaver Creek, Cloud's Creek, and Edisto), which together had more than 400 men, women, and children in connection—of whom some 130 (or 33 percent) were formal members.[23] Presbyterians, revivalistic Separate and Regular Baptists, and what Woodmason described as "an hundred other sects" were likewise on the march, setting in motion powerful currents that would eventually grow into a new culmination at the turn of the nineteenth century.[24] Considered against the background of colonial South Carolina's continuing religious development from 1670 and 1760, this Great Revival of 1800–1805 represented neither a sharp break nor a critical turning point in the history of religion in the American South but rather an outgrowth of nascent impulses that originated in the lowcountry in the years leading up to 1740. Indeed, by studying some of those impulses we have clearly seen that the main lines of development stand out clearly and definitely from the 1720s and 1730s, when religious revivals became a permanent part of the southern social pattern.

Notes

Preface

1. Donald G. Mathews, *Religion in the Old South* (Chicago: University of Chicago Press, 1977), xiii.

2. Ibid., 10–38; Samuel S. Hill, "A Survey of Southern Religious History," in Hill, ed., *Religion in the Southern States: A Historical Study* (Macon, Ga.: Mercer University Press, 1983), 383; Christine Leigh Heyrman, *Southern Cross: The Beginnings of the Bible Belt* (Chapel Hill: University of North Carolina Press, 1997), 9. It is important to note that Mathews wrote his book "not as the last word on southern religion, but the first word, an invitation to further discussion of the character, functions, and significance of religion in shaping and defining the South as a distinct part of the new American nation" (*Religion in the Old South*, xiii–xiv). For an excellent survey of recent work on religion in the early South that speaks to some of the ways in which the field of southern religious history has developed, see Jon F. Sensbach, "Religion in the Early South in an Age of Atlantic Empire," *Journal of Southern History* 73 (August 2007): 631–42. See also John B. Boles, "The Discovery of Southern Religious History," in Boles and Evelyn Thomas Nolen, eds., *Interpreting Southern History: Historiographical Essays in Honor of Stanford W. Higginbothan* (Baton Rouge: Louisiana State University Press, 1987), 510–48, and Sensbach, "Before the Bible Belt: Indians, Africans, and the New Synthesis of Eighteenth-Century Southern Religious History," in Beth Barton Schweiger and Donald G. Mathews, eds., *Religion in the American South: Protestants and Others in History and Culture* (Chapel Hill: University of North Carolina Press, 2004), 5–29.

3. Walter L. Robbins, ed., "John Tobler's Description of South Carolina (1754)," *South Carolina Historical Magazine* 71 (October 1970): 262.

4. Jack P. Greene, "Colonial South Carolina: An Introduction," in Greene, Rosemary Brana-Shute, and Randy J. Sparks, eds., *Money, Trade, and Power: The Evolution of Colonial South Carolina's Plantation Society* (Columbia: University of South Carolina Press, 2001), vii–viii; Greene, *Pursuits of Happiness: The Social Development of Early Modern British Colonies and the Formation of American Culture* (Chapel Hill: University of North Carolina Press, 1988), 50–52, 141–51.

5. Robbins, ed., "John Tobler's Description of South Carolina (1754)," 261.

6. Jon Butler, *Awash in a Sea of Faith: Christianizing the American People* (Cambridge: Harvard University Press, 1990); Thomas S. Kidd, *The Great Awakening: The Roots of Evangelical Christianity in Colonial America* (New Haven: Yale University Press, 2007); Sylvia R. Frey and Betty Wood, *Come Shouting Zion: African American Protestantism in the American South and the British Caribbean to 1830* (Chapel Hill: University of North Carolina Press, 1998).

7. S. Charles Bolton, *Southern Anglicanism: The Church of England in Colonial South Carolina* (Westport, Conn.: Greenwood Press, 1982); Daniel B. Thorpe, *The Moravian Community in Colonial North Carolina: Pluralism on the Southern Frontier* (Knoxville: University of Tennessee Press, 1995); Nicolas M. Beasley, *Christian Ritual and the Creation of British Slave Societies, 1650–1780* (Athens: University of Georgia Press, 2009).

8. Bolton, *Southern Anglicanism*, 56, 159, 162.

9. Extract from Bethabarba Diary, January 1761, *Records of the Moravians of North Carolina*, ed. Adelaide L. Fries, 11 vols. (Raleigh, N.C., 1922–1969), 1:234–36, quoted in Philip M. Hamer, George C. Rogers, Jr., and David R. Chestnutt, eds., *The Papers of Henry Laurens: Volume Three: Jan. 1, 1759–Aug. 31, 1763* (Columbia: University of South Carolina Press, 1972), 56n.

10. Robbins, ed., "John Tobler's Description of South Carolina (1754)," 260, 262.

11. Hugh Fisher, *A Preservative from damnable Errors, in the Unction of the Holy One* ([Boston], 1730), 31.

12. Patricia U. Bonomi, *Under the Cope of Heaven: Religion, Society, and Politics in Colonial America* (New York: Oxford University Press, 1986), 125.

13. Religion in the colonial Chesapeake has been the subject of several excellent studies in the past thirty years. See, for example, Rhys Isaac, *The Transformation of Virginia, 1740–1790* (Chapel Hill: University of North Carolina Press, 1982); John K. Nelson, *A Blessed Community: Parishes, Parsons, and Parishioners in Anglican Virginia, 1660–1776* (Chapel Hill: University of North Carolina Press, 2004); Dell Upton, *Holy Things and Profane: Anglican Parish Churches in Colonial Virginia* (Cambridge: MIT Press, 1986); Joan R. Gunderson, *The Anglican Ministry in Virginia, 1723–1775: A Study of Social Class* (New York: Garland , 1989).

14. Wesley M. Gewehr, *The Great Awakening in Virginia, 1740–1790* (Durham: Duke University Press, 1930), 40–166 (quotations on pp. 40, 106, 143).

15. For example, see Isaac, *The Transformation of Virginia*, 141–269; Heyrman, *Southern Cross*, 9–22.

16. Bonomi, *Under the Cope of Heaven*, 92.

17. Evan Haefeli, review of *Empires of God: Religious Encounters in the Early Modern Atlantic*, ed. Linda Gregerson and Susan Juster, *Journal of American History*, 98 (December 2011): 808–9.

18. Ned C. Landsman, *Crossroads of Empire: The Middle Colonies in British North America* (Baltimore: Johns Hopkins University Press, 2010); Richard A. Bailey, *Race and Redemption in Puritan New England* (New York: Oxford University Press, 2011); Chris Beneke and Christopher S. Grenda, eds., *The First Prejudice: Religious Tolerance and Intolerance in Early America* (Philadelphia: University of Pennsylvania Press, 2011); Linda Gregerson and Susan Juster, eds., *Empires of God: Religious Encounters in the Early*

Modern Atlantic (Philadelphia: University of Pennsylvania Press, 2011); Carla Gardina Pestana, *Religion and the Making of the British Atlantic World* (Philadelphia: University of Pennsylvania Press, 2009).

19. W. R. Ward, *The Protestant Evangelical Awakening* (Cambridge: Cambridge University Press, 1992); Mark A. Noll, *The Rise of Evangelicalism: The Age of Edwards, Whitefield, and the Wesleys* (Downers Grove, Ill.: InterVarsity Press, 2003).

Chapter 1. Libertines, Sectaries, and Enthusiasts

1. Gideon Johnston to bishop of Sarum [Salisbury], September 20, 1708, in Frank J. Kingberg, *Carolina Chronicle: The Papers of Commissary Gideon Johnston, 1707–1716* (Berkeley: University of California Press, 1946), 28. Although everyone living in the southwestern part of Carolina—Africans, Indians, and Europeans—might be called a settler, I have followed the convention of using the term to refer to white immigrants in general and free white immigrants in particular.

2. Frederick Lewis Weis, *The Colonial Clergy and the Colonial Churches of the Middle and Southern Colonies, 1607–1776* (Lancaster, Mass.: Society of the Descendants of the Colonial Clergy, 1938), 31, 36, 45, 51, 72, 100, 102; Steven B. Weeks, *Southern Quakers and Slavery: A Study in Institutional History* (Baltimore: The Johns Hopkins University Press, 1896), appendix; U.S. Bureau of Census, Department of Commerce, *Historical Statistics of the United States: Colonial Times to 1970*, 2 vols. (Washington, D.C.: U.S. Government Printing Office, 1975), 2:1168 (Ser. Z 15–17, compiled by Stella H. Sutherland). The term *formed congregation* is equated here with the word *church*. Compare Marcus Jernegan's use of the word *church* in Charles O. Paullin, *Atlas of the Historical Geography of the United States*, ed. John Wright (Washington, D.C.: Carnegie Institution of Washington and the American Geographical Society of New York, 1932), 49–50, plate 82.

3. Gideon Johnston to bishop of Sarum, September 8, 1708, in Klingberg, *Carolina Chronicle*, 19, 21–22, 27–28, 30.

4. Peter A. Coclanis, *The Shadow of a Dream: Economic Life and Death in the South Carolina Low Country, 1670–1920* (New York: Oxford University Press, 1989), 202n41.

5. "An Act for the making of Aliens Free of this Part of this Province, and for granting Liberty of Conscience to all Protestants," March 10, 1697, in Nicholas Trott, *The Laws of the British Plantations in America, Relating to the Church and the Clergy, Religion, and Learning* (London: B. Cowse, 1721), 74; *Oxford English Dictionary*, s.v. "several."

6. Petition of Joseph Boone, in Leo Francis Stock, ed., *Proceedings and Debates of the British Parliaments Respecting North America, 1542–1754*, 5 vols. (Washington, D.C.: Carnegie Institution of Washington), 3:116.

7. Gideon Johnston to bishop of Sarum, September 8, 1708, in Klingberg, *Carolina Chronicle*, 22.

8. M. Eugene Sirmans, *Colonial South Carolina: A Political History* (Chapel Hill: University of North Carolina Press, 1966), 17–74.

9. Petition of Joseph Boone, in Stock, *Proceedings and Debates*, 3:116.

10. Council to Proprietors, September 9, 1670, and March 4, 1671, *The Shaftesbury Papers and Other Records Relating to Carolina and the First Settlement on Ashley River Prior to the Year 1676*, ed. Langdon Cheves, vol. 5 of *Collections of the South Carolina Historical*

Society (Richmond: William Ellis Jones, 1897), 180, 276. Hereafter cited as Cheves, *Shaftesbury Papers.*

11. Mattie Erma Edwards Parker, ed., *North Carolina Charters and Constitutions, 1578–1698* (Raleigh: Carolina Charter Tercentenary Commission, 1963), 76. The eight original Carolina proprietors were Edward Hyde, 1st Earl of Clarendon; George Monck, 1st Duke of Albemarle; William Craven, 1st Earl of Craven; John Berkeley, 1st Baron Berkeley of Stratton; Lord Anthony Ashley Cooper; Sir George Carteret; Sir William Berkeley; and Sir John Colleton. See William S. Powell, *The Proprietors of Carolina* (Raleigh: North Carolina Tercentenary Commission, 1963). With the patronage of his relative the Duke of Albemarle, Colleton seems to have been the early leader of the group. After Colleton's death Anthony Ashley Cooper assumed this role.

12. Parker, *North Carolina Charters and Constitutions,* 77, 88; Wesley Frank Craven, *The Southern Colonies in the Seventeenth Century, 1607–1689,* vol. 1 of *A History of the South,* ed. Wendell H. Stephenson and E. Merton Coulter (Baton Rouge: Louisiana State University Press, 1949), 317–32; Charles McLean Andrews, *The Colonial Period in American History,* 4 vols. (New Haven: Yale University Press, 1934–1938), 3:183–87. See also James Lowell Underwood, "The Dawn of Religious Freedom in South Carolina: The Journey from Limited Tolerance to Constitutional Right," in *The Dawn of Religious Freedom in South Carolina,* ed. Underwood and W. Lewis Burke (Columbia: University of South Carolina Press, 2006), 1–2. As Richard Waterhouse points out, George Monck, Edward Hyde, John Berkeley, William Craven, and George Carteret had substantial influence at court. See Waterhouse, *A New World Gentry: The Making of a Merchant and Planter Class in South Carolina, 1670–1770* (New York: Garland, 1989), 2.

13. William L. Saunders, ed., *The Colonial Records of North Carolina,* 10 vols. (Raleigh: State of North Carolina, 1886–1890), 1 (1662–1712): 45.

14. In the spring of 1663 Puritans established a settlement in the Cape Fear region. It is important to note that the proprietors regularly corresponded with potential New England settlers. See Craven, *The Southern Colonies in the Seventeenth Century,* 318–20, 324–30.

15. N. H. Keeble, *The Restoration: England in the 1660s* (Oxford: Blackwell, 2001), 109–21. For the texts of these acts, see Alexander Luders et al., eds., *Statutes of the Realm,* "An Act for the Well Governing and Regulating of Corporations" (13 Car. II, stat. II., cap. 1); "An Act for the Uniformity of Public Prayers, and Administration of Sacraments, and other Rites and Ceremonies; and for Establishing the Form of Making, Ordaining and Consecrating Bishops, Priests and Deacons in the Church of England" (14 Car. II, cap. 4); "An Act to Prevent and Suppresse Seditious Conventicles" (16 Car. II, cap. 4); and "An Act for Restraining Nonconformists from Inhabiting in Corporations" (7 Car.II, cap. 2).

16. Parker, *North Carolina Charters and Constitutions,* 114. The Concessions and Agreement of January 7, 1665, was negotiated in London in the autumn of 1664 by William Yeamans on behalf of his father, Sir John Yeamans, the leader of a group of Barbadian adventurers planning a settlement at Port Royal. The proprietors encouraged Sir John to recruit New England settlers whom they believed would people the colony in large numbers. See Craven, *The Southern Colonies in the Seventeenth Century,* 329–31.

17. Lords Proprietors to Sir John Yeamans, January 11, 1664, in Cheves, *Shaftesbury Papers*, 51.

18. Parker, *North Carolina Charters and Constitutions*, 88–89, 104; Underwood, "The Dawn of Religious Freedom in South Carolina," 2.

19. *A Brief Description of the Province of Carolina, on the Coasts of Floreda, and more perticularly of the New Plantation begun by the English at Cape Feare, on that River now by them called Charles-River, the 29th of May, 1664* ... (London: Printed for Robert Horne, 1666), in Alexander S. Salley, Jr., ed., *Narratives of Early Carolina, 1650–1708* (1911; rpt., New York: Barnes & Noble, 1953), 71–72. Of course Charles II was generally disposed to be tolerant, but he issued both Carolina charters as the Cavalier Parliament set about circumscribing English nonconformity through the promulgation of the Clarendon Code.

20. Charles H. Lippy, "'Chastized by Scorpions': Christianity and Culture in Colonial South Carolina, 1669–1740," *Church History* 79 (June 2010): 253–70.

21. Lord Ashley to Governor Sayle, April 10, 1671, in Cheves, *Shaftesbury Papers*, 312. See also the endnotes in this volume, 476, notes to pages 279, 281.

22. For the text of the earliest version of the Fundamental Constitutions dated July 21, 1669, see Ruth S. Green, "The South Carolina Archives Copy of the Fundamental Constitutions, Dated July 21, 1669," *South Carolina Historical Magazine* 71 (April 1970): 86–100 (quotations on page 98). See also Mattie Erma E. Parker, "The First Fundamental Constitutions of Carolina," *South Carolina Historical Magazine* 71 (April 1970): 78–85. On the authorship of the Fundamental Constitutions, see J. R. Milton, "John Locke and the Fundamental Constitutions of Carolina," *Locke Newsletter* 21 (1990): 111–33.

23. Green, "The South Carolina Archives Copy of the Fundamental Constitutions," 98–99; Petition of Joseph Boone, in Stock, *Proceedings and Debates*, 3:116.

24. Green, "The South Carolina Archives Copy of the Fundamental Constitutions," 97, 99.

25. Ibid., 98.

26. Parker, *North Carolina Charters and Constitutions*, 181; John Locke, *The Works of John Locke: A New Edition, Corrected*, 10 vols. (London: Thomas Tegg, 1823), 10:194.

27. Parker, *North Carolina Charters and Constitutions*, 128; Articles of Agreement, April 26, 1669, in Cheves, *Shaftesbury Papers*, 91–93; Converse D. Clowse, *Economic Beginnings in Colonial South Carolina, 1670–1730* (Columbia: University of South Carolina Press, 1971), 14–17.

28. Quoted in Cheves, *Shaftesbury Papers*, 160.

29. See J. H. Lefroy, *Memorials of the Discovery and Early Settlement of the Bermudas or Somers Islands, 1511–1687*, 2 vols. (London: Longmans, Greeen, 1879), 2:298. How long the colonists aboard the *Carolina* stayed in Bermuda is unclear, but "the stern of the ship broke in" in the Bahamas. Quoted in Cheves, *Shaftesbury Papers*, 160. Yeamans indicated that the colonists were on the island for considerable time. In a letter from Barbados he wrote about the stormy voyage to the proprietors, noting "how by the hand of God through the violence of stormes and contrary winds your Fleete became dispersed." Once the *Carolina* limped into port in Bermuda, Yeamans added that "the refitting and waiting a faire oportunity had relapsed soe much time that I found myselfe

through necessity engaged to reterne from that Island hither." Sir John Yeamans to Lords Proprietors, November 15, 1670, in Cheves, *Shaftesbury Papers*, 217.

30. Governor Sayle to Lord Ashley, June 25, 1670, in Cheves, *Shaftesbury Papers*, 172.

31. Lefroy, *Memorials*, 2:171; Worthington C. Ford, "The Rev. Sampson Bond of the Bermudas." *Proceedings of the Massachusetts Historical Society*, 3rd. ser.,54 (1921): 289–318; Babette M. Levy, "Early Puritanism in the Southern and Island Colonies," *American Antiquarian Society Proceedings* 70 (1961): 188–90.

32. Governor Sayle to Lord Ashley, June 25, 1670, in Cheves, *Shaftesbury Papers*, 172.

33. Council to Proprietors, March 21, 1671, in Cheves, *Shaftesbury Papers*, 291. On Sayle, see Lefroy, *Memorials*, 2:117–18 passim; Michael Craton and Gail Saunders, *Islanders in the Stream: A History of the Bahamian People, Volume One: From Aboriginal Times to the End of Slavery* (Athens: University of Georgia Press, 1992), 74–79; Craven, *The Southern Colonies in the Seventeenth Century*, 335–37, 342–44; Levy, "Early Puritanism in the Southern and Island Colonies,"184–86, 188–89.

34. Quoted in Craton and Saunders, *Islanders in the Stream*, 79.

35. Council at Ashley river Remonstrance, March 16, 1671, in Cheves, *Shaftesbury Papers*, 290–91; Sirmans, *Colonial South Carolina*, 26.

36. William Owen to Robert Blaney, March 22, 1671, in Cheves, *Shaftesbury Papers*, 301.

37. Council at Ashley river Remonstrance, March 16, 1671, ibid., 291.

38. Sir John Yeamans to Lords Proprietors, November 15, 1670, ibid., 218.

39. William Owen to Robert Blayney, March 22, 1671, ibid., 301.

40. Richard S. Dunn, *Sugar and Slaves: The Rise of the Planter Class in the English West Indies, 1624–1713* (1972; rpt., New York: W.W. Norton, 1973), 112; Richard S. Dunn, "The English Sugar Islands and the Founding of South Carolina," *South Carolina Historical Magazine* 72 (April 1971): 81–93; Jack P. Greene, *Pursuits of Happiness: The Social Development of Early Modern British Colonies and the Formation of American Culture* (Chapel Hill: University of North Carolina Press, 1988), 42–43, 152–54; Virginia Bernhard, *Slaves and Slaveholders in Bermuda, 1616–1782* (Columbia: University of Missouri Press, 1999), 131–35 passim.

41. Lefroy, *Memorials*, 2:289.

42. Quoted in Ford, "The Rev. Sampson Bond," 300.

43. Governor Sayle to Lord Ashley, June 25, 1670, in Cheves, *Shaftesbury Papers*, 172. See also Lefroy, *Memorials*, 1:692; Ford, "The Rev. Sampson Bond," 306–7.

44. Lefroy, *Memorials*, 1:692.

45. Peter H. Wood, *Black Majority: Negroes in Colonial South Carolina from 1670 through the Stono Rebellion* (1974; rpt., New York: W.W. Norton, 1975), 21. It is significant that Gideon Johnston noted that Bermudians made up a substantial part of South Carolina's "Hotch potch." Walter B. Edgar has written that "in South Carolina, regardless of the island of origin, most settlers . . . were called 'Barbadians' (not a totally accurate appellation since settlers came from many different islands, including Bermuda and the Bahamas, which were the cultural heirs to Virginia and Massachusetts, not Barbados)": *South Carolina: A History* (Columbia: University of South Carolina Press, 1998), 48. For examples of some of the earliest Bermudians who came, see Agnes

Leeland Baldwin, *First Settlers of South Carolina,* Tricentennial Booklet Number 1 (Columbia: University of South Carolina Press, 1969). For later references, see John Lawson, *A New Voyage to Carolina; Containing the Exact and Natural History of That Country: Together with the Present State Thereof. And a Journal of a Thousand Miles, Travel'd Thro' Several Nations of Indians. Giving a Particular Account of Their Customs, Manners, & c.* (London, 1709), 7.

46. Lefroy, *Memorials,* 1:329.

47. Ibid., 2:324.

48. Ibid., 1:692; Ford, "The Rev. Sampson Bond," 301–5. See also Levy, "Puritanism in the Southern and Island Colonies," 188–90.

49. Lefroy, *Memorials,* 1:692.

50. Lefroy, *Memorials,* 2:320. On Smith's meeting with the Governor's Council, defiance of the council's order, and subsequent imprisonment, see ibid., 2:267–68. On Whaley, see ibid., 2:258 passim. On Smith's lawsuit, see ibid., 2:294–98. See also Bernhard, *Slaves and Slaveholders in Bermuda,* 137–40; Levy, "Early Puritanism in the Southern and Island Colonies," 187.

51. Lefroy, *Memorials,* 2:268.

52. Ibid., 1:692. On Seymour, see ibid., 2:186.

53. Ibid., 2:268.

54. Ibid., 2:277, 294. On *Heydon,* see ibid., 2:285–86 passim.

55. Ibid., 2:289. See also Bernhard, *Slaves and Slaveholders in Bermuda,* 137–40. The colonists appear to have spent several weeks in Bermuda. See note 29 above.

56. Lefroy, *Memorials,* 2:291.

57. Ibid., 2:293.

58. Bernhard, *Slaves and Slaveholders in Bermuda,* 137. The 1647 law is quoted on page 137.

59. Lefroy, *Memorials,* 2:293.

60. Ibid., 2:294.

61. Ibid., 2:329.

62. Ibid., 2:269. See also ibid., 2:319–20.

63. Ibid., 1:692.

64. Governor Sayle to Lord Ashley, June 25, 1670, in Cheves, *Shaftesbury Papers,* 172.

65. Lefroy, *Memorials,* 2:298–99.

66. Ibid., 2:200.

67. Ibid., 2:299.

68. "Mr. Carteret's Relation" [1670], in Cheves, *Shaftesbury Papers,* 166, 168.

69. Council to the Proprietors, 1670, ibid., 176. For an early reference to Albemarle Point, see Joseph West to Lord Ashley, June 27, 670, ibid, 174. For an important subsequent reference, see Lord Ashley to Gov. Sayle, April 10, 1671, ibid, 310. In 1680 Charleston was relocated across the Ashley River to Oyster Point.

70. Governor West to Lord Ashley, June 25, 1670, in Cheves, *Shaftesbury Papers,* 171.

71. Joseph West to Lord Ashley, June 27, 1670, ibid., 174. See also "Provisions at Ashley River," ibid., 178.

72. Joseph West to Lord Ashley, March 2, 1671, ibid., 268.

73. Council at Ashley river Remonstrance, March 16, 1671, ibid., 291–92. See also Charles H. Lesser, *South Carolina Begins: The Records of a Proprietary Colony, 1663–1671* (Columbia: South Carolina Department of Archives and History, 1995).

74. Council to the Proprietors, March 4, 1671, in Cheves, *Shaftesbury Papers,* 276.

75. Florence O'Sullivan to Lord Ashley, September 10, 1670, ibid., 189; Council to the Proprietors, September 9, 1670, ibid., 180.

76. Joseph West to Lord Ashley, March 2, 1671, ibid., 268; Council to Proprietors, September 9, 1670, ibid., 180–81.

77. Council to Proprietors, March 4, 1671, ibid., 276.

78. Joseph West to Lord Ashley, 1670, ibid., 203.

79. John Locke's summary of a letter by Maurice Mathews, now missing, dated circa September 15, 1670, ibid. [Locke's Carolina Memoranda], 259.

80. Governor Sayle to Lord Ashley, June 25, 1670, ibid., 71–72.

81. Council to Proprietors, September 9, 1670, ibid., 180.

82. Florence O'Sullivan to Lord Ashley, September 10, 1670, ibid., 189; Gov. West to Lord Ashley & c., March 21, 1671, ibid., 296.

83. John Culpepper's map, drawn in the summer of 1671, is reproduced from Cheves, *Shaftesbury Papers,* 5, frontpiece.

84. Council at Ashley river Remonstrance, March 16, 1671, ibid., 293–94; Gov. West to Lord Ashley, & c., March 21, 1671, ibid., 296. In March 1670 the first settlers elected Joseph Dalton, Robert Donne, Ralph Marshall, Paul Smith, and Joseph West to the council. The council's remonstrance was signed by Governor West, Florence O'Sullivan, Robert Donne, Stephen Bull, Paul Smith, and Ralph Marshall. Joseph Dalton served as the colony's register.

85. William Owen to Robert Blayney, March 22, 1671, ibid., 302. See also Sirmans, *Colonial South Carolina,* 26.

86. Apparently none of the acts from the 1670s or early 1680s survives. The titles of twenty-two statutes passed from May 1682 to April 1685 are listed in Thomas Cooper and David J. McCord, eds., *The Statutes at Large of South Carolina,* 10 vols. (Columbia: A. S. Johnston, 1836–1841), 2:v. Act nos. 1 and 2, "An Act for the observation of the Lord's Day" and "An Act for the suppression of Idle, Drunken and Swearing Persons" were both passed on May 26, 1682. Since statutes were normally to remain in force for a period of only twenty-three months, these measures were renewed by Act number 28, "An Act for reviving of several Acts of Parliament," which was passed on November 23, 1685. A new measure, Act number 74, was passed on December 11, 1691, combining language from the earlier laws. See ibid., 2:13, 68–70.

87. "An Act for the Better Observance of the Lord's Day," ibid., 2:68–70 (Act no. 74). There were of course a few exceptions to the prohibitions against working and travel. See also Underwood, "The Dawn of Religious Freedom in South Carolina," 23–26; Nicholas M. Beasley, *Christian Ritual and the Creation of British Slave Societies, 1650–1780* (Athens: University of Georgia Press, 2009), 40–41.

88. Council at Ashley river Remonstrance, March 21, 1671, in Cheves, *Shaftesbury Papers,* 292, 295; Joseph West to Lord Ashley, March 21, 1671, ibid., 296; "An Act for the Better Observance of the Lord's Day," in Cooper and McCord, *Statutes at Large,*

2:69 (Act no. 74). See also Joseph West to Lord Ashley, West to Sir George Carteret, and West to Sir Peter Colleton, March 2, 1671, in Cheves, *Shaftesbury Papers*, 268, 269, 273; John Stewart to William Dunlop, June 23, 1690, in J. G. Dunlop, ed., "Letters from John Stewart to William Dunlop," *South Carolina Historical Magazine* 32 (April–July 1931): 98; John Archdale, *A New Description of that Fertile and Pleasant Province of Carolina: with a Brief Account of its Discovery, Settling, and the Government Therof to this Time. With several Remarkable Passages of Divine Providence during my Time* (London: Printed for John Wyat, 1707), in Sally, *Narratives of Early Carolina*, 308–9 (hereafter cited as "Archdale's Description of Carolina").

89. Joseph West to Lord Ashley, March 2, 1671, in Cheves, *Shaftesbury Papers*, 268; Sirmans, *Colonial South Carolina*, 26–27. For a different view of South Carolina politics, see L. H. Roper, *Conceiving Carolina: Proprietors, Planters, and Plots, 1662–1729* (New York: Palgrave Macmillian, 2004), 41–67 passim.

90. John Locke's summary of a letter by Maurice Mathews, now missing, dated circa September 15, 1670, in Cheves, *Shaftesbury Papers* [Locke's Carolina Memoranda], 247–48, 259; William Owen to Robert Blayney, March 22, 1671, ibid., 302.

91. John Locke's summary of a letter by John Godfrey, now lost, circa July 1671, in ibid. [Locke's Carolina Memoranda], 350; Sirmans, *Colonial South Carolina*, 26–29. See also Dunn, "The English Sugar Islands and the Founding of South Carolina," 81–93; Richard Waterhouse, "England, the Caribbean, and the Founding of South Carolina," *Journal of American Studies* 9 (December 1975): 259–81; John P. Thomas, "The Barbadians in Early South Carolina," *South Carolina Historical Magazine* 31 (April 1930): 75–92; Wood, *Black Majority*, chapter 1. As Wesley Frank Craven underscores, not all Barbadian immigrants were Anglican: *The Colonies in Transition, 1660–1713* (New York: Harper & Row, 1968), 96. Nor were all "Barbadians" actually from Barbados. They included settlers from other English West Indian islands as well as the Atlantic colonies of Bermuda and the Bahamas. See Edgar, *South Carolina*, 48.

92. William Owen to Robert Blayney, March 22, 1671, in Cheves, *Shaftesbury Papers*, 304.

93. Ibid., 303 (emphasis added); Joseph West to Lord Ashley, September 3, 1671, ibid., 337–38.

94. John Locke's summary of a letter by Sir John Yeamans, now lost, circa July 1671, ibid. [Locke's Carolina Memoranda] , 349; Joseph West to Lord Ashley, September 3, 1671, ibid., 337.

95. Joseph West to Lord Ashley, September 3, 1671, ibid., 338. According to West, many of the colonists believed "Sir John intended to make [South Carolina] a Cape Fear settlement." It is important to note that the Cape Fear settlement had been abandoned in 1667 because of political infighting. See Craven, *The Southern Colonies in the Seventeenth Century*, 329–33.

96. Joseph West to Sir George Carteret, March 2, 1671, in Cheves, *Shaftesbury Papers*, 269. West repeated the same sentiments on March 2, 1671, in separate letters to Lord Ashley and Sir Peter Colleton. See *Shaftesbury Papers*, 268, 273.

97. Joseph West to Lord Ashley, September 3, 1671, ibid., 338; Anthony Ashley Cooper to Sir John Yeamans, December 15, 1671, ibid., 361; John Locke's summary of a letter

by Joseph West, now lost, circa July 1671, ibid. [Locke's Carolina Memoranda], 350. Richard Dunn classifies big Barbadian planters as owning sixty or more slaves and middling planters as owning from twenty to fifty-nine slaves. See his *Sugar and Slaves,* 92. Richard Waterhouse examines how these planters contributed to the formation of a colonial elite class in *A New World Gentry.*

98. "An Act or Order for the Publication and Execution of the Acts Concerning the Uniformity of Common Prayer," in Nicholas Trott, *The Laws of the British Plantations in America, Relating to the Church and the Clergy, Religion, and Learning,* 353–54; "An Act concerning Morning and Evening Prayer in Families," ibid., 354–56.

99. Anthony Ashley Cooper to Sir John Yeamans, June 20, 1672, Cheves, Shaftesbury Papers, 397–98.

100. Anthony Ashley Cooper to Joseph West and Council, June 20, 1672, ibid., 401; Proprietors to Governor and Council, May 18, 1674, ibid., 436.

101. Anthony Ashley Cooper to Sir John Yeamans, June 20, 1672, ibid., 397–98; Anthony Ashley Cooper to Joseph West and Council, June 20, 1672, ibid., 401. On Yeamans, see Thomas, "Barbadians in Early South Carolina," 79, 81; Craven, *The Southern Colonies in the Seventeenth Century,* 330–32, 336, 342–43.

102. John Dorrell and Hugh Wentworth to Lord Ashley, February 17, 1670, in Cheves, *Shaftesbury Papers*, 160. See also Sir John Hayden to Lords Proprietors, March 17, 1671, ibid., 281; Craton and Saunders, *Islanders in the Stream,* 79, 89, 92–95.

103. Lord Shaftesbury to Maurice Mathews, June 20, 1672, in Cheves, *Shaftesbury Papers,* 399. On South Carolina's population, see Joseph Dalton to Lord Ashley, January 20, 1672, ibid., 381–82 and 382n; Wood, *Black Majority,* 24–25. On recruiting efforts in colonies to the north, see John Locke's summary of a letter by Mathias Halsted to Lords Proprietors, now missing, circa August 1671, in Cheves, *Shaftesbury Papers* [Locke's Carolina Memoranda], 351–22; John Locke's summary of Halsted to Lord Ashley, now missing, circa March 1672, ibid. [Locke's Carolina Memoranda], 388.

104. Lord Shaftesbury to Joseph West, June 20, 1672, in Cheves, *Shaftesbury Papers,* 403; Wood, *Black Majority,* 24; Edgar, *South Carolina,* 88.

105. Lord Shaftesbury to Sir John Yeamans, June 20, 1672, in Cheves, *Shaftesbury Papers,* 398; Shaftesbury to Joseph West, June 20, 1672, ibid., 402; Shaftesbury to Governor and Council, June 20, 1672, ibid., 400.

106. Lord Shaftesbury to Joseph West, June 20, 1672, ibid., 402; Proprietors to Governor and Council, May 18, 1674, ibid., 434–35.

107. Sirmans, *Colonial South Carolina,* 29–34.

108. John Locke's summary of a letter by John Coming to Sir Peter Colleton, now missing, circa September 30, 1671, in Cheves, *Shaftesbury Papers* [Locke's Carolina Memoranda], 347.

109. Proprietors to Governor and Council, May 18, 1674, ibid., 437.

110. On South Carolina's population, see [Thomas Ashe], *Carolina; or a Description of the Present State of that Country, and the Natural Excellencies therof, viz., the Healthfulness of the Air, Pleasantness of the Place, Advantage and Usefulness of those Rich Commodities there plentifully abounding, which much encrease and flourish by the Industry of the Platers that daily enlarge that Colony* . . . (London: Printed for W. C., 1682), in Salley, *Narratives of*

Early Carolina, 158; Clowse, *Economic Beginnings in Colonial South Carolina*, 251; Coclanis, *The Shadow of a Dream*, 64.

111. Sirmans, *Colonial South Carolina*, chapter 3.

112. David Duncan Wallace, *The History of South Carolina*, 4 vols. (New York: American Historical Association, 1934), 1:95–96; Erskine Clarke, *Our Southern Zion: A History of Calvinism in the South Carolina Low Country, 1690–1990* (Tuscaloosa: University of Alabama Press, 1996), 30–32; Roper, *Conceiving Carolina*, 72; George Pratt Insh, *Scottish Colonial Schemes 1620–1686* (Glasgow: Maclehouse, Jackson, 1922), chapter 6; Bertrand Van Ruymbeke, *From New Babylon to Eden: The Huguenots and Their Migration to Colonial South Carolina* (Columbia: University of South Carolina Press, 2006), 71–96; Jo Anne McCormick, "The Quakers of Colonial South Carolina, 1670–1806," (Ph.D. dissertation, University of South Carolina, 1984), 20–30; Leah Townsend, *South Carolina Baptists, 1670–1805* (1935; rpt., Baltimore: Genealogical Publishing, 1978), 4–10; Daughters of the American Colonists, *Early Maine Records*, 4 vols. (n.p.: Maine Society Daughters of the American Colonists, Sir William Phips Chapter, 1934–1942), 4:261 (quotation); George Howe, *History of the Presbyterian Church in South Carolina*, 2 vols. (Columbia: Duffie & Chapman, 1870), 1:116–24, 185–86.

113. Proprietors to Council, October 18, 1690, quoted in Henry A. M. Smith, "The Ashley River: Its Seats and Settlements," *South Carolina Historical Magazine* 20 (January, 1919): 59; Waterhouse, "England, the Caribbean, and the Settlement of South Carolina," 260–63; Alexander S. Salley, Jr., "Governor Joseph Morton and Some of His Descendants," *South Carolina Historical Magazine* 5 (April 1904): 108–16; Alexander S. Salley, Jr., "Landgrave Daniel Axtell," *South Carolina Historical Magazine* 6 (October 1905): 174–76; Diane K. Bolton, "Stoke Newington: Growth," in *A History of the County of Middlesex: Volume VIII: Islington and Stoke Newington Parishes*, ed. T. F. T. Baker and C. R. Elrington (New York: Oxford University Press, 1985), 143; Langdon Cheves, "Blake of South Carolina," *South Carolina Historical Magazine* 1 (April 1900): 153–57.

114. John Oldmixon, *The British Empire in America* (London, 1708), in Salley, *Narratives of Early Carolina*, 329–30; Cheves, "Blake of South Carolina,"153–57; Alexander S. Salley, Jr., "The Family of the First Landgrave Thomas Smith," *South Carolina Historical Magazine* 28 (July 1927): 169–75; Smith, "The Ashley River," 162; Henry S. Burrage, "The Baptist Church of Kittery," *Collections and Proceedings of the Maine Historical Society*, 2nd ser., 9 (1898): 382–91; Townsend, *South Carolina Baptists*, 6–7; Edward Leodore Smith, "Landgrave Thomas Smith's Visit to Boston," *South Carolina Historical Magazine* 22 (April 1921): 60–64.

115. McCormick, "The Quakers of Colonial South Carolina," 20–34; Dunn, *Sugar and Slaves*, 103–6; Lord Ashley to Governor and Council, June 9, 1675, in Cheves, *Shaftesbury Papers*, 465; W. Scott Poole, "'Your liberty in that province': South Carolina Quakers and the Rejection of Religious Toleration," in Underwood and Burke, *The Dawn of Religious Freedom in South Carolina*, 165–83. See also Lord Shaftesbury to Andrew Percivall, June 9, 1675, in Cheves, *Shaftesbury Papers*, 464–65.

116. Randy J. Sparks, "Mary Fisher, Sophia Hume, and the Quakers of Colonial Charleston," in *South Carolina Women: Their Lives and Times*, ed. Marjorie Julian Spruill,

Valinda W. Littlefield, and Joan Marie Johnson, vol. 1 (Athens: University of Georgia Press, 2009), 40–59; Rebecca Larson, *Daughters of Light: Quaker Women Preaching and Prophesying in the Colonies and Abroad, 1700–1775* (Chapel Hill: University of North Carolina Press, 1999), 26, 65, 67, 232, 261, 311; George Fox to Friends in Charlestown, Carolina, December 23, 1683, in James Bowden, *The History of the Society of Friends in America,* vol. 2 (1850; rpt. Bedford, Mass.: Applewood Books, n.d.), 414; McCormick, "The Quakers of Colonial South Carolina," 25–26.

117. Howe, *History of the Presbyterian Church,* 1:78–85, 116–18; Insh, *Scottish Colonial Schemes,* 186–211, 278–79; Sirmans, *Colonial South Carolina,* 37, 40–41, 44; Linda G. Fryer, "Documents Relating to the Formation of the Carolina Company in Scotland, 1682," *South Carolina Historical Magazine* 99 (April 1998): 110–32; Leigh Eric Schmidt, *Holy Fairs: Scotland and the Making of American Revivalism,* 2nd ed. (Grand Rapids, Mich.: William B. Eerdmans , 2001), 51; John Stewart to William Dunlop, June 23, 1690, in Dunlop, "Letters from John Stewart to William Dunlop," 93.

118. Van Ruymbeke, *From New Babylon to Eden,* 72–74; Van Ruymbeke, "The Huguenots of Proprietary South Carolina: Patterns of Migration and Integration," in *Money, Trade, and Power: The Evolution of Colonial South Carolina's* Plantation Society, ed. Jack P. Greene, Rosemary Brana-Shute, and Randy J. Sparks (Columbia: University of South Carolina Press, 2001), 27–29, 41. In his earlier study Van Ruymbeke had estimated that about six hundred Huguenots migrated to South Carolina by 1710, but he subsequently revised his estimates downward.

119. Van Ruymbeke, *From New Babylon to Eden,* 97–121. Compare Jon Butler, *The Huguenots in America: A Refugee People in New World Society* (Cambridge: Harvard University Press, 1983), 91–143.

120. Coclanis, *The Shadow of a Dream,* 64–65; Wood, *Black Majority,* 131, 142–45. See also Clowse, *Economic Beginnings,* 251–52; Wood, *Black Majority,* 131, 142–45. In 1680 the population ranged from 1,000 to 1,200; in 1685 it stood between 2,500 and 2,700; in 1690 it rose to about 3,600; and in 1700 it hovered around 5,700.

121. Frederick Lewis Weis, *The Colonial Clergy and the Colonial Churches of the Middle and Southern Colonies,* 21, 36, 45, 72, 100, 102 and passim; Stephen B. Weeks, *Southern Quakers and Slavery:* appendix. The word *church* is used to refer to a formed congregation meeting regularly for public worship. Compare Marcus Jernegan's use of the term in Charles O. Paullin, *Atlas of the Historical Geography of the United States,* ed. John Wright (Washington, D.C.: Carnegie Institution of Washington and the American Geographical Society of New York, 1932), 49–50, plate 82. The per capita church ratio assumes a total population in 1701 of 5,700, with roughly 3,300 white residents and 2,400 black residents. Since all but a few black persons worshiped outside of these mostly white churches, a trend which was not reversed until after 1750, the per capita ratio was probably closer to 1 to 275.

122. Weis, *The Colonial Clergy and the Colonial Churches of the Middle and Southern Colonies,* 31, 36, 45, 51, 72, 100, 102; Howe, *History of the Presbyterian Church,* 1:70, 76–77, 79, 84, 86, 117, 122; "Extract of a Letter from Hugh Adams dated at Charletoun [*sic*] in Carolina Feb. 23, 1699/1700," printed in George E. Ellis et al. , eds.,"Diary of Samuel Sewall," *Massachusetts Historical Society Collections,* 5th ser., 6 (1879), 11. The measure

used here is strict: an ordained minister is defined here as one invested officially (as by the laying on of hands) with ministerial authority. Self- or unofficially invested lay preachers have not been included. Neither have assistants, licentiates, or exhorters. The sixteen nonconformist ministers include Gilbert Ashley and William Screven (Baptist); Benjamin Pierpont, John Cotton, Hugh Adams, and Joseph Lord (Congregational); Étienne Duscout, Florent-Phillippe Trouillard, Elias Prioleau, Pierre Robert, and Paul L'Escot (Huguenot); and Thomas Barret, Francis Makemie, Daniel Courtis, William Dunlop, and Archibald Stobo (Presbyterian). The Anglican ministers who settled include: Samuel Marshall, Phineas Rogers, Laurentius Van den Bosch, and Atkin Williamson.

123. Joseph Lord to Thomas Hinckley, February 21, 1699, in Solomon Lincoln et al., eds., "The Hinckley Papers," *Massachusetts Historical Society Collections,* 4th ser., 5 (1861): 305; Sirmans, *Colonial South Carolina,* 78, 162, 182–3, 187–91.

124. Gideon Johnston to SPG, July 5, 1710, in Klingberg, *Carolina Chronicle,* 57; Frederick Dalcho, *An Historical Account of the Protestant Episcopal Church in South Carolina from the First Settlement of the Province to the War of the Revolution* (Charleston: E. Thayer, 1820), 26–7.

125. Thomas Smith to SPG, January 16, 1708, reproduced by Alexander S. Salley, Jr., in "A Letter by the Second Landgrave Smith," *South Carolina Historical Magazine* 32 (January 1931): 62; Johnston to SPG, in Klingberg, *Carolina Chronicle,* 57. Williamson claimed he was ordained by the bishop of Lincoln, but many, including Thomas Smith and Gideon Johnston, doubted the claim. Still, in 1711 the South Carolina legislature granted him a pension. See S. Charles Bolton, *Southern Anglicanism: The Church of England in Colonial South Carolina* (Westport, Conn.: Greenwood Press, 1982), 193n3.

126. Thomas Smith to SPG, January 16, 1708, in Salley, "A Letter by the Second Landgrave Smith," 62; Francis Le Jau to SPG, February 19, 1710, in Frank J. Klingberg, *The Carolina Chronicle of Dr. Francis Le Jau, 1706–1717* (Berkeley: University of California Press, 1956), 73; John Stewart to William Dunlop, April 27, 1690, in Dunlop, "Letters from John Stewart to William Dunlop," 28. Stewart maintained that James Moore and Robert Quary successfully impeached Williamson's testimony in a trial as a result of the incident.

127. Thomas Smith to SPG, January 16, 1708, in Salley, "A Letter by the Second Landgrave Smith," 63; Francis Le Jau to SPG, February 19, 1710, in Klingberg, The *Carolina Chronicle of Dr. Francis Le Jau, 1706-1717,* 73. See also Stewart to Dunlop, April 27 and June 23, 1690, in Dunlop, "Letters from John Stewart to William Dunlop," 28, 28, 91. Some more recent historians, battling the older historiographical notion that the dissolute character of the Anglican clergy caused the Church of England to fall in decline, have attempted to bury the bear-cub episode. See Bolton, *Southern Anglicanism,* 86. Other historians have cited it as an example of the spiritual lethargy of seventeenth-century South Carolinians. See Jon Butler, *Awash in a Sea of Faith: Christianizing the American People* (Cambridge: Harvard University Press, 1990), 64. My emphasis is that the bear-cub episode represents deeply embedded lay hostility to the Anglican clergy in the seventeenth century. Among the weaknesses of the late Stuart English state church were the training and character of the lower clergy.

128. Parker, *North Carolina Charters and Constitutions,* 202, 227–28. Compare 181–82.

129. Sirmans, *Colonial South Carolina,* 38–42; Robert M. Weir, *Colonial South Carolina: A History* (Millwood, N.Y.: KTO Press, 1983), 64. Note that Morton was related to both the Blake and Axtell families.

130. John Stewart to William Dunlop, June 23, 1690, in Dunlop, "Letters from John Stewart to William Dunlop," 96. See the 1690 "Address to Seth Sothel" in William J. Rivers, *A Sketch of the History of South Carolina to the Close of Propriety Government by the Revolution of 1719* (Charleston: McCarter & Co., 1856).

131. Sirmans, *Colonial South Carolina,* 15, 38, 43–45.

132. Parker, *North Carolina Charters and Constitutions,* 152.

133. Sirmans, *Colonial South Carolina,* 44–46.

134. See John Stewart to William Dunlop, April 27, 1690, in Dunlop, "Letters of John Stewart to William Dunlop," 7–10, 14–15.

135. On the Huguenots' entanglement in South Carolina politics, see Butler, *The Huguenots in America,* 102–5. For a more detailed treatment see Van Ruymbeke, *From New Babylon to Eden,* 161–86.

136. Compare the 1665 charter in Parker, *North Carolina Charters and Constitutions* (91–104) with naturalization clauses in various versions of the Fundamental Constitutions (ibid., 152, 184, 206, 231).

137. John Stewart to William Dunlop, April 27, 1690, in Dunlop, "Letters from John Stewart to William Dunlop," 13.

138. Sirmans, *Colonial South Carolina,* 48–50; Cooper and McCord, *Statutes at Large,* 2:58–60 (Act no. 65).

139. John Stewart to William Dunlop, April 27, 1690, in Dunlop, "Letters from John Stewart to William Dunlop," 9.

140. "Archdale's Description of Carolina," in Salley, *Narratives of Early Carolina,* 298; Sirmans, *Colonial South Carolina,* 50–51, 61–62. By 1699 Huguenots were also prohibited from "being Owners and Masters of Vessels." See "Letter of Edward Randolph," in Salley, *Narratives of Early Carolina,* 209.

141. John Stewart to William Dunlop, June 23, 1690, in Dunlop, "Letters from John Stewart to William Dunlop," 98; Sirmans, *Colonial South Carolina,* 55–74; See also Cotton Mather to Anthony William Boehm, August 6, 1716, in Charles Francis Adams et al., "Diary of Cotton Mather, 1709–1724," *Massachusetts Historical Society Collections,* 7th ser., 8 (1912): 412.

142. John Stewart to William Dunlop, October 20, 1693, in Dunlop, "Letters from John Stewart to William Dunlop," 170–71.

143. John Stewart to William Dunlop, June 23, 1690 and October 20, 1693, ibid., 96, 170; Sirmans, *Colonial South Carolina,* 40, 46–47, 53–54; Howe, *History of the Presbyterian Church,* 1:128–30; Salley, "The Family of the First Landgrave Thomas Smith," 169–75.

144. Cheves, "Blake of South Carolina," 155–57; Sirmans, *Colonial South Carolina,* 56, 61–62; John Stewart to William Dunlop, April 27, 1690, in Dunlop, "Letters from John Stewart to William Dunlop," 11–12 (quotations).

145. Quoted in Sirmans, *Colonial South Carolina,* 62.

146. John Stewart to William Dunlop, April 27, 1690, in Dunlop, "Letters from John Stewart to William Dunlop," 9. On the Puritan domination of colonial government, see Sirmans, *Colonial South Carolina*, 61–74.

147. McCormick, ""The Quakers of South Carolina," 32–34; 40–43 (the 1696 Militia Act, part of a body of legislation known as Archdale's Laws, is quoted on page 43 from the City of Charleston *Year Book* [1883], 384); *A Collection of the Epistles from the Yearly Meeting of Friends in London to the Quarterly and Monthly Meetings in Great Briain, Ireland and Elsewhere, from 1675 to 1805; Being from the First Establishment of that Meeting to the Present Time* (Baltimore: Cole and Hewes, 1806), 70; Levy, *Early Puritanism in the Southern and Island Colonies*, 269; Greene, *The Quest for Power*, 476; John Stewart to William Dunlop, April 27, 1690, in Dunlop, "Letters from John Stewart to William Dunlop," 22; Sparks, "Mary Fisher, Sophia Hume, and the Quakers of Colonial Charleston," 46; Larson, *Daughters of Light*, 46–47, 64.

148. Townsend, *South Carolina Baptists*, 8; Henry A. M. Smith, "The Town of Dorchester, in South Carolina—A Sketch of Its History," *South Carolina Historical Magazine* 6 (April 1905): 82; Joseph Lord to Governor Thomas Hinkley, February 21, 1699, in Lincoln et al., "The Hinckley Papers," 305. In her will Elizabeth Blake provided "unto the building of an anabaptist Parsonage house in Charles Town fifty pounds," and "towards the maintenance of the minister of the People commonly called in way of derition Anabaptists twenty pounds per annum." Quoted in Townsend, *South Carolina Baptists*, 13.

149. These and the following quotations are from Henry S. Burrage, "Memoir of William Screven," *Collections and Proceedings of the Maine Historical Society*, 2nd ser., 1 (1889), 45–56; and "Some Added Facts Concerning Rev. William Screven," *Collections and Proceedings of the Maine Historical Society*, 2nd ser., 5 (1894): 275–84. See also, Burrage, "The Baptist Church in Kittery," *Collections and Proceedings of the Maine Historical Society*, 2nd ser., 9 (1898): 382–91; and Joshua Millet, *A History of the Baptists in Maine* (Portland, 1845), 24–28.

150. Townsend, *South Carolina Baptists*, 6–7, 58. Overlooking the extent to which people shuttled back and forth in the Atlantic world, Townsend suggests that Screven remained in Kittery until 1696. Ibid., 5.

151. Josiah Cotton, Manuscript History of the Cotton Family, and Diary, copied by W. G. Brooks from the original in possession of Roland Edwin Cotton, quoted in John Langdon Sibley, *Biographical Sketches of Graduates of Harvard University, in Cambridge, Massachusetts*, Vol. 1, the Classes of 1642-1658 (1873; rpt. Boston: Massachusetts Historical Society, 2010), 505. Hereafter cited as *Sibley's Harvard Graduates*. See also Sheila McIntyre and Len Travers, eds., *The Correspondence of John Cotton, Jr.* (Charlottesville: University of Virginia Press, 2009), 19–29, 573–74.

152. "Diary entries by John Cotton" in McIntyre and Travers, *The Correspondence of John Cotton, Jr.*, 581; Levy, "Puritanism in the Southern and Island Colonies," 264. George N. Edwards, *A History of the Independent or Congregational Church of Charleston South Carolina* (Boston: Pilgrim Press, 1947), 1, 4.

153. John Cotton to Rowland Cotton, July 16, 1698, in McIntyre and Travers, *The Correspondence of John Cotton, Jr.*, 574.

154. Quoted in *Sibley's Harvard Graduates,* 1:499. See also Mark Peterson, "The Plymouth Church and the Evolution of Puritan Religious Culture," *New England Quarterly* 66 (December 1993): 581–82, 587–88; Len Travers, "The Missionary Journal of John Cotton, Jr., 1666–1678," *Proceedings of the Massachusetts Historical Society,* 3rd ser., 109 (1997): 52–101.

155. Quoted in *Sibley's Harvard Graduates,1:* 498–500.

156. Cotton, "Diary entries by John Cotton," in McIntyre and Travers, *The Correspondence of John Cotton, Jr.,* 581–82; Perry Miller, "Jonathan Edwards and the Great Awakening," in *Errand into the Wilderness* (Cambridge: Harvard University Press, 1956), 160.

157. Cotton, "Diary entries by John Cotton," in McIntyre and Travers, *The Correspondence of John Cotton, Jr.,* 582; John Cotton to [unknown], August 1, 1699, ibid., 590.

158. John Cotton to Rowland Cotton, August 8, 1699, ibid., 594.

159. Cotton, "Diary entries by John Cotton," notational entry for January 2, 1699; John Cotton to Rowland Cotton, August 8, 1699, ibid., 582, 593.

160. John Cotton to Rowland Cotton, August 8, 1699, ibid., 594.

161. Quoted in *Sibley's Harvard Graduates,* 1:504. On Cotton's defense of infant baptism, see Joseph Lord to John Cotton, August 7 and September 5, 1699, in McIntyre and Travers, *The Correspondence of John Cotton, Jr.,* 591, 597–98.

162. John Cotton to Rowland Cotton, August 8, 1699, in McIntyre and Travers, *The Correspondence of John Cotton, Jr.,* 595.

163. Cotton, "Diary entries by John Cotton," ibid., 582–83.

164. Ibid., September 4 and September 8, 1699.

165. Theophilus Cotton to John Cotton, October 26, 1699, ibid., 600.

166. "Extract of a Letter from Mr. Hugh Adams dated at Charlestoun [*sic*] in Carolina Feb. 23 1699/1700," in Ellis et. Al., eds., "Diary of Samuel Sewall", 11–12.

167. Ibid.

168. Joseph Lord to Governor Thomas Hinckley, February 21, 1699, in Lincoln et al., "The Hinckley Papers," 305. Howe, *History of the Presbyterian Church,* 1:123–24; See also Clifford K. Shipton, *Sibley's Harvard Graduate: Biographical Sketches of Those Who Attended Harvard College,* Vol. 4., the Classes of 1690-1700 (Boston: Massachusetts Historical Society, 1933), 321–325; Petrona Royall McIver, "Wappetaw Congregational Church," *South Carolina Historical Magazine* 58 (January 1957), 34–37.

169. Quoted in Edwards, *History of the Independent or Congregational Church of Charleston,* 9.

170. On the location of the Wappetaw Church, see Christopher Clement Ohm and Ramona M. Grunden, "Where the Wappetaw Independent Congregational Church Stood . . . , Archaeological Testing at 38CH1682, Charleston County, SC," University of South Carolina Institute of Archaeology and Anthropolgy, *Books and Mauscripts* Book 201 (Columbia: University of South Carolina, 1998).

171. [William Hubbard] to John Archdale, June 26, 1696, "Archdale's Description of Carolina," in Salley, *Narratives of Early Carolina,* 299; Joseph B. Felt, *History of Ipswich, Essex, and Hamilton* (Cambridge, Mass.: Charles Folsom, 1834), 70–71; Shipton, *Sibley's Harvard Graduates,* 4:323. Susannah Wilborn was likely the daughter of John and

Elizabeth (Hart) Wilborn who emigrated from Massachusetts around 1691 and may have settled in South Carolina: Shipton, *Sibley's Harvard Graduates,* 4:323n8.

172. "Instructions for Emigrants from Essex County Mass., to South Carolina, 1697," in H. Roy Merrens, ed., *The Colonial South Carolina Scene: Contemporary Views, 1697–1774* (Columbia: University of South Carolina Press, 1977), 15.

173. [William Hubbard] to John Archdale, June 26, 1699, "Archdale's Description of Carolina," in Salley, *Narratives of Early Carolina,* 299.

174. "Archdale's Description of Carolina," ibid., 300, 302.

175. First Church at Dorchester, *Records of the First Church at Dorchester in New England, 1636–1734* (Boston: George H. Ellis, 1891), 13, 109; Henry A. M. Smith, "The Town of Dorchester, in South Carolina–A Sketch of Its History," *South Carolina Historical Magazine* 6 (April 1905): 61–66; Shipton, *Sibley's Harvard Graduates,* 4:101–105.

176. "Journal of the Elder William Pratt, 1695–1701," in Salley, *Narratives of Early Carolina,"* 195–96: *Records of the First Church at Dorchester in New England,* 145; Smith, "The Town of Dorchester, in South Carolina," 64.

177. "Journal of the Elder William Pratt," in Salley, *Narratives of Early Carolina,* 198–99; Smith, "The Town of Dorchester, in South Carolina," 67–78; William Sumner Appleton, *Records of the Descendants of William Sumner, or Dorchester, Mass.* (Boston: D. Clapp & Son, 1879), 3–4; Shipton, *Sibley's Harvard Graduates,* 4:103; McIntyre and Travers, *The Correspondence of John Cotton, Jr.,* 581–83, 589, 591, 593–95, 597.

178. "Journal of Elder William Pratt," in Salley, *Narratives of Early Carolina,* 197, 199.

Chapter 2. True-Blue Protestants

1. Leo Francis Stock, ed., *Proceedings and Debates of the British Parliaments Respecting North America, 1542–1754,* 5 vols. (Washington, D.C.: Carnegie Institution of Washington, 1924–1941), 3:115, 117–18; Thomas Cooper and David J. McCord, eds., *The Statutes at Large of South Carolina,* 10 vols. (Columbia: A. S. Johnston, 1836–1841), 2:232–33 (Act no. 222), 236–46 (Act no. 225). Granville signed and sealed the acts for himself, Lords Carteret and Craven, and Sir John Colleton.

2. Stock, *Proceedings and Debates of the British Parliaments,* 3:124. See also "Petition of Joseph Boone," February 28, 1706, ibid., 115–18.

3. Cooper and McCord, eds., *Statutes at Large,* 2:282–94; M. Eugene Sirmans, *Colonial South Carolina: A Political History* (Chapel Hill: University of North Carolina Press, 1966), 87–89; S. Charles Bolton, *Southern Anglicanism: The Church of England in Colonial South Carolina* (Wesport, Conn.: Greenwood Press, 1982), 25–28.

4. Based on their detailed analysis of a 1724 Anglican church census, Patricia U. Bonomi and Peter R. Eisenstadt estimate that "Anglicans may have drawn equal or gained a slight majority of adherents by 1730." See Bonomi and Eisenstadt, "Church Adherence in the Eighteenth-Century British American Colonies," *William & Mary Quarterly,* 3rd ser., 39 (April 1982): 256.

5. Cotton Mather to Anthony William Boehm, August 6, 1716, in Charles Francis Adams et al., "Diary of Cotton Mather, 1709-1724," *Massachusetts Historical Society Collections,* 7th ser., 8 (1912), 412; Daniel L. Brunner, *Halle Pietists in England: Anthony*

William Boehm and the Society for the Promoting of Christian Knowledge (Göttingen and Zürich: Vandenhoeck & Ruprecht, 1993), 46–47 passim.

6. Cotton Mather to Anthony William Boehm, August 6, 1716, in Adams et al., eds, "Diary of Cotton Mather, 1709-1724," 412.

7. Donald G. Mathews, *Religion in the Old South* (Chicago: University of Chicago Press, 1977), 6; Nicholas M. Beasley, *Christian Ritual and the Creation of British Plantation Societies, 1650–1780* (Athens: University of Georgia Press, 2009), 13–20 passim; Brian Hunt to the Secretary of the SPG, May 6, 1728, Society for the Propagation of the Gospel in Foreign Parts, *Records of the Society for the Propagation of the Gospel in Foreign Parts,* Series A (Letter Books, 1702–1737), 26 vols. (Microfilm), 21:99. See also Frederick Dalcho, *An Historical Account of the Protestant Episcopal Church in South Carolina from the First Settlement of the Province to the War of the Revolution* (Charleston: E. Thayer, 1820), and Bolton, *Southern Anglicanism,* passim.

8. Jon Butler, *Awash in a Sea of Faith: Christianizing the American People* (Cambridge: Harvard University Press, 1990), 32–34, 98–163. See also Butler, "Enlarging the Bonds of Christ: Slavery, Evangelism, and the Christianization of the White South, 1690–1790," in *The Evangelical Tradition in America,* ed. Leonard I. Sweet (Macon, Ga.: Mercer University Press, 1984), 87–130; Bolton, *Southern Anglicanism,* 19–20 passim.

9. Alexander S. Salley, Jr., ed., *Journals of the Commons House of Assembly of South Carolina For the Two Sessions of 1698* (Columbia: Historical Commission of South Carolina, 1914), 21; Sirmans, *Colonial South Carolina,* 77–78; Bolton, *Southern Anglicanism,* 21–22.

10. George Howe, *History of the Presbyterian Church in South Carolina,* 2 vols. (Columbia: Duffie & Chapman, 1870), 1:131; Langdon Cheves, "Blake of South Carolina," *South Carolina Historical Magazine* 1 (April 1900): 155–56.

11. Nicholas Trott, *The Laws of the British Plantations in America Relating to the Church and the Clergy, Religion and Learning* (London: B. Cowse, 1721), 74–75; Cooper and McCord, *Statutes at Large,* 2:133 (Act no. 154). For a detailed consideration of Huguenot naturalization, see Bertrand Van Ruymbeke, *From New Babylon to Eden: The Huguenots and Their Migration to Colonial South Carolina* (Columbia: University of South Carolina Press, 2006), 161–86. See also John Butler, *The Huguenots in America: A Refugee People in New World Society* (Cambridge: Harvard University Press, 1983), 101–5.

12. Salley, *Journals of the Commons House of Assembly of South Carolina For the Two Sessions of 1698,* 14, 18, 20, 21; "An Act to settle a Maintenance on a minister of the Church of England in Charlestown," in William Sumner Jenkins, ed., *Records of States of the United States of America: A Microfilm Compilation* [South Carolina], 107 reels (Washington, D.C.: Library of Congress Photoduplication Service, 1949), B.2. Session Laws, 1690-1869 (12 reels), S.C., Reel 1a (1690-1716).

13. Salley, *Journals of the Commons House of Assembly of South Carolina For the Two Sessions of 1698,* 28. Though the journal of the Commons House of Assembly does not record any opposition or debate on the 1698 Ministry Act, four prominent dissenters from Colleton County, John Alexander, Thomas Smith, Thomas Elliot, and William Elliot, were curiously cited "for their Contempt, in absenting themselves from ye Service of [the] House" when the measure was ratified on October 8. Ibid.

14. Mattie Erma Edwards Parker, ed., *North Carolina Charters and Constitutions, 1578–1698* (Raleigh: North Carolina Tercentenary Commission, 1963), 227–28, 238; Salley, *Journals of the Common House of Assembly of South Carolina for the Two Sessions of 1698*, 29–30; see also Sirmans, *Colonial South Carolina*, 73.

15. John Stewart to William Dunlop, April 27, 1690, in J. G. Dunlop, ed., "Letters from John Stewart to William Dunlop," *South Carolina Historical Magazine* 32 (April–July 1931): 3; "The Representation and Address of several of the Members of this present Assembly retur'd for Colleton County, and other the Inhabitants of this Province, whose names are hereunto subscribed," June 26, 1703, in William J. Rivers, *A Sketch of the History of South Carolina to the Close of the Proprietary Government by the Revolution of 1719* (Charleston: McCarter & Co., 1856), 454; Sirmans, *Colonial South Carolina*, 76–81.

16. John Archdale, *A New Description of that Fertile and Pleasant Province of Carolina: with a Brief Account of its Discovery, Settling, and the Government Thereof to this Time. With several Remarkable Passages of Divine Province during my Time* (London: John Wyat, 1707), in Alexander S. Salley, ed., *Narratives of Early Carolina, 1650–1708* (1911; rpt., New York: Barnes & Noble, 1946), 303; Bolton, *Southern Anglicanism*, 21.

17. "Representation and Address," June 23, 1703, in Rivers, *A Sketch of the History of South Carolina*, 454–55. Rivers includes the names of seventeen subscribers. Daniel Defore claimed that the petition was signed by 150 inhabitants. See *Party-Tyranny, or an Occasional Bill in Miniature; as now Practiced in Carolina. Humbly offered to the Consideration of both Houses of Parliament* (London, 1705), in Salley, *Narratives of Early Carolina*, 247.

18. "Representation and Address," June 23, 1703, in Rivers, *A Sketch of the History of South Carolina*, 457–58.

19. Ibid., 457–59; John Ash, *The Present State of Affairs in Carolina, by John Ash, Gent., Sent by several of the Inhabitants of that Colony, to deliver their Representation thereof to, and seek Redress from, the Lords Proprietors of that Province: Together with an Account of his Reception, by the Honourable the Lord Granvill, their Palatine, President, or Chief of the Proprietors* (London, 1706), in Alexander S. Salley, ed., *Narratives of Early Carolina, 1650–1708* (1911; rpt., New York: Barnes & Noble, 1953), 273.

20. Gideon Johnston to bishop of Sarum, September 20, 1708, in Frank J. Klingberg, ed., *Carolina Chronicle: The Papers of Commissary Gideon Johnston, 1707–1716* (Berkeley: University of California Press, 1946), 25; Sirmans, *Colonial South Carolina*, 80; Richard S. Dunn, *Sugar and Slaves: The Rise of the Planter Class in the English West Indies* (1972; rpt., New York: W. W. Norton, 1973), 133.

21. Joseph Lord to Governor Thomas Hinkley, February 21, 1699, in Solomon Lincoln et al., "The Hinckley Papers," *Massachusetts Historical Society Collections*, 4th ser., 5, 305; Sirmans, *Colonial South Carolina*, 78, 162, 182–83, 187–91.

22. Quoted in Beasley, *Christian Ritual and the Creation of British Slave Societies*, 66.

23. Gideon Johnston to bishop of Sarum, September 20, 1708, in Klingberg, *Carolina Chronicle*, 27; Sirmans, *Colonial South Carolina*, 79, 81; Bolton, *Southern Anglicanism*, 24.

24. Samuel Thomas, "A Memorial Relating to the State of the Church of England in the Province of South Carolina" (1705–1706), in "Documents Concerning Rev. Samuel Thomas, 1702–1707," *South Carolina Historical Magazine* 5 (January 1904): 34.

25. "Representation and Address," June 23, 1703, in Rivers, *A Sketch of the History of South Carolina,* 459; Cooper and McCord, *Statutes at Large,* 2:232–35 (Act no. 222), 236–46 (Act no. 225); Elizabeth (Axtell) Blake to Proprietors, May 16, 1704, in Daniel Defoe, *The Case of the Protestant Dissenters in Carolina, Shewing How a Law to prevent Occasional Conformity There, has ended in the Total Subversion of the Constitution in Church and State* (London, 1706), appendix, 43; Sirmans, *Colonial South Carolina,* 87; Butler, *The Huguenots in America,* 114; Robert M. Weir, *Colonial South Carolina: A History* (Millwood, N.Y.: KTO Press, 1983), 76.

26. Cooper and McCord, *Statutes at Large,* 2:232 (Act no. 222).

27. Stock, *Proceedings and Debates,* 3:122.

28. Cooper and McCord, *Statutes at Large,* 2:232 (Act no. 222); Stock, *Proceedings and Debates,* 3:122.

29. Cooper and McCord, *Statutes at Large,* 2:233 (Act no. 222); Stock, *Proceedings and Debates,* 3:122.

30. Sir Thomas Powys for Lord Granville, in Stock, *Proceedings and Debates,* 3:122. Hawles argued that "there were no churches erected." Ibid.

31. Cooper and McCord, *Statutes at Large,* 2:236, 238–40 (Act no. 225). See also 2:233 (Act no. 222); Sirmans, *Colonial South Carolina,* 87–88; Bolton, *Southern Anglicanism,* 25–26.

32. Cooper and McCord, *Statutes at Large,* 2:247 (Act no. 226).

33. Ibid., 2:245 (Act no. 225).

34. Quoted in Bolton, *Southern Anglicanism,* 25.

35. Ibid., 26.

36. Cooper and McCord, *Statutes at Large,* 2:240, 246 passim (Act no. 225).

37. Stock, *Proceedings and Debates,* 3:122–24.

38. Daniel Defoe, *Party-Tyranny, or an Occasional Bill in Miniature; as now Practiced in Carolina. Humbly offered to the Consideration of both Houses of Parliament,* in Salley, *Narratives of Early Carolina,* 259.

39. Defoe, *The Case of Protestant Dissenters in Carolina,* 29.

40. Stock, ed., *Proceedings and Debates,* 3:116–17.

41. "Representation and Address," June 23, 1703, in Rivers, *A Sketch of the History of South Carolina,* 460. Cooper and McCord, *Statutes at Large,* 2:251–53 (Act no. 228).

42. Alexander S. Salley, Jr., ed., *Journal of the Commons House of Assembly of South Carolina, November 20, 1706–February 8, 1706/7* (Columbia: The State Company, 1939), 4–5, 11; Cooper and McCord, *Statutes at Large,* 2:285 (Act no. 256).

43. Thomas Smith reported to the SPG in 1708 that when he and his father arrived in 1684 that they "found that there were two Ministers that professed themselves and were so reputed to be of the Established Church, according to the laws of England," Phineas Rogers and Atkin Williamson (Thomas Smith to SPG, January 16, 1708, in Alexander S. Salley, Jr., "A Letter by Second Landgrave Smith," *South Carolina Historical Magazine* 32 [January 1931]: 61–62.) Also, John Oldmixon related that a "Mr. Warmel

was sent over" around 1700 (John Oldmixon, *The History of the British Empire in America* [London, 1708], in Salley, ed., *Narratives of Early Carolina,* 364.) Neither Rogers, Williamson, nor Warmel is included in the list of Anglican ministers who served in South Carolina from 1696 to 1775 compiled by S. Charles Bolton, so by his count five clergy had arrived by the end of 1702. See *Southern Anglicanism,* 166–75.

44. Samuel Thomas to Rev. Dr. Woodward, January 29, 1702, in "Letters of the Rev. Samuel Thomas, 1702–1710," *South Carolina Historical and Genealogical Magazine* 4 (July 1903): 226.

45. Bonomi and Eisenstadt, "Church Adherence in the Eighteenth-Century British American Colonies," 247.

46. Salley, *Journals of the Commons House of Assembly of South Carolina for the Two Sessions of 1698,* 33.

47. Gideon Johnston to bishop of Sarum, September 20, 1708, in Klingberg, *Carolina Chronicle,* 27. See also Dalcho, *An Historical Account of the Protestant Episcopal Church in South Carolina,* 26–27, 63–70.

48. John Lawson, *A New Voyage to Carolina; Containing thte Exact Description and Natural History of That Country: Together with the Present State Thereof. And a Journal of a Thousand Miles, Travel'd Thro' Several Nations of Indians. Giving a Particular Account of Their Customs, Manners, &c.* (London, 1709), 3.

49. Gideon Johnston to bishop of Sarum, September 8, 1708 in Klingberg, *Carolina Chronicle,* 28–29.

50. Gideon Johnston to SPG, July 5, 1710, in Klingberg, *Carolina Chronicle,* 39–40. On Johnston's efforts, see Bolton, *Southern Anglicanism,* 31–36. On commissaries' efforts elsewhere, see G. M. Brydon, *Virginia's Mother Church and the Political Conditions under Which It Grew,* 2 vols. (Richmond, 1947), 1:225–40, 309–26.

51. Gideon Johnston to bishop of Sarum, September 20, 1708, Johnston to SPG, January 20, 1711, in Klingberg, *Carolina Chronicle,* 28, 78. The dissenter party provided a uniform bloc against Johnston, and their reaction took a predictable form. See Sirmans, *Colonial South Carolina,* 89–96.

52. Gideon Johnston to SPG, July 5, 1710, in Klingberg, *Carolina Chronicle,* 56–57.

53. Gideon Johnston, "Present State of the Clergy," in Arthur Henry Hirsh, *The Huguenots of Colonial South Carolina* (Durham: Duke University Press, 1928), 298; Johnston to the Secretary of the SPG, July 5, 1710 in Klingberg, *Carolina Chronicle,* 39, 51; Francis Le Jau quoted in Bonomi and Eisenstadt, "Church Adherence in the Eighteenth-Century British American Colonies," 252. See also Beasley, *Christian Ritual and the Creation of British Slave Societies,* 56–73, 85–98.

54. Charles Burnham to Gideon Johnston, April 4, 1716, in Klingberg, *Carolina Chronicle,* 163; Francis Le Jau to the Secretary of the SPG, August 5, 1709, in Klingberg, *The Carolina Chronicle of Dr. Francis Le Jau,* 58.

55. Samuel Thomas, "A Memorial Relating to the State of the Church of England in the Province of South Carolina" (1705–1706), in "Documents Concerning Rev. Samuel Thomas, 1702–1707," 37–38; Thomas to the Treasurer of the SPG, May 3, 1704, quoted in Beasley, *Christian Ritual and the Creation of British Plantation Societies,* 22.

56. Gideon Johston to bishop of Sarum, September 20, 1708, in Klingberg, *Carolina Chronicle*, 22.

57. William Screven to Elisha Callender, August 6, 1708, quoted in H.A. Tupper, ed., *Two Centuries of the First Baptist Church of South Carolina, 1683–1883* (Baltimore: R.H. Woodward and Company, 1889), 58.

58. Quoted in Patricia U. Bonomi, *Under the Cope of Heaven: Religion, Society, and Politics in Colonial America* (New York: Oxford University Press, 1986), 89–90.

59. Samuel Thomas, "A Memorial Relating to the State of the Church of England in the Province of South Carolina" (1705–1706), in "Documents Concerning Rev. Samuel Thomas, 1702–1707," 31–33; Babette M. Levy, "Early Puritanism in the Southern and Island Colonies." *American Antiquarian Society Proceedings* 70 (1961): 272–73.

60. Gideon Johnston to SPG, January 27 1710/11, in Klingberg, *Carolina Chronicle*, 72–73; Defoe, *The Case of the Protestant Dissenters in Carolina*, 12.

61. Thomas Nairne, *A Letter from South Carolina; Giving an Account of the Soil, Air, Product, Trade, Government, Laws, Religion, People, Military Strength, &c. of that Province: Together with the Manner and Necessary Charges of Settling a Plantation There, and the Annual Profit it Will Produce* (London: A. Baldwin, 1710), 45–46.

62. Nairne reported that there was only one Baptist congregation in the colony, for instance, but Anglican ministers conceded that they were "active beyond expression to increase the number of their Sectaryes" and had formed congregations stretching "towards the Southward," apparently all the way to Edisto. Francis Le Jau to Secretary of the SPG, August 10, 1713, in Klingberg, *The Carolina Chronicle of Dr. Francis Le Jau*, 134; "Report of Commissary Gideon Johnston to the Society for the Propagation of the Gospel about 1713," in Hirch, *The Huguenots of Colonial South Carolina*, 309. See also Leah Townsend, *South Carolina Baptists, 1670–1805* (1935; rpt., Baltimore: Genealogical Publishing, 1978), 12–13, 36–37, and chapter 1 passim. In sum, Baptists represented a significant minority of the dissenting population, about 20 percent during the first third of the the eighteenth century. On the western branch of the Cooper River, for instance, Samuel Thomas reported that there were seventy families living in two main settlements, Watboe and Wampee, in 1705 and 1706. Of these, he said that there were "about forty families of the profession of the Church of England, and 30. Families who dissent from the Church, these are more generally Anabaptists, and they have a preacher of that sort among them, one Lord's day in three." "A Memorial Relating to the State of the Church of England in the Province of South Carolina" (1705–1706), in "Documents Concerning Rev. Samuel Thomas, 1702–1707," 32.

63. Quoted in Butler, *The Huguenots in America*, 116. See also, "Report of Commissary Gideon Johnston to the Society for the Propagation of the Gospel about 1713," in Hirch, *The Huguenots of Colonial South Carolina*, 297–309; Bolton, *Southern Anglicanism*, 35; Van Ruymbeke, *From New Babylon to Eden*, 140.

64. Report of Commissary Gideon Johnston to the Society for the Propagation of the Gospel about 1713," in Hirch, *The Huguenots of Colonial South Carolina*, 309.

65. Frederick Lewis Weis, *The Colonial Clergy and the Colonial Churches of the Middle and Southern Colonies, 1607–1776* (Lancaster, Mass.: Society of the Descendants of the

Colonial Clergy, 1938), 29, 33, 39, 51–52, 78, 82–84, 86–87, 92, 100, 105; Dalcho, *Historical Account of the Protestant Episcopal Church*, 244–74, 284–302, 366–74.

66. Bolton, *Southern Anglicanism*, 166–69.

67. The Anglican survey of 1724 has been superbly analyzed by Patricia U. Bonomi and Peter B. Eisenstadt. See their "Church Adherence in the Eighteenth-Century British American Colonies," 253–62. The ministers' responses to the bishop of London are included in an unpaginated appendix following page 276, and all the calculations presented are based on those responses, using a standard multiplier of five to figure mean family size. Peter H. Wood (*Black Majority: Negroes in Colonial South Carolina from 1670 through the Stono Rebellion*, [1974; rpt., New York: W.W. Norton, 1975], 146–49) employs the same multiplier and provides population statistics for each parish as well as for the colony as a whole. See also Peter A. Coclanis, *The Shadow of a Dream: Economic Life and Death in the South Carolina Low Country, 1670–1920* (New York: Oxford University Press, 1989), 64.

68. Francis Varnod to the Secretary of the SPG, April 1, 1724, quoted in Bonomi and Eisenstadt, "Church Adherence in the Eighteenth-Century British American Colonies," 259.

69. See Bonomi and Eisenstadt, "Church Adherence in the Eighteenth-Century British American Colonies," appendix following page 276.

70. Beasley, *Christian Ritual and the Creation of British Plantation Societies*, 91; Cooper and McCord, *Statutes at Large*, 2:233 (Act no. 222).

71. Butler, "Enlarging the Bonds of Christ," 97–109.

72. Ira Berlin, *Many Thousands Gone: The First Two Centuries of Slavery in North America* (Cambridge: Harvard University Press, 1998), 8.

73. Philip D. Morgan, *Slave Counterpoint: Black Culture in the Eighteenth-century Chesapeake and Lowcountry* (Chapel Hill: University of North Carolina Press, 1998), 61; Coclanis, *The Shadow of a Dream*, 64.

74. Butler, *Awash in a Sea of Faith*, 130–51.

75. William Fleetwood, *A Sermon Preached before the Society for the Propagation of the Gospel in Foreign Parts, at the Parish Church of St. Mary-le-Bow, on Friday the 16th of February, 1710/11* (London: Joseph Downing, 1711), in Frank J. Klingberg, *Anglican Humanitarianism in Colonial New York* (Philadelphia: Church Historical Society, 1940), 205, 207. See also Thomas Secker, *A Sermon Preached before the Incorporated Society for the Propagation of the Gospel in Foreign Parts; at their Anniversary Meeting in the Parish-Church of St. Mary-le-Bow, on Friday, February 20, 1740–1* (London: J. and H. Pemberton, 1741), ibid., 213–33; William Warburton, *A Sermon Preached before the Incorporated Soceity for the Propagation of the Gospel in Foreign Parts; at their Anniversary Meeting in the Parish Church of St. Mary-le-Bow, on Friday, February 21, 1766* (London: E. Owen and T. Harrison,1766), 235–49; Butler, *Awash in a Sea of Faith*, 137–40; Butler, "Enlarging the Bonds of Christ," 101–2. Philip D. Morgan speaks of the emergence of paternalism in terms of an enlightened patriarchalism. See *Slave Counterpoint*, 284–96.

76. Fleetwood, *A Sermon Preached before the Society of the Propagation of the Gospel*, in Klingberg, *Anglican Humanitarianism in Colonial New York*, 203–4.

77. Ibid., 203–5, 207, 209–10.

78. Ibid., 203, 209, 211–12. Fleetwood spoke of "a *Blessed Medium*" in reference to the SPG's plantations in Barbados, which Christopher Codrington bequeathed to the Society in 1703. He suggested that the Codrington estates could serve as model plantations and that slave conversion there offered the Church of England a unique opportunity of "preaching *by Example.*" Ibid., 211. On the history the Codrington plantations, see Frank J. Klingberg, ed., *Codrington Chronicle: An Experiment in Anglican Altruism on a Barbados Plantation, 1710–1834* (Berkeley: University of California Press, 1949).

79. Klingberg, *The Carolina Chronicle of Dr. Francis Le Jau*, 134n179.

80. Francis Le Jau to Secretary of the SPG, January 26, 1715, and March 12, 1715, ibid., 146, 149.

81. Francis Le Jau to Secretary of the SPG, February 18, 1709, December 12, 1712, and August 10, 1713, ibid., 50, 125, 133.

82. "Instructions of the Clergy of South Carolina given to Mr. [Gideon] Johnston on his coming away for England, enlarged and explained by the said Mr. Johnston, and humbly presented to . . . the Society," March 4, 1712–1713, in Frank J. Klingberg, *An Appraisal of the Negro in Colonial South Carolina: A Study in Americanization.* (Washington, D.C.: Associated Publishers, 1941), 6.

83. Ibid.; Francis Le Jau to Secretary of the SPG, January 26, 1715, in Klingberg, *The Carolina Chronicle of Dr. Francis Le Jau*, 146.

84. Klingberg, *An Appraisal of the Negro in Colonial South Carolina*, 32, 55–61. See also Robert Olwell, *The Culture of Power in the South Carolina Low Country, 1740–1790* (Ithaca: Cornell University Press, 1998), 117n55.

85. "Instructions to the Clergy of South Carolina," in Klingberg, *An Appraisal of the Negro in Colonial South Carolina*, 6.

86. Richard Ludlam to the Secretary of the SPG, July 3, 1724, Records of the Society for the Propagation of the Gospel, quoted in Olwell, *Masters, Slaves & Subjects*, 118. There is a rich literature on attempts to convert slaves, with some historians stressing the importance of planter resistance, others the importance of slave resistance, and still others a lack of ministerial effort. See Sylvia R. Frey and Betty Wood, *Come Shouting to Zion: African American Protestantism in the American South and British Caribbean to 1830* (Chapel Hill: University of North Carolina Press, 1998), 63–117; Morgan, *Slave Counterpoint*, 420–37; Berlin, *Many Thousands Gone*, 142–76; Annette Laing, "'Heathens and Infidels'? African Christianization and Anglicanism in the South Carolina Low Country, 1700–1750," *Religion and American Culture: A Journal of Interpretation* 12, no. 2 (2002): 197–228. See also Bolton, *Southern Anglicanism*, 102–20.

87. Butler, "Enlarging the Bonds of Christ," 97–111.

88. Fleetwood, *A Sermon Preached before the Society for the Propagation of the Gospel*, in Klingberg, *Anglican Humanitarianism in Colonial New York*, 203–4.

89. Fleetwood, *A Sermon Preached before the Society for the Propagation of the Gospel*, in Klingberg, *Anglican Humanitarianism in Colonial New York*, 203–4, 206. See also Francis La Jau to Secretary of the SPG, September 18, 1711, in Klingberg, *The Carolina Chronicle of Dr. Francis Le Jau*, 102.

90. Parker, *North Carolina Charters and Constitutions,* 150, 164, 183. The word *power* was conspicuously added to the clause in one of the earliest revisions of the Fundamental Constitutions (March 1, 1670) and reflects and obvious attempt to quell any fears among prospective settlers—especially those from the West Indies—that their dominion over black slaves would be anything less than "absolute." For an older but still useful discussion of significance of this change as well as of the colony's seventeenth-century slave codes, see Thomas J. Little, "The South Carolina Slave Laws Reconsidered," *South Carolina Historical Magazine* 94 (April 1993): 86–101. Fleetwood stressed that Chrisitanization was entirely compatible with and reinforced secular law. See *A Sermon Preached before the Society for the Propagation of the Gospel,* in Klingberg, *Anglican Humanitarianism in New York,* 203–4, 206.

91. Clergy of South Carolina to Secretary of the SPG, March 10, 1724, *Records of the Society for the Propagation of the Gospel in Foreign Parts,* Series B (1701–1786), 25 vols. (Microfilm), 4:141.

92. Francis Le Jau to Secretary of the SPG, February 1, 1710, in Klingberg, *The Carolina Chronicle of Dr. Francis Le Jau,* 71. See also Gideon Johnston to bishop of Sarum, September 20, 1708, in Klingberg, *Carolina Chronicle,* 25; Sirmans, *Colonial South Carolina,* 80, 88–89, 93–95.

93. Gideon Johnston to bishop of Sarum, September 20, 1708; Johnson to Secretary of the SPG, July 5, 1710, in Klingberg, *Carolina Chronicle,* 24, 58. See also Francis Le Jau to Philip Stubs, July 3, 1707, in Klingberg, *The Carolina Chronicle of Dr. Francis Le Jau,* 29. On Stobo, see Jack C. Ramsay, Jr., "Archibald Stobo, Presbyterian Minister," *Journal of the Presbyterian Historical Society,* 37 (September 1959): 129–42.

94. Gideon Johnston to bishop of Sarum, September 20, 1708, in Klingberg, *Carolina Chronicle,* 23; Francis Le Jau to Secretary of the SPG, February 1, 1710, in Klingberg, *The Carolina Chronicle of Dr. Francis Le Jau,* 71.

95. Gideon Johnston to bishop of Sarum, September 20, 1708, in Klingberg, *Carolina Chronicle,* 23.

96. Chief Justice Nicholas Trott to the SPG, September 13, 1707, quoted in Bolton, *Southern Anglicanism,* 32. See also Klingberg, *Carolina Chronicle,* 18.

97. Gideon Johnston to bishop of Sarum, September 20, 1708, in Klingberg, *Carolina Chronicle,* 25.

98. Cooper and McCord, *Statutes at Large,* 2:137, 339, quoted in Thomas J. Curry, *The First Freedoms: Church and State in America to the Passage of the First Amendment* (New York: Oxford University Press, 1986), 59.

99. Curry, *The First Freedoms,* 59.

100. Francis Le Jau to Secretary of the SPG, August 5, 1709, in Klingberg, *The Carolina Chronicle of Dr. Francis Le Jau,* 58.

101. Gideon Johnston to the Secretary of the SPG, January 27, 1711, in Klingberg, *Carolina Chronicle,* 72–73. On Landgrave Thomas Smith's political tactics, see Sirmans, *Colonial South Carolina,* 81, 95.

102. Quoted in Bolton, *Southern Anglicanism,* 32–33. See also Sirmans, *Colonial South Carolina,* 96; Edward McCrady, *The History of South Carolina under the Proprietary Government, 1670–1719* (New York: Macmillian, 1897), 506–7. Governor Craven

seems to have been unusually catholic in his religious outlook indeed. For example, when Quaker preacher Thomas Chalkley landed in Charleston in 1713, he wrote, "I was several Times to visit the Governor, who was courteous and civil to me. He said, *I delivered Encouragement;* and spoke to several to be generous, and contribute to my Assistance. He meant an outward Maintenance; for he would have me encouraged to stay among them." Chalkley used the episode to instruct the governor in Quaker doctrine. "I told him, that tho'it might be a Practice with them, to maintain their Ministers, and pay them Money for preaching, it was contrary to our Principles to be paid for preaching agreeable to the Command of our great Maker, Christ Jesus, who said to his Ministers *Freely you have received, freely give:* So that we are limited by his Words, whatever others are: And those who take a Liberty, contrary to his Doctrine and Command, I think, must be *Antichrist's,* according to holy Scripture." Thomas Chalkley, *A Journal: Or Historical Account of the Life, Travels, and Christian Experiences of that Ancient, Faithful Servant of Jesus Christ, Thomas Chalkley* (London: Luke Hinde, 1751), 80.

103. "Instructions of the Clergy of South Carolina given to Mr. [Gideon] Johnston on his coming away for England, enlarged and explained by the said Mr. Johnston, and humbly presented to . . . the Society," March 4, 1712–1713, in Klingberg, *Carolina Chronicle,* 119–21, 126.

104. Ibid., 122–25.

105. Ibid., 121–22.

106. Quotations in Bolton, *Southern Anglicanism,* 93, 194n11. This paragraph is based on the material Bolton presents in chapter 5, pp. 87–94, 96 (Table 1). However, it is important to note again that Thomas Smith indicated to the SPG in a letter dated January 16, 1708, that there were two Anglican ministers laboring in the colony when he and his father arrived in 1684, Phineas Rogers and Atkin Williamson. Neither is included in the list of Anglican ministers who served in South Carolina from 1696 to 1775 compiled by Bolton, so by his count five clergy had arrived by the end of 1702 and twenty-six served from 1696 to 1719. See *Southern Anglicanism,* 87, 166–75.

107. Samuel Thomas, "A Memorial Relating to the State of the Church of England in the Province of South Carolina" (1705–1706), reprinted in "Documents Concerning Rev. Samuel Thomas, 1702–1707," 36.

108. "Instructions of the Clergy of South Carolina given to Mr. [Gideon] Johnston on his coming away for England, enlarged and explained by the said Mr. Johnston, and humbly presented to . . . the Society," March 4, 1712–1713, in Klingberg, *Carolina Chronicle,* 126.

109. Bolton, *Southern Anglicanism,* 96, Table 1, and chapter 5 passim.

110. Cooper and McCord, *Statutes at Large:* 1:58 (An Act for Supporting the Present Government under the Administration of the Honourable James Moore, Esq., the Present Goverour of the Same, or any Succeeding Governour, June 17, 1720).

111. Sirmans, *Colonial South Carolina,* 129–63; Weir, *Colonial South Carolina,* 94–111 (quotation on page 110).

112. Brian Hunt to Edmund Gibson, bishop of London, December 18, 1727, in Lambeth Palace Library, *The Fulham Papers at Lambeth Palace Library,* 20 reels (Microfilm, 2nd. ed., with additional reel), 42 vols. (London: World Microfilms, c.1970-c.1978),

11:39. Hereafter cited as *The Fulham Papers*. Lambeth Palace, London (General Correspondence, 1626–1800), 20 vols. (Microfilm),11:39.

113. Quoted in Weir, *Colonial South Carolina*, 110–11.

114. Alexander Cuming to Duke of Newcastle, July 14, 1730, British Public Record Office, Transcripts of records relating to South Carolina, 1663-1782, South Carolina Department of Archives and History, Columbia, 14:220.

115. Sirmans, *Colonial South Carolina*, 128.

116. William Guy to SPG, October 17, 1720, Society for the Propagation of the Gospel in Foreign Parts, *Records of the Society of the Propagation of the Gospel in Foreign Parts*, Series A (Letter Books, 1702–1737), 14:78–79.

117. W. T. Bull to the SPG, May 12, 1720, ibid., 14:74–75; Bull to Secretary of the SPG, August 12, 1720, ibid., 15:56–57. See also, Bolton, *Southern Anglicanism*, 38–39; Richard P. Sherman, *Robert Johnson: Proprietary and Royal Governor of South Carolina* (Columbia: University of South Carolina Press, 1966), 50–52.

118. Richard Ludlam to David Humphreys, March 25 1725, quoted in Klingberg, *An Appraisal of the Negro in Colonial South Carolina*, 48.

119. Clergy in South Carolina to the SPG, October 10, 1721, Society for the Propagation of the Gospel in Foreign Parts, *Records of the Society for the Propagation of the Gospel in Foreign Parts*, Series A (Letter Books, 1702–1737), 15:127. See also Bolton, *Southern Anglicanism*, 40.

120. Quoted in Beasley, *Christian Ritual and the Creation of British Slave Societies*, 59.

121. Quoted in Jack C. Ramsay, Jr., "Archibald Stobo, Presbyterian Minister," *Journal of the Presbyterian Historical Society* 37 (September 1959): 137.

122. Alexander S. Salley, Jr., ed., *Journal of the Commons House of Assembly of South Carolina, June 2, 1724–June 16, 1724* (Columbia: Historical Commission of South Carolina, 1944), 24–25. See also ibid., 5, 28, 44, 45, 47; Cooper and McCord, *Statutes at Large*, 2:137; Bolton, *Southern Anglicanism*, 41.

123. In addition, the governor had put dissenters on the defensive by questioning their loyalty, so they were especially eager to show "themselves Good Subjects to the King." See Salley, *Journal of the Commons House of Assembly of South Carolina, June 2, 1724–June 16, 1724*, 47, and chapter 3, below.

124. For an overview of both Nicholson's and Middleton's administrations and the crisis of the 1720s, see Sirmans, *Colonial South Carolina*, 129–59.

125. Arthur Middleton to Duke of Newcastle, May 17, 1728, British Public Record Office, Transcripts of records relating to South Carolina, 14:220.

126. Throughout the conflict Johnson kept the "good opinion" and "favour" of the people; only his refusal to "renounce all Obedience to the Lords Proprietors['] Authority" prevented him from continuing in his post. William Tredwell Bull to Secretary of the SPG, January 27, 1720, Society for the Propagation of the Gospel in Foreign Parts, *Records of the Society for the Propagation of the Gospel in Foreign Parts*, Series A (Letter Books, 1702–1737), 14:61–63; Memorial of Robert Johnson, British Public Record Office, Transcripts of records relating to South Carolina, 12:183.

127. Robert Johnson to Privy Council, November 7, 1727, British Public Record Office, Transcripts of records relating to South Carolina, 12:258–65.

Chapter 3. A Party of Seekers

1. Hugh Fisher, *A Preservative from Damnable Errors, in the Unction of the Holy One. A Sermon Preach'd, at the opening of a Presbytery at Charlestown in S. Carolina; some time before the Reverend Mr. Josiah Smith's Sermon (which he publish'd against it, with the Title, of Humane Impositions proved unscriptural & c.) and now published, (with the advice of some of the Reverend Ministers adhering to the Westminster Confession) to vindicate the Truths contained in it, from Mr. Smith's Mis-representations, and Exceptions. Together with a Postscript Containing some Remarks, upon Mr. Smith's Preface, and Sermon* ([Boston], 1730), 33.

2. *Three Letters from the Reverend Mr. G. Whitefield: viz. Letter I. To a Friend in London, concerning Archbishop Tillotson. Letter II. To the same, on the same Subject. Letter III. To the Inhabitants of Maryland, Virginia, North and South-Carolina, concerning their Negroes* (Philadelphia: B. Franklin, 1740). Referring to the Stono Rebellion, a smallpox epidemic in 1738, and an outbreak of yellow fever in 1739, Whitefield warned the southern colonists, "God first generally corrects us with Whips; if that will not do, he must chastise us with Scorpions": ibid., 16.

3. Christine Leigh Heyrman, *Southern Cross: The Beginnings of the Bible Belt* (Chapel Hill: University of North Carolina Press, 1997), 23. In emphasizing the obstacles revivalists encountered in claiming "the soul of the South," Heyrman recovers something of the time dimensions involved in the rise of southern evangelicalism.

4. S. Charles Bolton, *Southern Anglicanism: The Church of England in Colonial South Carolina* (Westport, Conn.: Greenwood Press, 1982), 37–62; Patricia U. Bonomi, *Under the Cope of Heaven: Religion, Society, and Politics in Colonial America* (New York: Oxford University Press, 1986), 91–92.

5. Alexander Garden to Edmund Gibson, bishop of London, December 28, 1733, in Lambeth Palace Library, *The Fulham Papers at Lambeth Palace Library*, 20 reels (Microfilm 2nd. ed., with additional reel), 42 vols. (London: World Microfilms, c.1970-c.1978), 11:39 Hereafter cited as *The Fulham Papers*. On the economy in the early royal era, see Peter A. Coclanis, *The Shadow of a Dream: Economic Life and Death in the South Carolina Low Country, 1670–1920* (New York: Oxford University Press, 1989), chapter 3. Using quantitative data culled from Naval Officer Shipping Lists and available price series, the historian Stephen G. Hardy estimates that the compound growth rate of the value of rice exported from the colony was 13.9 percent per year from 1722 to 1738: "Colonial South Carolina's Rice Industry and the Atlantic Economy: Patterns of Trade, Shipping, and Growth, 1715–1775," in Jack P. Greene, Rosemary Brana-Shute, and Randy J. Sparks, eds., *Money, Trade, and Power: The Evolution of Colonial South Carolina's Plantation Society* (Columbia: University of South Carolina Press, 2001), 112.

6. Alexander Garden to Edmund Gibson, bishop of London, May 15, 1735, in *The Fulham Papers*, 10:7–10; Richard P. Sherman, *Robert Johnson: Proprietary & Royal Governor of South Carolina* (Columbia: University of South Carolina Press, 1966), 120.

7. M. Eugene Sirmans, *Colonial South Carolina: A Political History, 1663–1763* (Chapel Hill: University of North Carolina Press, 1966), 183–85.

8. Alexander Garden, *Take Heed How Ye Hear: A Sermon Preached in the Parish Church of St. Philip Charles-Town, in South Carolina on Sunday the 13th of July, 1740. With a Preface,*

containing some Remarks on Mr. Whitefield's Journals (Charleston: Peter Timothy, 1741), 25, 28–29.

9. Alexander S. Salley, Jr., ed., *Journal of the Commons House of Assembly of South Carolina, June 2, 1724–June 16, 1724* (Columbia: Historical Commission of South Carolina, 1944), 44. Petition of Archibald Stobo, 1722, Society for the Propagation of the Gospel in Foreign Parts, *Records of the Society of the Propagation of the Gospel in Foreign Parts,* Series A (Letter Books, 1702–1737), 26 vols. (Microfilm), 16:107–10.

10. Salley, *Journal of the Commons House of South Carolina, June 2, 1724–June 16, 1725,* 44; Governor Francis Nicholson to Edmund Gibson, Bishop of London, August 5, 1724, in *The Fulham Papers,* 9:156–57. See also Richard Ludlam to David Humphreys, March 25 1725, quoted in Frank J. Klingberg, *An Appraisal of the Negro in Colonial South Carolina: A Study in Americanization* (Washington, D.C.: Associated Publishers, 1941), 48; Bolton, *Southern Anglicanism,* 39–41; Ruth M. Winton, "Governor Francis Nicholson's Relations with the Society for the Propagation of the Gospel in Foreign Parts, 1701–1727," *Historical Magazine of the Protestant Episcopal Church* 17 (1948): 274–86.

11. Salley, *Journal of the Commons House of Assembly of South Carolina, June 2, 1724–June 16, 1724,* 24.

12. John Archdale, *A New Description of that Fertile and Pleasant Province of Carolina: with a Brief Account of its Discovery, Settling, and the Government Thereof to this Time. With several Remarkable Passages of Divine Providence during my Time* (London: Printed for John Wyat, 1707), in Alexander S. Salley, Jr., ed., *Narratives of Early Carolina, 1650–1708* (1911; rpt., New York: Barnes & Noble, 1953), 304. Hereafter cited as "Archdale's Description of Carolina."

13. See Garden, *Take Heed How Ye Hear,* 30–37; Jon Butler, *The Huguenots in America: A Refugee People in New World Society* (Cambridge: Harvard University Press, 1983), 116–20; Bertrand Van Ruymbeke, *From New Babylon to New Eden: The Huguenots and Their Migration to Colonial South Carolina* (Columbia: University of South Carolina Press, 2006), 142–45.

14. Garden, *Take Head How Ye Hear,* 36.

15. Butler, *The Huguenots in America,* 130; Peter H. Wood, *Black Majority: Negroes in Colonial South Carolina from 1670 through the Stono Rebellion* (1974; rpt., New York: W. W. Norton, 1975), 149.

16. Garden, *Take Heed How Ye Hear,* 30–32; Van Ruymbeke, *From New Babylon to Eden,* 142–43. See also Hillel Schwartz, *The French Prophets: The History of a Millenarian Group in Eighteenth-Century England* (Berkeley: University of California Press, 1980).

17. Garden, *Take Heed How Ye Hear,* 33–34.

18. Ibid., 35–36.

19. Clergy of South Carolina to bishop of London, October 1, 1724, in *The Fulham Papers,* 9:154–55.

20. Alexander Garden to Edmond Gibson, bishop of London, April 20, 1731, in *The Fulham Papers,* 9:254–55; *South Carolina Gazette,* January 8, May 27, 1732; Richard Beale Davis, *Intellectual Life in the Colonial South, 1585–1763,* 3 vols. (Knoxville: University of Tennessee Press, 1978) 3:607–8, 619, and 698; Bolton, *Southern Anglicanism,* 132–34.

21. *South Carolina Gazette,* October 14, 1732; John Walsh, "'Methodism' and the Origins of English-Speaking Evangelicalism," in Mark A. Noll, David W. Bebbington, and George A. Rawlyk, eds., *Evangelicalism: Comparative Studies of Popular Protestantism in North America, the British Isles, and Beyond, 1700–1990* (New York: Oxford University Press, 1994), 23–24, 35n16. In August 1740, as Walsh points out, George Whitefield reported that one evangelical convert in Charleston "in an extraordinary manner, burnt nearly forty pounds' worth of books written by such authors as Chubb, Foster, etc.," suggesting that although few South Carolinians actually embraced deism, deist works were in fact read in the colony: George Whitefield, *Journals, 1737–1741, to which is prefixed his "Short Account" (1746) and "Further Account" (1747)* (1756; rpt., Gainesville, Fla.: Scholars Facsimiles and Reprints, 1969), 451 (August 21, 1740).

22. *South Carolina Gazette,* August 12, September 23 and 30, October 28, and November 4 and 11, 1732. Whitmarsh wrote of his religious views:

> I'm not High-Church, or Low Church, nor Tory, nor Whig,
> No flatt'ring young Coxcomb, nor formal old Prig.
> Not eternally talking, nor silently quaint
> No profligate Sinner, nor pragmatical Saint,
> I'm not vain of my Judgment, nor pinn'd on a Sleeve
> Nor implicitly any Thing can I believe.

23. Alexander Garden to Edmund Gibson, bishop of London, May 24, 1725, The Fulham Papers (General Correspondence, 1626–1800), 9:176–77. Garden claimed that his efforts to impose Anglican ceremonial on his parishioners were being undermined by John La Pierre, who deviated from prayer-book liturgy by baptizing a child from St. Philip's at the home of the infant's parents. See Bolton, *Southern Anglicanism,* 42. On the privatization of the ritual of baptism, see Nicholas M. Beasley, *Christian Ritual and the Creation of British Slave Societies, 1650–1780* (Athens: University of Georgia Press, 2009), 64–73.

24. Alexander Garden to Edmund Gibson, bishop of London, June 28, 1729, and November 8, 1732, The Fulham Papers (General Correspondence, 1626–1800), 9:239–40, 266–67; *South Carolina Gazette,* October 8, 1732; Bolton, *Southern Anglicanism,* 44–48; Van Ruymbeke, *From New Babylon to Eden,* 151, 154–55.

25. Alexander Garden to Edmund Gibson, bishop of London, June 28, 1729, The Fulham Papers (General Correspondence, 1626–1800), 9:239–40.

26. William Guy to Secretary of the SPG, June 19, 1727, Society for the Propagation of the Gospel in Foreign Parts, *Records of the Society for the Propagation of the Gospel in Foreign Parts,* Series A (Letter Books, 1702–1737), 20:81; Francis Varnod to Secretary of the SPG, May 4, 1727, ibid., 20:79–80.

27. Francis Varnod to Secretary of the SPG, May 4, 1727, ibid, 20:81; Brian Hunt to Edmund Gibson, bishop of London, December 18, 1727, The Fulham Papers (General Correspondence, 1626–1800), 9:139.

28. Clergy of South Carolina to Secretary of the SPG, January 2, 1728, Society for the Propagation of the Gospel in Foreign Parts, *Records of the Society of for the Propagation of the Gospel in Foreign Parts,* Series A (Letter Books, 1702–1737), 20:104–6.

29. Garden, *Take Heed How ye Hear*, 37.

30. See ibid., 27–30.

31. "Archdale's Description of Carolina," in Salley, *Narratives of Early Carolina*, 308–9, 311.

32. Ibid., 284; Brooks Holifield, *Theology in America* (New Haven: Yale University Press, 2003), 77. A feeling of intense crisis usually precedes any generalized religious awakening. See John B. Boles, "Evangelical Protestantism in the Old South: From Religious Dissent to Cultural Dominance," in Charles Reagan Wilson, ed., *Religion in the South* (Jackson: University Press of Mississippi, 1985), 13–34.

33. Frederick Lewis Weis, *The Colonial Clergy and the Colonial Churches of the Middle and Southern Colonies, 1607–1776* (Lancanster, Mass.: Society of the Descendants of the Colonial Clergy, 1938), 108–39 passim; Steven B. Weeks, *Southern Quakers and Slavery: A Study in Institutional History* (Baltimore: Johns Hopkins University Press, 1896), appendix; Jo Anne McCormick, "The Quakers of Colonial South Carolina, 1670–1807" (Ph.D. dissertation, University of South Carolina, 1984), 37–38; George Howe, *History of the Presbyterian Church in South Carolina*, 2 vols. (Columbia: Duffie & Chapman, 1870), 1:165–201; Leah Townsend, *South Carolina Baptists, 1670–1805* (1935; rpt. Baltimore: Genealogical Publishing, 1978), 1–60. White immigration fell off sharply in the early decades of the eighteenth century, and mortality and morbidity rates remained frightfully high until at least the 1740s. See Robert M. Weir, *Colonial South Carolina: A History* (Millwood, N.Y.: KTO Press, 1983), 123, 147, 205–7, 209–10. Demographic trends obviously helped to shape the larger pattern of church growth. On Quakers leaving the Society, see Francis Le Jau to Secretary of the SPG, March 13, 1708, in Frank J. Klingberg, ed., *The Carolina Chronicle of Dr. Francis Le Jau, 1706–1717* (Berkeley: University of California Press, 1956), 37; and Sophia Hume, *An Exhortation to the Inhabitants of the Province of South-Carolina, To bring their Deeds to the Light of Christ, in their own Consciences* (1748; rpt. London: Luke Hinde, 1752), 29–32.

34. [Thomas Nairne], *A Letter from South Carolina; Giving an Account of the Soil, Air, Product, Trade, Government, Laws, Religion, People, Military Strength, &c. of that Province; Together with the Manner and necessary Charges of Settling a Plantation there, and the Annual Profit it will produce* (London: A. Baldwin, 1710), 46; Peter A. Coclanis, *The Shadow of a Dream: Economic Life and Death in the South Carolina Low County, 1670–1920* (New York: Oxford University Press, 1991), 64, estimates through an interpolation that the white population stood at roughly 5,115 in 1710. McCormick, "The Quakers of Colonial South Carolina," 30–31, suggests that approximately one hundred Quakers settled in the colony by 1700.

35. Thomas Chalkley, *A Journal: Or Historical Account of the Life, Travels, and Christian Experience of that Ancient, Faithful Servant of Jesus Christ, Thomas Chalkley* (London: Luke Hinde, 1751), 80; McCormick, "The Quakers of Colonial South Carolina," 60.

36. William Piggott, "An Introduction to the Following Minnitts," in Mabel L. Webber, ed., "The Records of the Quakers in Charles Town," *South Carolina Historical Magazine* 28 (January–July 1927): 26.

37. Francis Le Jau to Secretary, March 13, 1708, and December 11, 1712, in Klingberg, *The Carolina Chronicle of Dr. Francis Le Jau*, 37, 124; Piggott, "An Introduction to the

Following Minnitts," in Webber, "The Records of the Quakers in Charles Town," 26; McCormick, "The Quakers of Colonial South Carolina," 46–49.

38. John Fothergill, *An Account of the Life and Travels in the Work of the Ministry of John Fothergill* (London: Luke Hinde, 1753), 184, 190; Charles Town Meeting Minute Book, January 3, 1723/4, in Webber, "The Records of the Quakers in Charles Town," 39; McCormick, "The Quakers of Colonial South Carolina," 66–86.

39. Susan O'Brien, "A Transatlantic Community of Saints: The Great Awakening and the First Evangelical Network, 1735–1755," *American Historical Review* 91 (October 1986), 811–32; O'Brien, "Eighteenth-Century Publishing Networks in the First Years of Transatlantic Evangelicalism," in Noll, Bebbington, and Rawlyk, *Evangelicalism*, 38–57; Walsh, "'Methodism' and the Origins of English-Speaking Evangelicalism," 20–25.

40. Thomas S. Kidd, *The Great Awakening: The Roots of Evangelical Christianity in Colonial America* (New Haven: Yale University Press, 2007), 70–71; Howe, *History of the Presbyterian Church in South Carolina*, 1:128–30, 185; Sirmans, *Colonial South Carolina*, 53–54, 80–81, 93–94. See also, George C. Rogers, Jr., *Evolution of a Federalist: William Loughton Smith of Charleston (1758–1812)* (Columbia: University of South Carolina Press, 1962), 401 (genealogical chart); Clifford K. Shipton, ed., *Sibley's Harvard Graduates: Biographical Sketches of Those Who Attended Harvard College*, Vol. 7, 1722–1725 (Boston: Massachusetts Historical Society, 1945), 569–85.

41. Josiah Smith, *The Greatest Sufferers Not always the Greatest Sinners. A Sermon Delivered in Charlestown, in the Province of South-Carolina, February 4. 1727,8. Then Occasioned by the Terrible Earthquake in New-England* (Boston, 1730), i; Benjamin Colman, Preface to Josiah Smith, *A Discourse Delivered at Boston, on July 11, 1726: Then Occassion'd by the Author's Ordination. And now Published at the Request of Several Gentlemen, who were Present at the Delivery of it* (Boston: S. Gerrish and T. Hancock, 1726), i; Sirmans, *Colonial South Carolina*, 93–94; Shipton, *Sibley's Harvard Graduates*, 7:569.

42. Colman, Preface to Smith, *A Discourse Delivered at Boston, on July 11. 1726*, i–ii. The English minister who arrived in Bermuda may have been Presbyterian John Paul, not James Paul. See Shipton, *Sibley's Harvard Graduates*, 7:570.

43. Colman, Preface to Smith, *A Discourse Delivered at Boston, on July 11, 1726*, i–iii; Shipton, *Sibley's Harvard Graduates*, 7:569; Kidd, *The Great Awakening*, 70–71. See also Smith, *A Sermon Preached in Boston, July 10th, 1726. And now Published at the Desire of several Gentlemen then Present* (Boston, 1727).

44. Kidd, *The Great Awakening*, xiv.

45. Josiah Smith, *A Sermon Preached in Boston, July 10th, 1726* , 1–2; *South Carolina Gazette*, January 12, 1740.

46. Smith, *A Sermon Preached in Boston, July 10th, 1726*, 3, 5–9. For additional analysis, see Kidd, *The Great Awakening*, 71.

47. Smith, *A Sermon Preached in Boston, July 10th, 1726*, 11, 13–14, 21, 23, 25, passim.

48. Smith, *A Discourse Delivered at Boston, on July 11, 1726*, 1, 3, 18, 20–22, passim.

49. Shipton, *Sibley's Harvard Graduates*, 7:571; Howe, *History of the Presbyterian Church*, 1:185; Jack C. Ramsay, Jr., "Archibald Stobo, Presbyterian Minister," *Journal of the Presbyterian Historical Society* 37 (September 1959): 135–37.

50. Quoted in Clifford K. Shipton, ed., *Sibley's Harvard Graduates: Biographical Sketches of Those Who Attended Harvard College,* Vol. 4, the classes of 1690–1700 (Boston: Massachusetts Historical Society, 1933), 324.

51. Smith, *The Greatest Sufferers Not always the Greatest Sinners,* i–ii.

52. Smith, *A Discourse Delivered at Boston, on July 11, 1726,* 18; *The Duty of Parents to Instruct their Children: Being the Substance of Several Sermons Preach'd at Cainhoy, in the Province of South-Carolina, Anno Dom. 1727. Now Contracted into One Discourse* (Boston: D. Henchman, 1730), i.

53. Smith, *The Duty of Parents to Instruct their Children,* i; Smith, *The Young Man Warned: Or, Solomon's Counsel to his Son: A Sermon Delivered at Cainhoy, in the Province of South-Carolina, Anno Dom. 1729* (Boston: D. Henchman, 1730), 31. See also *Solomon's Caution Against the Cup: A Sermon Delivered at Cainhoy, in the Province of South-Carolina. March 30. 1729* (Boston: D. Henchman, 1730).

54. Smith, *The Duty of Parents to Instruct their Children,* i–ii.

55. Howe, *History of the Presbyterian Church in South Carolina,* 1:189. See also Erskine Clarke, *Our Southern Zion: A History of Calvinism in the South Carolina Low Country, 1690–1990* (Tuscaloosa: University of Alabama Press, 1996), 47–48; Davis, *Intellectual Life in the Colonial South,* 2:764. The precise founding date of the Charleston or South Carolina Presbytery is a minor mystery. Other names for the organization include the Old South Carolina Presbytery, the Scotch Presbytery, and the Presbytery of the Province. Howe, *History of the Presbyterian Church in South Carolina,* 1:189–90. Ramsay suggests a founding date of around 1724, not 1727. See "Archibald Stobo, Presbyterian Minister," 137. For background and revealing insight into the origins of the Charleston Presbytery, see Josiah Smith, *Humane Impositions Proved Unscriptural, or, the Divine Right of Private Judgement* (Boston: D. Henchman, 1729) ii; Smith, *The Divine Right of Private Judgement Vindicated. In Answer to the Reverend Mr. Hugh Fisher's Postscript, Annex'd to his Preservative from Damnable Errors, in Unction of the Holy One* (Boston: n.p., 1730), 20–21; Hugh Fisher, *A Preservative from Damnable Errors, in the Unction of the Holy One,* 32, 49–50 passim. It is not entirely unlikely that Smith preached *The Greatest Sufferers Not always the Greatest Sinners* at the Charleston Presbytery shortly after he first returned to the colony, though he may have delivered it as a Sunday sermon at the Independent church with several ministers in attendance.

56. Howe, *History of the Presbyterian Church,* 1:191.

57. Fisher, *A Preservative from Damnable Errors, in the Unction of the Holy One,* 33. Here Fisher aptly describes the controversy as a street fight over religious truth.

58. Smith, *Humane Impositions Proved Unscriptural, or, the Divine Right of Private Judgement,* ii; *No New Thing to be Slander'd. A Sermon Preach'd at Cainhoy, in the Province of South-Carolina, Sept. 27. 1730. And now Publish'd for the Satisfaction of the Author's People, and to rectify the Opinion, which some had conceiv'd of his Principles, Particularly relating to the Errors of Arius and Arminius* (Boston, 1730), 23 (postscript). In the latter piece (p. 21) Smith says: "To speak in one comprehensive Word, I know not of one Article in the [Westminster] Assemblies shorter Catechism but what I freely assent to. Nor can I say, I disbelieve any thing in their Confession, unless where it appears to Me, to give the Magistrate too great and extended a Power in the Church; where it asserts the Office

of Ruling Elders as distinct from those that preach; and where it in so may Words declares, 'That a Man may not marry any of his Wife's Kindred, nearer in Blood, than he may of his own.'"

59. Smith, *Humane Impositions Proved Unscriptural, or, the Divine Right of Private Judgement,* ii, 8–9, 11.

60. Ibid., 2, 6, 7, 8, 10.

61. Fisher, *A Preservative from Damnable Errors, in the Unction of the Holy One*, 2–3, 5, 24, 31.

62. Ibid., 32, 49–50. Smith reprinted his letter in *The Divine Right of Private Judgment Vindicated* (pp. 20–21), indicating that what he wrote "was purely to *Banter.*"

63. Fisher, *A Preservative from Damnable Errors, in the Unction of the Holy One,* 2, 42.

64. Ibid., 42, partly quoting another minister, Thomas Manton (1620–1677), who wrote a well-known commentary on the book of Jude.

65. On Smith's contention that Fisher's Presbytery sermon was altered for publication in light of the press appearance of his own, see *The Divine Right of Private Judgment Vindicated,* 1–3, 6. On Fisher's admitted improvements and enlargements, see *A Preservative from Damnable Errors, in the Unction of the Holy One,* 34. There is no reason to believe that Smith was wholly mistaken, and since Fisher had a copy of his published sermon in hand before he sent his to press, I have considered it accordingly, as it appears, as Smith contended, that one version of it was preached, another published.

66. Fisher, *A Preservative from Damnable Errors, in the Unction of the Holy One,* 41–42, 51, 55, 59–61. Fisher maintained throughout that neither he nor any of the other subscribers denied Smith's party the liberty to examine the *Westminster Confession* or any Christian doctrine according to the Bible, let alone that he used the words *impose* or *imposition* in his Presbytery sermon on subscription. Never, Fisher said, did he argue "for People's pinning their faith upon other Men's sleeves," as Smith charged.

67. Smith, *The Divine Right of Private Judgment Vindicated,* 9, 22–23, 30. Whereas Smith wrote this piece to dispute Fisher's sermon point by point, *No New Thing* was penned because of the "Whispers of disaffected Persons" in his own congregation. Fisher's *Preservative from Damnable Errors* struck Cainhoy with a thunderclap, sending the church into a convulsion, with some absenting themselves from communion in protest. "You ought to have been with Me, and seen, what I had to offer in my Defense, before you censur'd and left Me," Smith admonished the congregation. "Some of you are verily Guilty concerning Me," he added, "in that you have heard and been too much influenc'd by the Misrepresentation of my Principles, and conceal'd it from Me." Having pontificated upon the history and causes of slander, and noting that Bassett and Porter had also refused to own the *Westminster Confession,* Smith launched into a lengthy apologia. Smith, *No New Thing to be Slander'd,* 14. On disaffection in the Caihhoy church, see also *The Divine Right of Private Judgment Vindicated,* 6.

68. Josiah Smith to Benjamin Colman, October 12, 1730, quoted in Howe, *History of the Presbyterian Church,* 1:191.

69. Smith, *The Divine Right of Private Judgment Vindicated,* 49.

70. Smith, *No New Thing to be Slander'd,* 22 (postscript).

71. Hugh Fisher, *The Divine Right of Private Judgment, Set In a True Light: A Reply to the Reverend Mr. Josiah Smith's Answer, to a Postscript Annex'd to a Sermon . . . Together with, Remarks on the Reverend Mr. Nathan Bassett's Appendix* (Boston, 1731), 99–100.

72. Howe, *History of the Presbyterian Church in South Carolina,* 1:201–6. Laypeople flexed their muscle in other ways, solidifying the breach between subscribers and non-subscribers in some cases by taking a firm stand against the discomposition of tradition. In 1732 an Edisto layman deeded several slaves "for the perpetual maintenance, out of their yearly labor, of a Presbyterian minister who owns the holy Scriptures for his only rule of Faith and practice, and who, agreeably to the holy Scriptures of the Old and New Testaments, shall own the Westminster Confession of Faith, with the Larger and Shorter Catechisms, as a test of his orthodoxy." Three years later another layman bequeathed monies "for the maintenance of a minister of the gospel, according to the Presbyterian profession, who is, or shall be thereafter, from time to time regularly called and settled on John's Island, in Colleton county . . . and who shall acknowledge and subscribe the Westminster Confession of Faith as the confession of his faith, and shall firmly believe and preach the same to the people there committed, or which shall hereafter be committed to his care and pastoral inspection." See Circular Church Records, Charleston, South Carolina, quoted in Howe, *History of the Presbyterian Church in South Carolina,* 1:202. Will of Robert Ure [dated 1735], ibid., 1:207.

73. Josiah Smith to Benjamin Colman, November 7, 1735, quoted in Howe, *History of the Presbyterian Church in South Carolina,* 1:206–7.

74. Isaac Watts to Benjamin Coleman, October 12, 1739, in Henry F. Jenks et al., eds., "Letters from Dr. Isaac Watts," *Proceedings of the Massachusetts Historical Society,* 2nd ser., 9 (Boston: Massachusetts Historical Society, 1895): 370; Josiah Smith, *A Sermon, Preached at Charlestown, South-Carolina, in the Year 1739,* 2nd ed. (Charleston: Robert Wells, 1773), 23. See also Smith, *A Sermon Deliver'd at Charles-town, in South Carolina: the Lord's Day after the Funeral, and Sacred to the Memory of the Reverend Mr. Nathan Bassett, who Exchang'd this for a Better Life, June 26th 1738* (Boston: S. Kneeland and T. Green, 1739).

75. Robert L. Meriwether, *The Expansion of South Carolina, 1729–1765* (Kingsport, Tenn.: Southern Publishers, 1940), 33–109. See also Arlin C. Migliazzo, *To Make This Land Our Own: Community, Identity, and Cultural Adaptation in Purrysburg Township, South Carolina, 1732–1865* (Columbia: University of South Carolina Press, 2007).

76. Extract of the Memoir of David Witherspoon, in J. G. Wardlaw, *Genealogy of the Wardlaw Family* (Yorkville, S.C., 1910), 10; Meriwether, *The Expansion of South Carolina,* 43, 79, 80n, 84.

77. French-speaking Reformed Protestants, mostly Swiss, gathered a congregation in Purrysburg in 1732; their minister Joseph Bugnion, who was Swiss Reformed, received Anglican ordination in London before arriving in the colony. Gabriel Falk, a Swedish Lutheran minister, also labored in the township. A Presbyterian congregation was established in Williamsburg and already by 1736 the "Irish Protestants" had secured the services of a Scotch-Irish minister, Robert Heron. Swiss and German Reformed clergymen, Bartholomew Zouberbuhler, Sr., and Christian Theus, began

holding services in New Windsor and Saxe-Gotha by the end of the decade. Lutheran and German Reformed congregations in Purrysburg and Orangeburg grew up in the 1730s around lay preachers. The Brandenburg judge and physician John Frederick Holzendorf read "Postille" sermons to early German-speaking settlers at Purrysburg. A Toggenburg goldsmith, John Ulrich Giessendanner, a wayfaring Pietist who had dabbled in mystical Illuminism in Switzerland and Germany, was "called by the people" at Orangeburg to be their resident minister, his congregation consisting of "all kinds of religionists." Across the colony to the east and north, Welsh Tract Baptists in Queensboro took cooperative action and founded the Welsh Neck Baptist Church in January 1738. Meriwether, *The Expansion of South Carolina*, 39–40, 57, 67, 84, 96; Migliazzo, *To Make This Land Our Own*, 149–154; South Carolina Synod of the Lutheran Church in America, *History of the Lutheran Church in South Carolina* (Columbia: R. L. Bryan, 1971), 15–30. Hereafter cited as *History of the Lutheran Church in South Carolina*

78. *History of the Lutheran Church in South Carolina*, 11–31; Meriwether, *The Expansion of South Carolina*, 33–76.

79. Albert B. Faust and Gaius M. Brumbaugh, *Lists of Swiss Emigrants in the Eighteenth Century to the American Colonies: Two Volumes in One* (Baltimore: Genealogical Publishing, 1968), quoted in *History of the Lutheran Church in South Carolina*, 12.

80. "Testimony at hearings about John Giessendanner," 1716, reprinted in Hugh George Anderson, "The European Phase of J. U. Giessendanner's Life," *South Carolina Historical Magazine* 67 (July 1966): 132.

81. "Fragment of Governor Tobler's Diary," February 11, 1737–March 18, 1737, in Charles G. Cordle, ed., "The John Tobler Manuscripts: An Account of German-Swiss Emigrants in South Carolina, 1737," *Journal of Southern History* 5 (February–November 1939): 87. The entry quoted is for February 17, 1737.

82. Ibid., 87.

83. Ibid. Zouberbuhler suffered furious abuse not only on the trip over; when he arrived at New Windsor other reform-minded clergy commented on his lack of "inner warmth and piety" in their correspondence with their colleagues back home, saying privately that his congregation seemed to be as "sheep without a shepherd." Samuel Urlsperger, *Ausführliche Nachricht von den Saltzburgischen Emigranten, die sich in Amerika niedergelassen haben*, 18 vols. (Halle: Verlegung des Waysenhauses, 1735–1752), 1:2350, 2385, quoted in *History of the Lutheran Church in South Carolina*, 41–42. Joseph Bugnion, a French-speaking Swiss minister who took Anglican orders before leaving London in 1732, was forced to abandon his ministry in Purrysburg in less than a year; he was no more popular in the lowcountry parish of St. James, Santee, where he was subsequently transferred. In 1735 he was dismissed at Alexander Garden's request. Bugnion's successor at Purrysburg, "a French student" and an understudy of the Anglican-Reformed minister, went the way of his mentor. The laity "chased him away," charging him with living "a wicked life and of mixing in bad affairs." A few months later, another reordained Swiss Reformed minister, Henry Chiffele, arrived. He was well liked and a vast improvement over Bugnion and his student, but despite his best efforts he simply did not "know the German language very well," which put him at a distinct disadvantage in the cultural babble of Purrysburg. German-speaking Lutherans and Reformed

preferred the services performed by a lay reader, John Frederick Holzendorf. They took their children to the Lutheran pastors across the Savannah River at Ebenezer to have them baptized, and they also went there to get married, Chiffele "being unwilling and unable to marry them in the German language." Urlsperger, *Ausführliche Nachricht von den Saltzburgischen Emigranten, die sich in Amerika niedergelassen haben,* 1:368, 1037, 2162, quoted in William J. Hinke, "The Origin of the Reformed Church in South Carolina," *Journal of the Presbyterian Historical Society* 3 (December 1906): 369–71.

84. See John Catron, "The Atlantic World Origins of African American Christianity" (Ph.D. dissertation, University of Florida, 2008).

85. *History of the Lutheran Church in South Carolina,* 46.

86. Giessendanner moved to Marburg to enroll at the university, but he dropped out after a year. Prior to his leaving Lichtensteig in 1714, he had spent time as a goldsmith's apprentice in Halle, Germany, the epicenter of Pietism. At least by the early 1700s he was styling himself a lay teacher, and by the time he struck out for Marburg he was facing opposition from local officials for his radical tendencies. Anderson, "The European Phase of J. U. Giessendanner's Life," 129–30. On the growth and spread of Pietism, see Dale W. Brown, *Understanding Pietism* (Grand Rapids, Mich.: William B. Eerdmans, 1978), chapter 1.

87. Ringgli's testimony is quoted in Anderson, "The European Phase of J. U. Giessendanner's Life," 133.

88. John Giessendanner to Mr. Paravicini, April 23, 1737, ibid., 135.

89. Samuel Urlsperger, *Ausführliche Nachricht von den Saltzburgischen Emigranten, die sich in Amerika niedergelassen haben,* 1, 2174 quoted in Hinke, "The Origin of the Reformed Church in South Carolina," 373. Before accepting his ministerial call Giessendanner married his long-time housekeeper "to prevent & obviate any cause offence or scandal." Quoted in Hinke, *Ministers of the Reformed Congregations in Pennsylvania & Other Colonies in the 18th Century* (Lancaster, Penn.: Historical Commission of the Evangelical and Reformed Church, 1951), 325. Copy available at the Lutheran Theological Seminary Library, Columbia, S.C.

90. Hans Wernhard Trachsler, *Kurtzverfasste Reiss-Beschreibung eines, neulich aus der in West-Indien gelegenen Landschaft Carolina, in sein Vaterland Zurückgekommenen Lands-Angehürigen, samt Bericht von dieses Lands Art, Natur, and Eigenschaften* (Zürich: Bürklischer Druckerey, 1738) quoted in Hinke, *Ministers of the Reformed Congregations,* 373; Peter Rowe as quoted by Samuel Dibble, marginal note in Gottfried Dellman Bernheim, *History of the German Settlements and of the Lutheran Church in North and South Carolina* (Philadelphia: Lutheran Bookstore, 1872), 113; copy available at the Lutheran Theological Seminary Library, Columbia, S.C. In addition to Giessendanner, other clergymen were active and influential. Swiss Reformed minister Christian Theus, brother of colonial South Carolina's best-known portrait painter, came to the colony as a theological candidate. He was ordained in 1739 and settled at Saxe-Gotha, where he ministered to the congregation of St. John's, Congaree, for more than fifty years. *History of the Lutheran Church in South Carolina,* 58–65. Down the road in Orangeburg, Theus's colleague, John Ulrich Giessendanner's nephew and namesake, John, was delivering sermons in "to the Inexpressible satisfaction" of his German-Swiss, German, English,

and French adherents. He, too, had arrived as a theology student and been ordained in 1739. Shortly thereafter, in 1741, English settlers from Amelia, "observing him to be a Man of Learning, Piety and Knowledge in the holy Scriptures, prevailed with him to officiate in preaching once Every fortnight in English, which he . . . performed very articulate and Intelligible." Moreover, "above four score of the Dutch [read *Deutsch*] and English Inhabitants of Orangeburg and the adjoining plantations" signed a formal petition in 1744 after Bartholomew Zouberbuhler, Jr., applied to the South Carolina Council to obtain Anglican ordination so that he might preach in the township with state support. Supporters of the younger Giessendanner were incensed. They claimed that Zouberbuhler, trained in the Orthodox Reformed tradition like his father, had been encouraged "by some wicked Persons, in one part of the Township" who were endeavoring "to kick Mr. Giessendanner out of the church." Apparently he publicly rebuked them for Sabbath-breaking as well as for "Great Irregularitys, and disorders." *South Carolina Council and Upper House Journals, 1721–1775*, South Carolina Department of Archives and History, Columbia, 11: 139-43 (May 6, 1744).

91. The story of the Ashley River Baptists is somewhat unusual, however, because it is rather well documented—exceptionally so for these critical years. See Ashley River Baptist Church (Charleston District, S.C.), Records, 1736–1769 (Microfilm), Southern Baptist Historical Library and Archives, Nashville, May 24, 1736–May 25, 1769. (Hereafter cited as Records of the Ashley River Baptist Church). The records, which commence in 1736 when Ashley River Baptist congregation founded an independent "Branch of ye visible Church of Christ" in the wake of a New Light schism, constitute the earliest comprehensive extant records of any Baptist church in the South—a literal quarry of information that can be mined profitably to explore the rise of evangelicalism in the colony. Ibid, May 24, 1736, frame 1. See also the piece I co-edited with Sarah E. Kegley, "Records of the Ashley River Baptist Church, 1736–1769," *South Carolina Baptist Historical Quarterly* 27 (November 2001): 3–32. The manuscript records are now at Furman University, and though they have been edited and published, all the following references are from a microfilm copy available from the Southern Baptist Convention Historical Commission Historical Commission, Nashville. (Publication Number 1090). Frame numbers shall hereafter be omitted.

92. Records of the Ashley River Baptist Church, May 24, 1736, June 9, 1740; Morgan Edwards, *Materials Towards A History of the Baptists*, edited by Eve B. Weeks and Mary B. Warren, 2 vols. (Danielsville, Ga.: Heritage Papers, 1984), 2:124–25; Towsend, *South Carolina Baptists*, 32–33.

93. Records of the Ashley River Baptist Church, March 18, 1738; South Carolina Commons House Journals, 1705–1775, South Carolina Department of Archives and History, Columbia, April 26, May 1, 3, 1745. See also Edwards, *Materials Towards A History of the Baptists*, 2:121–22, 124–26, 151–52; Townsend, *South Carolina Baptists*, 14n; David Benedict, *A General History of the Baptist Denomination in America, and Other Parts of the World*, 2 vols. (Boston: Lincoln and Edmonds, 1813), 2.: 121-26. The five points of Calvinism are: unconditional election, limited (particular) atonement, total depravity, irresistible grace, and the final perseverance of the saints. It appears that the disagreements in the Charleston church initially began about the time Isaac Chanler arrived

in the colony in 1733. According to contemporary sources, one of the members of the Stono branch, William Elliot, Jr., was suspended from communion for espousing "Arminian" sentiments. This "occasioned a schism into which was drawn his father and several others." William Elliot, Sr., the wealthy patriarch of the family, had donated the lot upon which the Charleston Baptist church was built, and he reportedly "sent to England for one Mr. Ingram a Minister holding the same Tenets with himself." Edwards, *Materials Towards A History of the History of the Baptists,* 2:122; South Carolina Commons House Journals, 1705–1775, April 26, 1745. Six of the twenty-one constituent members of the Stono Baptist Church (or 28.57 percent) were members of the Elliot family.

94. Records of the Ashley River Baptist Church, March 14–15, 1741, May 24, 1736, March 18 and June 17–18, 1738. The complex story of the various Baptist groups in British America, their theological orientation and relative numbers from place to place and over time, is told clearly and succinctly by Robert G. Gardner, *Baptists of Early America: A Statistical History, 1639–1790* (Atlanta: Georgia Baptist Historical Society, 1983), 14–63.

95. See Thomas Cooper and David J. McCord, eds., *The Statutes at Large of South Carolina,* 10 vols. (Columbia, S.C.: A. S. Johnston, 1836–1841), 3:661; Edwards, *Materials Towards A History of the History of the Baptists,* 2:120–23, 124–26, 151–53; Townsend, *South Carolina Baptists,* 14–17, 54–6. Around the turn of the eighteenth century Charleston Baptists adopted the Calvinistic *London Confession of Faith* (1689). It does not appear that they had ever held to the laying on of hands.

96. South Carolina Commons House Journals, 1705–1775, May 1, 1745; *South Carolina Gazette,* September 26–October 3, 1741 (postscript).

97. Edwards, *Materials Toward A History of the Baptists,* 2:122; South Carolina Commons House Journals, 1705–1775, January 26, February 14, April 26, May 1, and May 3, 1745.

98. Records of the Ashley River Baptist Church, June 19–20, September 17–18, December 12, 1737, and September 21, 1740. On Susannah Baker, see Francis Varnod's 1726 census of St. George's Parish, reprinted in Klingberg, *An Appraisal of the Negro in Colonial South Carolina,* 58–60, as well as the analysis in Wood, *Black Majority,* 159–66.

99. Townsend, *South Carolina Baptists,* 34n.

100. Edwards, *Materials Towards A History of the Baptists,* 2:126; Records of the Ashley River Baptist Church, March 18, 1738.

101. For a list of Chanler's publications, see Townsend, *South Carolina Baptists,* 34n, and 282n. Chanler apparently attempted to institute the ritualistic "laying on of hands" at the Euhaw Baptist Church in St. Helena's Parish in 1746, "but the thing created disturbance" and he "desisted from attempting to introduce the rite": Edwards, *Materials Towards A History of the Baptists,* 2:132.

102. See Noll, Bebbington, Rawlyk, "Introduction," in *Evangelicalism,* 6; Kidd, *The Great Awakening,* xiv.

103. Records of the Ashley River Baptist Church, December 12, 1737, and June 9, 1740.

104. Ibid., June 9, 1740, September [n.d.] 1742, and December 14, 1745. See also Beasley, *Christian Ritual in and the Creation of British Slave Societies,* 90–95. The Ashley River

Church considered only eighteen cases of sinful or disorderly conduct from 1736 to 1769. Of the total number of people cited, seven (or 39 percent) were charged with drunkenness. Next to these were cases involving adultery and absentia; there were four each, representing 22 percent of the overall sum respectively. Finally, two cases (11 percent) dealt with "evil speaking" and "using ill words . . . in Publick company," and one (6 percent) concerned "maintaining an Error in Doctrine of a very bad Consequence." See Little and Kegley, "Records of the Ashley River Baptist Church."

105. Records of the Ashley River Baptist Church, June 12, 1738, December 14, 1745.

106. Ibid., December 11, 1738, September 10, 1739.

107. John B. Boles, "Introduction," in Boles, ed., *Masters and Slaves in the House of the Lord: Race and Religion in the American South* (Lexington: University Press of Kentucky, 1988), 13. Apparently the Ashley River congregation later became mostly black (see chapter 5 below).

108. Sylvia R. Frey and Betty Wood, *Come Shouting to Zion: African American Protestantism in the American South and the British Caribbean to 1830* (Chapel Hill: University of North Carolina Press, 1998), xi–xii, 35, 76–79, 82–83; Mechal Sobel, *Trabelin' On: The Slave Journey to an Afro-Baptist Faith* (1979: rpt. Princeton: Princeton University Press, 1988), xii–xxiv, 100–101.

Chapter 4. A Hammer and a Fire

1. "A letter from Mrs. Bryan to her Sister," October 1739, in [William Hutson,] *Living Christianity, delineated, in the Diaries and Letters of two Eminently pious Persons, lately deceased; vis. Mr. Hugh Bryan, and Mrs. Mary Hutson, Both of South Carolina. With a Preface by the Reverend Mr. John Conder, and the Reverend Mr. Thomas Gibbons* (London: J. Buckland, 1760), 18–19, 20, 22. Catherine Bryan strongly urged her sister to read Whitefield's writings. In a revealing postscript she added: "one thing I woul'd have you observe is that I felt and experienced those things I tell you of, before I had read Mr. Whitefield's works on the New-Birth or Justification, or heard, or thought any such things were to be felt or known, so that I would not have you think that I was led away by him with his Enthusiastick notions, as the world is pleas'd to call them." Ibid., 23. For an example of one of Whitefield's works on regeneration to which Bryan may very well have been referring, see *The Nature and Necessity of our New Birth in Christ Jesus, in Order to Salvation* (London, 1737). Whitefield mentions Catherine Bryan's conversion in his journal. See George Whitefield, *Journals, 1737–1741, to which is prefixed his "Short Account" (1746) and "Further Account" (1747)* (1756; rpt., Gainesville, Fla.: Scholars Facsimilies and Reprints, 1969), 437. See also Alan Gallay, *The Formation of a Planter Elite: Jonathan Bryan and the Southern Colonial Frontier* (Athens: University of Georgia Press, 1989), 33–34. On Whitefield, see Harry S. Stout, *The Divine Dramatist: George Whitefield and the Rise of Modern Evangelicalism* (Grand Rapids, Mich.: William B. Eerdmans, 1991); Frank Lambert, *"Pedlar in Divinity": George Whitefield and the Transatlantic Revivals* (Princeton: Princeton University Press, 1994).

2. "A letter from Mr. Hugh Bryan to his Sister, giving an account of his experiences towards God," undated, in Hutson, *Living Christianity, delineated*, 11, 13–14; "A letter from Mr. Hugh Bryan to his Child," July 16, 1740, ibid., 23–24. See also Harvey H. Jackson,

"Hugh Bryan and the Evangelical Movement in Colonial South Carolina," *William and Mary Quarterly*, 3rd ser., 43 (October 1986): 594–614; Leigh Eric Schmidt, *Holy Fairs: Scotland and the Making of American Revivalism*, 2nd ed. (Grand Rapids, Mich.: William B. Eerdmans, 2001).

3. Isaac Chanler, *New Converts Exhorted to Cleave to the Lord. A Sermon on Acts XI 23 Preach'd July 30, 1740, at a Wednesday Evening-lecture, in Charlestown, Set Up at the Motion, and the Desire of the Rev. Mr. Whitefield; with a Brief Introduction Relating to the Character of that Excellent Man . . . With Preface by the Reverend Mr. Cooper of Boston, N.E.* (Boston: D. Fowle for S. Kneeland and T. Green, 1740), 5. See also Whitefield, *Journals*, 43–44. Whitefield's visits to South Carolina have been the focus of several studies. See, for example, William Howland Kenney III, "Alexander Garden and George Whitefield: The Significance of Revivalism in South Carolina, 1738–1741," *South Carolina Historical Magazine* 71 (January 1970): 1–16; David T. Morgan, Jr., "George Whitefield's Ministry in Georgia and the Carolinas, 1739–1740," *Georgia Historical Quarterly* 54 (December 1970): 517–39; Morgan, "The Consequences of George Whitefield's Ministry in Georgia and the Carolinas, 1739–1740," *Georgia Historical Quarterly* 55 (January 1971): 62–82; Morgan, "The Great Awakening in South Carolina, 1740–1745," *South Atalntic Quarterly* 70 (Autumn 1971): 595–606; and Andrew T. Nelson, "Enthusiasm in Carolina, 1740," *South Atlantic Quarterly* 44 (October 1945): 397–405. S. Charles Bolton also feature's Whitefield's ministry in *Southern Anglicanism: The Church of England in Colonial South Carolina* (Westport, Conn.: Greenwood Press, 1982), 50–56. For a good bibliography of sources on the Great Awakening, see Thomas S. Kidd, *The Great Awakening: A Brief History with Documents* (Boston: Bedford / St. Martin's, 2008).

4. Alexander Garden, *Take Heed How Ye Hear: A Sermon Preached in the Parish Church of St. Philip Charles-Town, in South Carolina, on Sunday the 13th of July, 1740. With a Preface, containing some Remarks on Mr. Whitefield's Journals* (Preface, 1–33, and Sermon, 1–38, paginated separately) (Charleston: Peter Timothy, 1741), Preface, 6, 12.

5. Whitefield, *Journals*, 440.

6. See Whitefield, *Journals*, 150, 153–54; Morgan, "The Consequences of George Whitefield's Ministry in the Carolinas and Georgia, 1739–1740," 73–74. Whitefield boarded the *Minerva* on January 16, 1741, and apparently spent several days in Charleston harbor awaiting passage abroad. Continuing to preach and visit with his "many friends," he noted that the ship sailed "over Charleston bar" on January 24. Whitefield, *Journals*, 509.

7. Frank Lambert, *Inventing the "Great Awakening"* (Princeton: Princeton University Press, 1999), 13. See also Alan Heimert and Perry Miller, eds., *The Great Awakening: Documents Illustrating the Crisis and Its Consequences* (Indianapolis: Bobbs-Merrill, 1967), xxv–xxviii. On Whitefield's 1739 travels in America, see Whitefield, *Journals*, October 30 to December 2 (Middle Colonies), December 3 to 10 (Maryland), December 11 to 18 (Virginia), and December 19 to 31 (North Carolina), 334–79.

8. Whitefield, *Journals*, 379–80.

9. Ibid., 380–81. On historical explorations of the slave insurrection, see Mark M. Smith, *Stono: Documenting and Interpreting a Southern Slave Revolt* (Columbia: University of South Carolina Press, 2005).

10. Whitefield, *Journals*, 159–60.

11. Ibid., 381–82.

12. Josiah Smith, *A Sermon, preached at Charlestown, South-Carolina, in the Year 1739*, 2nd ed. (Charleston: Robert Wells, 1773), 3–4. In this critical piece, a sermon on Psalm 38: 2 ("For thine arrows stick fast in me"), Smith reveals what he thought the Great Awakening was an awakening to:

> People know not what they say, when they raise clamours, and cry out, against a severe and searching ministry. It is the glory of the Gospel, that it is the power of God to them that believe; it is the honour of God's word that it can reach the soul, and prick the heart. . . . It is even enumerated among the glories and triumphs of the Redeemer, "When he girds his sword upon his thigh, and his right hand teaches terrible things; when his arrows are sharp in the hearts of his enemies, and the people fall under him." What a glorious sermon was that, when three thousand were pricked in their hearts, and cried out, what shall we do to be saved? For my own part, I shall ever honour the names of those ministers in the church, who have been *Sons of thunder*, and whose sermons have been like pointed arrows, in the consciences of their hearers. If the awakening of people into a sense of their undone and wretched condition, by nature; if making them humble, and leading them to despair of salvation, out of Christ: I say, if this be criminal; if this be a reproach to their character, many of our modern writers are very safe. But to prophesy smooth things, and to cry out peace, where there is no peace, is a character I shall never be ambitious of.

13. Whitefield, *Journals*, 382.

14. Ibid., 382. See also *South Carolina Gazette*, January 19, 1740. On Whitefield's innovative preaching, see Stout, *The Divine Dramatist*.

15. Whitefield, *Journals*, 383; Garden, *Take Heed How Ye Hear*, "Preface," 12–13, 17, 25–26.

16. Garden, *Take Heed How Ye Hear*, "Preface," 12, 26; Whitefield, *Journals*, 382–83.

17. Whitefield, *Journals*, 383–84.

18. George Whitefield, *Three Letters from the Reverend Mr. G. Whitefield: vis. Letter I. To a Friend in London, concerning Archbishop Tillotson. Letter II. To the same, on the same Subject. Letter III. To the Inhabitants of Maryland, Virginia, North and South-Carolina, concerning their Negroes* (Piladelphia: B. Franklin, 1740). See also Alexander Garden, *Six letters to the Rev. Mr. George Whitefield. The First, Second and Third, on the Subject of Justification. The Fourth containing Remarks on a Pamphlet, entitled, the Case between M. Whitefield and Dr. Stebbing state, &c. The Fifth containing Remarks on Mr. Whitefield's two Letters concerning Archbishop Tillotson, and the Book entitled, the Whole Duty of Man. The Sixth, containing Remarks on Mr. Whitefield's second Letter, concerning Archbishop Tillotson, and on his Letter concerning the Negroes*, 2nd ed. (Boston: T. Fleet, 1740). Whitefield's first and third letters were written on January 18 and 23, 1740, respectively. The second was written on March 28. However, the two letters on Tillotson and Whitefield's letter on Richard Allestree's *Whole Duty of Man* will be considered first. Garden published the fifth of his six letters in the *South Carolina Gazette* on April 26, 1740.

19. Whitefield, *Three Letters,* 2–3.

20. Ibid., 2–4. Whitefield claimed that Wesley coined the expression about Tillotson: "My dear and honoured Friend . . . first spoke it in a private Society, when he was expounding Part of St. Paul's Epistle to the Romans, and proving the Doctrine of Justification in the Sight of God, by Faith alone, in Contradistinction to good Works," he wrote. Ibid., 2. Whitefield emphasized that Tillotson, who was born the son of a Puritan clothier, had no excuses. He "had his Education amongst those who did truly preach Christ, and yet afterwards, [in his writings,] preach'd Doctrines as contrary to the Articles to which he subscribed as Darkness is contrary to Light." Ibid., 4. Here he again speaks of Tillotson's heterodoxy.

21. Ibid., 4–5.

22. Ibid., 12.

23. George Whitefield, *A Letter from the Rev. Mr. Whitefield from Georgia, to a Friend in London, showing the Fundamental Error of a Book, Entitled The Whole Duty of Man* (Charleston: Peter Timothy, 1740), 3–4.

24. Whitefield, *Three Letters,* 15.

25. Georgia, which prohibited slavery, was excluded from the title of Whitefield's letter, though there was much bending of the rules. Georgia planters leased slaves and South Carolinians brought slaves with them to the province. Thus, while Whitefield did not specifically address Georgians in the letter, he no doubt was aware of the southern context.

26. Whitefield, *Three Letters,* 13, 16; Whitefield, *A Letter from the Rev. Mr. White-field from Georgia, to a Friend in London, shewing the Fundamental Error of the Book, entitled The Whole Duty of Man,* 3, 10. See also Whitefield, *Journals,* 384–85 passim.

27. Whitefield, *Three Letters,* 13, 16.

28. Ibid., 13–14.

29. Ibid., 15–16. Compare William Fleetwood, *A Sermon Preached before the Society for the Propagation of the Gospel in Foreign Parts, at the Parish Church of St. Mary-le-Bow, on Friday the 16th of February, 1710/11. Being the Day of their Anniversary Meeting* (London: Joseph Downing, 1711), in Frank J. Klingberg, *Anglican Humanitarianism in Colonial New York* (Philadelphia: Church Historical Society, 1940), 197–212.

30. *South Carolina Gazette,* March 1, 1740. Smith's letter of January 9 was published in the *Gazette,* January 19, 1740. See also February 2, 9, 16, and 23, 1740; Heimert and Miller, eds., *The Great Awakening,* 62–63; Thomas S. Kidd, *The Great Awakening: The Roots of Evangelical Christianity in America* (New Haven: Yale University Press, 2007), 71–72; Morgan, "The Great Awakening in South Carolina," 596–97.

31. *South Carolina Gazette,* January 29, 1741; February 16, 1740.

32. Ibid., January 19, 1740.

33. Ibid., February 16, 1740.

34. Ibid., January 19, 1740.

35. Ibid, March 29, 1741.

36. Ibid., February 2, 9, and 16, 1740. The preponderance of evidence suggests that "Arminius" was in fact Alexander Garden, and since there is no reason to believe otherwise, I have identified him as such.

37. Ibid., February 9, 1740. See also February 16, 23, March 8, 22, 29, July 5, September 6, and October 9, 1740. In a short letter to Timothy appearing in the January 22, 1741, issue, Smith noted that he planned to send the last installment of his response to Arminius to be printed (with Garden's reply) in pamphlet form.

38. Ibid., February 2, 1740.

39. Ibid., February 2, 9, 1740.

40. Ibid., February 9, 23, 1740.

41. *Regeneration, and Testimony of the Spirit. Being the Substance of Two Sermons Lately Preached in the Parish Church of St. Philip, Charles-Town, in South-Carolina. Occasioned by some Erroneous Notions of Certain Men who call themselves Methodists* (Charleston: Peter Timothy, 1740), i, 1–3, 13. See also Garden, *Take Heed How Ye Hear.* Garden did less to defend his own position in the latter sermon (which was preached in July), focusing instead on attacking the enthusiasm of the new lights. The same can generally be said of the sermons included in his *Six letters to the Rev. Mr. George Whitefield.*

42. Garden, *Regeneration, and Testimony of the Spirit,* 12, 16–17, 21, 24–45.

43. Ibid., 1, 21.

44. Of course, by no means did Anglican ministers present a unified front. See Bolton, *Southern Anglicanism,* 53, and below.

45. Garden, *Regeneration, and Testimony of the Spirit,* i, 21. See also p. 13.

46. Garden, *Take Heed How Ye Hear,* 19; *Regeneration, and Testimony of the Spirit,* i.

47. *South Carolina Gazette,* March 29, 1740.

48. Whitefield, *Journals,* 400 (March 18, 1740); *South Carolina Gazette,* March 22, 1740.

49. *South Carolina Gazette,* March 22, 1740.

50. *Some Queries, Concerning the Operation of the Holy Spirit, Answered. Delivered at a Lecture held at the Baptist-Meeting-House-in Charles-Town, South-Carolina: And now published at the earnest Request of Some of the Hearers* (Philadelphia: B. Franklin, 1740). This piece was likely authored by Thomas Simmons. Morgan Edwards (*Materials Towards A History of the Baptists,* edited by Eve B. Weeks and Mary B. Warren, 2 vols. [Danielsville, Ga.: Heritage Papers, 1984], 2:122) recorded that Whitefield's coming "caused a revival" in Simmons's congregation. A print notice dated Saturday, March 15, announced that Whitefield was to "preach twice" that day, but there was no subsequent report on the size of the audiences at either Charleston Baptist or the Independent Church (where the itinerant preached on Saturday afternoon) in the notice dated Monday, March 17. See *South Carolina Gazette,* March 22, 1740.

51. Whitefield, *Journals,* 398–99 (March 15, 1740). In a revealing notation concerning his March visit to the Baptist church, Whitefield wrote that he "was much pleased, when I heard afterwards, that from the same pulpit, a person not long ago had preached, who denied the doctrine of original sin, the divinity and Righteousness of our Lord, and the operation of God's Blessed Spirit upon the soul." Here it is possible that he could have been referring to Robert Ingram, who died in 1738, but it is more probable that he was referring to Henry Heywood, who arrived in 1739 to replace Ingram. After the Ashley River and Stono Baptists split from the Charleston congregation, it was agreed that Chanler and Ingram would submit attendance

reports to the metropolitan church twice each year (May and November) and "sit down in Christian communion at ye Lords Table when ye ministers of Each Branch of ye Church are to Take their turns in Preaching as before." Records of the Ashley River Baptist Church, 1736–1769, May 13, 1736. Presumably this tradition continued after Heywood arrived at Stono. Heywood stood opposed to Whitefield, and, according to Morgan Edwards, "translated to English Dr. Whitby's treatise on Original sin," together with a defense of the exposition "against Dr. Gill." Morgan Edwards, *Materials Towards A History of the Baptists,* 2:152 See also *South Carolina Gazette,* June 25, 1741 (postscript).

52. *South Carolina Gazette,* February 23, 1740. See also Whitefield, *Journals,* 399–400 (March 16 and 17, 1740); *South Carolina Gazette,* March 22 and 29, 1740.

53. *South Carolina Gazette,* March 29, 1740.

54. Ibid., March 29, 1740; Whitefield, *Journals,* 400 (March 17, 1740).

55. *South Carolina Gazette,* January 19, 1740.

56. Whitefield, *Journals,* 398 (March 14, 1740).

57. Ibid., 397–98 (March 14, 1740). See also Garden, *Take Heed How Ye Hear,* "Preface," 17–20. I have considered both accounts in the story of this famous episode.

58. Whitefield, *Journals,* 398 (March 14, 1740).

59. Garden, *Take Heed How Ye Hear,* 17. In his sermon Garden traced the history of Charleston's "*Balls* and *Assemblies*" and provided an "Account and Description" of each. He then offered an explanation of why he did not preach against them. See ibid., 18–20.

60. Morgan, "The Great Awakening in South Carolina," 597–98.

61. Whitefield, *Journals,* 399. See also Garden, *Six letters to the Rev. Mr. George Whitefield,* 5–6.

62. Garden, *Six letters to the Rev. Mr. George Whitefield,* 5–7.

63. Whitefield, *Journals,* 400 (March 18, 1740). See also ibid., 399 (March 16, 1740); *South Carolina Gazette,* March 29, April 11, 1740.

64. Alexander Garden to Edmund Gibson, bishop of London, April 24, 1740, in Lambeth Palace Library, *The Fulham Papers at Lambeth Palace Library,* 20 reels (Microfilm 2nd. ed., with additional reel), 42 vols. (London: World Microfilms, c.1970-c.1978), 10:74. Hereafter cited as *The Fulham Papers.*

65. *South Carolina Gazette,* April 11, June 14, 1740.

66. Whitefield, *Journals,* 437 (June 30, 1740).

67. Whitefield, *Three Letters,* 16.

68. Whitefield, *Journals,* 437–38 (July 1, 1740).

69. Hutson, *Living Christianity, delineated,* 33; Whitefield, *Journals,* 438 (July 1, 1740).

70. Lewis Jones to Commissary Garden, St. Helen's South Carolina, and Jones to [Secretary], August 15, 1740. Both letters are quoted in Klingberg, *An Appraisal of the Negro in Colonial South Carolina: A Study in Americanization* (Washington, D.C.: Associated Publishers, 1941), 70–71.

71. Whitefield refers to Thomas Buer as "Mr. B . . ." in his journal. Buer, one of Whitefield's many supporters in South Carolina, was an elder at Bethel Presbyterian Church. Whitefield, *Journals,* 438, 445 (July 3 and 22, 1740). See also *South Carolina*

Gazette, July 25, 1740; George Howe, *History of the Presbyterian Church in South Carolina,* 2 vols. (Columbia: Duffie & Chapman, 1870), 1:203.

72. *South Carolina Gazette,* July 18, 1740; Whitefield, *Journals,* 441, 445 (July 13 and July 23, 1740). On the extent of this July preaching tour, see the *South Carolina Gazette,* July 12, 18, and 25, 1740; Whitefield, *Journals,* 438–46 (July 3 to July 25, 1740).

73. *South Carolina Gazette,* July 25, 1740; Whitefield, *Journals,* 441 (July 12, 1740).

74. Whitefield, *Journals,* 439–41 (July 7, 8, 9 and 12, 1740).

75. Ibid., 441 (July 12, 1740).

76. Ibid., 442–43 (July 19, 1740).

77. See ibid., 443 (notation following entry for July 19, 1740). Whitefield appeared before the court on three occasions, on Tuesday, Wednesday, and Thursday, July 15–17. He prosecuted his appeal and posted a surety bond on Friday, July 18.

78. See ibid., 398 (March 14, 1740); Garden, *Take Heed How Ye Hear,* 18.

79. *South Carolina Gazette,* July 25, 1740.

80. Ibid., July 25, 1740. See also Bolton, *Southern Anglicanism,* 51–52; Kenney, "Alexander Garden and George Whitefield," 10–11; Morgan, "The Consequences of George Whitefield's Ministry in the Carolinas and Georgia," 67–68; Morgan, "The Great Awakening in South Carolina," 600–601."

81. Alexander Garden to Bishop Sherlock, February 1, 1750, in *The Fulham Papers,* 10:134–35. See also Garden, *Take Heed How Ye Hear,* "Preface," 7–10. Francis Guichard, the French minister to whom Garden referred, was an ordained Anglican minister, though he preached at the Huguenot Church.

82. See Bolton, *Southern Anglicanism,* 42–49.

83. Ibid., 41. On the nature of authority in colonial British America, see Jack P. Greene, "Independence, Improvement, and Authority: Toward a Framework for Understanding the Histories of the Southern Backcountry during the Era of the American Revolution," in Ronald Hoffman, Thad W. Tate, and Peter J. Albert, eds., *An Uncivil War: The Southern Backcountry during the American Revolution* (Charlottesville: University Press of Virginia, 1985), 3–36.

84. Garden, *Take Heed How Ye Hear,* "Preface," 11. See also Greene, "Independence, Improvement, and Authority," 21–25, 33–35; Bolton, *Southern Anglicanism,* 43.

85. Whitefield, *Journals,* 445–46 (July 23 and 25, 1740); Bolton, *Southern Anglicanism,* 47–48, 167–69. William Orr was a Presbyterian who had taken Anglican orders.

86. Garden, *Take Heed How Ye Hear,* "Preface," 12–13.

87. (Boston: T. Fleet, 1740), 22.

88. Garden, *Take Heed How Ye Hear,* "Preface," 11; *Six letters to the Rev. Mr. George Whitefield,* 20.

89. Whitefield, *Journals,* 439, 442 (July 6 and July 13, 1740); Garden, *Take Heed How Ye Hear,* 15. See also Garden, *Take Heed How Ye Hear,* "Preface," 3–6, 16. As Garden correctly observed, he preached his sermon on July 13, not July 20 as Whitefield recorded.

90. Garden, *Take Heed How Ye Hear,* "Preface," 15–17; Whitefield, *Journals,* 441, 443 (July 13 and 20, 1740).

91. Whitefield, *Journals,* 443, 445 (July 20 and 24, 1740); Howe, *History of the Presbyterian Church,* 1:202–3. Five of Whitefield's journal entries for late August are

mislabeled. Monday, July 22, should read July 21; Tuesday, July 23, should read July 22; Wednesday, July 24 (cited above), should read July 23; Thursday, July 25, should read July 24; and Friday, July 26, should read July 25.

92. Whitefield, *Journals,* 447–49 (August 2, 4, 17). Two of the dates referred to here should read Sunday, August 3, not August 2, and Monday, August 18, not August 17. See also Gallay, *The Formation of a Planter Elite,* 34.

93. Whitefield, *Journals,* 450–51 (August 24, 1740); *South Carolina Gazette,* September 6, 1740. The date referred to in Whitefield's journal should read Monday, August 25, not August 24. On the significance of Whitefield's reading list, see Susan O'Brien, "Eighteenth-Century Publishing Networks in the First Years of Transatlantic Evangelicalism," in Mark A. Noll, David W. Bebbington, and George A. Rawlyk, eds., *Evangelicalism: Studies in Popular Protestantism in North America, the British Isles, and Beyond, 1700–1990* (New York: Oxford University Press, 1994), 38–57.

94. Whitefield, *Journals,* 450–51 (August 24 [i.e., 25], 1740).

95. *South Carolina Gazette,* July 12, 1740.

96. Ibid., September 6, 1740; Andrew Croswell, *An Answer to the Rev. Mr. Garden's Three First Letters to the Rev. Mr. Whitefield. With an Appendix Concerning Mr. Garden's Treatment of Mr. Whitefield, &c.* (Boston: S. Kneelend and T. Green, 1741), 5–6, 50, 52–53; Kenney, "Alexander Garden and George Whitefield," 13. Kenney provides especially insightful analysis in his article. See also Leigh Eric Schmidt, "'A Second and Glorious Reformation': The New Light Extremism of Andrew Croswell," *William and Mary Quarterly,* 3rd ser., 43 (April 1986): 217–18; Kidd, *The Great Awakening,* 121.

97. Isaac Chanler, *New Converts Exhorted to Cleave to the Lord,* "Preface," i–iv; "Author's Introduction," v–vi; "Sermon," 4–5, 11. See also Whitefield, *Journals,* 443–44 (July 20, 1740).

98. Whitefield, *Journals,* 444, 451 (July 20 and August 24 [i.e., 25], 1740).

99. Ibid., 443, 450–52 (July 20 and August 24 [i.e., 25], 1740).

Chapter 5. The Kingdom of Heaven

1. David Ramsay, *History of South Carolina, From its First Settlement in 1670 to the Year 1808,* 2 vols. (1809; rpt. Newberry, S.C.: W. J. Duffie, 1858), 2:251; Frederick Dalcho, *An Historical Account of the Protestant Episcopal Church in South Carolina form the First Settlement of the Province to the War of the Revolution* (Charleston: E. Thayer, 1820), 180–83. Among the other ministers known to have attended the meetings of the religious and literary society were John Joachim Zubly, pastor of the Wappetaw Independent church in Christ's Church Parish, and Philip Morrison, pastor of the Charleston's Scots Presbyterian church. Ministers such as Josiah Smith, Presbyterian pastor James Edmonds, and Baptist revivalist Oliver Hart may also have attended. See George Howe, *History of the Presbyterian Church in South Carolina,* 2 vols. (Columbia: Duffie & Chapman, 1870), 1:264–67, 271–72; Leah Townsend, *South Carolina Baptists, 1670–1805* (1935; rpt. Baltimore: Genealogical Publishing, 1978), 20–23, 118. Among the lay members were several notables such as Gabriel Manigault, Daniel Crawford, Christopher Gadsden, Henry Laurens, John Rattray, and Benjamin Smith. With the exception of Manigault, all of these men were serving in the South Carolina Commons House of

Assembly at the time. See Jack P. Greene, *The Quest for Power: The Lower Houses of Assembly in the Southern Royal Colonies, 1689–1776* (Chapel Hill: University of North Carolina Press, 1963), 475–88.

2. William Henry Lyttleton to Board of Trade, September 1, 1759, British Public Record Office, Transcripts of records relation to South Carolina, 1663-1782, South Carolina Department of Archives and History, Columbia, 28:213. See also Richard Clarke, *The Prophetic Numbers of Daniel and John Calculated: In Order to Show the Time, when the Day of Judgment for the First Age of the Gospel, is to be Expected: and the Setting Up the Millennial Kingdom of the Jehovah and His Christ,* 3rd ed. (Philadelphia: William Bradford, 1759). The second edition of the Clarke's sermon is advertised in the *South Carolina Gazette* for March 3, 1759.

3. Philip Johns, a free black man brought up on charges of "promoting and encouraging an insurrection" later that summer, was almost certainly influenced by Clarke. See Robert Olwell, *Masters, Slaves & Subjects: The Culture of Power in the South Carolina Low Country, 1740–1790* (Ithaca: Cornell University Press, 1998), 136–37; John Scott Strickland, "Across Space and Time: Conversion, Community, and Cultural Change among South Carolina Slaves" (Ph.D. dissertation, University of North Carolina, 1985), 109–113.

4. Ramsay, *History of South Carolina,* 2:251–52. See also Desiree Hirst, *Hidden Riches: Traditional Symbolism from the Renaissance to Blake* (New York: Barnes & Noble, 1964); George C. Rogers, Jr., *Evolution of a Federalist: William Loughton Smith of Charleston (1758–1812)* (Columbia: University of South Carolina Press, 1962), 61–69. Nine months after Clarke left the colony a number of provincial elites took subscriptions for "his writings in explanation of scripture prophecies." *South Carolina Gazette,* December 8, 1759. Furthermore, in 1808 David Ramsay wrote that "the present generation will have the opportunity of judging . . . his commentaries [on whether] the general conversion of the Jews will take place between the present day and the year 1835." *History of South Carolina,* 2:252. In addition to *The Prophetic Numbers of Daniel and John Calculated,* Clarke published several other works that circulated widely throughout the Atlantic world. These included *A Spiritual Voice to the Christian Church, and to the Jews; In an Explanation of the Sabbatical Year of Moses by the Gospel of Jesus Christ . . .* (London: J. Townsend, 1760) and *A Second Warning to the World, by the Spirit of Prophecy. In an explanation of the mysteries in the Feast of Trumpets on the First Day of the Seventh Month...* (London: J. Townsend, 1760).

5. Ramsay, *History of South Carolina,* 2:251. Henry Laurens was among Clarke's most zealous followers. See, for example, Henry Laurens to John Ettwein, April 7, 1762, in Philip M. Hamer, George C. Rogers, Jr., and David R. Chesnuttt, eds., *The Papers of Henry Laurens: Volume Three: Jan. 1, 1759–Aug. 31, 1763* (Columbia: University of South Carolina Press, 1972), 93–94.

6. Charles Martin to Secretary of the SPG, February 24, 1759, Society for the Propagation of the Gospel in Foreign Parts, *Records of the Society for the Propagation of the Gospel in Foreign Parts,* Series B (General Correspondence, 1701–1786), 25 vols. (Microfilm): 5:14.

7. Oliver Hart, Diary, October 27, 1754, South Carolina Baptist Collection, Furman University, Greenville, S.C. (hereafter cited as Hart, MS Diary); Clarke, *The Prophetic Numbers of Daniel and John Calculated*, 3, 17.

8. Josiah Smith, *The Character, Preaching, & c. of the Reverend Mr. Geo. Whitefield, Impartially represented and supported, in a Sermon Preach'd in Charlestown, South-Carolina, March 26. Anno Domini 1740* (Philadelphia: B Franklin, 1740), 22–24. See also Alexander Garden, *Take Heed How Ye Hear: A Sermon Preached in the Parish Church of St. Philip Charles-Town, in South Carolina, on Sunday the 13th of July, 1740. With a Preface, containing some Remarks on Mr. Whitefield's Journals* (Charleston: Peter Timothy, 1741), 30–37; Hugh Fisher, *A Preservative from Damnable Errors, in the Unction of the Holy One. A Sermon Preach'd, at the Opening of a Presbytery at Charlestown in S. Carolina; some time before the Reverend Mr. Josiah Smith's Sermon (which he publish'd against it, with the Title, of Humane Impositions proved unscriptural & c.) and now published, (with the advice of some of the Reverend Ministers adhering to the Westminster Confession to vindicate the Truths contained in it, from Mr. Smith's Mis-representations, and Exceptions. Together with a Postscript Containing some Remarks, upon Mr. Smith's Preface, and Sermon* [Boston], 1730. 2, 42. In January 1740, while his imagination was "a little heated," Smith remarked that when Whitefield preached in Charleston "the Pulpit seem'd almost to be the Tribunal, and the preacher himself, if the Comparison may be pardon'd, the Great Judge, cloathed in Flames, and adjudging a guilty World to penal Fire." *South Carolina Gazette*, January 19 and February 16, 1740.

9. Smith, *The Character, Preaching, & c. of the Reverend Mr. Geo. Whitefield*, 22–23; Clarke, *The Prophetic Numbers of Daniel and John Calculated*, 4.

10. George Whitefield, *Journals, 1737–1741, to which is prefixed his "Short Account" (1746) and "Further Account" (1747)*, (1756; rpt. Gainesville, Fla.: Scholars Facsimilies and Reprints, 1969), 502 (December 10, 1740). See also Matthew Mulcahy, "'Melancholy and Fatal Calamities'; Disaster and Society in Eighteenth-Century South Carolina," in Jack P. Greene, Rosemary Brana-Shute, and Randy J. Sparks, eds., *Money, Trade, and Power: The Evolution of Colonial South Carolina's Plantation Society* (Columbia: University of South Carlina Press, 2001), 278–98; Thomas S. Kidd, *The Great Awakening: The Roots of Evangelical Christianity in America* (New Haven: Yale University Press, 2007), 76–78.

11. Josiah Smith, *The Burning of Sodom, with its Moral Causes, Improved in a Sermon, Preach'd at Charlestown South-Carolina, after a most Terrible Fire, which broke out on Nov. 18, 1740* (Boston: D. Fowler, 1741), unpaginated author's preface and pages 4, 6, 13, and 21.

12. Ibid., 20–22.

13. Ibid., 5, 13–14.

14. Ibid., 13, 17; Whitefield, *Journals*, 506 (January 10, 1740). See also Alan Gallay, *The Formation of a Planter Elite: Jonathan Bryan and the Southern Colonial Frontier* (Athens: University of Georgia Press, 1989) 42–43; Harvey H. Jackson, "Hugh Bryan and the Evangelical Movement in Colonial South Carolina," *William and Mary Quarterly*, 3rd ser., 43 (October 1986): 601–3.

15. *South Carolina Gazette,* January 8, 1741 (postscript).

16. Ibid., January 8, 1741 (postscript), March 27, 1742.

17. Ibid., January 8 (postscript) and January 22, 1741; Alexander Garden to bishop of London, January 28, 1741, in Lambeth Palace Library, *The Fulham Papers at Lambeth Palace Library,* 20 reels (Microfilm 2nd. Ed., with additional reel), 42 vols. (London: World Microfilms, c. 1970-c.1978), 10:95-96. Hereafter cited as *The Fulham Papers.*

18. Whitefield, *Journals,* 507, 509 (January 10, 11, and 18, 1741); *South Carolina Gazette,* January 22, 1741.

19. *South Carolina Gazette,* January 29, 1741.

20. Ibid., January 29, 1741. See also Josiah Smith, *No New Thing to be Slander'd. A Sermon Preach'd at Cainhoy, in the Province of South-Carolina, Sept. 27. 1730. And now Publish'd for the Satisfaction of the Author's People, and to rectify the Opinion, which some had conceiv'd of his Principles, Particularly relating to the Errors of Arius and Arminius* (Boston, 1720), 3.

21. *South Carolina Gazette,* June 25, 1741.

22. Ibid., July 2, 1741.

23. Ibid., July 30, 1741.

24. Ibid., July 30, 1741.

25. Ibid., June 25, 1741.

26. Ibid., July 2, 1741.

27. Ibid., July 30, 1741.

28. Ibid., September 26, 1741 (Internal quotation marks omitted).

29. Ibid., July 2, 1741.

30. Ibid., July 30, 1741. See also ibid., July 2, 1741.

31. Ibid., September 26, October 10, 1741.

32. Sophia Hume, *An Exhortation to the Inhabitants of the Province of South-Carolina, To bring thier Deeds to the Light of Christ, in their own Consciences* (1748; rpt. London: Luke Hinde, 1752), 17, 28–30, 32, 44, 81–84. See also Rebecca Larson, *Daughters of Light: Quaker Women Preaching and Prophesying in the Colonies and Abroad, 1700–1775* (Chapel Hill: University of North Carolina Press, 1999), 65, 67, 70–71, 73–74, 76, 78–79, 84; Randy J. Sparks, "Mary Fisher, Sophia Hume, and the Quakers of Colonial Charleston: 'Women Professing Godliness.'" in Marjorie Julian Spruill, Valinda W. Littlefield, and Joan Marie Johnson, eds., *South Carolina Women: Their Lives and Times,* vol. 1 (Athens: University of Georgia Press, 2009), 40–59.

33. Hume, *An Exhortation to the Inhabitants of the Province of South-Carolina,* 3–5, 29, 41, 75.

34. Ibid., 3–4. See also Hume, *An Epistle to the Inhabitants of South-Carolina, containing Sundry Observations Proper to Be Considered by Every Professor of Christianity in General* (1750; rpt. London: Luke Hinde, 1754).

35. Whitefield, *Journals,* 451 (August 24 [i.e., 25], 1740).

36. J. H. Easterby, R. Nicholas Oldsbert, and Terry Lipscomb, eds., *The Colonial Records of South Carolina: The Journal of the Commons House of Assembly,* 13 vols. (Columbia: Historical Commission, 1951–1986), 3:380–82, 388, 407; Jackson, "Hugh Bryan and the Evangelical Movement in Colonial South Carolina," 606–7; Leigh Eric Schmidt, "'The Grand Prophet,' Hugh Bryan: Early Evangelicalism's Challenge to the

Establishment and Slavery in the Colonial South," *South Carolina Historical Magazine* 87 (October 1986): 238–50; Gallay, *The Formation of a Planter Elite*, 45–46; Strickland, "Across Space and Time," 152–56.

37. "A letter of Mr. Hugh Bryan to his daughter Mrs. E——T——, October 3, 1741, in [William Hutson], *Living Christianity, delineated, in the Diaries and Letters of two Eminently pious Persons, lately deceased; vis. Mr. Hugh Bryan, and Mrs. Mary Hutson, Both of South Carolina. With a Preface by the Revernd Mr. John Conder, and the Reverend Mr. Thomas Gibbons* (London: J. Buckland, 1760), 54; *South Carolina Gazette*, January 8, 1741, March 6, 1742; Elise Pinckney, ed., *The Letterbook of Eliza Pinckney, 1739–1762* (Chapel Hill: University of North Carolina Press, 1972), 27–30; Jackson, "Hugh Bryan and the Evangelical Movement in Colonial South Caroliina," 607–9. See also *Boston Weekly Post-Boy*, May 3.

38. *South Carolina Gazette*, March 6, 1742.

39. *South Carolina Gazette*, March 27 and April 3, 1742; South Carolina Council and Upper House Journals, 1721–1775, 38 vols., South Carolina Department of Archives and History, Columbia, 8:37 (April 10, 1742); 40–41 (May 25, 1742); Gallay, *The Formation of a Planter Elite*, 45–46; Strickland, "Across Space and Time," 156–57. See also Josiah Smith, *A Funeral Discourse, Sacred to the Memory of Mr. Joseph Moody, Lately a Deacon of this Church. Delivered June 30. 1766. At Charles-Town, in South Carolina* (Charleston: Peter Timothy, 1766). Smith turned at the end of the discourse and spoke to slaves. "I can't conclude," he said, "without speaking to the *negroes*—you have lost a *master*, a *father!*—*my* father, *my* father, *the chariot of Israel, and the horsemen thereof;* yea, he was a servant of servants, a *servant* to you *all*, for the gospel of Christ—He knew what it was, to *save* one soul *from death*, tho' the soul of a *negro*. You remember the pains he took every sabbath-day, to bring you to a sight and sense of your apostacy; . . . to bring you unto *all* holy obedience, obedience to *God*, obedience to your *masters*, obedience to the *household* of faith, obedience to *yourselves* . . . So I am persuaded, with the great apostle, he was ready, not only to be bound, but to go to prison, and even to die" (pp. 13–14).

40. *South Carolina Gazette*, April 17 and 24, 1742.

41. Josiah Smith, *Jesus persecuted in His Disciples. A Sermon Preach'd in Charlestown, South-Carolina; Anno Dom. 1742* (Boston: S. Kneeland and T. Green, 1745), 5, 7, 9.

42. Ibid., 6, 9–10, 14.

43. Ibid., 9, 13–16.

44. Ibid., 17–18. The spring of 1742 is often considered to be the nadir of the evangelical movement's progress in South Carolina. See Kidd, *The Great Awakening*, 79–80; David T. Morgan, Jr., "The Consequences of George Whitefield's Ministry in the Carolinas and Georgia," 1739–1740, *Georgia Historical Quarterly* 55 (January 1971): 72.

45. *South Carolina Gazette*, July 11, 1743.

46. Josiah Smith, *A Zeal of* GOD *Encourag'd and Guarded: A Sermon Preach'd at Charlestown, in the Province of South-Carolina; March 3d. 1744,5* (Boston: S. Kneeland and T. Green, 1745), 19–20.

47. Smith, *The Character, Preaching, &c. of the Reverend Mr. Geo. Whitefield*, 3. On one of Whitefield's visits during the mid-1740s, see the *South Carolina Gazette*, November 11, 1745. On this occasion Whitefield "preached twice in Mr. Smith's meeting." While in

Charleston at the end of the month Whitefield reported that he preached "as usual in this Town, twice a Day." See George Whitefield to Mr. John Sims, November 30, 1745, in John W. Christie, ed., "Newly Discovered Letters of George Whitefield, 1744–46," *Journal of the Presbyterian Historical Society* 32 (June 1954): 73. See also *Boston Gazette,* June 17, 1746.

48. John Newton to Rev. T. Haweis, January 21, 1763, in Newton, *Letters, Originally Published Under the Signatures of Omicron and Vigil By the Reverend Mr. John Newton, Minister of the Gospel in London; To which is Prefixed, An Authentic Narrative of Some Remarkable and Interesting particulars in the Life of Mr. Newton. Communicated in a Series of Letters to the Reverend Mr. Haweis, Rector of Aldwincle, Northamptonshire* (Philadelphia: Printed by John M'Culloch for W. Young, 1788), 78–79 passim.

49. Ramsay, *History of South Carolina,* 2:273.

50. See, for example, the following selected list of short titles of sermons written and published after 1749: *Sermons on Several Important Subjects* (Boston: Edes and Gill, 1757); *The Church of Ephesus Arraign'd* (Charleston: Charles Crouch, 1768); *Success a Great Proof of St. Paul's Fidelity* (Charleston: Charles Crouch, 1770); *Death the End of All Men* (Charleston: Robert Wells, 1771); *The Broken Heart Relieved* (Charleston: Robert Wells, 1773); *St. Paul's Victory and Triumph* (Charleston: Robert Wells, 1774).

51. Howe, *History of the Presbyterian Church,* 1:264 (quotations); Circular Church, Register of the Corporation, Volume 1 (1696–1796), South Carolina Historical Society, Charleston, S.C., December 9 and 15, 1754, February 13, 1757, and August 26, 1759. Edmonds was born in London about 1720. He seems to have arrived in the colony in 1752 or 1753. Edmonds was preceded at the Independent Meeting House by Samuel Fayerweather.

52. Howe, *History of the Presbyterian Church,* 1:248–50.

53. Records of Stoney Creek Church, William Hutson's Register, Presbyterian Historical Society, Montreat, N.C., June 8, 1743. See also "Register Kept by the Rev. Wm. Hutson, of Stoney Creek Independent Congregational Church and (Circular) Congregational Church in Charles Town S.C. 1743–1760," *South Carolina Historical Magazine* 38 (October 1937): 21 (hereafter cited as Hutson, "Register of Stoney Creek Church"); Howe, *History of the Presbyterian Church,* 2:249–250.

54. Hutson, "Register of Stoney Creek Church," 21–22. In general, the articles of faith bound members to the doctrines and creeds of the *Westminster Confession*. However, there was one important distinction with regard to church government. Article 24 of the Stoney Creek Confession stated that "no one church hath any priority or superintendency above or over another, and that every church ought to be organical; that an elder or elders, a deacon or deacons, ought to be elected in every congregation, according to those holy qualifications laid down in the word of God, and that the said elders and deacons so chosen ought solemnly to be ordained with prayer and laying on the hand of the eldership. That such churches as have not officers so ordained are disorderly; there being something yet wanting." This stemmed from a belief that "a true church is not national or parochial" and explains why the members of the church were considered "Independent Presbyterians." Records of the Stoney Creek Church, William Hutson's Register, June 8, 1743; Howe, *History of the Presbyterian Church,* 1:249–250.

55. Records of the Stoney Creek Church, William Hutson's Register, June 8, 1743–January 18, 1756, July 7, 1756–1760; Hutson, Diary, February 27, 1757–March 8, 1761, South Carolina Historical Society; Hutson, *Living Christianity, delineated,* "Preface," iii; "Extract of a Letter from the Rev. Mr. William Hutson of South-Carolina to Mr. Dennis De Berdt, Merchant in London, relating to the Life and Character of Mr. Hugh Bryan," May 21, 1745, in *Living Christianity, delineated,* 1–6; Howe, *History of the Presbyterian Church,*1:264–65. See also Susan O'Brien, "A Transatlantic Community of Saints: The Great Awakening and the First Evangelical Network, 1735–1755," *American Historical Review* 91 (October 1986):811–32; O' Brien, Eighteenth-Century Publishing Networks in the First Years of Transatlantic Evangelicalism," in Mark A Noll, David W. Bebbington, and George A. Rawlyk, eds., *Evangelicalism: Studies in Popular Protestantism in North America, the British Isles, and Beyond, 1700–1990* (New York: Oxford University Press, 1994), 38–57. Following the example of Whitefield, Hutson visited and preached at numerous Independent and Presbyterian churches south of Charleston, including Stoney Creek, Wando Neck, Dorchester, Pon Pon, Beaufort, James Island, and Beech Hill. What is more, he frequented many Baptist congregations in the region, including the Charleston and Euhaw Baptist churches.

56. Archibald Simpson, *Journals and Sermons, 1748–1784*, South Carolina Historical Society, Charleston (Microform), 64 microfiches [Spartanburg, S.C.: Reprint Co., distributor, 1981], 1748 and June 12, 1754 (hereafter cited as Simpson, *Journals*); Howe, *History of the Presbyterian Church,* 1:273–74.

57. Simpson, *Journals,* June 12, 1754. According to his lengthy journal account, Simpson said Whitefield was "entirely byased by the Accounts He has received from the Orphanhouse" and "Affirmed all the devilish falsehooods that were Said Against me by my enemies . . . as if He had Seen them all." He "appealed to the Eternal God of truth" that everything Whitefield had heard was "purely the Malice of Hell," writing, "I never told a known falsehood at the Orphanhouse or anywhere else about the affairs between him and me." He also wrote that "it was nothing but the Cruel treatment I met with there which drove me . . . away in poverty, misery, and sickness [and] the curses imprecations dreadful threatenings and denunciations of the most terrible judgements against me of a Mad Ennthusiastick Woman." Simpson does not elaborate on his cruel treatment, nor does he mention anything else about the "Enthusiastick Woman," though she was apparently the reason why Whitefield accused him of sexual impropriety.

58. Ibid., June 17, 1754, March 8, 1755, January 28, 1765, and January 6, 1768. See also the entry for December 5, 1764.

59. See Simpson, *Journals,* 1754–1761; 1769–1771; 1771–1772.

60. Ibid., May 17–19, 26, June 23, November 1, 1754.

61. Ibid., Oct 11, 1754. The following journal entries are suggestive of his activities.

> July 23, 1756: Rode 35 miles to James Island as there is not [regular] preaching there; was lost in the woods but got over the next day. Prevented from preaching by violent rain in the forenoon. At 12 o'clock preached to about thirty people. Admitted two young women converted by my labors; admitted their father, a wonderful conversion!

June 12, 1757: This day preached to very Crowded Auditory, the Church Minister being at this time Indisposed from Jonah 1.6. The spirit of the Lord was indeed wonderfully present with my soul and seemed most remarkably to bl[e]ss his own word. People were greatly moved and melted down under the Word.

62. In 1765 and 1766, for instance, Simpson made several trips to Salt Ketcher Creek in Colleton County. "The people of the neighborhood," he wrote, "were originally of the church of England, and had no desire for the preaching of the gospel till two families of the name of Dunham, from the Bethel [Presbyterian] church, Pon Pon, and another from the same, by the name of Hamilton, moved among them." Afterward "they . . . resolved on establishing gospel worship among them, and I commenced to assist them." Simpson, *Journals*, April 3, 1766.

63. Commenting on the death of one Presbyterian minister, for instance, Simpson noted that "Rev. [Samuel] Hunter hath been in the province about twenty years, which is very extraordinary, few ministers living half that time in this country, which is so sickly and fatal to people in our way." Simpson, *Journals*, June 23, 1754.

64. Ibid., July 23, 1756.

65. Ibid., April 16–17, 24, 1759; Howe, *History of the Presbyterian Church*, 1:290–92.

66. Howe, *History of the Presbyterian Church*, 1:285–300, 329–44. See also Peter N. Moore, *World of Toil and Strife: Community Transformation in Backcountry South Carolina, 1750–1805* (Columbia: University of South Carolina Press, 2007), 3, 7, 8, 32–37, 97–98 passim.

67. Simpson, *Journals*, May 26, 1759.

68. South Carolina Synod of the Lutheran Church in America, *History of the Lutheran Church in South Carolina* (Columbia: R. L. Bryan, 1971), 11–92 (hereafter cited as *History of the Lutheran Church in South Carolina*); Gilbert P. Voigt, *German and German-Swiss Element in South Carolina, 1732–1752*, Bulletin of the University of South Carolina, no. 133 (Columbia: University of South Carolina, 1922), 8–33; William J. Hinke, "The Origin of the Reformed Church in South Carolina," *Journal of the Presbyterian Historical Society* 3 (December 1906): 367–71; Gottfried Dellman Bernheim, *History of the German Settlements and the Lutheran Church in North and South Carolina* (1872; rpt., Spartanburg, S.C.: Reprint Company, n.d.), 81–171; Robert L. Meriwether, *The Expansion of South Carolina, 1729–1765* (Kingsport, Tenn.: Southern Publishers,1949), 42–65; Theodore G. Tappert, "The Influence of Pietism in Colonial American Lutheranism," in Ernest Stoeffler, ed., *Continental Pietism and Early American Christianity* (Grand Rapids, Mich.: William B. Eerdmans, 1976), 13–33; James Tanis, "Reformed Pietism in Colonial America," in Stoeffler, *Continental Pietism and Early American Christianity*, 34–73; Dale W. Brown, *Understanding Pietism* (Grand Rapids, Mich.: William B. Eerdmans, 1978), 27–82.

69. "Fragment of Governor Tobler's Diary," February 11–March 18, 1737, in Charles G. Cordle, ed., "The John Tobler Manuscripts: An Account of German-Swiss Emigrants in South Carolina, 1737," *Journal of Southern History* 5 (February–November 1939): 86.

70. Walter L. Robbins, ed., "John Tobler's Description of South Carolina (1754)," *South Carolina Historical Magazine* 71 (October 1970): 261–62.

71. Ibid., 261; Tappert, "The Influence of Pietism in Colonial American Lutheranism," 13–33; Tanis, "Reformed Pietism in Colonial America," 34–73; On the contemporary German terminology, see Brown, *Understanding Pietism*, 35–136.

72. "Jacob Wever's Confession," reprinted in Bernheim, *History of the German Settlements*, 198–202.

73. Ibid., 200; Richard Maxwell Brown, *The South Carolina Regulators* (Cambridge: Harvard University Press, 1963), 19–20; Theodore G. Tappert and John W. Doberstein, eds., *The Journals of Henry Melchoir Muhlenburg*, 3 vols. (Philadelphia: Mulenberg Press, 1942–1945), 2:578–79 (hereafter cited as Muhlenberg, *Journals*).

74. Muhlenberg, *Journals*, 2:579.

75. See Muhlenberg, *Journals*, 2:577–80.

76. Ibid., 2:581, 589–90, 592; Robbins, "John Tobler's Description of South Carolina (1754)," 263; *History of the Lutheran Church in South Carolina*, 23–77; Johann G. Freiderichs to Friedrich Wagner, June 26, 1755, in Simon Hart and Harry J. Kreider, *Lutheran Church in New York and New Jersey, 1722–1760; Lutheran Records in the Ministerial Archive of the Staatsarchive, Hamburg, Germany* (Ann Arbor.: Edwards Brothers, 1962), 389–90.

77. Morgan Edwards, *Materials Towards A History of the Baptists*, edited by Eve B. Weeks and Mary B. Warren, 2 vols. (Danielsville, Ga.: Heritage Papers, 1984), 2:120–43, 151–59; Townsend, *South Carolina Baptists*, 14–110.

78. Isaac Chanler, *The Doctrines of Glorious Grace Unfolded, defended, and practically Improved . . . With an Appendix containing some Remarks on the Works of Mr. James Foster . . . Particularly the Controversy concerning Mysteries in Religion, and the Use of Reason in Matters of Faith* (Boston: S. Keeland and T. Green, 1744); Ashley River Baptist Church (Charleston District, S.C.), Records, 1736–1769 (Microfilm), Southern Baptist Historical Library and Archives, Nashville, May 26, 1744, June 14, 1752 (hereafter cited as Records of the Ashley River Baptist Church); Edwards, *Materials Towards A History of the Baptists*, 2:125–26; George Whitefield to Jonathan Barber, December 16, 1745, and Whitefield to John Cennick, May 2, 1746 (postscript), in John W. Christie, ed., "Newly Discovered Letters of George Whitefield, 1745–1746," *Journal of the Presbyterian Historical Society* 32 (June 1954): 77, 85.

79. Isaac Chanler, *The Qualifications of a Gospel Minister for and Duty in studying rightly to divide the Word of Truth: And the Duty of those who do partake of the Benefit of his Labours Towards Him, Fully, Plainly, and Impartially Represented in Two Sermons on 2 Tim., 2:15. Preached at the Ordination of the Reverend Philip James, at the Welsh Tract, on Pee Dee River in South Carolina, April 4, 1743* (Boston: S. Kneeland and T. Greene, 1743), 7; Records of the Ashley River Baptist Church, n.d., 1745; Edwards, *Materials Towards A History of the Baptists*, 2:126–28; Townsend, *South Carolina Baptists*, 61–64.

80. John Fordyce to Secretary of the SPG, October 24, 1743, Society for the Propagation of the Gospel in Foreign Parts, *Records of the Society for the Propagation of the Gospel in Foreign Parts*, Series B (General Correspondence, 1701–1786), 11:233; Fordyce to Secretary of the SPG, November 4, 1743, ibid., 12:92. See also Edwards, *Materials Towards A History of the Baptists*, 2:127; S. Charles Bolton, *Southern Anglicanism: The Church of England in Colonial South Carolina* (Westport, Conn.: Greenwood Press, 1982), 65–66.

81. Edwards, *Materials Towards A History of the Baptists,* 2:125, 130–33; Townsend, *South Carolina Baptists,* 36–39; Whitefield, *Journals,* 447 (August 2, 1740); Isaac Chanler, *The State of the Church of Christ, both Militant and Triumphant, Consider'd and Improv'd, For the Consolation of Saints and for the Awakening of secure Sinners; For the Promoting of a Catholick Love Amongst the Godly of Every Denomination, and of Universal Holiness. Being the Substance of Two Sermons Now Drawn Up in one Discourse, from Acts XIV.22, Occasioned by the Death of the Rev. Mr. William Tilly, Late Minister of the Gospel on Edisto-island who Departed this Life April 13, 1744* (Charleston: Peter Timothy, 1745).

82. Oliver Hart, "Extracts from the Diary of Rev. Oliver Hart, from A.D. 1740 to A.D. 1780," Yearbook [City of Charleston, S.C.] (1896), 378; Edwards, *Materials Towards A History of the Baptists,* 2:124; Townsend, *South Carolina Baptists,* 20–22, 25n.

83. Wood Furman, *History of the Charleston association of Baptist churches in the State of South-Carolina; with an appendix containing the principal circular letters to the churches* (Charleston: J. Hoff, 1811), 8–9; Townsend, *South Carolina Baptists,* 111; Horace Fraser Rudisill, *The Diaries of Evan Pugh, 1762–1801* (Florence, S.C.: St. David's Society, 1993), 14 (November 8, 1762) (quotation). Evan Pugh and lay representatives from Euhaw did not attend the 1751 conference.

84. Hart, "Extracts from the Diary of Rev. Oliver Hart," 378; Journal of John Gano, quoted in "Biography of John Gano," in *The Southern Light, Independent, Religious and Literary Journal, Set for the Defense of the Truth, and Devoted to the Diffusion of Knowledge* 1, no. 9 (September 1856): 323.

85. "Extracts from the Diary of Rev. Oliver Hart," 380; Hart, MS Diary, August 23, 26, September 15, 18, 23, October 10, 66, 27, 1754; Townsend, *South Carolina Baptists,* 21–22; Kidd, *The Great Awakening,* 256–57.

86. Records of the Ashley River Baptist Church, May 28, 1750–March 10, 1755; Townsend, *South Carolina Baptists,* 34–35; Edwards, *Materials Towards A History of the Baptists,* 2:126.

87. Hart, "Extracts from the Diary of Rev. Oliver Hart," 390; Edwards, *Materials Towards A History of the Baptists,* 2:130–33; Townsend, *South Carolina Baptists,* 39–41.

88. Edwards, *Materials Towards A History of the Baptists,* 2:138–39; Townsend, *South Carolina Baptists,* 47–50; Pugh Diary entry for May 19, 1763, in Rudisill, *The Diaries of Evan Pugh,* 22.

89. Edwards, *Materials Towards A History of the Baptists,* 2:126–29, 134–38; Townsend, *South Carolina Baptists,* 61–110.

90. Edwards, *Materials Towards A History of the Baptists* , 2:127–28.

91. Extract from Bethabarba Diary, January 1761, *Records of the Moravians of North Carolina,* ed. Adelaide L. Fries, 11 vols. (Raleigh, N.C., 1922–1969), 1:234–36, quoted in Hamer, Rogers, and Chestnutt, *The Papers of Henry Laurens,* 56n.

92. John Ettwein to Henry Laurens, March 20, 1762; Laurens to Ettwein, April 7, 1762, in Hamer, Rogers, and Chestnutt, *The Papers of Henry Laurens,* 3:91–94.

93. John Ettwein to Henry Laurens, June 24, 1762, ibid., 102–3.

94. John Ettwein to Henry Laurens, March 2, 1763; Laurens to Ettwein, March 19, 1763, ibid., 356–57, 373–74.

95. Henry Laurens to John Ettwein, April 7, 1762; Laurens to Ettwein, March 19, 1763, ibid., 92–93, 374.

Chapter 6. Wrestling with God

1. Archibald Simpson, *Journals and Sermons, 1748–1784*, South Carolina Historical Society, Charleston (Microform) 64 microfiches [Spartanburg, S.C.: Reprint Co., distributor, 1981], July 10, 1756 (hereafter cited as Simpson, *Journals*).

2. Ibid., April 19, 1755.

3. Ibid., July 10, 1756.

4. Ibid., October 2, 1756.

5. Ibid., November 28, 1756.

6. Ibid., October 17 and November 30, 1756.

7. Ibid., January 17, 1757.

8. Ibid., February 4, 11, 18; April 20; June 4, 12, 21, 1757.

9. Ibid., Sept 9, 18; December 4, 1757; January 15, May 17, 1758.

10. John B. Boles, "Evangelical Protestantism in the Old South: From Religious Dissent to Cultural Dominance," in Charles Reagan Wilson, ed., *Religion in the South* (Jackson: University Press of Mississippi, 1985), 15.

11. *"A letter from Mrs. Bryan to her Sister,"* October 1739, in [William Hutson], *Living Christianity, delineated, in the Diaries and Letters of two Eminently pious Persons, lately deceased; vis. Mr. Hugh Bryan, and Mrs. Mary Hutson, Both of South Carolina. With a Preface by the Reverend Mr. John Conder, and the Reverend Mr. Thomas Gibbons* (London: J. Buckland, 1760), 18–19.

12. Isaac Chanler, *New Converts Exhorted to Cleave to the Lord. A Sermon on Acts XI 23. Preach'd July 30, 1740, at a Wednesday Evening-lecture, in Charlestown, Set up at the Motion, and the Desire of the Rev. Mr. Whitefield; With a Brief Introduction Relating to the Character of that Excellent Man . . . With Preface by the Reverend Mr. Cooper of Boston, N.E.* (Boston: D. Fowle for S. Kneeland and T. Green, 1740), 5.

13. Simpson, *Journals*, June 4, 1757; January 6, 1768.

14. See ibid., entry for January 15, 1758.

15. Alexander S. Salley, Jr., ed., *Journal of the Commons House of Assembly of South Carolina, June 2, 1724–June 16, 1724* (Columbia: Historical Commission of South Carolina, 1944), 24.

16. William Orr to the Secretary of the SPG, September 30, 1742, in William L. Saunders, ed., *The Colonial Records of North Carolina*, 10 vols. (Raleigh: State of North Carolina, 1886–1890), 4:609.

17. Charles Woodmason, *The Carolina Backcountry on the Eve of the Revolution: The Journal and Other Writings of Charles Woodmason, Anglican Itinerant*, ed. Richard J. Hooker (Chapel Hill: University of North Carolina Press, 1953), 105.

18. Ibid., 20, 47, 51.

19. Ibid., 6. On the population of the backcountry, see Peter A. Coclanis, *The Shadow of a Dream: Economic Life and Death in the South Carolina Low Country, 1670–1920* (New York: Oxford University Press, 1989), 68. On the settlement and development of the

backcountry, see Robert L. Meriwether, *The Expansion of South Carolina, 1729–1765* (Kingsport, Tenn.: Southern Publishers, 1940); Rachel N. Klein, *Unification of a Slave State: The Rise of the Planter Class in the South Carolina Backcountry, 1760–1808* (Chapel Hill: University of North Carolina Press, 1990).

20. Walter L. Robbins, ed., "John Tobler's Description of South Carolina (1754)," *South Carolina Historical Magazine* 71 (October 1970): 262–63. See also Robbins, ed., "John Tobler's Description of South Carolina (1753)," *South Carolina Historical Magazine* 71 (July 1970): 147n.

21. Ibid., 260–63.

22. John Pearson to Philip Pearson, May 5, 1764, quoted in Leah Townsend, *South Carolina Baptists, 1670–1805* (1935; rpt., Baltimore: Genealogical Publishing, 1978), 124.

23. Morgan Edwards, *Materials towards a History of the Baptists,* edited by Eve B. Weeks and Mary B. Warren, 2 vols. (Danielsville, Ga.: Heritage Papers, 1984), 2:124–25; Towsend, *South Carolina Baptists,* 153–55. Edwards estimated that there were 315 men, women, and children connected to Beaver Creek, Cloud's Creek, and Edisto. The estimate for Broad River is based on the number of families said to have been connected. This estimate was reached by calculating the number of families (18) by 5.

24. Woodmason, *The Carolina Backcountry on the Eve of the Revolution,* 13.

Bibliography

Primary Sources

A Brief Description of the Province of Carolina, on the Coasts of Floreda, and more perticularly of the New Plantation begun by the English at Cape Feare, on that River now by them called Charles-River, the 29th of May, 1664. Wherein is set forth the Healthfulness of the Air; the Fertility of the Earth, and Waters; and the great Pleasure and Profit will accrue to those that shall go thither to enjoy the same. Also, Directions and advice to such as shall go thither whether on their own accompts or to serve under another. Together with a most accurate Map of the whole Province (London: Printed for Robert Horne, 1666). In *Narratives of Early Carolina, 1650–1708,* edited by Alexander S. Salley, Jr. 1911. Reprint, New York: Barnes & Noble, 1953.

A Collection of the Epistles from the Yearly Meeting of Friends in London to the Quarterly and Monthly Meetings in Great Britain, Ireland and Elsewhere, from 1675 to 1805; Being from the First Establishment of that Meeting to the Present Time. Baltimore: Cole and Hewes, 1806.

Adams, Charles Francis, Nathaniel Paine, Burrett Wendell, and Worthington Chauncey Ford, eds. "Diary of Cotton Mather, 1709–1724." *Massachusetts Historical Society Collections,* 7th ser., vol. 8. Boston: Massachusetts Historical Society, 1912.

Appleton, William Sumner. *Record of the Descendants of William Sumner, of Dorchester, Mass.* Boston: D. Clapp & Son, 1879.

Archdale, John. *A New Description of that Fertile and Pleasant Province of Carolina: with a Brief Account of its Discovery, Settling, and the Government Thereof to this Time. With several Remarkable Passages of Divine Providence during my Time* (London: Printed for John Wyat, 1707). In *Narratives of Early Carolina, 1650–1708,* edited by Alexander S. Salley, Jr. 1911. Reprint, New York: Barnes & Noble, 1953.

Ash, John. *The Present State of Affairs in Carolina, by John Ash, Gent., Sent by several of the Inhabitants of that Colony, to deliver their Representation thereof to, and seek Redress from, the Lords Proprietors of that Province: Together with an Account of his Reception, by the Honourable the Lord Granville, their Palatine, President, or Chief of the Proprietors* (London, 1706). In *Narratives of Early Carolina, 1650–1708,* edited by Alexander S. Salley, Jr. 1911. Reprint, New York: Barnes & Noble, 1953.

[Ashe, Thomas]. *Carolina; or a Description of the Present State of that Country, and the Natural Excellencies therof, viz., the Healthfulness of the Air, Pleasantness of the Place, Advantage and Usefulness of those Rich Commodities there plentifully abounding, which much encrease and flourish by Industry of the Planters that daily enlarge that Colony. Published by T. A. Gent, Clerk on Board his Majesties Ship the Richmond, which was sent out in the Year 1680, with particular Instructions to enquire into the Stat of that Country, by his Majesties Special Command, and Return'd this Present Year, 1682* (London: Printed for W. C., 1682). In *Narratives of Early Carolina, 1650–1708*, edited by Alexander S. Salley, Jr. 1911. Reprint, New York: Barnes & Noble, 1953.

Ashley River Baptist Church (Charleston District, S.C.). Records, 1736–1769. (Microfilm). Southern Baptist Historical Library and Archives, Nashville.

Bond, Sampson. *The Sincere Milk of the Word, for the Children of Barmuda. In a Short Plain Catechism.* Boston: Green and Allen, 1699.

British Public Record Office, Transcripts of records relating to South Carolina, 1663–1782. South Carolina Department of Archives and History, Columbia.

Chalkley, Thomas. *A Journal: Or Historical Account of the Life, Travels, and Christian Experiences of that Ancient, Faithful Servant of Jesus Christ, Thomas Chalkley.* London: Luke Hinde, 1751.

Chanler, Isaac. *The Doctrines of Glorious Grace Unfolded, defended, and practically Improved: Herein the Fall of Mankind in the First Adam, and the Methods of Divine Sovereignty in the Effectual Recovery of a Chosen Remnant by Christ the Second Adam, are Declared, and Set in a Scriptural Light. With an Answer to Principal and Most Popular Objections: and in the Whole Many Scriptures Plainly Opened, and Their Seeming Contradictions Reconciled: With an Appendix, containing some Remarks on the Works of Mr. James Foster. In this the Absurd and Dangerous Nature of Socinianism is Laid Open; the Important Doctrines of our Blessed Savior's Divinity and Satisfaction Defended Against His Exceptions; and Diverse Other Useful Points Considered; Particularly the Controversy concerning Mysteries in Religion, and the Use of Reason in Matters of Faith.* Boston: S. Kneeland and T. Green, 1744.

———. *New Converts Exhorted to Cleave to the Lord. A Sermon on Acts XI 23 Preach'd July 30, 1740, at a Wednesday Evening-lecture, in Charlestown, Set Up at the Motion, and the Desire of the Rev. Mr. Whitefield; With a Brief Introduction Relating to the Character of that Excellent Man . . . With Preface by the Reverend Mr. Cooper of Boston, N.E.* Boston: D. Fowle for S. Kneeland and T. Green, 1740.

———. *The Qualifications of a Gospel Minister for and Duty in studying rightly to divide the Word of Truth: And the Duty of those who do partake of the Benefit of his Labours Towards Him, Fully, Plainly, and Impartially Represented in Two Sermons on 2 Tim., 2:15. Preached at the Ordination of the Reverend Philip James, at the Welsh Tract, on Pee Dee River in South Carolina, April 4, 1743.* Boston: S. Kneeland and T. Greene, 1743.

———. *The State of the Church of Christ, both Militant and Triumphant, Consider'd and Improv'd, For the Consolation of Saints and for the Awakening of secure Sinners; For the Promoting of a Catholick Love Amongst the Godly of Every Denomination, and of Universal Holiness. Being the Substance of Two Sermons Now Drawn Up in one Discourse, from Acts XIV.22. Occasioned by the Death of the Rev. Mr. William Tilly, Late Minister of the*

Gospel on Edisto-island who Departed this Life April 13, 1744. Charleston: Peter Timothy, 1744.

Cheves, Langdon, ed. *The Shaftesbury Papers and Other Records Relating to Carolina and the First Settlement on Ashley River Prior to the Year 1676*, vol. 5 of *Collections of the South Carolina Historical Society*. Richmond: William Ellis Jones, 1897.

Christie, John W., ed. "Newly Discovered Letters of George Whitefield, 1745–1746." *Journal of the Presbyterian Historical Society* 32 (June 1954): 69–90.

Circular Congregational Church (Charleston, S.C.). Records, 1732– (bulk 1800–1910s). South Carolina Historical Society, Charleston.

Clarke, Richard. *The Prophetic Numbers of Daniel and John Calculated: In Order to Show the Time, when the Day of Judgment for the First Age of the Gospel, is to be Expected: and the Setting Up the Millennial Kingdom of the Jehovah and His Christ*. 3rd ed. Philadelphia: William Bradford, 1759.

———. *A Second Warning to the World, by the Spirit of Prophecy. In an Explanation of the Mysteries in the Feast of Trumpets on the First Day of the Seventh Month. . . .* London: J. Townsend, 1760.

———. *A Spiritual Voice to the Christian Church, and to the Jews; In an Explanation of the Sabbatical Year of Moses by the Gospel of Jesus Christ: . . .* London: J. Townsend, 1760.

Cooper, Thomas, and David J. McCord, eds. *The Statutes at Large of South Carolina*. 10 vols. Columbia: A. S. Johnston, 1836–1841.

Cordle, Charles G., ed. "The John Tobler Manuscripts: An Account of German-Swiss Emigrants in South Carolina, 1737." *Journal of Southern History* 5 (February–November 1939): 83–97.

[Croswell, Andrew]. *An Answer to the Rev. Mr. Garden's Three First Letters to the Rev. Mr. Whitefield. With an Appendix Concerning Mr. Garden's Treatment of Mr. Whitefield, & c.* Boston: S. Kneelend and T. Green, 1741.

Daughters of the American Colonists, Sir William Phips Chapter (Maine). *Early Maine Records*, 4 vols. N.p.: Maine Society Daughters of the American Colonists, Sir William Phips Chapter, 1934–1942.

[Defoe, Daniel]. *The Case of Protestant Dissenters in Carolina, Shewing How a Law to prevent Occasional Conformity There, has ended in the Total Subversion of the Constitution in Church and State. Recommended to the serious Consideration of all that are true Friends of our present Establishment*. London, 1706.

[Defoe, Daniel]. *Party-Tyranny, or an Occasional Bill in Miniature; as now Practiced in Carolina. Humbly offered to the Consideration of both Houses of Parliament* (London, 1705). In *Narratives of Early Carolina, 1650–1708*, edited by Alexander S. Salley, Jr. 1911. Reprint, New York: Barnes & Noble, 1953.

Dunlop, J. G., ed., "Letters from John Stewart to William Dunlop," *South Carolina Historical Magazine* 32 (January–July 1931): 1–33.

Easterby, J. H., R. Nicholas Oldsbert, and Terry Lipscomb, eds. *The Colonial Records of South Carolina: The Journal of the Commons House of Assembly*. 13 vols. Columbia: Historical Commission of South Carolina, 1951–1986.

Edwards, Morgan. *Materials Towards A History of the Baptists*. 2 vols. Edited by Eve B. Weeks and Mary B. Warren. Danielsville, Ga.: Heritage Papers, 1984.

Ellis, George E., William H. Whitmore, Henry Warren Torry, and James Russell Lowell, eds. "Diary of Samuel Sewall, 1699 / 1700–1714." *Massachusetts Historical Society Collections*, 5th ser., vol. 6. Boston: Massachusetts Historical Society, 1879.

First Church at Dorchester (Dorchester, Boston, Mass.). *Records of the First Church at Dorchester in New England, 1636–1734.* Boston: George H. Ellis, 1891.

Fisher, Hugh. *The Divine Right of Private Judgment, Set In a True Light: A Reply to the Reverend Mr. Josiah Smith's Answer, to a Postscript Annex'd to a Sermon, Entituled A Preservative from Damnable Errors, in the Unction of the Holy One. Together with, Remarks on the Reverend Mr. Nathan Bassett's Appendix.* Boston, 1731.

———. *A Preservative from Damnable Errors, in the Unction of the Holy One. A Sermon Preach'd, at the Opening of a Presbytery at Charlestown in S. Carolina; some time before the Reverend Mr. Josiah Smith's Sermon (which he publish'd against it, with the Title, of Humane Impositions proved unscriptural &c.) and now published, (with the advice of some of the Reverend Ministers adhering to the Westminster Confession) to vindicate the Truths contained in it, from Mr. Smith's Mis-representations, and Exceptions. Together with a Postscript Containing some Remarks, upon Mr. Smith's Preface, and Sermon.* [Boston], 1730.

Fleetwood, William. *A Sermon Preached before the Society for the Propagation of the Gospel in Foreign Parts, at the Parish Church of St. Mary-le-Bow, on Friday the 16th of February, 1710/1. Being the Day of Their Anniversary Meeting* (London: Joseph Downing, 1711). In *Anglican Humanitarianism in Colonial New York*, by Frank J. Klingberg (Philadelphia: Church Historical Society, 1940).

Fothergill, John. *An Account of the Life and Travels in the Work of the Ministry of John Fothergill.* London: Luke Hinde, 1753.

Garden, Alexander. *The Doctrine of Justification According to the Scriptures, and the Articles, and Homilies of the Church of England, Explained and Vindicated. In a Letter to Mr. A. Croswell of Groton, in New England. Being a Reply to the said Mr. Croswell's Answer to Mr. Garden's Three First Letters to Mr. Whitefield. With a Postscript.* Charleston: Peter Timothy, 1742.

———. *Regeneration, and Testimony of the Spirit. Being the Substance of Two Sermons Lately Preached in the Parish Church of St. Philip, Charles-Town, in South-Carolina. Occasioned by some Erroneous Notions of Certain Men who call themselves Methodists.* Charleston: Peter Timothy, 1740.

———. *Six letters to the Rev. Mr. George Whitefield. The First, Second and Third, on the Subject of Justification. The Fourth containing Remarks on a Pamphlet, entitled, the Case between M. Whitefield and Dr. Stebbing state, &c. The Fifth containing Remarks on Mr. Whitefield's two Letters concerning Archbishop Tillotson, and the Book entitled, the Whole Duty of Man. The Sixth, containing Remarks on Mr. Whitefield's second Letter, concerning Archbishop Tillotson, and on his Letter concerning the Negroes.* 2nd ed. Boston: T. Fleet, 1740.

———. *Take Heed How Ye Hear: A Sermon Preached in the Parish Church of St. Philip Charles-Town, in South Carolina, on Sunday the 13th of July, 1740. With a Preface, containing some Remarks on Mr. Whitefield's Journals.* Charleston: Peter Timothy, 1741.

Green, Ruth S., ed. "The South Carolina Archives Copy of the Fundamental Constitutions, Dated July 21, 1669." *South Carolina Historical Magazine* 71 (April 1970): 86–100.

Hamer, Philip M., George C. Rogers, Jr., and David R. Chestnutt, eds. *The Papers of Henry Laurens: Volume Three: Jan. 1, 1759–Aug. 31, 1763*. Columbia: University of South Carolina Press, 1972.

Hart, Oliver, Diary, August 4, 1754–October 27, 1754. South Carolina Baptist Historical Collection, James B. Duke Library, Furman University.

———. "Extracts from the Diary of Rev. Oliver Hart, from A.D. 1740 to A.D. 1780." Yearbook [City of Charleston, S.C.] (1896): 375-401.

Hutson, R. W., ed. "Register Kept by the Rev. Wm. Hutson, of Stoney Creek Independent Congregational Church and (Circular) Congregational Church in Charles Town S.C. 1743–1760." *South Carolina Historical Magazine* 38 (January 1937): 21–36.

Hutson, William, Diary, 1757–1761. South Carolina Historical Society, Charleston.

[Hutson, William]. *Living Christianity, delineated, in the Diaries and Letters of two Eminently pious Persons, lately deceased; vis. Mr. Hugh Bryan, and Mrs. Mary Hutson, Both of South Carolina. With a Preface by the Reverend Mr. John Conder, and the Reverend Mr. Thomas Gibbons.* London: J. Buckland, 1760.

Hume, Sophia. *An Epistle to the Inhabitants of South-Carolina, containing Sundry Observations Proper to Be Considered by Every Professor of Christianity in General.* 1750. Reprint, London: Luke Hinde, 1754.

———. *An Exhortation to the Inhabitants of the Province of South-Carolina, To bring their Deeds to the Light of Christ, in their own Consciences.* 1748. Reprint, London: Luke Hinde, 1752.

Jenkins, William Sumner, ed. *Records of the States of the United States of America: A Microfilm Compilation.* [South Carolina] 107 reels. Washington, D.C.: Library of Congress Photoduplication Service, 1949.

Jenks, Henry F., Edward L. Pierce, Edward J. Young, and Charles C. Smith, eds. "Letters from Dr. Isaac Watts." *Proceedings of the Massachusetts Historical Society*, 2nd ser., vol. 9, 331–410. Boston: Massachusetts Historical Society, 1895.

"Journal of the Elder William Pratt, 1695–1701." In *Narratives of Early Carolina, 1650–1708*, edited by Alexander S. Salley, Jr. 1911. Reprint, New York: Barnes & Noble, 1953.

Klingberg, Frank J., ed. *The Carolina Chronicle of Dr. Francis Le Jau, 1706–1717.* Berkeley: University of California Press, 1956.

———. *Carolina Chronicle: The Papers of Commissary Gideon Johnston, 1707–1716.* Berkeley: University of California Press, 1946.

———. *Codrington Chronicle: An Experiment in Anglican Altruism on a Barbados Plantation, 1710–1834.* Berkeley: University of California Press, 1949.

Lambeth Palace Library, *The Fulham Papers at Lambeth Palace Library*, 20 reels (Microfilm, 2nd. Ed., with additional reel), 42 vols. London: World Microfilms, c. 1970–c.1978.

Lawson, John. *A New Voyage to Carolina; Containing the Exact and Natural History of That Country: Together with the Present State Thereof. And a Journal of a Thousand Miles, Travel'd Thro' Several Nations of Indians. Giving a Particular Account of Their Customs, Manners, &c.* London, 1709.

Lefroy, J. H. *Memorials of the Discovery and Early Settlement of the Bermudas or Somers Islands, 1511–1687.* 2 vols. London: Longmans, Green, 1879.

"Letter of Edward Randolph." In *Narratives of Early Carolina, 1650–1708*, edited by Alexander S. Salley, Jr. 1911. Reprint, New York: Barnes & Noble, 1953.

Lincoln, Solomon, Alonzo H. Quint, Williams Latham, and Joseph Palmer, eds. "The Hinckley Papers." *Massachusetts Historical Society Collections*, 4th ser., vol. 5, 1–308. Boston: Massachusetts Historical Society, 1861.

Locke, John. *The Works of John Locke: A New Edition, Corrected.* 10 vols. London: Printed for Thomas Tegg, 1823.

Luders, Alexander, Thomas Edlyn Tomlins, J. France, John Raithby, and W. E. Taunton, eds. *Statutes of the Realm* [1101–1713]. 11 vols. London: Record Commission, 1810–1828.

McIntyre, Sheila, and Len Travers, eds. *The Correspondence of John Cotton, Jr.* Charlottesville: University of Virginia Press, 2009.

Nairne, Thomas. *A Letter from South Carolina; Giving an Account of the Soil, Air, Product, Trade, Government, Laws, Religion, People, Military Strength, &c. of that Province: Together with the Manner and Necessary Charges of Settling a Plantation There, and the Annual Profit it Will Produce.* London: A. Baldwin, 1710.

Newton, John. *Letters, Originally Published Under the Signatures of Omicron and Vigil By the Reverend Mr. John Newton, Minister of the Gospel in London. To which is Prefixed, An Authentic Narrative of Some Remarkable and Interesting particulars in the Life of Mr. Newton. Communicated in a Series of Letters to the Reverend Mr. Haweis, Rector of Aldwincle, Northamptonshire.* Philadelphia: Printed by John M'Culloch for W. Young, 1788.

Oldmixon, John, *The British Empire in America* (London, 1708). In *Narrative of Early Carolina, 1605–1708*, edited by Alexander S. Salley, Jr. 1911. Reprint, New York: Barnes & Nobel, 1953.

Parker, Mattie Erma Edwards , ed. *North Carolina Charters and Constitutions, 1578–1698.* Raleigh: Carolina Charter Tercentenary Commission, 1963.

Pinckney, Elise, ed. *The Letterbook of Eliza Pinckney, 1739–1762.* Chapel Hill: University of North Carolina Press, 1972.

Records of Stoney Creek Church, William Hutson's Register, Presbyterian Historical Society, Montreat, N.C.

Robbins, Walter L., ed. "John Tobler's Description of South Carolina (1753)." *South Carolina Historical Magazine* 71 (July 1970): 141–61.

———. "John Tobler's Description of South Carolina (1754)." *South Carolina Historical Magazine* 71 (October 1970): 257–65.

Rudisill, Horace Fraser, ed. *The Diaries of Evan Pugh, 1762–1801.* Florence, S.C.: St. David's Society, 1993.

Salley, Alexander S., Jr., ed. *Journal of the Commons House of Assembly of South Carolina, November 20, 1706–February 8, 1706/7.* Columbia: The State Company, 1939.

———. *Journal of the Commons House of Assembly of South Carolina, June 2, 1724–June 16, 1724.* Columbia: Historical Commission of South Carolina, 1944.

———. *Journals of the Commons House of Assembly of South Carolina For the Two Sessions of 1698.* Columbia: Historical Commission of South Carolina, 1914.

———. "A Letter by the Second Landgrave Smith." *South Carolina Historical Magazine* 32 (January 1931): 61–63.

Saunders, William L., ed. *The Colonial Records of North Carolina.* 10 vols. Raleigh: State of North Carolina, 1886–1890.

Secker, Thomas. *A Sermon Preached before the Incorporated Society for the Propagation of the Gospel in Foreign Parts; at their Anniversary Meeting in the Parish-Church of St. Mary-le-Bow, on Friday, February 20, 1740–1* (London: J. and H. Pemberton, 1741). In *Anglican Humanitarianism in Colonial New York*, by Frank J. Klingberg. Philadelphia: Church Historical Society, 1940.

Simpson, Archibald, *Journals and Sermons, 1748–1784.* South Carolina Historical Society, Charleston (Microform), 64 microfiches [Spartanburg, S.C.: Reprint Co., distributor, 1981].

Smith, Josiah. *The Broken Heart Relieved: A Sermon, Preached at Charlestown, South-Carolina, March the 27th, 1763.* Charleston: Robert Wells, 1773.

———. *The Burning of Sodom, with its Moral Causes, Improved in a Sermon, Preach'd at Charlestown South-Carolina, after a most Terrible Fire, which broke out on Nov. 18, 1740.* Boston: D. Fowler, 1741.

———. *The Character and Duty of Minister and People, Represented in a Sermon on I Thess: V, 12, 13. Delivered March 24, 1736. at the Ordination of the Reverend Mr. John Osgood, to the Pastoral Charge of the Congregational Church at Dorchester. Now Published at the Request and Charge of the People in General.* Charleston: Lewis Timothy, 1736.

———. *The Character, Preaching, & c. of the Reverend Mr. Geo. Whitefield, Impartially represented and supported, in a Sermon Preach'd in Charlestown, South-Carolina, March 26. Anno Domini 1740.* Philadelphia: B. Franklin, 1740.

———. *The Church of Ephesus Arraign'd: The Substance of Five Short Sermons, Contracted into One. Delievered 1760, at Charles-Town, South-Carolina.* Charleston: Charles Crouch, 1768.

———. *Death the End of All Men: A Sermon, Sacred to the Memory of the Reverend John Thomas, Pastor of the Independent Congregation at Charlestown in South-Carolina, who Died at New-York, September 19th, 1771. AEtat 26.* Charleston: Robert Wells, 1771.

———. *A Discourse Delivered at Boston, on July 11, 1726: Then Occasion'd by the Author's Ordination. And now Published at the Request of Several Gentlemen, who were Present at the Delivery of it.* Boston: S. Gerrish and T. Hancock, 1726.

———. *The Divine Right of Private Judgment Vindicated. In Answer to the Reverend Mr. Hugh Fisher's Postscript, Annex'd to his Preservative from Damnable Errors, in Unction of the Holy One.* Boston, 1730.

———. *The Duty of Parents to Instruct their Children: Being the Substance of Several Sermons Preach'd at Cainhoy, in the Province of South-Carolina, Anno Dom. 1727. Now Contracted into One Discourse.* Boston: D. Henchman, 1730.

———. *A Funeral Discourse, Sacred to the Memory of Mr. Joseph Moody, Lately a Deacon of this Church. Delivered June 30. 1766. At Charles-Town, in South Carolina.* Charleston: Peter Timothy, 1766.

———. *The Greatest Sufferers Not always the Greatest Sinners. A Sermon Delivered in Charlestown, in the Province of South-Carolina, February 4. 1727,8. Then Occasioned by the Terrible Earthquake in New-England.* Boston, 1730.

———. *Humane Impositions Proved Unscriptural, or, the Divine Right of Private Judgement. A Sermon Preached at the Opening of Presbytery in Charlstown in the Province of South Carolina, March 5th. 1728,9.* Boston: D. Henchman, 1729.

———. *Jesus persecuted in His Disciples. A Sermon Preach'd in Charlestown, South-Carolina; Anno Dom. 1742.* Boston: S. Kneeland and T. Green, 1745.

———. *No New Thing to be Slander'd. A Sermon Preach'd at Cainhoy, in the Province of South-Carolina, Sept. 27. 1730. And now Publish'd for the Satisfaction of the Author's People, and to rectify the Opinion, which some had conceiv'd of his Principles, Particularly relating to the Errors of Arius and Arminius.* Boston, 1730.

———. *St. Paul's Victory and Triumph: The Substance of Six Short Sermons Contracted into Three: Delivered at Charlestown, South-Carolina, in the year 1769.* Charleston: Robert Wells, 1774.

———. *A Sermon Deliver'd at Charles-town, in South Carolina: the Lord's Day after the Funeral, and Sacred to the Memory of the Reverend Mr. Nathan Bassett, who Exchang'd this for a Better Life, June 26th 1738.* Boston: S. Kneeland and T. Green, 1739.

———. *A Sermon, Preached at Charlestown, South-Carolina, in the Year 1739.* 2nd ed. Charleston: Robert Wells, 1773.

———. *A Sermon Preached in Boston, July 10th, 1726. And now Published at the Desire of several Gentlemen then Present.* Boston, 1727.

———. *Sermons on Several Important Subjects: Viz. Prejudices Rectified. The Rain Imbibed, an Emblem of Grace. The Shortness of Time, a Motive to Moderation. The Grave, without any Order. The Immortality of the Soul. The Great Day. The Effects of Divine Fury. The Necessity of Practice. Solomon's Caution Against the Cup. The Character and Employment of Good Angels.* Boston: Edes and Gill, 1757.

———. *Solomon's Caution Against the Cup: A Sermon Delivered at Cainhoy, in the Province of South-Carolina. March 30. 1729.* Boston: D. Henchman, 1730.

———. *Success a Great Proof of St. Paul's Fidelity: Sacred to the Memory of the Reverend George Whitefield, A.M. Chaplain to the Right Honourable the Countess of Huntingdon. Who Departed this Life, at Newberry-Port, on Lord's Day Morning, September 30, 1770. Aetatis 56. Delivered October 18, 1770, at Charles-Town, in South Carolina.* Charleston: Charles Crouch, 1770.

———. *The Young Man Warned: Or, Solomon's Counsel to his Son. A Sermon Delivered at Cainhoy, in the Province of South-Carolina, Anno Dom. 1729.* Boston: D. Henchman, 1730.

———. *A Zeal of GOD Encourag'd and Guarded: A Sermon Preach'd at Charlestown, in the Province of South-Carolina; March 3d. 1744, 5.* Boston: S. Kneeland and T. Green, 1745.

Society for the Propagation of the Gospel in Foreign Parts, *Records of the Society for the Propagation of the Gospel in Foreign Parts,* Index to letter series A, B, and C. (Microfilm). Introduction by Belle Pridmore. 1 reel. Yorkshire, England: Micro Methods, 1964.

———. *Records of the Society for the Propagation of the Gospel in Foreign Parts,* Series A (Letter Books, 1702–1737). 26 vols. (Microfilm). Introduction by Belle Pridmore. 8 reels. Yorkshire, England: Micro Methods, 1964.

———. *Records of the Society for the Propagation of the Gospel in Foreign Parts,* Series B (Letters, 1701–1786). 25 vols. (Microfilm). Introduction by Belle Pridmore. 14 reels. Yorkshire, England: Micro Methods, 1964.

———. *Records of the Society for the Propagation of the Gospel in Foreign Parts,* Series C (Letters, 1635–1812). 15 vols. (Microfilm). Introduction by Belle Pridmore. 5 reels. Yorkshire, England: Micro Methods, 1964.

Some Queries, Concerning the Operation of the Holy Spirit, Answered. Delivered at a Lecture held at the Baptist-Meeting-House-in Charles-Town, South-Carolina: And now published at the earnest Request of Some of the Hearers. Philadelphia: B. Franklin, 1740.

South Carolina Commons House Journals, 1705–1775. South Carolina Department of Archives and History, Columbia.

South Carolina Council and Upper House Journals, 1721–1775. South Carolina Department of Archives and History, Columbia.

South Carolina Gazette. South Carolina Historical Society, Charleston.

Stock, Leo Francis, ed. *Proceedings and Debates of the British Parliaments Respecting North America, 1542–1754.* 5 vols. Washington, D.C.: Carnegie Institution of Washington, 1924–1941.

Tappert, Theodore G., and John W. Doberstein, eds. *The Journals of Henry Melchoir Muhlenburg.* 3 vols. Philadelphia: Mulenberg Press, 1942–1945.

Thomas, Samuel. "Documents Concerning Rev. Samuel Thomas, 1702–1707." *South Carolina Historical Magazine* 5 (January 1904): 21–55.

———. "Letters of the Rev. Samuel Thomas, 1702–1710." *South Carolina Historical and Genealogical Magazine* 4 (July 1903): 221–30.

Trott, Nicholas. *The Laws of the British Plantations in America, Relating to the Church and the Clergy, Religion, and Learning.* London: B. Cowse, 1721.

Warburton, William. *A Sermon Preached before the Incorporated Society for the Propagation of the Gospel in Foreign Parts; at their Anniversary Meeting in the Parish Church of St. Mary-le-Bow, on Friday, February 21, 1766* (London: E. Owen and T. Harrison, 1766). In *Anglican Humanitarianism in Colonial New York,* by Frank J. Klingberg. Philadelphia: Church Historical Society, 1940.

Webber, Mabel L., ed. "The Records of the Quakers in Charles Town." *South Carolina Historical Magazine* 28 (January–July 1927): 22–43, 94–107, 176–97.

Whitefield, George. *Journals, 1737–1741, to which is prefixed his "Short Account" (1746) and "Further Account" (1747),* facsimile reproduction of the 1905 edition of William Wale with an introduction by William V. Davis. Gainesville, Fla.: Scholars Facsimiles and Reprints, 1969.

———. *A Letter from the Rev. Mr. Whitefield from Georgia, to a friend in London, shewing the Fundamental Error of a Book, Entitled The Whole Duty of Man.* Charleston: Peter Timothy, 1740.

———. *The Nature and Necessity of our New Birth in Christ Jesus, in Order to Salvation. A Sermon Preached in the Church of St. Mary Radcliffe, in Bristol. By George Whitefield, A.B. of Pembroke College, Oxford. Published at the Request of several of the Hearers.* 2nd ed. London: C. Rivington, 1737.

———. *Three Letters from the Reverend Mr. G. Whitefield: viz. Letter I. To a Friend in London, concerning Archbishop Tillotson. Letter II. To the same, on the same Subject. Letter III. To the Inhabitants of Maryland, Virginia, North and South-Carolina, concerning their Negroes.* Philadelphia: B. Franklin, 1740.

Woodmason, Charles. *The Carolina Backcountry on the Eve of the Revolution: The Journal and Other Writings of Charles Woodmason, Anglican Itinerant*, ed. Richard J. Hooker. Chapel Hill: University of North Carolina Press, 1953.

Secondary Sources

Books

Andrews, Charles McLean. *The Colonial Period in American History.* 4 vols. New Haven: Yale University Press, 1934–1938.

Bailey, Richard A. *Race and Redemption in Puritan New England.* New York: Oxford University Press, 2011.

Baldwin, Agnes Leeland. *First Settlers of South Carolina.* Tricentennial Booklet Number 1. Columbia: University of South Carolina Press, 1969.

———. *First Settlers of South Carolina, 1670–1700.* Easley, S.C.: Southern Historical Press, 1985.

Beasley, Nicholas M. *Christian Ritual and the Creation of British Slave Societies, 1650–1780.* Athens: University of Georgia Press, 2009.

Benedict, David. *A General History of the Baptist Denomination in America, and Other Parts of the World.* 2 vols. Boston: Lincoln and Edmonds, 1813.

Beneke, Chris, and Christopher S. Grenda, eds. *The First Prejudice: Religious Tolerance and Intolerance in Early America.* Philadelphia: University of Pennsylvania Press, 2011.

Berlin, Ira. *Many Thousands Gone: The First Two Centuries of Slavery in North America.* Cambridge: Harvard University Press, 1998.

Bernhard, Virginia. *Slaves and Slaveholders in Bermuda, 1616–1782.* Columbia: University of Missouri Press, 1999.

Bernheim, Gottfried Dellman. *History of the German Settlements and of the Lutheran Church in North and South Carolina.* 1872. Reprint, Spartanburg, S.C.: Reprint Company, n.d.

Bolton, S. Charles. *Southern Anglicanism: The Church of England in Colonial South Carolina.* Westport, Conn.: Greenwood Press, 1982.

Bonomi, Patricia U. *Under the Cope of Heaven: Religion, Society, and Politics in Colonial America.* New York: Oxford University Press, 1986.

Bowden, James. *The History of the Society of Friends in America.* 2 vols. 1850–1854. Reprint, Bedford, Mass.: Applewood Books, n.d.

Bowes, Frederick P. *The Culture of Early Charleston.* Chapel Hill: University of North Carolina Press, 1942.

Bridenbaugh, Carl. *Myths and Realities: Societies of the Colonial South.* Baton Rouge: Louisiana State University Press, 1952.

Brown, Dale W. *Understanding Pietism.* Grand Rapids, Mich.: William B. Eerdmans, 1978.

Brown, Richard Maxwell. *The South Carolina Regulators.* Cambridge: Harvard University Press, 1963.

Brunner, Daniel L. *Halle Pietists in England: Anthony William Boehm and the Society for the Promoting of Christian Knowledge.* Göttingen and Zürich: Vandenhoeck & Ruprecht, 1993.

Brydon, George MacLaren. *Virginia's Mother Church and the Political Conditions under Which It Grew.* 2 vols. Richmond: Virginia Historical Society, 1947.

Butler, Jon. *Awash in a Sea of Faith: Christianizing the American People.* Cambridge: Harvard University Press, 1990.

———. *The Huguenots in America: A Refugee People in New World Society.* Cambridge: Harvard University Press, 1983.

Caldecott, Alfred. *The Church in the West Indies.* 1898. Reprint, London: Frank Cass, 1970.

Cappon, Lester J. *Atlas of Early American History: The Revolutionary Era, 1760–1790.* Princeton: Princeton University Press, 1976.

Carroll, B. R. *Historical Collections of South Carolina: Embracing Many Rare and Valuable Pamphlets, and Other Documents, Relating to the History of That State, From Its First Discovery to Its Independence in the Year 1776.* 2 vols. New York: Harper & Brothers, 1836.

Clarke, Erskine. *Our Southern Zion: A History of Calvinism in the South Carolina Low Country, 1690–1990.* Tuscaloosa: University of Alabama Press, 1996.

Clowse, Converse D. *Economic Beginnings in Colonial South Carolina, 1670–1730.* Columbia: University of South Carolina Press, 1971.

Coclanis, Peter A. *The Shadow of a Dream: Economic Life and Death in the South Carolina Low Country, 1670–1920.* New York: Oxford University Press, 1989.

Crane, Verner W. *The Southern Frontier, 1670–1732.* Durham: Duke University Press, 1928.

Craton, Michael, and Gail Saunders. *Islanders in the Stream: A History of the Bahamian People, Volume One: From Aboriginal Times to the End of Slavery.* Athens: University of Georgia Press, 1992.

Craven, Wesley Frank. *The Colonies in Transition, 1660–1713.* New York: Harper & Row, 1968.

———. *The Southern Colonies in the Seventeenth Century, 1607–1689.* Vol. 1 of *A History of the South,* edited by Wendell H. Stephenson and E. Merton Coulter. Baton Rouge: Louisiana State University Press, 1949.

Curry, Thomas J. *The First Freedoms: Church and State in America to the Passage of the First Amendment.* New York: Oxford University Press, 1986.

Dalcho, Frederick. *An Historical Account of the Protestant Episcopal Church in South Carolina from the First Settlement of the Province to the War of the Revolution.* Charleston: E. Thayer, 1820.

Davis, Richard Beale. *Intellectual Life in the Colonial South, 1585–1763.* 3 vols. Knoxville: University of Tennessee Press, 1978.

Dunn, Richard S. *Sugar and Slaves: The Rise of the Planter Class in the English West Indies, 1624–1713.* 1972. Reprint, New York: W.W. Norton, 1973.

Edgar, Walter B. *South Carolina: A History.* Columbia: University of South Carolina Press, 1998.

Edgar, Walter B., Louise N. Bailey, et al., eds. *Biographical Directory of South Carolina House of Representatives.* 5 vols. Columbia: University of South Carolina Press, 1974–1993.

Edwards, George N. *A History of the Independent or Congregational Church of Charleston South Carolina.* Boston: Pilgrim Press, 1947.

Faust, Albert B., and Gaius M. Brumbaugh. *Lists of Swiss Emigrants in the Eighteenth Century to the American Colonies. Two Volumes in One.* Baltimore: Genealogical Publishing, 1968.

Felt, Joseph B. *History of Ipswich, Essex, and Hamilton.* Cambridge, Mass.: Charles Folsom, 1834.

Frey, Sylvia R., and Betty Wood. *Come Shouting Zion: African American Protestantism in the American South and the British Caribbean to 1830.* Chapel Hill: University of North Carolina Press, 1998.

Furman, Wood. *History of the Charleston Association of Baptist Churches in the State of South-Carolina; with an appendix containing the principal circular letters to the churches.* Charleston: J. Hoff, 1811.

Gallay, Alan. *The Formation of a Planter Elite: Jonathan Bryan and the Southern Colonial Frontier.* Athens: University of Georgia Press, 1989.

Games, Allison. *Migration and the Origins of the English Atlantic World.* Cambridge: Harvard University Press, 1999.

Gardner, Robert G. *Baptists of Early America: A Statistical History, 1639–1790.* Atlanta: Georgia Baptist Historical Society, 1983.

Gaustad, Edwin Scott. *Historical Atlas of Religion in America.* Rev. ed. New York: Harper & Row, 1976.

Gewehr, Wesley M. *The Great Awakening in Virginia, 1740–1790.* Durham: Duke University Press, 1930.

Greene, Jack P. *Pursuits of Happiness: The Social Development of Early Modern British Colonies and the Formation of American Culture.* Chapel Hill: University of North Carolina Press, 1988.

———. *The Quest for Power: The Lower Houses of Assembly in the Southern Royal Colonies, 1689–1776.* Chapel Hill: University of North Carolina Press, 1963.

Greene, Jack P., and J. R. Pole, eds. *Colonial British America: Essays in the New History of the Early Modern Era.* Baltimore: Johns Hopkins University Press, 1984.

Gregerson, Linda, and Susan Juster, eds. *Empires of God: Religious Encounters in the Early Modern Atlantic.* Philadelphia: University of Pennsylvania Press, 2011.

Gunderson, Joan R. *The Anglican Ministry in Virginia, 1723–1775: A Study of Social Class.* New York: Garland, 1989.

Harlow, Vincent T. *A History of Barbados, 1625–1685.* Oxford: Clarendon Press, 1926.

Hart, Simon, and Harry J. Kreider, eds. *Lutheran Church in New York and New Jersey, 1722–1760: Lutheran Records in the Ministerial Archive of the Staatsarchive, Hamburg, Germany.* Ann Arbor: Edwards Brothers, 1962.

Heimert, Alan, and Perry Miller, eds., *The Great Awakening: Documents Illustrating the Crisis and Its Consequences.* Indianapolis: Bobbs-Merrill, 1967.

Heyrman, Christine Leigh. *Southern Cross: The Beginnings of the Bible Belt.* Chapel Hill: University of North Carolina Press, 1997.

Hinke, William J. *Ministers of the Reformed Congregations in Pennsylvania & Other Colonies in the 18th Century.* Lancaster, Penn.: Historical Commission of the Evangelical and Reformed Church, 1951.

Hirsh, Arthur Henry. *The Huguenots of Colonial South Carolina.* Durham: Duke University Press, 1928.

Hirst, Desiree. *Hidden Riches: Traditional Symbolism from the Renaissance to Blake.* New York: Barnes & Noble, 1964.

Hofstadter, Richard. *America at 1750: A Social Portrait.* New York: Alfred A. Knopf, 1971.

Holifield, Brooks. *Theology in America.* New Haven: Yale University Press, 2003.

Howe, George. *History of the Presbyterian Church in South Carolina.* 2 vols. Columbia: Duffie & Chapman, 1870.

Insh, George Pratt. *Scottish Colonial Schemes 1620–1686.* Glasgow: Maclehouse, Jackson, 1922.

Isaac, Rhys. *The Transformation of Virginia, 1740–1790.* Chapel Hill: University of North Carolina Press, 1982.

Johnson, Allen, et al., eds. *Dictionary of American Biography.* 21 vols. New York: Charles Scribner's Sons, 1928.

Keeble, N. H. *The Restoration: England in the 1660s.* Oxford: Blackwell, 2001.

Kidd, Thomas S. *The Great Awakening: A Brief History with Documents.* Boston: Bedford / St. Martin's, 2008.

———. *The Great Awakening: The Roots of Evangelical Christianity in Colonial America.* New Haven: Yale University Press, 2007.

Klein, Rachel N. *Unification of a Slave State: The Rise of the Planter Class in the South Carolina Backcountry, 1760–1808.* Chapel Hill: University of North Carolina Press, 1990.

Klingberg, Frank J. *An Appraisal of the Negro in Colonial South Carolina: A Study in Americanization.* Washington, D.C.: Associated Publishers, 1941.

Lambert, Frank. *Inventing the "Great Awakening."* Princeton: Princeton University Press, 1999.

———. *"Pedlar in Divinity": George Whitefield and the Transatlantic Revivals.* Princeton: Princeton University Press, 1994.

Landsman, Ned. C. *Crossroads of Empire: The Middle Colonies in British North America.* Baltimore: Johns Hopkins University Press, 2010.

Larson, Rebecca. *Daughters of Light: Quaker Women Preaching and Prophesying in the Colonies and Abroad, 1700–1775.* Chapel Hill: University of North Carolina Press, 1999.

Lesser, Charles H. *South Carolina Begins: The Records of a Proprietary Colony, 1663–1671.* Columbia: South Carolina Department of Archives and History, 1995.

Linder, Suzanne Cameron. *Anglican Churches in Colonial South Carolina: Their History and Architecture.* Charleston: Wyrick and Company, 2000.

Lippy, Charles H., ed. *Religion in South Carolina.* Columbia: University of South Carolina Press, 1993.

Lumpkin, William L. *Baptist Foundations in the South: Tracing through the Separates the Influence of the Great Awakening, 1754–1787.* Nashville: Broadman Press, 1961.

Mathews, Donald G. *Religion in the Old South.* Chicago: University of Chicago Press, 1977.

Manross, William W. *The Fulham Papers in the Lambeth Palace Library: American Colonial Section—Calendars and Indexes.* Oxford: Clarendon Press, 1965.

McCrady, Edward. *The History of South Carolina under the Proprietary Government, 1670–1719.* New York: Macmillan, 1897.

———. *The History of South Carolina under the Royal Government, 1719–1776.* 1899. Reprint, New York: Russell & Russell, 1969.

Meriwether, Robert L. *The Expansion of South Carolina, 1729–1765.* Kingsport, Tenn.: Southern Publishers, 1940.

Merrens, H. Roy, ed. *The Colonial South Carolina Scene: Contemporary Views, 1697–1774* Columbia: University of South Carolina Press, 1977.

Migliazzo, Arlin C. *To Make This Land Our Own: Community, Identity, and Cultural Adaptation in Purrysburg Township, South Carolina, 1732–1865.* Columbia: University of South Carolina Press, 2007.

Millet, Joshua. *A History of the Baptists in Maine.* Portland, 1845.

Moore, Peter N. *World of Toil and Strife: Community Transformation in Backcountry South Carolina, 1750–1805.* Columbia: University of South Carolina Press, 2007.

Morgan, Philip D. *Slave Counterpoint: Black Culture in the Eighteenth-century Chesapeake and Lowcountry.* Chapel Hill: University of North Carolina Press, 1998.

Mulcahy, Matthew. *Hurricanes and Society in the British Greater Caribbean, 1624–1783.* Baltimore: Johns Hopkins University Press, 2006.

Nelson, John K. *A Blessed Community: Parishes, Parsons, and Parishioners in Anglican Virginia, 1660–1776.* Chapel Hill: University of North Carolina Press, 2004.

Nelson, Louis P. *The Beauty of Holiness: Anglicanism and Architecture in Colonial South Carolina.* Chapel Hill: University of North Carolina Press, 2009.

Noll, Mark A. *The Rise of Evangelicalism: The Age of Edwards, Whitefield, and the Wesleys.* Downers Grove, Ill.: InterVarsity Press, 2003.

Ohm, Christopher Clement, and Ramona M. Grunden. *Where the Wappetaw Independent Congregational Church Stood . . . , Archaeological Testing at 38CH1682, Charleston County, SC.* University of South Carolina Institute of Archaeology and Anthropology *Books* and Manuscripts Book 201. Columbia: University of South Carolina, 1998.

Olwell, Robert *Masters, Slaves & Subjects: The Culture of Power in the South Carolina Low Country, 1740–1790.* Ithaca: Cornell University Press, 1998.

Paullin, Charles O. *Atlas of the Historical Geography of the United States,* edited by John Wright. Washington, D.C.: Carnegie Institution of Washington and the American Geographical Society of New York, 1932.

Pestana, Carla Gardina. *The English Atlantic in an Age of Revolution, 1640–1661.* Cambridge: Harvard University Press, 2004.

———. *Religion and the Making of the British Atlantic World.* Philadelphia: University of Pennsylvania Press, 2009.

Powell, William S. *The Proprietors of Carolina.* Raleigh: North Carolina Tercentenary Commission, 1963.

Ramsay, David. *History of South Carolina, From its First Settlement in 1670 to the Year 1808.* 2 vols. 1809. Reprint, Newberry, S.C.: W. J. Duffie, 1858.

Rivers, William J. *A Sketch of the History of South Carolina to the Close Proprietary Government by the Revolution of 1719.* Charleston: McCarter & Co., 1856.

Rogers, George C., Jr. *Evolution of a Federalist: William Loughton Smith of Charleston (1758–1812).* Columbia: University of South Carolina Press, 1962.

Roper, L. H. *Conceiving Carolina: Proprietors, Planters, and Plots, 1662–1729.* New York: Palgrave Macmillan, 2004.

Rowland, Lawrence S., Alexander Moore, and George C. Rogers, Jr. *The History of Beaufort County, South Carolina. Volume 1, 1514–1861.* Columbia: University of South Carolina Press, 1996.

Salley, Alexander S., Jr. *The History of Orangeburg County, South Carolina, from Its Settlement to the End of the Revolution.* Orangeburg, S.C.: R. Lewis Berry, 1898.

Schmidt, Leigh Eric. *Holy Fairs: Scotland and the Making of American Revivalism.* 2nd ed. Grand Rapids, Mich.: William B. Eerdmans, 2001.

Schwartz, Hillel. *The French Prophets: The History of a Millenarian Group in Eighteenth-Century England.* Berkeley: University of California Press, 1980.

Sherman, Richard P. *Robert Johnson: Proprietary and Royal Governor of South Carolina.* Columbia: University of South Carolina Press, 1966.

Shipton, Cifford K. *Sibley's Harvard Graduates: Biographical Sketches of Those Who Attended Harvard College.* Vol. 4., the Classes of 1690–1700. Boston: Massachusetts Historical Society, 1933.

———. *Sibley's Harvard Graduates: Biographical Sketches of Those Who Attended Harvard College.* Vol. 6., the Classes of 1713–1721. Boston: Massachusetts Historical Society, 1942.

———. *Sibley's Harvard Graduates: Biographical Sketches of Those Who Attended Harvard College.* Vol. 7., the Classes of 1722–1725. Boston: Massachusetts Historical Society, 1945.

———. *Sibley's Harvard Graduates: Biographical Sketches of Those Who Attended Harvard College.* Vol. 9., the Classes of 1731–1735. Boston: Massachusetts Historical Society, 1956.

Sibley, John Langdon. *Biographical Sketches of Graduates of Harvard University, in Cambridge, Massachusetts.* Vol. 3., the Classes of 1678–1689. 1873. Reprint, Boston: Massachusetts Historical Society, 2010.

Sirmans, M. Eugene. *Colonial South Carolina: A Political History.* Chapel Hill: University of North Carolina Press, 1966.

Smith, Mark M. *Stono: Documenting and Interpreting a Southern Slave Revolt.* Columbia: University of South Carolina Press, 2005.

Sobel, Mechal. *Trabelin' On: The Slave Journey to an Afro-Baptist Faith.* 1979. Reprint, Princeton: Princeton University Press, 1988.

South Carolina Synod of the Lutheran Church in America. *History of the Lutheran Church in South Carolina.* Columbia: R. L. Bryan, 1971.

Spurr, John. *The Restoration Church of England, 1646–1689.* New Haven: Yale University Press, 1991.

Stout, Harry S. *The Divine Dramatist: George Whitefield and the Rise of Modern Evangelicalism.* Grand Rapids, Mich.: William B. Eerdmans, 1991.

Thompson, Ernest Trice. *Presbyterians in the South.* 3 vols. Richmond: John Knox Press, 1963–1973.

Thorpe, Daniel B. *The Moravian Community in Colonial North Carolina: Pluralism on the Southern Frontier.* Knoxville: University of Tennessee Press, 1995.

Townsend, Leah. *South Carolina Baptists, 1670–1805.* 1935. Reprint, Baltimore: Genealogical Publishing, 1978.

Tupper, H.A., ed. *Two Centuries of the First Baptist Church of South Carolina, 1683–1883.* Baltimore: R.H. Woodward and Company, 1889.

Upton, Dell. *Holy Things and Profane: Anglican Parish Churches in Colonial Virginia.* Cambridge: MIT Press, 1986.

U.S. Department of Commerce, Bureau of the Census. *Historical Statistics of the United States: Colonial Times to 1970.* 2 volumes. Washington, D.C.: U.S. Government Printing Office, 1975.

Van Ruymbeke, Bertrand. *From New Babylon to Eden: The Huguenots and Their Migration to Colonial South Carolina.* Columbia: University of South Carolina Press, 2006.

Voigt, Gilbert P. *German and German-Swiss Element in South Carolina, 1732–1752.* Bulletin of the University of South Carolina No. 113. Columbia: University of South Carolina, 1922.

Wallace, David Duncan. *The History of South Carolina.* 4 vols. New York: American Historical Association, 1934.

Ward, W. R. *The Protestant Evangelical Awakening.* Cambridge: Cambridge University Press, 1992.

Wardlaw, J. G. *Genealogy of the Wardlaw Family.* Yorkville, S.C., 1910.

Waterhouse, Richard. *A New World Gentry: The Making of a Merchant and Planter Class in South Carolina, 1670–1770.* New York: Garland, 1989.

Weeks, Steven B. *Southern Quakers and Slavery: A Study in Institutional History.* Baltimore: Johns Hopkins Press, 1896.

Weir, Robert M. *Colonial South Carolina: A History.* Millwood, N.Y.: KTO Press, 1983.

Weis, Frederick Lewis. *The Colonial Clergy and the Colonial Churches of the Middle and Southern Colonies, 1607–1776.* Lancaster, Mass.: Society of the Descendants of the Colonial Clergy, 1938.

———. *The Colonial Clergy of Virginia, North Carolina, and South Carolina.* 1955. Reprint, Baltimore: Genealogical Publishing Co., 1976.

Wood, Peter H. *Black Majority: Negroes in Colonial South Carolina from 1670 through the Stono Rebellion.* 1974. Reprint, New York: W. W. Norton, 1975.

Articles and Essays

Anderson, Hugh George. "The European Phase of J. U. Giessendanner's Life." *South Carolina Historical Magazine* 67 (July 1966): 129–37.

"Biography of John Gano." In *The Southern Light, an Independent, Religious and Literary Journal, Set for the Defense of the Truth, and Devoted to the Diffusion of Knowledge,* edited by E. L. Whatley. Vol. 1, no. 9 (September 1856): 321–29. Edgefield, S.C.: Simkins, Durisoe & Co., 1856.

Boles, John B. "The Discovery of Southern Religious History." In *Interpreting Southern History: Historiographical Essays in Honor of Stanford W. Higginbothan*, edited by John B. Boles and Evelyn Thomas Nolen, 510–48. Baton Rouge: Louisiana State University Press, 1987.

———. "Evangelical Protestantism in the Old South: From Religious Dissent to Cultural Dominance." In *Religion in the South*, edited by Charles Reagan Wilson, 13–34. Jackson: University Press of Mississippi, 1985.

———. "Introduction." In *Masters and Slaves in the House of the Lord: Race and Religion in the American South*, edited by John B. Boles, 1–18. Lexington: University Press of Kentucky, 1988.

Bolton, Diane K. "Stoke Newington: Growth." In *A History of the County of Middlesex: Volume VIII: Islington and Stoke Newington Parishes*, edited by T. F. T. Baker and C. R. Elrington, 143–51. New York: Oxford University Press, 1985.

Bonomi, Patricia U., and Peter R. Eisenstadt. "Church Adherence in the Eighteenth-Century British American Colonies." *William & Mary Quarterly*, 3rd ser., 39 (April 1982): 245–86.

Burrage, Henry S. "The Baptist Church in Kittery." *Collections and Proceedings of the Maine Historical Society*, 2nd ser., 9 (1898): 382–91.

———. "Memoir of William Screven." *Collections and Proceedings of the Maine Historical Society*, 2nd ser., 1 (1889): 45–56.

———. "Some Added Facts Concerning Rev. William Screven." *Collections and Proceedings of the Maine Historical Society*, 2nd ser., 5 (1894): 275–84.

Butler, Jon. "Enlarging the Bonds of Christ: Slavery, Evangelism, and the Christianization of the White South, 1690–1790." In *The Evangelical Tradition in America*, edited by Leonard I. Sweet, 87–130. Macon, Ga.: Mercer University Press, 1984.

———. "Enthusiasm Described and Decried: The Great Awakening as Interpretive Fiction." *Journal of American History* 69 (September 1982): 305–25.

Cheves, Langdon. "Blake of South Carolina." *South Carolina Historical Magazine* 1 (April 1900): 153–66.

Dunn, Richard S. "The English Sugar Islands and the Founding of South Carolina." *South Carolina Historical Magazine* 72 (April 1971): 81–93.

Fleming, James H. "Richard Marsden, Wayward Clergyman." *William and Mary Quarterly*, 3rd ser., 11 (October 1954): 578–91.

Ford, Worthington C. "The Rev. Sampson Bond of the Bermudas." *Proceedings of the Massachusetts Historical Society*, 3rd. ser., 54 (1921): 289–318.

Fryer, Linda G. "Documents Relating to the Formation of the Carolina Company in Scotland, 1682." *South Carolina Historical Magazine* 99 (April 1998): 110–32

Greene, Jack P. "Colonial South Carolina and the Caribbean Connection." *South Carolina Historical Magazine* 88 (December 1987): 192–210.

———. "Colonial South Carolina: An Introduction." In *Money, Trade, and Power: The Evolution of Colonial South Carolina's Plantation Society*, edited by Jack P. Greene, Rosemary Brana-Shute, and Randy J. Sparks, vii–xiii. Columbia: University of South Carolina Press, 2001.

———. "Independence, Improvement, and Authority: Toward a Framework for Understanding the Histories of the Southern Backcountry during the Era of the American

Revolution." In *An Uncivil War: The Southern Backcountry during the American Revolution,* edited by Ronald Hoffman, Thad W. Tate, and Peter J. Albert, 3–36. Charlottesville: University Press of Virginia, 1985.

Haefeli, Evan. Review of *Empires of God: Religious Encounters in the Early Modern Atlantic,* edited by Linda Gregerson and Susan Juster. *Journal of American History* 98 (December 2011): 808–9.

Hall, David D. "Religion and Society: Problems and Reconsiderations." In *Colonial British America: Essays in the New History of the Early Modern Era,* edited by Jack P. Greene and J. R. Pole, 317–44. Baltimore: Johns Hopkins University Press, 1984.

Hardy, Stephen G. "Colonial South Carolina's Rice Industry and the Atlantic Economy: Patterns of Trade, Shipping, and Growth, 1715–1775. In *Money, Trade, and Power: The Evolution of Colonial South Carolina's Plantation Society,* edited by Jack P. Greene, Rosemary Brana-Shute, and Randy J. Sparks, 108–40. Columbia: University of South Carolina Press, 2001.

Hill, Samuel S. "A Survey of Southern Religious History." In *Religion in the Southern States: A Historical Study,* edited by Samuel S. Hill, 383–423. Macon, Ga.: Mercer University Press 1983.

Hinke, William J. "The Origin of the Reformed Church in South Carolina." *Journal of the Presbyterian Historical Society* 3 (December 1906): 367–89.

Jackson, Harvey H. "Hugh Bryan and the Evangelical Movement in Colonial South Carolina." *William and Mary Quarterly,* 3rd ser., 43 (October 1986): 594–614.

Jones, Lewis P. "South Carolina." In *Religion in the Southern States: A Historical Study,* edited by Samuel S. Hill, 263–88. Macon, Ga.: Mercer University Press, 1983.

Kelsey, R. W. "Swiss Settlers in South Carolina." *South Carolina Historical Magazine* 23 (July 1922): 85–91.

Kenney, William Howland, III. "Alexander Garden and George Whitefield: The Significance of Revivalism in South Carolina, 1738–1741." *South Carolina Historical Magazine* 71 (January 1970): 1–16.

Laing, Annette. "'Heathens and Infidels'? African Christianization and Anglicanism in the South Carolina Low Country, 1700–1750. *Religion and American Culture: A Journal of Interpretation* 12, no. 2 (2002):197–228.

———. "'A Very Immoral and Offensive Man': Religious Culture, Gentility, and the Strange Case of Brian Hunt, 1727." *South Carolina Historical Magazine* 103 (January 2002): 6–29.

Levy, Babette M. "Early Puritanism in the Southern and Island Colonies." *American Antiquarian Society Proceedings* 70 (1961): 69–348.

Lippy, Charles H. "'Chastized by Scorpions': Christianity and Culture in Colonial South Carolina, 1669–1740." *Church History* 79 (June 2010): 253–70.

Little, Thomas J. "'Adding to the Church Such As Shall Be Saved': The Growth in Influence of Evangelicalism in Colonial South Carolina, 1740–1775. In *Money, Trade, and Power: The Evolution of Colonial South Carolina's Plantation Society,* edited by Jack P. Greene, Rosemary Brana-Shute, and Randy J. Sparks, 363–82. Columbia: University of South Carolina Press, 2001.

———. "The Origins of Southern Evangelicalism: Revivalism in the South Carolina Lowcountry, 1700–1740." *Church History* 75 (December 2006): 768–808.

———. "The South Carolina Slave Laws Reconsidered." *South Carolina Historical Magazine* 94 (April 1993): 86–101.

Little, Thomas J., and Sarah E. Kegley. "Records of the Ashley River Baptist Church, 1736–1769." *South Carolina Baptist Historical Quarterly* 27 (November 2001): 3–32.

McIver, Petrona Royall. "Wappetaw Congregational Church." *South Carolina Historical Magazine* 58 (January 1957): 34–47.

Miller, Perry. "Jonathan Edwards and the Great Awakening." In *Errand into the Wilderness,* by Perry Miller, 153–66. Cambridge: Harvard University Press, 1956.

Milton, J. R. "John Locke and the Fundamental Constitutions of Carolina," *Locke Newsletter* 21 (1990): 111–33.

Moore, Alexander. "Public Politics and Private Faith: Huguenot Political Acculturation in South Carolina, 1687–1707." In *The Dawn of Religious Freedom in South Carolina,* edited by James Lowell Underwood and W. Lewis Burke, 114–25. Columbia: University of South Carolina Press, 2006.

Morgan, David T., Jr. "The Consequences of George Whitefield's Ministry in the Carolinas and Georgia, 1739–1740." *Georgia Historical Quarterly* 55 (January 1971): 62–82.

———. "George Whitefield's Ministry in Georgia and the Carolinas, 1739–1740." *Georgia Historical Quarterly* 54 (December 1970): 517–39.

———. "The Great Awakening in South Carolina, 1740–1745." *South Atlantic Quarterly* 70 (Autumn 1971): 595–606.

Mulcahy, Matthew. "'Melancholy and Fatal Calamities': Disaster and Society in Eighteenth-Century South Carolina." In *Money, Trade, and Power: The Evolution of Colonial South Carolina's Plantation Society,* edited by Jack P. Greene, Rosemary Brana-Shute, and Randy J. Sparks, 278–98. Columbia: University of South Carolina Press, 2001.

Nelson, Andrew T. "Enthusiasm in Carolina, 1740." *South Atlantic Quarterly* 44 (October 1945): 397–405.

Noll, Mark A., David W. Bebbington, and George A. Rawlyk. "Introduction." In *Evangelicalism: Studies in Popular Protestantism in North America, the British Isles, and Beyond, 1700–1990,* edited by Mark A. Noll, David W. Bebbington, and George A. Rawlyk, 3–6. New York: Oxford University Press, 1994.

O'Brien, Susan. "Eighteenth-Century Publishing Networks in the First Years of Transatlantic Evangelicalism." In *Evangelicalism: Studies in Popular Protestantism in North America, the British Isles, and Beyond, 1700–1990,* edited by Mark A. Noll, David W. Bebbington, and George A. Rawlyk, 38–57. New York: Oxford University Press, 1994.

———. "A Transatlantic Community of Saints: The Great Awakening and the First Evangelical Network, 1735–1755." *American Historical Review* 91 (October 1986): 811–32.

Osborn, Byrle J. "Governor Joseph West, A Seventeenth Century Forgotten Man Rediscovered." *New York Genealogical and Biographical Record* 65 (1934): 202–5.

Parker, Mattie Erma E. "The First Fundamental Constitutions of Carolina." *South Carolina Historical Magazine* 71 (April 1970): 78–85.

Peterson, Mark. "The Plymouth Church and the Evolution of Puritan Religious Culture." *New England Quarterly* 66 (December 1993): 570–93.

Poole, W. Scott. "'Your liberty in that province': South Carolina Quakers and the Rejection of Religious Toleration." In *The Dawn of Religious Freedom in South Carolina*, edited by James Lowell Underwood and W. Lewis Burke, 165–83. Columbia: University of South Carolina Press, 2006.

Ramsay, Jack C., Jr. "Archibald Stobo, Presbyterian Minister." *Journal of the Presbyterian Historical Society* 37 (September 1959): 129–42.

Salley, Alexander S., Jr. "The Family of the First Landgrave Thomas Smith." *South Carolina Historical Magazine* 28 (July 1927): 169–75.

———. "Governor Joseph Morton and Some of His Descendants." *South Carolina Historical Magazine* 5 (April 1904): 108–16.

———. "Landgrave Daniel Axtell." *South Carolina Historical Magazine* 6 (October 1905): 174–76.

Schmidt, Leigh Eric. "'The Grand Prophet,' Hugh Bryan: Early Evangelicalism's Challenge to the Establishment and Slavery in the Colonial South." *South Carolina Historical Magazine* 87 (October 1986): 238–50.

———. "'A Second and Glorious Reformation': The New Light Extremism of Andrew Croswell." *William and Mary Quarterly*, 3rd ser., 43 (April 1986): 214–44.

Sensbach, Jon F. "Before the Bible Belt: Indians, Africans, and the New Synthesis of Eighteenth-Century Southern Religious History." In *Religion in the American South: Protestants and Others in History and Culture*, edited by Beth Barton Schweiger and Donald G. Mathews, 5–29. Chapel Hill: University of North Carolina Press, 2004.

———. "Religion in the Early South in an Age of Atlantic Empire." *Journal of Southern History* 73 (August 2007): 631–42.

Smith, Edward Leodore. "Landgrave Thomas Smith's Visit to Boston." *South Carolina Historical Magazine* 22 (April 1921): 60–64.

Smith, Henry A. M. "The Ashley River: Its Seats and Settlements." *South Carolina Historical Magazine* 20 (January 1919): 3–51.

———. "Joseph West: Landgrave and Governor." *South Carolina Historical Magazine* 19 (October 1918): 189–93.

———. "Purrysburgh." *South Carolina Historical Magazine* 10 (October 1909): 187–219.

———. "The Town of Dorchester, in South Carolina—A Sketch of Its History." *South Carolina Historical Magazine* 6 (April 1905): 62–95.

———. "The Upper Ashley; And the Mutations of Families." *South Carolina Historical Magazine* 20 (July 1919): 151–98.

Sparks, Randy J. "Mary Fisher, Sophia Hume, and the Quakers of Colonial Charleston: 'Women Professing Godliness.'" In *South Carolina Women: Their Lives and Times*, vol. 1, edited by Marjorie Julian Spruill, Valinda W. Littlefield, and Joan Marie Johnson, 40–59. Athens: University of Georgia Press, 2009.

Stout, Harry S. "George Whitefield in Three Countries." In *Evangelicalism: Studies in Popular Protestantism in North America, the British Isles, and Beyond, 1700–1990*, edited by Mark A. Noll, David W. Bebbington, and George A. Rawlyk, 58–72. New York: Oxford University Press, 1994.

Tanis, James. "Reformed Pietism in Colonial America." In *Continental Pietism and Early American Christianity*, edited by Ernest Stoeffler, 34–73. Grand Rapids, Mich.: William B. Eerdmans, 1976.

Tappert, Theodore G. "The Influence of Pietism in Colonial American Lutheranism." In *Continental Pietism and Early American Christianity*, edited by Ernest Stoeffler, 13–33. Grand Rapids, Mich.: William B. Eerdmans, 1976.

Thomas, John P. "The Barbadians in Early South Carolina." *South Carolina Historical Magazine* 31 (April 1930): 75–92.

Travers, Len. "The Missionary Journal of John Cotton, Jr., 1666–1678." *Proceedings of the Massachusetts Historical Society*, 3rd ser., 109 (1997): 52–101.

Underwood, James Lowell. "The Dawn of Religious Freedom in South Carolina: The Journey from Limited Tolerance to Constitutional Right." In *The Dawn of Religious Freedom in South Carolina*, edited by James Lowell Underwood and W. Lewis Burke, 1–57. Columbia: University of South Carolina Press, 2006.

Van Ruymbeke, Bertrand. "The Huguenots of Proprietary South Carolina: Patterns of Migration and Integration." In *Money, Trade, and Power: The Evolution of Colonial South Carolina's Plantation Society*, edited by Jack P. Greene, Rosemary Brana-Shute, and Randy J. Sparks, 26–48. Columbia: University of South Carolina Press, 2001.

Voigt, Gilbert P. "Cultural Contributions of German Settlers to South Carolina." *South Carolina Historical Magazine* 53 (October 1952): 183–89.

———. "Religious Conditions among German-Speaking Settlers in South Carolina, 1732–1774." *South Carolina Historical Magazine* 56 (April 1955): 59–66.

———. "Swiss Notes on South Carolina." *South Carolina Historical Magazine* 21 (July 1920): 93–104.

Walsh, John. "'Methodism' and the Origins of English-Speaking Evangelicalism." In *Evangelicalism: Studies in Popular Protestantism in North America, the British Isles, and Beyond, 1700–1990*, edited by Mark A. Noll, David W. Bebbington, and George A. Rawlyk, 19–37. New York: Oxford University Press, 1994.

Waterhouse, Richard. "England, the Caribbean, and the Founding of South Carolina." *Journal of American Studies* 9 (December 1975): 259–81.

Webber, Mabel L. "Joseph West, Landgrave and Governor: More Details Concerning Him." *South Carolina Historical Magazine* 40 (July 1939): 79–80.

Winton, Ruth M. "Governor Francis Nicholson's Relations with the Society for the Propagation of the Gospel in Foreign Parts, 1701–1727." *Historical Magazine of the Protestant Episcopal Church* 17 (1948): 274–86.

Dissertations and Theses

Catron, John. "The Atlantic World Origins of African American Christianity." Ph.D. dissertation, University of Florida, 2008.

Clark, Marion W. "German Churches in South Carolina Prior to 1787." B.D. thesis, Lutheran Theological Southern Seminary, 1966.

Laing, Annette. "'All Things to All Men': Popular Religious Culture and the Anglican Mission in Colonial America, 1701–1750." Ph.D. dissertation, University of California, Riverside, 1995.

Long, Ronald Wilson. "Religious Revivalism in the Carolinas and Georgia, 1740–1805." Ph.D. dissertation, University of Georgia, 1968.

McCormick, Jo Anne. "The Quakers of Colonial South Carolina, 1670–1806." Ph.D. dissertation, University of South Carolina, 1984.

Morgan, David Taft, Jr. "The Great Awakening in the Carolinas and Georgia, 1740–1775." Ph.D. dissertation, University of North Carolina, 1968.

Strickland, John Scott. "Across Space and Time: Conversion, Community, and Cultural Change among South Carolina Slaves." Ph.D. dissertation, University of North Carolina, 1985.

Index

CPSIA information can be obtained at www.ICGtesting.com
Printed in the USA
LVOW11*2114011114

411543LV00003B/7/P